JESUS AS
THEY SAW HIM

JESUS

AS

THEY

SAW HIM

NEW TESTAMENT INTERPRETATIONS OF JESUS

William Barclay

HARPER & ROW, PUBLISHERS

New York, Evanston
and London

LIBRARY OF CONGRESS CATALOG CARD NUMBER: 62-1527

CONTENTS

13632

6 CONTENTS

FOREWORD

THE chapters of this book began life as articles in the pages of the *British Weekly,* although many of them have been extensively revised and rewritten. I have therefore first of all to thank the Rev. Denis Duncan, B.D., the editor of that paper, for permission to republish them in this form.

The aim of this book is to bring together the titles and the interpretations of Jesus which we meet in the New Testament. Obviously such a book cannot be complete, but I have tried to make it as comprehensive as I could. In order to make it comprehensive I have had to use a certain amount of repetition. This book is one of a trilogy and the first two volumes of the trilogy are *The Mind of Jesus* and *Crucified and Crowned.* In these two books the titles *Son of Man* and *Lord* in particular were discussed; but it seemed to me, since the three books are designed to be read separately as well as together, that it was impossible to write a book on the New Testament interpretations of Jesus without dealing again with these two words. So I have dealt with them again, and, while the exposition of their meaning is unchanged, the treatment of them is much fuller.

I have tried as far as possible to give all illustrative passages in full. I was well aware that the reader in many cases would not have at hand the books of the inter-testamental period which have been quoted, and years of teaching have made me pessimistically aware that, even when the necessary books lie to hand, references will not always be looked up! I have therefore as a general rule tried to quote in full all passages cited, even from the New Testament itself.

As always, my most sincere and cordial thanks are due to the Rev. David L. Edwards, Miss Kathleen Downham and Miss Jean Cunningham of the SCM Press for unwearied patience, constant encouragement and most valuable advice. I should like to thank my wife for much wearisome work in the preparation and correction of the manuscript.

No one can send out a book on a subject like this without a feeling of its complete inadequacy. I can only hope and pray that as the writing of it has opened to me something of the inexhaustible wonder of Jesus Christ, so the reading of it will do something of that for others.

WILLIAM BARCLAY

Trinity College
Glasgow
July 1962

1

JESUS

IT can very often happen that a name given to a man can be a one-word summary of what he has done and of what he is. That is specially the case with names which were not given to a person at his birth and at his entry into the world, but which are rather titles which were given to a man in virtue of his deeds. So the impact of Alexander on the world is summed up in his title Alexander the Great; the relationship of William to England is summed up in his title William the Conqueror. Ethelred goes down to history as Ethelred the Unready, and Mary as Bloody Mary, titles in which the character of each is summed up. Elizabeth is Gloriana, the name in which the splendour of the Elizabethan age is summed up. Francis of Assisi is the Troubadour of Christ, a name which is a witness to his joy in Christ. Judas Maccabaeus by his very name is the Hammer of the enemies of Israel, as Edward the First was the Hammer of the Scots. The function of John in history is summed up in his title John the Baptizer; the politics and the character of Simon are contained in his title Simon the Zealot. All this is specially true of Jesus. All through the New Testament we find men giving Jesus titles which are at one and the same time affirmations and confessions of their faith in him and summaries of what they believed him to be. It is these titles that we are about to study. But before we turn to the titles, we must first look at the name of Jesus itself.

In the Gospels this is by far the commonest name of our Lord, for in them he is called by this simple name almost six hundred times. It is at first sight an astonishing fact that in the four

9

Gospels the expression *Jesus Christ* occurs only four times, in Mark 1.1; Matt. 1.1; John 1.17; 17.3; and the expression the Lord *Jesus* occurs only twice, and in both cases there is doubt about it. In Luke 24.3 the reading is doubtful, and Mark 16.19 is not part of the original Gospel. When the Gospel writers thought of their Lord, it was the name Jesus which came automatically to their minds and to their lips, and this is a very significant fact.

(i) The name Jesus underlines the real humanity of our Lord. To us the name Jesus is a holy and a sacred name, and we would account it almost blasphemy to give it to any child or to call any person by it. But in New Testament times it was one of the commonest of names. It is the Greek form by which three Hebrew Old Testament names are regularly represented—Joshua (e.g. Ex. 17.10); Jehoshua (e.g. Zech. 3.1); Jeshua (Neh. 7.7). There are indeed two occasions in the AV in which Joshua is very confusingly called Jesus. In Acts 7.45 we read that the fathers brought the tabernacle into the land of Palestine with Jesus. In Heb. 4.8 it is said that, if Jesus had been able to give the people rest, there would have been no need to speak of still another day. In both these cases Jesus is Joshua, a fact which is made clear in all the more modern translations.

There were at least five High Priests who were called Jesus. In the works of the historian Josephus there appear about twenty people called Jesus, ten of whom were contemporary with our Lord. One of the best known and most important books of the Apocrypha, the book usually known by the name Ecclesiasticus, is the work of Jesus the son of Sirach. In the New Testament itself we come on Jesus Justus, the friend of Paul (Col. 4.11), and the sorcerer of Paphos is called Bar-Jesus (Acts 13.6). In the contemporary census and taxation returns found amoung the papyri the name Jesus often occurs.

A very interesting possible occurrence of the name Jesus

is in Matt. 27.18. There are certain manuscripts which give Jesus as the first name of Barabbas. The RSV notes this reading, and both Moffatt and the NEB accept it as correct, so that the translation of that verse becomes: 'Which would you like me to release to you—Jesus Bar-Abbas, or Jesus called Messiah?' If that reading is correct, as it well may be, the choice before the mob is even more vivid and dramatic.

By the second century the name Jesus was vanishing as an ordinary name. Amongst the Jews it vanished because it had become a hated name by which no Jew would call his son; and amongst the Christians it had vanished because it was too sacred for common use.

The consistent use of the name Jesus in the Gospels underlines the humanity of Jesus. To those who had known him, lived with him, talked with him, walked with him, eaten with him, Jesus was no unearthly, inhuman, demigod figure; he was a man among men.

(ii) But, ordinary though it was, the name Jesus was nonetheless a highly significant name. In the ancient world names were really meaningful, and they often described some special characteristic about the child to whom they were given. So, for instance, both Samuel and Saul means *asked for,* and are names given to a child who had come in answer to many prayers. The name Jesus was given to our Lord, as the New Testament story tells, by the direct instruction of God (Matt. 1.21). It is significant that the Jewish Rabbis had a saying: 'Six persons received their names before they were born, namely, Isaac, our great lawgiver Moses, Solomon, Josiah, Ishmael, and the Messiah.' Jewish belief was that God would say what the name of his Messiah must be.

The name Jesus held a very special meaning for both Jew and Greek. In both languages it is a name which is capable of becoming a one-word summary of the work that its bearer came to do.

(*a*) In Hebrew the names Joshua and Jehoshua, which, as we have seen, become Jesus in Greek, mean, 'Jehovah is my help,' or, 'Jehovah is rescue,' or, 'The help of Jehovah.' 'You shall give him the name Jesus,' the angel said, 'for he will save his people from their sins' (Matt. 1.21). The very name stamps Jesus as Saviour. He is God's divinely appointed and divinely sent Rescuer, whose function it is to deliver men from their sins. He came to rescue men from the estrangement and the alienation from God which is the consequence of their past sins, and for the future to liberate them from the bondage to sin, from the moral frustration and the continuous and inevitable defeat which are the result of sin. He came to bring friendship for fear, and victory for defeat.

This is in fact a meaning of the name Jesus which all true Jews would recognize. In Ecclesiasticus Jesus the Son of Sirach speaks of Joshua the son of Nun (Jesus the son of Nave is what he calls him): 'Jesus the son of Nave was valiant in the wars, and was the successor of Moses in prophecies, who according to his name was made great for the saving of the elect of God' (Ecclus. 46.1). Joshua the son of Nun, Jesus the son of Nave, as his name denotes, rescued his people from their enemies; Jesus of Nazareth is the great Rescuer from sin.

(*b*) The Greeks connected the name Jesus with the verb *iasthai*, which means *to heal*. There is no real connection between the two words except in sound, but the Greeks made much of Jesus as the healer of the bodies and the souls of men.

Clement of Alexandria quotes the saying of John (1 John 2.2); 'And he is the propitiation for our sins,' and comments, 'Jesus who heals (*ho iōmenos*) both our body and soul.'[1] In one of his lectures to those who were receiving instruction

---

[1] *Paidagogos* 3.12.

preparatory to becoming members of the Church Cyril of
Jerusalem works this out more fully: 'He is called Jesus by
a fitting name, as having the appellation from his salutary
healing . . . Jesus means, according to the Hebrew, *Saviour*,
but in the Greek tongue *The Healer*, since he is the
physician of souls and bodies, curer of spirits, curing the
blind in body, and leading minds into the light, healing the
visibly lame, and guiding the steps of sinners to repentance . . .
If, therefore, anyone is suffering in soul from sins, there is
the physician for him.'

To the Greek mind the very name Jesus identified our
Lord as the great healer of the bodies and the souls of men,
the one who alone could bring health to the body in its
pain and cleansing to the soul infected with the disease of sin.

It is no accident that our Lord was called by the name
Jesus. That name sums up the things which he came into
the world to do and which only he can do. He came to
be the divine Rescuer who alone can deliver men from the
consequences and from the grip of sin; he came to be the
divine Physician who alone can bring healing to the bodies
and the souls of men.

> Jesus! the name that charms our fears,
>   That bids our sorrows cease;
> 'Tis music in the sinner's ears,
>   'Tis life, and health, and peace.

1 *Catechetical Lectures* 10.4,13.

2

MAN

IT may come as something of a surprise to us to find that
in the New Testament Jesus is on more than one occasion
plainly, bluntly and unequivocally called a man. In Greek
there are two words for *man*. There is *anthrōpos,* which is
the word for man as a human being. It is the generic word
for man as a representative and specimen of humanity. There
is the word *anēr,* which describes a man rather as a husband
and a father, as an individual person, as a male member
of the human species. In the New Testament Jesus is called
by both of these words.

It might not be so very surprising to find Jesus called a
man by those who, so to speak, did not know him very
well, and who had never come into close, intimate, personal
contact with him; and there are instances when that is so.
When John the Baptizer saw Jesus, he said: 'This is he of
whom I spoke when I said, "After me a man (*anēr*) is
coming who takes rank before me"; for before I was born
he already was' (John 1.30). The invitation of the woman
of Samaria was: 'Come and see a man (*anthrōpos*) who
has told me everything I ever did' (John 4.29). In explaining
his cure the man born blind said: 'The man (*anthrōpos*)
called Jesus made a paste and smeared my eyes with it'
(John 9.11). When Pilate presented Jesus to the people in
his despairing effort not to crucify him, he said: 'Behold the
Man!' (*anthrōpos*). It could be said that all these people,
with the possible exception of John the Baptizer, knew Jesus
only very briefly and in no way intimately.

But there are other occasions in which Jesus is called

'man' in very different circumstances. In the first recorded sermon delivered by a Christian preacher Peter spoke of Jesus as 'Jesus of Nazareth a man *(anēr)* attested to you by God with mighty works and wonders and signs which God did through him in your midst' (Acts 2.22, RSV). In the Pastoral Epistles, which come from a time when Christian thought about Jesus was much more highly developed, it is said: 'There is one God, and also one mediator between God and men, Christ Jesus, himself man' *(anthrōpos)* (I Tim. 2.5). It can be seen that the Church had no hesitation in using the word man of Jesus. Here is something which is very significant.

(i) It shows us that those who actually companied with Jesus found him fully and naturally a man. He did not seem to them to be some indeterminate person from some halfway land in which human and divine were intermingled; he did not seem to them a kind of Greek demigod, neither fully human or fully divine; he did not seem to them to be so divine as to be inhuman. There was nothing unnatural about him. He was a man among men, as fully a man as they were men, and they found no difficulty in calling him a man. Shakespeare's Mark Antony described Julius Caesar:

> His life was gentle, and the elements
> So mix'd in him that Nature might stand up
> And say to all the world, 'This was a man!'

Any Christology must begin from the historical fact that those who lived and walked and ate and talked and companied with Jesus saw absolutely nothing unnatural and abnormal about him. His manhood was complete.

(ii) From this a very great and basic truth follows. Jesus was clearly fully man; yet it is equally clear that 'God was in Christ'. In a unique sense God and man; it must mean that there is no uncrossable and unbridgeable gulf between manhood and godhead; manhood is such that God can enter into it. In the old creation story God said: 'Let us make man in our own image, after our own likeness' (Gen. 1.26). Man bears the image of God; there is an intimate connection between God and man. He whom his companions would regard as a man in the fullest sense of the term was also the Son of God. Manhood is such that God can take it upon himself and enter into it.

(iii) This fearless use of the word man to describe Jesus has been made the basis of a certain kind of Christology. It has been made the foundation of what is called Adoptianist Christology. To put it at its simplest, this Christology says that Jesus was a man, who proved himself to be so fit a weapon for the purposes of God that God uniquely equipped him and uniquely entered into him, thereby adopting him as his Son.

Let us return to the saying of Peter in his first Christian sermon in Acts 2.22. In the AV it is said that Peter spoke of 'Jesus of Nazareth, a man approved of God among you by miracles and wonders and signs'. We may first note how the humanity of Jesus is triply stressed. He is called simply by his human name Jesus with no addition to it whatsoever; he is said to be of Nazareth, and thereby he is given a local, actual, human habitation; he is called a man, *anēr,* a human being in the full sense of the term. Next we look at the word which the AV translates *approved,* in Greek *apodedeigmenon. Apodeiknumi* from which *apodedeigmenon* is the perfect participle passive can mean to prove, to demonstrate, and that is the sense in which the AV takes the word. In this passage of the AV the word *approved* does not mean that God looked upon Jesus with favour, or, as we say, with approval; it means that God proved, demonstrated who Jesus was by miracles and signs. This use of the word *approve* is

found in Shakespearean language contemporary with the AV.
In the *Merchant of Venice* (iii. 2) Shakespeare has:

> In religion
> What damned error, but some sober brow
> Will bless it and approve it with a text!

There the word *approve* means in modern English to prove,
provide proof of. Thus both the *Twentieth Century New
Testament* and J. B. Phillips say that Jesus was a man whose
mission was *proved* by his miracles; Weymouth, Moffatt and
Knox all use the word *accredited*. Here the idea is that Jesus
was attested by his miracles; they proved him to be in a
unique relationship with God. But *apodedeigmenon* could
equally well mean *designated for office*. It is in actual fact
the regular Greek word for the man who was designated
for the imperial power, designated as the successor of the
reigning Emperor. Thus in *The Beginnings of Christianity*
Cadbury translates it *appointed*. The meaning would then be
that Jesus was a man appointed by God to a special task.

It so happens that in this passage there is an alternative
Greek reading. It is true that *apodedeigmenon* is the reading
of the manuscripts which are generally considered to be best;
but in the Western Text there is the reading *dedokimasmenon*,
which is the perfect participle passive of the verb *dokimazō*
which means *to test*. *Dedokimasmenos* is the word to describe
some one who has undergone and satisfied some test. It can,
for instance, be used of metal which has been tested and
which has been found to be clear of all alloy; and, even
more suggestive, in the papyri it can be used for a doctor
who has passed his examinations and who is fully qualified
to practise. This line of thought would mean that Jesus had,
so to speak, satisfied every test, and had so been accepted
by God as the instrument and agent of his purposes.

If we build on this idea, we come to the conception of

Jesus as a person who throughout the first thirty years of his life was being tested in every way by God, a person who by his love, his fidelity, his obedience, his faith proved himself to be the person for whom God was seeking, a person who was progressively and completely equipped by God's purposes, and who was finally adopted as the Son of God, to do God's special work of redeeming the world.

It is natural to ask when this adoption took place, when it was, so to speak, finalised. Those who have thought along those lines have usually held that this adoption by God took place at the Baptism of Jesus. Once again in the New Testament manuscripts we have an interesting variant reading. The voice which came to Jesus at his baptism said: 'Thou art my Son, my Beloved; on thee my favour rests' (Mark 1.11; Matt. 3.17; Luke 3.22). This voice is composed of two Old Testament quotations, consisting of parts of Ps. 2.7 and Isa. 42.1. But in the manuscripts of Luke there is an alternative reading. In it the Isaiah quotation is dropped and the quotation from Ps. 2.7 is extended and the words of the voice become: 'Thou art my Son, my Beloved; this day I have begotten thee.' If this is the correct reading, then we could say that at that moment the man Jesus was completely and perfectly adopted by God as his Son—and the fact that that reading exists shows that there were some in the early Church who were prepared to take it in that sense.

It may be said that this is the simplest and the earliest of all Christologies. It says quite simply that Jesus was a man who by his love and his gentleness, his goodness and his obedience so approved himself to God that God could take him and specially and uniquely equip him until he was able to adopt him as his Son and so to use him for the work of the redemption of the world. What is conserved here is the certainty that those who knew Jesus when he was here in the flesh were quite certain that he was no freak, no half-

and-half creature, no demigod walking in some no man's land between humanity and divinity; he was to them a man among men. What this conception fails to conserve is the essential connection between God and Jesus, between the Father and the Son, which, the thinkers of the Church began to see, must not be an acquired connection but a connection that goes back to the very nature and essence and being of Jesus Christ. Adoptianist Christology provided men with a vivid, dramatic and intelligible picture of Jesus, but in the end men felt that it was a conception which did not go far enough.

However that may be, the New Testament writers did not hesitate to call Jesus man in the fullest sense of the term; and we rejoice in his manhood, for it means that somehow manhood and godhead are in him connected together, and that he who is our Lord and Saviour is also our brother man.

3

GOD

ONE of the most vexed questions in Christian thought and language is whether or not we can directly and simply call Jesus God. In his book *Christ and the Christian* Nels Ferré has pointed out that Nathaniel Micklem has said that the assertion, 'Jesus is God', is a shocking heresy.[1] On the other hand, Christian devotion has never hesitated to call Jesus God. This began very early. Not long after the last book in the New Testament had been written, Ignatius of Antioch could speak about 'the blood of God'.[2] 'There is one Physician,' he says, 'who is both flesh and spirit, born yet not born, who is God in man.'[3] He urges his people to act in such a way that Jesus may be 'our God in us'.[4] He speaks of Jesus as 'the God who has given you wisdom'.[5] Charles Wesley in his great hymn sings his love and praise to Jesus:

> Amazing love! how can it be
> That Thou, my God, shouldst die for me?

Isaac Watts writes:

> Forbid it, Lord, that I should boast,
> Save in the death of Christ, my God.

No one can doubt or deny the fact that this is the way in which love and devotion have spoken and sung throughout the centuries, but is this a real New Testament interpretation of Jesus? Let us examine the evidence.

It is when we begin to examine the evidence that we run into

---

[1] Nels Ferré, *Christ and the Christian*, 39; Nathaniel Micklem, *Ultimate Questions*, 131. [2] *Ephesians* 1.1.
[3] *Ephesians* 7.2. [4] *Ephesians* 15.3. [5] *Smyrnaeans* 1.1.

very real difficulties. The evidence is not extensive. But we shall find that on almost every occasion in the New Testament on which Jesus seems to be called God there is a problem either of textual criticism or of translation. In almost every case we have to discuss which of two readings is to be accepted or which of two possible translations is to be accepted. Herein lies the proof that this is in fact a way of speaking which men found it difficult to use.

We shall examine the evidence of the New Testament section by section.

(i) In the first three Gospels this way of speaking does not occur at all.

(ii) In the Fourth Gospel there are three relevant passages, two of which are beset with problems either of translation or of text, and one of which is clear and definite.

(a) In the AV John 1.1 reads: 'In the beginning was the Word, and the Word was with God, and *the Word was God.'* For long the newer translations continued this rendering, with the exception of Moffatt and Goodspeed, who both render: 'The Word was divine.' If the translation of the AV is too much, the translation of Moffatt and Goodspeed is too little. In a case like this we cannot do other than go to the Greek, which is *theos ēn ho logos. Ho* is the definite article, *the*, and it can be seen that there is a definite article with *logos*, but not with *theos*. When in Greek two nouns are joined by the verb to be and when both have the definite article, then the one is fully identified with the other; but when one of them is without the article, it becomes more an adjective than a noun, and describes rather the class or the sphere to which the other belongs.

An illustration from English will make this clear. If I say, '*The* preacher is *the* man,' I use the definite article before both preacher and man, and I thereby identify the preacher with some quite definite individual man whom I have in mind.

But, if I say, 'The preacher is man,' I have omitted the definite article before man, and what I mean is that the preacher must be classified as a man, he is in the sphere of manhood, he is a human being.

John has no definite article before *theos,* God. The *Logos,* therefore, is not identified as God or with God; the word *theos* has become adjectival and describes the sphere to which the *Logos* belongs. We would, therefore, have to say that this means that the *Logos* belongs to the same sphere as God; without being identified with God the *Logos* has the same kind of life and being as God. Here the NEB finds the perfect translation: 'What God was, the Word was.'

This passage then does not identify the *Logos* and God; it does not say that Jesus was God, nor does it call him God; but it does say that in his nature and being he belongs to the same class as God, and is in the same sphere of life as God.

(*b*) The second passage is in John 1.18. Here the AV has: 'No man hath seen God at any time; the only begotten Son, which is in the bosom of the Father, he hath declared him.' The problem here is that there are three different readings in the Greek manuscripts.

1. Certain manuscripts read simply *the only begotten one* without any noun at all. This reading is not well supported and may be disregarded.

2. Certain manuscripts read *the only begotten Son (huios),* and the reading is well supported.

3. Certain manuscripts read *the only begotten God (theos),* and this reading has what is very probably the best manuscript support of all.

We now turn to the translators, and we find that they fully realise the problem which the textual evidence has set them. Weymouth, the RSV, the NEB all put *the only Son* in the text of their translation, and all indicate that there is an

alternative possibility that instead of *Son* we should read *God*.
The NEB suggests as an alternative translation: 'The only
One, himself God, the nearest to the Father's heart has made
him known.' Kingsley Williams, who does not annotate, also
retains *Son*.

But there is another group of translators who accept the
reading *theos*, God, and who translate in various ways. The
Twentieth Century New Testament translates: 'God the only
Son, who is ever with the Father—he has revealed him.'
Goodspeed translates: 'It is the divine Only Son, who leans
upon his Father's breast, that has made him known', which
indeed seems to translate both readings at one and the same
time. Moffatt translates: 'Nobody has ever seen God, but God
has been unfolded by the divine One, the only Son, who lies
upon the Father's breast', which, like the rendering of Goodspeed, is a conflation of both readings.

There is obvious difficulty here. It is a first principle of textual criticism that the more difficult reading is always the
reading which is more likely to be the original. An easy saying
is not likely to be turned by a scribe into a difficult one; but
a difficult saying is quite likely to be simplified by a scribe
as he copies it. Now here the word *God* is a far more difficult
reading then the word *Son,* and the textual evidence for
it is good[1]; we would therefore accept the reading *theos;* and

[1] Since this is so important and so problematic a passage we give the
manuscript evidence.
The only begotten One (with no noun) is the reading of certain
manuscripts of the Latin Vulgate, possibly the old Syriac, the Diates-
saron of Tatian, Cyril of Jerusalem, Nonnus, and Nestorius.
The only begotten Son is the reading of Codex Alexandrinus, one of
the correctors of Codex Ephraemi Rescriptus, Family I, many of
the later uncials, the Latin Versions, the Curetonian, Harcleian,
and Palestinian old Syriac, the Armenian and the Ethiopian Versions,
two out of five quotations of the passage in Clement of Alexandria,
six out of seven in Eusebius, seven out of seven in Athanasius,
Gregory Nazianzen, Theodore of Mopsuestia, Chrysostom, two out
of three quotations in the Latin translation of Irenaeus, Tertullian,

here it does seem that the Son is called God, that the word God is applied to Jesus, although once again it is more accurate to say, not that the Son is identified with God, but that it is affirmed that the being of the Son is the being of God, that Father and Son belong to the same sphere of godhead. The difficulty about this passage is that there is so much genuine uncertainty about it that it would be quite unsafe to build any argument upon it.

(c) The third passage in the Fourth Gospel is the cry of love and devotion of Thomas in John 20.28, in which Thomas greets the Lord whose victory he had doubted with the impassioned words, 'My Lord and my God!' About this passage there is no doubt, but it must be remembered that this is not the verdict of a theologian but the reaction of the loving heart.

(iii) We now turn to the letter to the Hebrews. The relevant passage there is Heb. 1.8,9. In this passage the writer to the Hebrews is seeking to prove from prophecy the superiority of the Son, and in order to do so he cites texts from Ps. 45.6,7 and Isa. 61.1. Here the problem is not a problem of text, but of translation. The translators fall into three groups.

(a) The AV translates:

Hilary, seven out of seven quotations in Victorinus, two out of three quotations in Ambrosiaster.
The only begotten God is the reading of Codex Sinaiticus, Codex Vaticanus, the original scribe of Codex Ephraemi Rescriptus, Codex Regius, the original scribe of the Washington Codex, Codex Koridethianus, possibly the valuable minuscule 33, the Syriac Peshitto and the margin of the Syriac Harcleian, the Egyptian Versions; one codex of the Ethiopic Version and Ambrosiaster on one occasion confuse the two readings. 'The only begotten God' is also read by Valentinus as cited by Irenaeus and Clement of Alexandria, three out of five quotations in Clement of Alexandria, three out of three in Origen. Basilides, Didymus, Epiphanius, Gregory of Nyssa, Cyril, one out of three quotations in the Latin version of Irenaeus, and Jerome.

But unto the Son he saith:
Thy throne, O God, is for ever and ever
. . . .
Therefore, God, even thy God, hath anointed thee
with the oil of gladness above thy fellows.

That translation is followed by the RSV (with a note that
an alternative translation is possible), Weymouth, and
Kingsley Williams. In this rendering the Son is definitely
addressed as God in the first quotation, but not in the second.

(b) Of the second group of translators Moffatt may be
taken as typical. He translates:

He says of the Son:
God is thy throne for ever and ever
. . . .
Therefore God, thy God, has consecrated thee,
with the oil of rejoicing above my comrades.

This is the alternative rendering noted by the RSV and is
also the translation of the *Twentieth Century New Testament*
and of Goodspeed. In this rendering the vocative 'O God'
in v. 8 has become a nominative, and there is no suggestion
that the Son is called God.

(c) Of the third group the New English Bible is the representative. It translates:

But of the Son,
Thy throne, O God, is for ever and ever
. . . .
Therefore, O God, thy God has set thee above thy fellows,
by anointing with the oil of exultation.

In the second clause the alternative translation, 'God, who
is thy God,' is noted; but in the NEB in the actual text in both
halves of the passage the Son is uniquivocally addressed as God.

This is a passage in which no one would wish to be dogmatic.
In both cases both translations are perfectly possible, although
we would say as a personal opinion that the Greek reads

more naturally in the first part as, 'Thy throne, O God, is for ever and ever,' and in the second part as, 'God, thy God, hath anointed thee.' But, whatever translation we accept, we once again see that the matter stands in such doubt that it would be very unsafe to base any firm argument upon it.

(iv) We now turn to the General Epistles. In them we have two passages, one fairly certain and one doubtful.

(a) In II Peter 1.1 the writer speaks of the precious faith we have received through the righteousness *of God and our Saviour Jesus Christ*. All the newer translations (Weymouth in a footnote) render the last phrase the righteousness of *our God and Saviour Jesus Christ*, which is undoubtedly the correct translation. There Jesus Christ is quite definitely called God.

(b) The other passage is I John 5.20. Here the problem is not a problem either of text or translation, but of connection and interpretation. There are no material differences between the renderings of the various translators, and we quote the translation of the NEB:

> We know that the Son of God has come and given us understanding to know him who is real; indeed we are in him who is real, since we are in his Son Jesus Christ. This is the true God, this is eternal life.

The problem is, to whom does the statement, 'This is the true God,' refer? Does it refer to God, or does it refer to Jesus Christ? It is hardly possible to be certain, although, to express again a personal opinion, the run of the section seems to make it refer to Jesus Christ. But once again the doubt is such that we could not base any firm argument on the passage.

(v) We turn next to the Revelation. The revelant fact about the Revelation is not that it definitely and directly calls Jesus God but that it unhesitatingly takes Old Testament pictures and descriptions which belong to God and applies them to Jesus Christ. That is to say, it consistently speaks of the Risen Lord in terms of God. And here we may note that the Revelation has nothing at all to say about Jesus in the days of his flesh; it is the Risen Lord with which it is entirely concerned. We may take a passage like Rev. 1.13-16. John sees in the midst of the seven golden lampstands 'one like a son of man, robed down to his feet, with a golden girdle round his breast. The hair of his head was white as snow-white wool, and his eyes flamed like fire; his feet gleamed like burnished brass refined in a furnace, and his voice was like the sound of rushing waters.' That is a description taken directly from the description of the Ancient of Days in Dan. 10.5-7 and of the voice of God in Ezek. 43.2. That is to say, the John of the Revelation has described the Risen Christ in precisely the same terms as the Old Testament writers use to describe God. He thereby clearly indicates that he would have called Jesus God.

(vi) We turn next to the undoubted letters of Paul. In these letters we have to consider certain facts and two particular passages.

(a) It is not doubtful that Paul thought of Jesus Christ in terms of God. He says of Jesus that he was in the *form* of God. (Phil. 2.6). He then goes on to say that Jesus was found in human *form* (Phil. 2.8, RSV), where the AV renders that he was found in *fashion* as a man. The RSV somewhat misleadingly translates two Greek words by the English word *form*, whereas the AV correctly distinguishes between them. In the first instance the word is *morphē*, which means the unchanging and unchangeable essential nature of a thing; the second word is *schēma*, which means the changing and altering external form of a person or a thing. For instance, a man has always the unchanging *morphē* of manhood; that is what he essentially is; but he will have different *schēmata*, different outward forms, in babyhood, childhood, youth, maturity and old age. A tulip, a rose, a chrysanthemum, a marigold, a daffodil, a delphinium all have the same *morphē*, the same essential nature, for they are all flowers; but they have very different outward *schēmata*, outward forms. Paul says that Jesus was in the *morphē* of God; that is to say, the essential nature of Jesus is the same as the essential nature of God; but he says that Jesus was found in the *schēma* of a man; that is to say, he temporarily took the form of manhood upon him. The NEB renders the Greek well here. In translating the word *morphē* it renders the passage: 'The divine nature was his from the first.' In translating the word *schēma* it says that he was 'revealed in human shape.' This passage leaves us in no doubt that Paul believed that the nature of Jesus is the nature of God.

The second passage is in Col. 2.9 where Paul says of Jesus: 'In him the whole fulness of deity dwells bodily' (RSV). The NEB renders: 'It is in Christ that the complete being of the Godhead dwells embodied.' Here again there is the affirmation of faith that Jesus is not explicable on any human terms.

On these general grounds we may say with certainty that Paul believed in the deity of Jesus Christ.

(*b*) When we come to particular passages the certainty is very much less. There are two passages which we must consider.

The first is Romans 9.5. The difficulty of this passage is neither in text nor in translation; the difficulty is in punctuation; and here the original manuscripts are of no help to us, for in them there was no punctuation at all, nor was there even any space between the words. The writing simply runs straight on. The translators of this passage punctuate it in two ways. Of the one method of punctuation the AV may be taken as typical:

> Whose (that is, the Jews) are the fathers, and of whom as concerning the flesh Christ came, who is over all, God blessed for ever. Amen.

In that translation there is a comma after 'all', and therefore
the phrase 'God blessed for ever' refers back to Christ, and
therefore Jesus is definitely called God. This translation is
followed by Weymouth and the *Twentieth Century New
Testament,* and is referred to in a footnote as a possibility by
the RSV.

Of the other method of punctuation the NEB may be taken
as typical, although it refers to the first method in a footnote
as a possibility:

> Theirs are the patriarchs, and from them in natural
> descent sprang the Messiah. May God, supreme above
> all, be blessed for ever! Amen.

In that rendering there is a full stop after Messiah or Christ,
and the words after that become, not a reference to Christ,
but an ascription of praise to God. This rendering is followed
by the RSV, by Kingsley Williams, by Moffatt, who underlines the separation of the words even further by enclosing
them in brackets, and by Goodspeed, who prefaces them with
a dash.

Here again is a case in which few will wish to be dogmatic.
Both punctuations are equally possible, although, to express
no more than an opinion, we would say that the Greek reads
more naturally as an ascription of praise to God, especially
when we remember the presence of the closing Amen.

The second passage is in Col. 2.2, and is a very difficult
passage. The meaning of this passage turns on the meaning
of the word *mustērion,* mystery. In Greek religious thought a
mystery is not something mysterious in the modern sense of
the term. A mystery in New Testament language is, first,
something which has been revealed by God to man and which
man could not have discovered for himself; and, second,
something which is hidden and obscure to the outsider, but
clear and meaningful to the initiate. The thing itself may be

very simple, but its meaning is only open to those to whom
it has been granted to know it and to see it. We shall take
three renderings of this passage.

First there is the rendering of the AV: It is Paul's desire for
the Colossians,

> 'that their hearts might be comforted, being knit to-
> gether in love, and unto all riches of the full assurance
> of understanding, to the acknowledgment (i.e. the know-
> ledge) of the full mystery of God, and of the Father
> and of Christ.'

This is one of the rare occasions when the AV is actually in
error, for it is clear in the Greek that the mystery of God is
in fact nothing other than Christ himself.

The rendering of the RSV corrects the error:

> That their hearts may be encouraged as they are knit
> together in love, to have all the riches of assured under-
> standing and the knowledge of God's mystery, of Christ,
> in whom are hid all the treasures of wisdom and
> knowledge.

This corrects the error and gives the true sense of the passage.

The rendering of the NEB still further clarifies the passage:

> I want them to continue in good heart and in the unity
> of love, and to come to the full wealth of conviction
> which understanding brings, and grasp God's secret. That
> secret is Christ himself; in him lie hidden all God's
> treasures of wisdom and knowledge.

Jesus Christ is the mystery of God, the revealed truth of
God, the one in whom to the Christian the secret of the love
of God is full displayed. This is natural and easy to understand. Paul's prayer is that the Colossians should strive to
come to a knowledge of Jesus Christ, because Jesus Christ is
God's mystery, God's revelation to those who accept him of
his truth and of his love.

But it is just possible to translate this passage in an entirely different way. It could mean that it is Paul's aim that the Colossians should come to a knowledge of 'the mystery of the God Christ', that is to say, that they should come to a knowledge of the secret truth which the God Christ brought to men. No modern translator accepts this rendering, although certain ancient translators did, and it is mentioned by Cullmann as a possibility.[1]

Our conclusion then in regard to Paul is that in general there is no doubt that he thought of Jesus Christ in terms of God, but that the passages in which he may have called Jesus by the title of God are so doubtful that once again no firm argument can be based upon them.

(vii) Finally we turn to the Pastoral Epistles. In them there are two passages to be considered.

(a) The first passage is Titus 2.13. The renderings of this passage fall into two groups. Of the first group the AV is typical. It translates:

> Looking for the blessed hope and the glorious appearing of the great God and our Saviour Jesus Christ.

In that rendering 'the great God' and 'our Saviour Jesus Christ' are distinguished and are different persons. Moffatt and Kingsley Williams follow this translation and the RSV and the NEB refer to it as a possibility in a footnote.

Of the second group the NEB is typical:

> Looking forward to the happy fulfilment of our hopes when the splendour of our great God and Saviour Christ Jesus will appear.

With this translation the RSV, Weymouth, the *Twentieth Century New Testament,* and Goodspeed agree.

This is closely parallel to II Peter 1.1, and it is probable

[1] *The Christology of the New Testament* p. 313.

that the second translation which identified God and our Saviour Jesus Christ is correct.

(b) The second passage is in I Tim. 3.16, which is in fact a fragment of a Christian hymn. In this case there is a textual variant which makes the translation uncertain. The renderings fall into two groups. The AV renders:

> And without controversy great is the mystery of godliness: God was manifest in the flesh.

The RSV refers to this as a possibility in a footnote.

The other rendering is, as in the RSV:

> Great indeed, we confess, is the mystery of our religion: He was manifested in the flesh.

With this reading the literal translation is in fact 'who was manifested in the flesh.' This is the translation of the RSV, the NEB, Weymouth, Moffatt, the *Twentieth Century New Testament* and Kingsley Williams.

Clearly the consensus of opinion is much in favour of the second rendering which eliminates the word God.[1]

Here then is the sum total of the New Testament evidence for the application of the name God to Jesus Christ. In the first three Gospels Jesus is never called God. In the Fourth Gospel Jesus is unequivocally called God only in the cry of the adoring heart of Thomas (John 20.28). There is no doubt that Paul thought of Jesus in terms of God, but there is no passage in his letters in which Jesus is called God beyond any doubt. In the General Epistles it is possible that Jesus is called God in I John 5.20, but by no means certain. The probability is that he is called God in II Peter 1.1 and in

---

[1] The variant reading in the manuscripts comes from a confusion very easily made. The earliest manuscripts are uncials, that is, written in capital letters, and contractions are freely used. The word for 'God' is *theos* and the word for 'who' is *hos*; *theos* is contracted into ΘC and *hos* is written OC. Obviously confusion is easy.

Titus 2.13. The result of this examination is that there is only one passage in the New Testament, John 20.28, where there is no doubt that Jesus is called God.

There is a curious problem here. If it were possible to take all the passages in the New Testament in which Jesus *may* be called God and to put them together, the evidence would be very strong, but the curious fact is that so many of the passages involve a doubt either of text or of translation. It may well be that there is a reason for this strange situation. It may well be that the early Church did think and speak of Jesus as God, but that there was a certain hesitancy to write this down, as it were, in cold print. In the language of adoration it sounded completely fitting; but the theology of the mind hesitated completely to accept the verdict of the heart. It was one thing to speak or sing of Jesus as God; it was quite another thing to write it down in black and white. It is extremely significant that on the one occasion when there is no argument, in the case of Thomas, the statement is not a theological proposition but a lover's cry; it is not the product of intellectual reasoning but of intense personal emotion. That is why, I think we can still without hesitation call Jesus God in a hymn of adoration while to state it as a theological dogma still evokes a certain hesitancy. It is this very fact which produced the strangely confused evidence of the New Testament itself. In view of this let us go on to ask what the New Testament writers meant when they thought of Jesus in terms of God.

To begin with, one thing is clear. With the exception of Luke all the New Testament writers were Jews. The Jews were and still are intense monotheists; and, therefore, if any Jew thought of Jesus in terms of God, he was certainly not setting Jesus up as a rival God or even as a second God. Nothing that they said or thought could lessen the lonely holiness of God.

It is further clear that Jesus never set himself on an equality with God nor did he identify himself with God. Jesus' own name for God is Father, and the characteristic and essential attitude of sonship is loving and trusting obedience to the father. Time and again we find Jesus at prayer to God. Again and again he slipped away to be alone with God and to draw strength from God. In Gethsemane he prayed to be enabled to accept the will of God (Matt. 26.36-46; Mark 14.32-42; Luke 22.40-46). On the Cross he prayed: 'My God, my God why hast thou forsaken me?' (Matt. 27.46; Mark 15.34). No one can possibly hold that Jesus was praying to himself. Even if we call Jesus God, we must see that he lived in continual obedience and trust to the God who was his Father.

Still further, when we study the books in which Jesus is called God, or in which he is unmistakably thought of in terms of God, we do not go very far before we are confronted with a paradox. As we have seen, in the Revelation John does not hesitate to attach to Jesus Old Testament descriptions of God (e.g. Rev. 1.13-15), but in that very same book the Risen Christ is repeatedly shown to us as speaking of 'My God.' He says to Sardis: 'I have not found any work of yours completed in the eyes of my God.' He says to Philadelphia: 'He who is victorious—I will make him a pillar in the temple of my God' (Rev. 3.2,12). Certainly the writer of the Revelation regarded Jesus as God, and yet at the same time God was Jesus' God even in the state of his glory.

It may well be that the writer to the Hebrews calls Jesus God (Heb. 1.8). Yet this very same writer vividly shows us Jesus in Gethsemane praying to God with loud cries and tears (Heb. 5.7). Certainly the writer to the Hebrews thought of Jesus in terms of God, but equally certainly he saw nothing unnatural in the sight of Jesus praying desperately and agonisingly to God.

Certainly Paul thought of Jesus as God, but this same Paul

can write: 'When all things are thus subject to him (Jesus), then the Son himself will also be made subordinate to God, who made all things subject to him, and thus God will be all in all' (I Cor. 15.28). Paul could and did think of Jesus as God without in any way losing the conviction of the lonely supremacy of God.

Nowhere does this paradox stand out more clearly than in the Fourth Gospel. No one can doubt that John thought of Jesus in terms of God; and yet there is no book where Jesus speaks so often of being *sent* to do God's will. 'This is eternal life: to know thee who alone art truly God, and Jesus Christ whom thou hast sent (John 17.3). Nowhere is the father-son relationship of Jesus to God more magnificently stated, and nowhere is the obedience of Jesus to God more consistently stressed. 'It is meat and drink for me to do the will of him who sent me until I have finished his work' (John 4.34). In no book is the unique relationship of Jesus to God more continuously stressed, and yet in no book is God more truly God, controlling and directing every word and action of Jesus.

The paradox of the Fourth Gospel reaches its highest tension in two sayings of Jesus. Jesus said: 'My Father and I are one' (John 10.30). And Jesus said: 'The Father is greater than I' (John 14.28). After his resurrection Jesus said to Mary Magdalene: 'Go to my brothers and tell them that I am now ascending to my Father and your Father, my God and your God' (John 20.17). No Gospel so clearly sets out Jesus in terms of this double idea of deity and subjection to deity, of godhead and subjection to God.

If this is to be understood, we must start from Jesus' saying: 'My Father and I are one' (John 10.30). Wherein did that oneness, that unity, that identity lie? We shall find the key to this in Jesus' prayer for his own people. In his prayer for his disciples and for all who will come to believe in him Jesus prayed that 'they may be one as we are one' (John 17.22).

This is clearly to say that the unity, the oneness between Christian and Christian must be the same as the unity, the oneness between Jesus and God. We must then argue from the known to the unknown and from the seen to the unseen. Wherein lies the oneness, the unity, between Christian and Christian? It is Jesus' prayer for his people that the love the Father had for him may be in them (John 17.26). The badge of Christian discipleship is that they should obey the new commandment and that they should have love one for another (John 13.33,34). This is to say as clearly as it can be said that the oneness, the unity between Christian and Christian is a oneness and a unity of love. *It, therefore, follows that the unity between Jesus and God is a unity of love.* The unity of Jesus and God is the unity of a personal relationship. No one would claim that this is all that there is to say, but here is something which we can understand. It may well be that, when we move into a world of philosophic and metaphysical essences and substances and beings and the like, we have not only moved into a world which is unintelligible to the ordinary mind, but also that we may well have in fact taken the wrong turning. It may be that we should seek and find the relationship of Jesus to God in a world of personal relationships—which is a realm which we all understand because we are persons.

If the relationship between God and Jesus is a relationship of utter and perfect love, then light shines. If there exists between Jesus and God this complete and perfect personal relationship, then the heart of Jesus and the heart of God, the mind of Jesus and the mind of God, are perfectly one. What in fact did Jesus say in what may well be regarded as the supreme saying of the Fourth Gospel? He said: 'Anyone who has seen me has seen the *Father*' (John 14.9). It is not: 'Anyone who has seen me has seen *God*'; it is: 'Anyone who has seen me has seen the *Father*.' In Jesus we do not see

God's *omnipotence*, for there were times when Jesus was hungry and weary and on the point of physical collapse. In Jesus we do not see God's *omnipresence*, for Jesus in the days of his flesh was as subject to the laws of space and time as any other man. In Jesus we do not see God's *omniscience*, for there were things which Jesus did not know. He did not, for instance, know the time of his return. In Jesus we do not see the great *world-sustaining, world-directing* power of God, for when Jesus was on this earth God was still sustaining, controlling and directing his universe. What we do see in Jesus is *the Father*, and that very word expresses a personal relationship. In Jesus we see perfectly and completely revealed the heart of God for man, the mind of God for man, the attitude of God towards man, the personal relationship which God wills to exist between himself and man. It is precisely here that Paul's great saying comes in: 'God was in Christ reconciling the world to himself' (II Cor. 5.19).

Nels Ferré has somewhere a wise saying. You can, he says, say that Jesus is God, but you cannot say that God is Jesus. God was still directing his universe in omniscience, omnipotence and omnipresence, when the man Jesus was on this earth; but in this man Jesus we see absolutely, perfectly, completely, uniquely, unrepeatably God as God is in his personal relationship with men.

Christian devotion in every age is right when it calls Jesus God, for human categories are not enough to contain him, for he is beyond a doubt the incarnate love of the heart of God for men. No man can know God as God is in himself, for no human mind can comprehend infinity, nor do we need to comprehend it. What we can see in Jesus is God in his attitude and in his relationship to men, and that is all we need to know. That is what we see perfectly enmanned in Jesus, and that is why it is right to call Jesus God.

4

SON OF DAVID

IT might well be said that of all the titles which are applied to Jesus Son of David is most Jewish, most deeply rooted in the history, the tradition, and the expectation of the Jewish people.

For the Jews there never had been and there never would be a king like David, for David was the man after God's own heart. To David God had made the great promise: 'Your house and your kingdom shall be made sure for ever before me; your throne shall be established for ever' (II Sam. 7.16). It was, therefore, only to be expected that, when the Jews dreamed of a golden age, they connected it with a king of David's line. The oldest and the most popular idea of the Messiah was that God would send to his people a king such as David had been, a king who would deliver his people, a king who would restore the greatness of Israel, and lead them to a glory such as they had never known before.

This was the dream of Isaiah: 'Of the increase of his government and of peace there shall be no end, upon the throne of David and over his kingdom, to establish and to uphold it with justice and with righteousness from this time forth and for evermore' (Isa. 9.7). It was out of the stump of Jesse that the shoot was to come (Isa. 11.1). This was the dream of Jeremiah: 'Behold the days are coming, says the Lord, when I will raise up for David a righteous Branch, and he shall reign as king and deal wisely, and shall execute justice and righteousness in the land' (Jer. 23.5). 'They shall serve the Lord their God and David their king, whom I will raise up for them' (Jer. 30.9). 'David shall never lack a man

38

to sit on the throne of the house of Israel' (Jer. 33.17). This was the dream of Amos: 'In that day I will raise up the booth of David that is fallen, and repair its breaches, and raise up its ruins, and rebuild it as in the days of old' (Amos 9.11). This was the dream of Zechariah: 'On that day the Lord will put a shield about the inhabitants of Jerusalem so that the feeblest among them on that day shall be like David, and the house of David shall be like God' (Zech. 12.8). It was the dream of Hosea that the day would come when the children of Israel would 'return and seek the Lord their God and David their king' (Hos. 3.5). This was the dream of Ezekiel, who heard God say: 'I will set up over them one shepherd, my servant David, and he shall feed them; he shall feed them and be their shepherd. And I, the Lord, will be their God, and my servant David shall be prince among them' (Ezek. 34.23,24). 'My servant David shall be king over them, and they shall all have one shepherd' (Ezek. 37.24).

It is quite true that the dream of the Messiah changed. When the situation so deteriorated that it became plain that no human means could ever mend it, then the hope of a champion and liberator of David's line began to be displaced by the hope of a divine superhuman Messiah, or by the hope of the direct intervention of God, and of all the apocalyptic events of the last days. But, whatever were the hopes and the speculations of the Rabbis and of the scholars, to the heart of the ordinary people the dream of the king of David's line was still very dear. In fact the first time that the actual expression 'Son of David' occurs is in the Psalms of Solomon, midway through the first century BC. It is the prayer of the poet and patriot who wrote these Psalms: 'Behold, O Lord, and raise up unto them their king, the son of David, at the time in which thou seest, O God, that he may reign over thy servant Israel' (Ps. Sol. 17.23). The hope of the king of David's line never died.

Roman imperial policy sheds a flood of light on the dearness of this dream to the Jews. Eusebius, quoting Hegesippus, tells us that, after the conquest of Jerusalem in AD 70 Vespasian gave orders that all who belonged to the lineage of David should be sought out, in order that none of the royal family should be left among the Jews. And as late as AD 90 Domitian was following the same policy, for Eusebius writes of him: 'Domitian commanded that the descendants of David should be slain'.[1] Even as late as that the Roman thought it possible that a descendant of David could still become a focus of trouble and a rallying point for national patriotic sentiment.

Not infrequently in the New Testament Jesus is referred to as the Son of David. Particular stress is laid on his physical descent from David. Matthew begins his Gospel: 'The book of the genealogy of Jesus Christ, the Son of David' (Matt. 1.1). Gabriel's promise to Mary in Luke's Gospel is that the Lord God will give to the child she will bear 'the throne of his father David' (Luke 1.32). Paul speaks of Jesus Christ 'who was descended from David according to the flesh' (Rom. 1.3). In the Pastoral Epistles the instruction is: 'Remember Jesus Christ, risen from the dead, descended from David' (II Tim. 2.8). In the Revelation the Risen Lord is called 'the Lion of the tribe of Judah, the Root of David' (Rev. 5.5). 'I am the root and offspring of David,' he says, 'the bright morning star' (Rev. 22.16). In the same way, the descent of Joseph from David is stressed in order to guarantee the lineage of Jesus (Matt. 1.20; Luke 1.27; 2.4).

It was for the Messiah who was the Son of David that the people were waiting. 'Does not Scripture say,' they said, 'that the Messiah is to be of the family of David?' (John 7.42). Fairly frequently in the Gospels, especially in Matthew, as one would expect in the most Jewish of the Gospels, Jesus is

[1] *Ecclesiastical History* 3.12 and 19.

addressed as the Son of David. He was so called by the two
blind men (Matt. 9.27); by the people when he healed the
blind and dumb demoniac (Matt. 12.13); by the Syro-
Phoenician woman (Matt. 15.22); by the blind man or blind
men in Jericho (Matt. 20.30,31; Mark 10.47,48; Luke 18.38,
39); by the crowds in the streets of Jerusalem and the children
in the Temple courts (Matt. 21.9,15).

It can be seen that it was the simple people who called
Jesus Son of David, especially when they were astonished at
his power, or when they desired the help of that power for
themselves, and, when they did so call him, they were clearly
greeting him as the long-expected Messiah.

But there was one occasion when Jesus quite definitely
accepted this title, yet as definitely laid it down that it was
not enough. The incident is related in all the first three Gospels
(Matt. 22.41-45; Mark 2.35-37; Luke 20.41-44). Jesus asked
the Pharisees what they had to say about the Messiah. They
answered that the Messiah was the Son of David. Jesus then
drew their attention to Ps. 110.1, which was universally accepted as Messianic. In the argument the assumption is that
David wrote the Psalm. The Psalm begins: 'The Lord said to
my Lord, Sit at my right hand, until I put your enemies under
your feet.' The first *Lord* is God, for God is the speaker; the
second *Lord* is the Messiah, the conquering liberator and
triumphant champion who is to come. It has already been
stated by the Pharisees that the Messiah is the *Son* of David;
but in the Psalm David calls the Messiah *Lord*. This means
that the expression *Son* of David is not in itself enough to
describe Jesus, for he is *Lord* of David too.

Jesus was indeed Son of David by physical descent; and he
was indeed Son of David in that all the Messianic hopes and
promises were fulfilled in him. But the very words of that
Psalm, which speak of his enemies being put under his feet,
lend themselves to the interpretation of the Messiah as a

mighty warrior and conquering king who was to subdue in military conquest the enemies of David, and that is precisely the interpretation of the Messiah which Jesus had once and for all refused and put aside. In that sense Jesus was not the Son of David; he was something very different and something far more.

So, then, Son of David is the most Jewish of all the titles of Jesus, and Jesus accepted that title, because it was his by right, but he also transcended it; and in so doing he laid down his connection with the past, but he also laid it down that in himself he had brought to men something which not only fulfilled the dreams of the past, but which also far transcended them.

5

SON OF GOD

IT may well be true to say that of all the titles of Jesus the title Son of God comes most automatically to our lips; and yet it may also be true to say that of all the titles of Jesus it is the title of which the meaning is least clearly defined in our minds.

That the idea of Jesus as Son of God was central to the thought of the Church from the beginning there is no doubt. Mark's Gospel opens: 'The beginning of the gospel of Jesus Christ, the Son of God' (Mark 1.1); and, even if the phrase Son of God is not part of the original text of the Gospel, it nevertheless shows the terms in which the early Church thought of Jesus. Similarly, it is generally agreed that Acts 8.37 is not part of the original text of the book; but it is the expression of the faith and belief of the early Church. It is the statement of the conditions of baptism made by Philip to the Ethiopian. Philip told the Ethiopian that, if he believed with all his heart, he could be baptised; and the Ethiopian answered: 'I believe that Jesus Christ is the Son of God.' Whether or not that statement is part of the original text of Acts, it is certainly the baptismal confession of the early Church. John wrote: 'If a man acknowledges that Jesus is the Son of God, God dwells in him and he dwells in God' (I John 4.15). 'Who is victor over the world but he who believes that Jesus is the Son of God? (I John 5.5). The letter is addressed to 'those who give their allegiance to the Son of God' (I John 5.13). And since the First Letter of John is part of the front-line battle for orthodoxy in face of Christological heresy, John's insistent use of the title is all the more significant.

43

It is further clear, according to the New Testament narrative, that it was this title, or rather the claim to this title, which was the principal charge against Jesus in the eyes of the orthodox Jewish authorities. When Jesus spoke of 'My Father', as John tells the story, 'This made the Jews still more determined to kill him, because he was not only breaking the Sabbath, but, by calling God his own Father, he claimed equality with God' (John 5.17,18). 'Are you the Messiah, the Son of God?' was the question of the High Priest to Jesus, and it was a question intended and designed to produce a self-incriminating answer (Matt. 26.63,64; Mark 14.61,62; Luke 22.69,70). And it was exactly that claim which the crowds took up in their taunts to Jesus on the Cross: 'Did he trust in God? Let God rescue him, if he wants him—for he said he was God's Son' (Matt. 27.42,43). 'We have a law,' the Jews said, 'and by that law he ought to die, because he claimed to be Son of God' (John 19.7). Clearly the claim to be the Son of God was precisely the blasphemy with which Jesus was charged.

It is further true that the New Testament Letters make it abundantly clear that there is no stratum of New Testament thought in which the conception of Jesus as the Son of God is not basic and fundamental. Jesus is designated the Son of God in power (Rom. 1.3). It is the Son of God, Jesus Christ, that Paul and Silvanus and Timothy preached to the Corinthians (II Cor. 1.19). It is by faith in the Son of God, who loved him and gave himself for him, that Paul lives (Gal. 2.20). To come to the knowledge of the Son of God is the very essence of a mature Christian faith (Eph. 4.13). The essence of the distinction between Jesus and the prophets, the former bearers to men of the revelation of God, is that Jesus is a Son (Heb. 4.14). Apostasy is a recrucifixion of the Son of God (Heb. 6.6). The man who has spurned the Son of God cannot hope to escape the consequences of his action (Heb. 10.29).

The Son of God appeared for the very purpose of undoing
the devil's work (I John 3.8). The Son of God came to give
men understanding of him who is real (I John 5.20). The
letter to Thyatira begins: 'These are the words of the Son of
God' (Rev. 2.18). One of the commonest descriptions of God
is to call God the God and Father of our Lord Jesus Christ
(Rom. 15.6; II Cor. 1.3; 2.30; Eph. 1.3; Col. 1.3; I Peter 1.3;
Rev. 1.6). The Second Letter of John speaks of Jesus Christ,
the Father's Son (II John 3).

It is clear that the idea of Jesus as Son of God is written
into the theology, the devotion, and the liturgy of the New
Testament Church.

In the Fourth Gospel there is a special manifestation of
all this. The Fourth Gospel has a characteristic way of referring to Jesus as 'the Son' and of showing him referring to
himself by that title. 'The Father loves the Son and has
entrusted him with all authority. He who puts his faith in the
Son has hold of eternal life; but he who disobeys the Son shall
not see that life' (John 3.35,36). 'The Father does not judge
anyone but has given full jurisdiction to the Son; it is his will
that all should pay the same honour to the Son as to the
Father. To deny honour to the Son is to deny it to the Father
who sent him' (John 5.22,23). 'It is my Father's will that
everyone who looks upon the Son and puts his faith in him
shall possess eternal life' (John 6.40). All over the Fourth
Gospel we find references to the Son, in such a way that
the phrase 'the Son' quite clearly is not so much a description
of a relationship as it is a title, and almost the description of
an office.

Very closely connected with this is the way in which Jesus
is constantly shown in the Fourth Gospel speaking about
'My Father'. 'You must not turn my Father's house into a
market,' he said (John 2.16). 'I have come accredited by my
Father' (John 5.43). 'I am revealing in words what I saw in

my Father's presence' (John 8.39). 'If I am not acting as my Father would, do not believe me' (John 10.37). 'There are many dwelling-places in my Father's house' (John 14.2). 'Anyone who loves me will heed what I say; then my Father will love him, and we will come to him and make our dwelling with him' (John 14.23). The word of the Risen Christ to Mary is: 'I am ascending to my Father and your Father, to my God and your God' (John 20.17). Clearly there is the closest personal relationship between Jesus and God. He is uniquely 'the Son', and God is uniquely to him 'my Father'.

Let us then try to find out something of the meaning of the title Son of God. We must begin by noting that this is not a title which either Jesus or Christian theology invented. It is in fact a title with a long and varied history.

(i)   In the Old Testament *the angels* are called the sons of God. The old Genesis story tells how the sons of God saw that the daughters of men were fair and came down and took to wife such as they chose (Gen. 6.2). In the prologue of the drama of the book of Job we read that there was a day when the sons of God came to present themselves before the Lord and Satan also came among them (Job 1.6). We read of the day of creation when the morning stars sang together and all the sons of God shouted for joy (Job 38.7). Certainly in the Old Testament the angels are called the sons of God, but it has to be noted, as the writer to the Hebrews pointed out, that no individual angel is ever called the Son of God (Heb. 1.5).

(ii)   In the Old Testament *the nation of Israel* is called the son of God. It is the message and the demand of God to Pharaoh: 'Thus says the Lord, Israel is my first-born son, and I say to you, Let my son go that he may serve me' (Ex. 4.22, 23). Hosea heard God say: 'When Israel was a child, I loved him, and out of Egypt I called my son' (Hos. 11.1). It is possible to speak of God's chosen nation as God's son.

(iii)   If the nation as a whole was the son of God, then it was natural to speak of *the king of the nation* as being God's son in a special sense. In Ps. 89.27 we read: 'I will make him the (AV my) firstborn.' It was God's promise in regard to Solomon: 'I will be his father, and he shall be my son' (II Sam. 7.14). In a special sense God's chosen king of God's chosen people was God's son.

(iv)   In Luke's genealogy of Jesus, the lineage of Jesus is traced back to *Adam,* who, as Luke says, 'was the son of God' (Luke 3.38). And in the beatitudes of Jesus *the peace-makers* are called the sons of God (Matt. 5.9).

(v)   The heathen world was well acquainted with the calling of men sons of God. Pagan mythology was full of heroes who owed their birth to the union of a god with a mortal maid. Hercules was the son of Alkmene and Zeus; Achilles was the son of Thetis the goddess and Peleus the mortal man. It was a commonplace for nations and races to trace their origin back to some divine founder. And in the Hellenistic world it was a commonplace for kings to provide themselves with pedigrees stretching back to the gods. So the Ptolemies of Egypt traced their origin back to a god, and Alexander the Great provided himself with a lineage stemming from Zeus. The ancient world was very familiar with stories of heroes and demigods who claimed an origin which made them sons of the gods.

It is further to be noted, and this is a point to which we shall return, that Son of God was a title of the Messiah. In the Book of Enoch, written between the Testaments, the promise of God is: 'I and my Son will be united with them for ever in the paths of uprightness in their lives; and you shall have peace' (Enoch 105.2). The same title occurs in II (4) Esdras, written early in the second century AD. There the writer says: 'My Son the Messiah shall be revealed' (II [4] Esd. 7.28,29). My Son shall reprove the nations . . .

for their ungodliness (II [4] Esd. 13.37). 'No one upon the earth can see my Son but in the power of his day' (II [4] Esd. 13.52).

This use of the title can be seen in the New Testament itself. In Matthew Peter's confession at Caesarea Philippi is: 'You are the Messiah, the Son of the living God' (Matt. 16.16). The question of the High Priest to Jesus at his trial is: 'Are you the Messiah, the Son of God?' (Matt. 26.63; cp. Mark 14.61). The narrative of Luke again shows how the two titles were equated. 'Tell us,' said the Jews, 'are you the Messiah?' 'If I tell you' said Jesus, 'you will not believe me; and if I ask questions, you will not answer.' Then he went on: 'But from now on, the Son of Man will be seated at the right hand of Almighty God.' 'You are the Son of God, then?' they all said (Luke 22.67-70). It is clear from the New Testament that Son of God is a known Messianic title.

Let us now turn to the Gospels themselves in order to see Jesus' own consciousness of sonship, as it appears in their account of his life and teaching. If we accept the record of the Gospels as in any way valid, it is clear that from the beginning to the end of his life Jesus lived in the unique consciousness of his own sonship.

(i) When Jesus was a lad of twelve, as Luke tells the story, on his first visit to the Passover in Jerusalem he lingered behind after his parents had set out for home. They sought him and found him in the temple, and gently chided him for causing them anxiety. His answer was: 'Did you not know that I was bound to be in my Father's house?' (Luke 2.49). We may well see here what we might call the dawn of Jesus' articulate consciousness of his own special relationship with God. This becomes even clearer when we set Mary's question beside Jesus' answer. The question was: 'My son, why have you treated us like this? Your father and I have been searching for you in great anxiety' (Luke 2.48). In his answer Jesus

gently but definitely takes the word Father and gives it
directly to God. Jesus' realisation of his position and his
task had begun.

(ii) It was precisely that consciousness which came to
Jesus in the moment of his baptism, for it was then that the
voice spoke to him: 'Thou art my Son, my Beloved; on thee
my favour rests' (Mark 1.11; Matt. 3.17; Luke 3.22). It
was in the consciousness of his sonship that he entered upon
his ministry and set out on his task.

(iii)   In the temptations the tempter began his attacks on
Jesus by saying: 'If you are the Son of God' (Matt. 4.3,6;
Luke 4.3,9). There are two things involved here. (a) The
very form of the tempter's attack invites Jesus to have doubts
about his own sonship. '*If* you are the Son of God.' It is
as if the tempter said to him: 'Are you sure that the whole
thing is not a delusion? Are you sure that you are not only
imagining you are God's Son?' The sure way to paralyse a
man's actions is to make him doubt his destiny. If at that
moment Jesus had allowed a doubt to creep like a canker into
his mind, he could not have gone on. (b) Given that he
was the Son of God, Jesus had to find some way of expressing that sonship in action. Here in the temptation story
he is confronted with the choice between expressing his
conviction of sonship in the conventional, nationalistic,
materialistic terms, or of expressing it in terms of an obedience
to God which could only end on the Cross. The entire background of the temptation story is the consciousness of Jesus
of his own sonship, and in the temptation there came to Jesus
the twofold temptation to doubt his own sonship and to express it in the wrong way.

(iv)   As Jesus' days in the flesh began to march to their
inevitable conclusion, and as the Cross became not a distant
shadow, but an immediate certainty, the same voice came again
to Jesus on the Mount of Transfiguration. 'This is my Son,

my Beloved,' God said, 'on whom my favour rests; listen to him' (Matt. 17.5; Mark 9.7; Luke 9.35). Jesus was armed with the consciousness of sonship as he steadfastly set his face to go to Jerusalem.

(v) Through the last days of Jesus' earthly life this consciousness runs like a dominant theme. It emerges in the parable of the wicked husbandmen (Matt. 21.33-43; Mark 12.1-12; Luke 20.9-19). In that parable the vineyard is Israel (Isa. 5.1-7), the owner of the vineyard is God, the husbandmen are the leaders and the rulers of Israel, the orthodox authorities. To request the rental for the vineyard the master first sents a series of servants, and, when they are repelled and ill-treated and killed, he sends his son. The servants are the prophets who were rejected and persecuted in their day and generation; the son is Jesus himself. The whole pattern of that parable distinguishes between the *servants* and the *son*, and does so deliberately. And by that very distinction Jesus distinguishes and separates himself from the prophets. They are *servants;* he is *the son.* True, he is in the prophetic succession, but he is more than a prophet and other than a prophet, as a son is more and other than a servant. Here in this parable Jesus deliberately confronts men with himself as the Son.

(vi) The very essence of the story of Gethsemane is that Jesus is talking to his Father (Matt. 26.36-42; Mark 14.32-39; Luke 22.39-44). In this scene Jesus is not so much praying to God as holding a conversation with his Father, which for him was one and the same thing. In Mark's account this is vividly underlined. In Mark we hear Jesus praying: 'Abba, Father!' (Mark 14.36). Here is one of the most astonishing and moving moments in the Gospel narrative. *Abba* was the Aramaic word by which a little child called his father in the home circle in Palestine in the days of Jesus, as *jaba* is in Arabic today. In other words, this is the Aramaic for the English word Daddy.

Translation is impossible, but there is no word which so shows the intimate relationship between Jesus and God. The essence of Gethsemane is still the experience of Jesus of the father-hood of God.

(vii) From Gethsemane Jesus went to his trial before the High Priest. There the High Priest challenged him with a question: 'Are you the Messiah, the Son of God?' Jesus answered: 'It is as you say' (Matt. 26.63,64; Mark 14.61,62; Luke 22.69). Jesus was well aware that in giving that answer he was signing his own death warrant. There is a very real sense in which Jesus went to his death for the sake of the conviction that God was his Father, and that he was the Son of God. This was the truth which it was impossible for him to hide or to deny.

(viii) From the trial before the High Priest and before Pilate Jesus went to the Cross. Here again he was met with the same temptation as had confronted him in the wilderness. The passers-by jeered at him. 'Come down from the cross and save yourself, if you are indeed the Son of God.' 'Did he trust in God? Let God rescue him, if he wants him—for he said he was God's Son' (Matt. 27.40,43). Here again there is the temptation to doubt his sonship, and this time it must have come to Jesus with redoubled force. Could his consciousness really be justified? Could God be his Father and yet allow this to happen? Was a cross any kind of place on which to find him who was the Son of God? This is the assault on the one conviction on which the whole life and being of Jesus depended. If that central citadel of his consciousness could be stormed, then his whole world was bound to disintegrate into tragic fragments. That God was his Father was the one truth which Jesus must clutch to himself or perish.

(ix) And to that truth he did victoriously cling, for it is with complete confidence in it that he died. As Luke tells the story, the last words of Jesus on the Cross were: 'Father, into thy hands I commit my spirit' (Luke 23.46). There is even more in that final committal than meets the eye at first glance. It is a quotation of Ps. 31.5. That verse was the first prayer which every Jewish mother taught her child to pray, when he went to bed at night before the dark came down. Jesus died with a child's prayer on his lips. But the significant thing is that to the verse of the Psalm, to the old prayer, he had added one word, the word *Father*. All things had conspired to wrest from him the conviction that God was his Father and that he was God's Son, but in spite of everything he had held triumphantly to it.

It is easy to see that in the first three Gospels we are presented with a picture of Jesus as a person whose life was begun, continued and ended in the consciousness that in a unique sense he was the Son of God, and whose whole work was sustained by that conviction.

When we turn to the Fourth Gospel, we find that it has a characteristic way of referring to Jesus as The Son. In it Jesus is The Son *par excellence*. We have to bring out the difference by writing the words with capital letters. 'The Father loves the Son and has entrusted him with all authority. He who puts his faith in the Son has hold of eternal life, but he who disobeys the Son shall not see that life' (3.35,36). 'The Father ... has given full jurisdiction to the Son; it is his will that all should pay the same honour to the Son as to the Father. To deny honour to the Son is to deny it to the Father who sent him' (5.22,23). Everywhere in the Fourth Gospel The Son and The Father are correlative terms. The Son is rather more a title than a description of Jesus.

Very closely connected with that is the fact that in the Fourth Gospel Jesus is continuously depicted as speaking of My Father. 'You must not turn my Father's house into a market,' he said when he cleansed the Temple (2.16). 'I have come accredited by my Father, and you have no welcome for me' (5.43). 'If I am not acting as my Father would, do not believe me' (10.37). 'There are many dwelling-places in my Father's house' (14.2). 'Anyone who loves me will heed what I say; then my Father will love him, and we will come to him and make our dwelling with him' (14.23). 'I have disclosed to you everything that I heard from my Father' (15.15). Jesus said to Mary Magdalene: 'I am now ascending to my Father and your Father, my God and your God' (20.17). All through the Fourth Gospel Jesus speaks of 'My Father', in a way that connects him quite uniquely with God.

We may further note, as being kin to this, what we might call the characteristic liturgical definition of God in the New Testament as the God and Father of our Lord Jesus Christ (Rom. 15.6; II Cor. 1.3; Eph. 1.3; Col. 1.3; I Peter 1.3; Rev. 1.6). The connection of Jesus with God is so close that he can only be described in terms of God and God can only be described in terms of him.

Into the pattern of this investigation there must now come another piece. Throughout the New Testament *men* are called sons of God; it was in fact precisely to give them that sonship that Jesus came into this world and lived and died. John describes the very essence of the Christian life: 'To all who did receive him, to those who have yielded him their allegiance, he gave the right to become children of God, not born of any human stock, or by the fleshly desire of a human father, but the offspring of God himself' (John 1.13). 'If you know that he (God) is righteous, you must recognize that every man who does right is his child. How great is the love that the Father has shown to us! We were called God's children, and such we are . . . Here and now, dear friends, we are God's children (I John 2.29; 3.1,2). 'All who are moved by the Spirit of God are sons of God' (Rom. 8.14). 'The created universe waits with eager expectation for God's sons to be revealed' (Rom. 8.19). 'Through faith you are all sons of God in union with Christ Jesus' (Gal. 3.26). 'You are therefore no longer a slave but a son, and if a son, then also by God's own act an heir' (Gal. 4.7). 'The Lord disciplines those whom he loves; he lays the rod on every son whom he acknowledges' (Heb. 12.6).

We have already seen how in Gethsemane (Mark 14.36) Jesus called God by the word Abba, the most intimate possible word, the word by which a little child called his father in the home circle; and it is Paul's insistence that it is open to men to do the same. 'The Spirit you have received is not a spirit of slavery leading you back into a life of fear, but a Spirit that makes us sons, enabling us to say, Abba! Father!' (Rom. 8.15). 'To prove that you are sons, God has sent into our hearts the Spirit of his Son, crying, Abba! Father!' (Gal. 4.6). Even such an intimacy with God as that is open to men.

Are we then to go on to say that there is open to men exactly the same sonship of God as was possessed by Jesus Christ? Can we say that it is quite possible for a man to be the son of in the same sense as Jesus Christ was the Son of God? To state that question is to answer it. When a man prays he does not so much say, *My* Father, as he says, Our Father. It is always clear in the New Testament that a man possesses his sonship by grace, while Jesus possessed his sonship as a right. A man enters into sonship by adoption, while Jeus Christ is Son in his being. We would not describe any man as The Son, with capital letters, as we describe Jesus Christ. Still less could any man say: 'Anyone who has seen me has seen the Father' (John 14.9). There is clearly in the sonship of Jesus a unique quality. A man may be *a son* of God; Jesus is *The Son* of God.

Let us then turn back to the New Testament to see if we can find out what was in the mind and the heart of those who called Jesus the Son of God.

(i) From the linguistic point of view the phrase Son of God could well mean simply *God-like*. Hebrew is not strong in adjectives and frequently it uses the phrase 'son of' followed by an abstract noun instead of an adjective. So Hebrew can speak of 'a son of peace' (Luke 10.6) where we would speak of a peaceable man. Barnabas can be called 'a son of consolation' (Acts 4.36) where we would speak of a consoling, or a comforting, or a sympathetic man. James and John are called 'sons of thunder' (Mark 3.17), where we would speak of thunderous or explosive characters. The peace-makers are called 'sons of God' (Matt. 5.9), where we would say that they are doing a God-like work. Are we then to say that when Jesus is called the Son of God that this is the equivalent of an adjective and that it means no more than God-like?

That the phrase Son of God can have that meaning there is no doubt; and that on one occasion it actually has that meaning there is equally no doubt. When Jesus died on the Cross the centurion who was in charge of the crucifixion paid him his astonished tribute of admiration. But Matthew and Mark have one version of that tribute while Luke has another. According to the first two Gospels the centurion said: 'Truly this man was a son of God' (Matt. 27.54; Mark 15.39). It is to be noted that the AV wrongly renders the phrase *the* Son of God; there is no *the* in the Greek, and this error is corrected in all the modern translations. In the same passage Luke (23.47) has, as the AV translates it: 'Certainly this was a righteous man', or, as the RSV and the NEB translate it: 'Certainly (NEB: beyond all doubt) this man was innocent.' The word which the AV translates 'righteous' and which the RSV and the NEB tranlate 'innocent' is *dikaios* which basically means 'just'. What the centurion in effect said was: 'This man has been condemned as a criminal and has died on a cross, but beyond a doubt he was a good man.' Here the phrase 'a son of God' and 'a good man' are used as identical.

Can we say that we have our clue here? Shall we go on to say that, when Jesus is called the Son of God, it means no more than that he was a specially good and God-like man? This explanation goes some distance towards the truth but falls short of the whole truth, because, if this was the explanation, Jesus would consistently be called *a* son of God, as in fact the centurion did call him, and not *the* Son of God, as in fact he was usually called. This explanation fails to do justice to the uniqueness which the use of the definite article gives to the phrase.

It is suggested that the title The Son of God is to be consistently interpreted as a Messianic title, and that it denotes Jesus as the Messiah. To a certain extent that is quite certainly true, and there are certain occasions when the title is certainly used in a Messianic sense.

(a)   To the western modern mind one of the most puzzling usages of this title in regard to Jesus is its consistent use by those who were demon-possessed. Mark tells us that, when the unclean spirits saw Jesus, they would fall at his feet and cry aloud: 'You are the Son of God' (Mark 3.11; cp. Luke 4.41). The cry of the Gerasene demoniac was: 'What do you want with me, Jesus, Son of the Most High God?' (Mark 5.7; Matt. 8.29; Luke 8.28). But, set against its background, this is the easiest of all the uses of the title to explain.

In the ancient world all illness was held to be due to the action of demons. It does not matter whether this is to be taken as literally true, or whether it is a primitive way of expressing the cause of illness which modern medicine would express differently. The important point is that the man who was ill was completely convinced that he was in fact demon-possessed. He was certain that the demons were occupying his body and his mind, and he had identified himself with them. Now it was the conviction that, when the Messiah came, he would defeat and destroy the demons; that was an essential part of the Messianic work and function. If then a demon-possessed man was confronted with Jesus, and if he had the idea that Jesus was the Messiah, his whole instinct was to recoil in terror, because, if Jesus was the Messiah, that was the end of the demons, and, as the man saw it because of his self-identification with the demons, the end of himself. Quite certainly when the demon-possessed man called Jesus 'The Son of the Most High God', and shrank away from him in terror, he was under the conviction that he was the Messiah, and that he was about to destroy the demons and the man with them. This is a clear case of the use of Son of God in a Messianic sense.

(b) In this line of thought the examination of certain parallel passages in the same or in different Gospels is highly illuminating.

When Philip had attached himself to Jesus, he went to find Nathanael. 'We have met the man spoken of by Moses in the law', he said. 'It is Jesus, son of Joseph, from Nazareth.' After his initial doubts Nathanael was convinced and this confession of faith was: 'Rabbi, you are the Son of God; you are King of Israel' (John 1.45,49). In that passage Jesus is the one who has been foretold, the Son of God, the King of Israel; that is to say, he is the Messiah.

The three Gospels tell the story of Peter's confession and discovery at Caesarea Philippi, but they have different versions of Peter's words. In Mark Peter anwers: 'You are the Messiah' (Mark 8.28). In Luke Peter's answer is: 'God's Messiah' (Luke 9.20). In Matthew Peter's answer is: 'You are the Messiah, the Son of the living God' (Matt. 16.16). There again it is clear that on the lips of Peter the title Son of God is a Messianic title.

When we study the different versions of the question of

the High Priest to Jesus at his trial together with Jesus'
answer to it, we again have a clear case of Son of God
being used as a title of the Messiah, or indeed as being
identical with the title Messiah. In Matthew (26.63) the
question of the High Priest is: 'By the living God I charge
you to tell us: Are you the Messiah, the Son of God?' In
Mark (14.61) the question is: 'Are you the Messiah, the
Son of the Blessed One?' In Luke the dialogue is fuller and
the matter is even clearer (22.67-70). 'Tell us,' said the
Jewish authorities, 'are you the Messiah?' Jesus answered:
'If I tell you, you will not believe me; and, if I ask questions,
you will not answer. But from now on the Son of Man will
be seated at the right hand of Almighty God.' 'You are the
Son of God, then?' they all said. Here quite clearly Son of
God and Messiah are the same thing.

The same situation confronts us when we examine the
taunts flung at Jesus by the passing crowds and by others
when he hung upon his cross. Matthew (27.40) has it, they
said: 'Come down from the cross and save yourself if you
are indeed the Son of God.' And then they go on to say
(27.43): 'Let God rescue him, if he wants him—for he said
he was God's son.' Mark (15.32 has: 'Let the Messiah, the
King of Israel, come down from the cross. If we see that
we shall believe.' Luke (23.35) has: 'Now let him save himself, if this is God's Messiah (NEB: God's Anointed), his
Chosen'. The crowds go on to say (23.37): 'If you are the
King of the Jews save yourself.' The impenitent thief taunts
Jesus (23.39): 'Are you not the Messiah? Save yourself, and
us.' Here again it is clear that King of Israel and Son of
God are both Messianic titles, and are different ways of de-
scribing Jesus as the Messiah. To believe that Jesus is
Messiah is to believe that he is Son of God. 'I now believe,'
Martha said to Jesus, 'that you are the Messiah, the Son of
God who was to come into the world' (John 11.27).

Whatever else may remain doubtful, it is not doubtful that
Son of God is a Messianic title, and at least sometimes describes Jesus as the Messiah of God.

And yet even after we have said that there remains something to be said. At the trial of Jesus before the High Priest
the answer and the claim of Jesus produced in the High
Priest and in the orthodox Jews a feeling of horror, as of
those faced with an ultimate blasphemy (Matt. 26.65; Mark
63,64). The reaction is more than the reaction to a messianic
pretender. There had been many and many a false messiah,
and such figures had not been greeted with a horror like this.
Judaism had not mobilised all its forces to eliminate a false
messiah before. It seems clear that the Jews were perfectly
conscious that the claim of Jesus was more than the claim to
be the Messiah.

We may well set against that Matthew's account of the
events during the storm at sea. It ends with the men in
the boat falling at Jesus' feet and saying: 'Truly you are the
Son of God' (Matt. 14.22-33). These words of the disciples
are not a credal confession; they are not the summary of
a carefully wrought out theology; they are the cry of the
adoring heart. Much of New Testament thought is moving
before the days of creeds and confessions and speculations,
and before the attempts to relate religious experience to
philosophic thought and categories, and it may well be true
to say that when men called Jesus Son of God they were
often doing no more than call him Messiah, and that sometimes the language is not the language of reasoned theology
or thought at all but the outrush in devotion of the loving
and adoring heart.

It will very greatly help us to understand the content of
this phrase, if we trace the way in which it is used of Jesus,
and the connections in which it is used of Jesus, throughout
the New Testament.

(i) The uniqueness of the sonship of Jesus is repeatedly stressed. Jesus is not simply the Son of God; he is God's *only* Son. No one has ever seen God; God's only Son, who is nearest to the Father's heart has made him known (John 1.18). In his love God sent into the world his *only* Son (John 3.16). The uniqueness of the sonship of Jesus is never doubted and never questioned. On one occasion Paul seems to see in the resurrection a guarantee and demonstration of that uniqueness, for he says of Jesus: 'He was declared Son of God by a mighty act in that he rose from the dead (Rom. 1.3).

(ii) This uniqueness comes from a quite unique connection with God. 'My Father and I are one,' Jesus said (John 10.30). The Son only does what he sees the Father doing (John 5.19,20). The Son does nothing on his own authority; he has been taught by the Father (John 8.28). The Father is in him and he is in the Father (John 10.38). What the Father has said to him is what the Son speaks (12.50). To see the Son is to see the Father (John 14.9-11). The Son can speak of himself and the Father as 'we'. Of the man who does the will of the Father it is said: 'We will come and make our dwelling with him' (John 14.23). To dishonour the Son is to dishonour the Father; to hate the Son is to hate the Father; and to love and honour the Son is to love and honour the Father (John 5.23; 8.49,54; 15.23,24). The Father is glorified in the Son and the Father's glory belongs to the Son (John 14.31; 17.1: Luke 9.26). He has been accredited by the Father and has been given royal power by the Father (John 5.43; Luke 22.28,29). He can speak of the Temple as his Father's house, and because of that takes to himself the right to cleanse it (John 2.16). Whatever else the phrase Son of God means, it certainly means that Jesus was uniquely connected with God.

(iii) This unique connection means that the Son has

been entrusted by the Father with a unique authority. 'Everything,' said Jesus, 'is entrusted to me by my Father' (Matt. 11.27; Luke 10.22). The Father has entrusted the Son with all authority (John 3.35). Even as he went to the Cross Jesus was well aware that the Father had entrusted everything to him (John 13.3). 'All that the Father has is mine' (John 16.15). In particular the Son is entrusted with judgment. 'The Father does not judge anyone, but has given full jurisdiction to the Son' (John 5.22). To the Son the Father has delegated and entrusted his full authority.

(iv) This unique connection means that the Son has unique knowledge of the Father, and therefore the Son alone can reveal God to men and bring men to God. 'The Father knows me and I know the Father' (John 10.15). 'No man comes to the Father except by me' (John 14.6). 'I am revealing in words what I saw in my Father's presence' (John 8.38). 'No one knows the Son but the Father, and no one knows the Father but the Son, and those to whom the Son may choose to reveal him' (Matt. 11.27; Luke 10.21,22). The Son's knowledge of the Father is such that none else can possess it, but the Son possesses it in order to lead others into it, and to the Father.

(v) This leads us directly to the great and supreme function of the Son. *The Son has the unique and only place in God's scheme of salvation. The Son is the object of saving faith.* It is the man who believes in the Son who has eternal life (John 3.16). 'He who puts his faith in the Son has hold of eternal life, but he who disobeys the Son shall not see that life' (John 3.36). 'It is my Father's will,' Jesus says in the Fourth Gospel, 'that everyone who looks upon the Son and puts his faith in him shall possess eternal life' (John 6.40). To deny the Son is to be without the Father; to acknowledge the Son is to have the Father (I John 2.22,23). If a man acknowledges that Jesus is the Son of God, God dwells in him and he dwells in God (I John 4.15). The Son has the unique place in the Father's scheme and plan of salvation, and for him there is no possible substitute.

This means that *a Christian is a man who gives his allegiance to Jesus Christ the Son*. He who disobeys the Son shall not see eternal life: God's wrath rests upon him (John 3.36). The commandment of God is that the Christian must give allegiance to Jesus Christ (I John 3.23). John's letter is addressed to those who give allegiance to the Son of God (I John 5.13). 'The man who puts his faith in him (the Son) does not come under judgment; but the unbeliever has already been judged because he has not given allegiance to God's only Son' (John 3.18). Allegiance to the Son is the condition of salvation.

We may put this in another way. *The Son is the life-giver.* 'As the Father has life-giving power in himself, so has the Son, by the Father's gift' (John 5.26). The Christian life is a life shared with the Father and the Son (I John 1.3). God sent his only Son into the world to bring us life (I John 4.9). 'He who possesses the Son has life indeed; he who does not possess the Son has not that life' (I John 5.11,12).

Finally, it has to be noted that the Son is *the bringer of salvation*, and consistently this is indissolubly connected with the death of the Son. This is the consistent thought of Paul. God reconciled us to himself by the death of his Son (Rom. 5.10). God sent his Son as a sacrifice for sin (Rom. 8.3). God did not spare his own Son, but surrendered him for us all (Rom. 8.32). God speaks of God's son 'who loved me and sacrificed himself for me' (Gal. 2.20). The Son was sent to purchase the freedom of those who were under the law (Gal. 4.4). It is in the Son that there are procured our release and our forgiveness (Col. 1.13). It is the Son who delivers men from the terrors of the judgment to come (I Thess. 1.10).

This is equally consistently the thought of John. We are cleansed from every sin by the blood of Jesus, God's Son (I John 1.7). The Son appeared in the world for the purpose of undoing the devil's work (I John 3.8). God sent his Son as the remedy for the defilement of our sins, and to be the Saviour of the world (I John 4. 10,14).

This remedy involved a union with the Son in which we enter into .his life. Through him Christians are shaped into his likeness (Rom. 8.29). Christians are called to share in his life (I Cor. 1.9). The life which Paul lives is the life of Christ in him, by faith in the Son of God (Gal. 2.20). Through the Son of God men can grow into that full manhood which is the stature of Christ (Eph. 4.13).

Here there is the work of the Son. The Son has a unique connection with God; the Son has a unique place in God's scheme of salvation; the work of the Son is done through the sacrifice of the Son; and the result of that work is that men share the life of the Son.

Let us then try to sum up the meaning and the implications of this title Son of God, when it is applied to Jesus.

(i) It obviously implies a unique intimacy between God and Jesus. There is no closer relationship than the relationship between God and Jesus. This side of the matter is summed up in the saying: 'My Father and I are one' (John 10.30).

(ii) But, intimate as this relationship is, it never becomes equality, still less identity. The Father is always distinguished from the Son; and the Son keeps his place as Son, and the Father retains his supremacy as Father. This emerges in two ways. It emerges in the saying of Jesus: 'The Father is greater that I' (John 14.28). And it emerges in the frank recognition that there are certain things which are not known even to the Son, but which are known only by the Father. In relation to his return Jesus said: 'But about that day or that hour no one knows, not even the angels in heaven, not even the Son; only the Father' (Mark 13.32; Matt. 24.36). The relationship is still a father-son relationship in which Father and Son retain the places that a father and son must have.

(iii) This relationship therefore issues in certain things. It issues in a *unique obedience*. The perfect son is the son who obeys his father's will; and in that sense Jesus is the perfect Son. 'It is meat and drink for me,' he said, 'to do the will of him who sent me until I have finished his work' (John 4.34). 'I cannot act by myself . . . My aim is not my own will but the will of him who sent me' (John 5.30). 'I came down from heaven, not to do my own will, but the will of him who sent me' (John 6.38).

The Gospels may well be read as a series of incidents in which Jesus seeks or accepts the will of God. The divine drama can be read as series of crucial moments in which Jesus seeks and accepts the will of God. As a boy in the Temple he was seeking to find out what God wanted him to do with his life. At his baptism he offerend himself to God that God might use him as he wished. In his temptations he was seeking to find out the way in which God wished him to carry out the task which he had given him to do. At the Transfiguration he was seeking the approval of the will of God before he set out on the last journey to Jerusalem. In Gethsemane he fought the bitter battle with human horror of a cross in order to accept the will of God. At his trial he is in effect saying that he will choose the will of God rather than the will of men, no matter what the cost. On the cross he is still inflexibly holding to the path which God had marked out for him. Jesus' life was begun, continued and ended in obedience to the will of God, because in fact that must always be the essence of the life of any son in relation to his father.

Jesus' sonship is expressed in his perfect obedience to God.

It is here that we are to find the meaning of what is called his *sinlessness*. To say that Jesus was sinless is not the best way in which the quality of the life of Jesus may be expressed. The inadequacy in such a description of the life of Jesus lies in the fact that the word *sinless* is a negative word, and would express abstention from evil rather than positive good. The sinlessness of Jesus was not a merely negative condition in which he refused evil; it was much more a positive and continuous and unfailing acceptance of the will of God for himself.

(iv) This unique intimacy of Jesus with God and his unique obedience to God issue in a unique knowledge of God. No one knows the Father but the Son (Matt. 11.27). There is much more than intellectual knowledge here. A teacher's difficulty in teaching his students seldom, almost never, lies in their intellectual inadequacy. It is not that they are incapable in the intellectual and mental sense. The difficulty lies in the fact that either they will not accept the discipline and the toil of learning, or that they are completely out of sympathy with him, and their minds will not take in what he has to say. The preacher's difficulty is not that his people *cannot* understand what he seeks to say; it is that they *refuse* to understand. This is to say that teaching and learning depend on more than the wisdom and the technique of the teacher and the mental and intellectual calibre of the student. They depend at least as much on the establishment of a relationship of fellowship and sympathy between the one who teaches and those who are taught. Jesus' knowledge of God was not a knowledge which came from mental and intellectual distinction; it came rather from a fellowship with God in which God could communicate himself to Jesus as to no other person.

(v) This unique intimacy, unique obedience and unique knowledge issued in a unique power. However we may explain or interpret any single incident, it is unquestionable that Jesus possessed unique and special powers. The fact is that Jesus was such that he could be entrusted with power which in the hands of anyone else would do far more harm than good. He could do what he did because he was what he was.

It is just here that we come on the real significance of the use of the title Son of God in regard to Jesus in the Gospels. It would be true to say that sometimes when we read the Gospels we get the impression that Jesus lived and moved in an atmosphere of astonishment. Again and again people were astonished at him. The writers of the Gospels seem to have ransacked the Greek dictionary for words to express their amazement at Jesus Christ. The Gospels writers use four main words to express the astonishment of those who saw, and listened to, Jesus. We give in brackets the number of times that each of these words occurs in the Gospels. They use the word *thaumazein,* which means *to wonder* or *to marvel* (Matt.: 6; Mark: 2; Luke: 6). They use the word *existēmi,* which means *to be astonished* or *to be amazed* (Matt.: 1; Mark: 3; Luke: 1). This is a strong word which means to be out of oneself with astonishment. They use the word *thambeisthai* which means to be astounded (Mark: 2). They use the word *ekplēssesthai,* which means *to be suddenly shocked or amazed* with such violence that a man is almost driven out of his senses (Matt.: 4; Mark: 5; Luke: 3).

The astonishment of men in the presence of Jesus is connected in particular with two things.

(i) It is connected with his miracles. Men are astonished at the stilling of the storm (Matt. 8.27; Luke 8.25; Mark 6.51); at the healing of the epileptic boy (Luke 9.43); at the healing of the Gerasene demoniac (Mark 5.20) at the raising of Jairus' daughter (Mark 5.42; Luke 8.56); and on many another occasion.

(ii) It is connected with the teaching of Jesus. Men are

astonished at his teaching in the synagogue in Nazareth
(Matt. 13.54; Luke 4.22); at his answer to the question about
the tribute money (Matt. 22.22; Luke 20.26); at his
teaching about riches and rich men (Matt. 19.25; Mark 10.
26); at the way in which he dealt with the Sadducees (Matt.
22.33).

Jesus' ministry began, continued and ended in astonishment.
And it may be that the most revealing astonishment of all
is in a statement of Mark about Jesus as he went on the
last journey to Jerusalem: 'They were on the road going up
to Jerusalem, Jesus leading the way; *and the disciples* were
filled with awe; while those who followed behind were afraid'
(Mark 10.32). The real astonishment was not so much about
what Jesus said or did as it was about Jesus himself. It was
when men were confronted with him that they were astounded
and amazed.

Here we believe is the meaning of this title as it appears
in the Gospels themselves. In the Gospels we have not yet
reached the time of systematic theology; we are still in
the time of immediate, personal reaction to Jesus Christ.
Confronted with him, men knew themselves in the presence
of one who was nearer to God than anyone they had ever
seen or met before, of one who had the wisdom of God on
his lips, and the power of God on his hands, of one who in
the most unique way was for them the way to God. Their
instictive reaction was a feeling of wondering adoration, and
that adoration made them certain that, whatever else was
true of Jesus, human categories were unable to contain him,
and they therefore called him Son of God. In the first instance
this is the instinctive reaction of the human heart. In the
first instance it is devotion far more than it is theology. But
from then on it became the unfinished, and the unfinishable,
task to define wherein that special relationship lay.

6

SON OF MAN

IF we are to place any reliance at all upon the Gospel records as we possess them, Son of Man was quite certainly Jesus' most personal and most deliberately chosen title for himself. The title Son of Man occurs about 82 times in the New Testament. With one exception all these occurrences are in the Gospels. The one exception is the saying of Stephen in Acts 7.56: 'Behold, I see the heavens opened, and the Son of Man standing at the right hand of God.' Further, of the remaining occurrences of this title, all but one are on the lips of Jesus himself, and the one exception is a quotation of the words of Jesus. The one exception is the question of the crowd in Jerusalem in the last days, following upon Jesus' prediction of his own crucifixion. 'We have heard from the law that the Christ remains for ever. How can you say that the Son of Man must be lifted up? Who is this Son of Man?' (John 12.34). If we are to accept the evidence of the Gospels, here is a title of Jesus which to all intents and purposes no one uses of Jesus except himself. Clearly this is Jesus' self-chosen name for himself. And equally clearly, if that be so, we are under special obligation to try to discover what he meant by it and why he used it.

Right at the beginning of our investigation we are confronted with an initial difficulty. Ordinarily Jesus spoke Aramaic; in Aramaic 'son of man' is *bar nasha;* and *bar nasha* is not a title, but the normal Aramaic expression for 'a man', a human being, a member of the human race. If a Rabbi was telling a story or a parable about a man, he would naturally begin: 'There was a *bar nasha ...*' The phrase is simply the ordinary, indefinite expression for 'a man'.

This is equally true of the Hebrew of the Old Testament in which the corresponding phrase is *ben adam*. In the Old Testament again and again *ben adam* is simply a human being and frequently occurs as a strict parallel to the word *man*. 'God is not a man that he should lie,' says Balaam, 'or a son of man that he should repent' (Num. 23.19). When the Book of Isaiah speaks of the importance of justice and righteousness (Isa. 56. 2), we read: 'Blessed is the man who does this and the son of man who holds it fast.' When Jeremiah is telling of the doom of Edom (Jer. 49.18), he says: 'As when Sodom and Gomorrah and their neighbour cities were overthrown, says the Lord, no man shall dwell there, no son of man shall sojourn in her.' The advice of the Psalmist is: 'Put not your trust in princes, in a son of man in whom there is no help' (Ps. 146.3). 'What is man that thou art mindful of him,' the Psalmist asks, 'and the son of man that thou dost care for him?' (Ps. 8.4). It is clear that the natural and obvious meaning of the expression 'son of man' is nothing more than 'a man'.

There is in Ezekiel a specialised use of this phrase 'son of man.' It occurs in Ezekiel more than 90 times, always as an address by God to Ezekiel. 'Son of man,' says God to Ezekiel, 'stand upon your feet and I will speak with you' (2.1). 'Son of man, eat what is offered to you, eat this scroll, and go, speak to the house of Israel' (3.1). 'Son of man, go, get you to the house of Israel, and speak with my words to them' (3.4). In the case of Ezekiel the expression 'son of man' denotes Ezekiel's humanity, with all its attendant weakness and frailty and ignorance, in contrast with the strength, the knowledge and the glory of God.

It is on this human side of the expression that certain interpreters have fastened. Their interpretations have taken four main lines.

(a) It is suggested that when Jesus used the title Son

of Man he was speaking in terms of the human part of his
nature, and that when he used the term Son of God he was
speaking in terms of the divine side of his nature. There are
two difficulties there. First, it is in fact when he uses the
term Son of Man that Jesus makes many of his greatest and
most divine statements and claims. Second, to partition Jesus'
life into times when he spoke humanly as Son of Man and
divinely as Son of God is to leave him a split personality
when in point of fact in Jesus the divine and the human,
man and God, were one unity.

(b) E. F. Scott in *The Kingdom and the Messiah* quotes
two interesting interpretations of the title Son of Man. It
is suggested that, when Jesus called himself Son of Man, he
was thinking of himself as The Man, The Representative
Man, The Man in whom humanity finds its peak and its
example and its consummation. F. W. Robertson wrote:
'There was in Jesus no national peculiarity or individual
idiosyncrasy. He was not the son of the Jew, or the son of
the carpenter; not the offspring of the mode of living and
thinking of that particular century. He was The Son of Man.'
Again, this theory falls on two grounds. First, it is too
abstract to have emerged at all in the world of New Testament
thought. Second, once again we have to note that it was
precisely in terms of Son of Man that Jesus made many of
his most superhuman claims and statements.

(c) E. Abbott produced a thoughtful but rather involved
explanation of Jesus' use of the term Son of Man. He thought
that Jesus was using the title against two backgrounds, against
the background of Ezekiel and against the background of
Psalm 8. The Ezekiel background speaks of the frailty, the
humiliation, the weakness of man; the Psalm 8 background
speaks about what can only be called the divinity of man.
'What is man that thou art mindful of him, and the son of
man that thou dost care for him? Yet thou hast made him

little less than God, and does crown him with glory and honour' (Ps. 8.4,5). In these verses the Psalmist conjoins man's present weakness and man's infinite divine potentiality. So Abbott believed that 'by his adoption of the expresive title Son of Man Jesus sought to intimate that he stood for the divine potentiality in human nature. He was the Man in whom God had revealed himself, and whose victory would deliver all men from their bondage.' That is undoubtedly a very attractive suggestion, but the trouble about it is that it is so complicated that it is impossible to see anyone understanding what Jesus really meant, if he did use the title Son of Man in that way.

(d) It has been suggested that, when Jesus used the title Son of Man, he was deliberately contrasting himself with, and deliberately disowning, the visions of a Messiah who was a supernatural figure of might and power and an apocalyptic wonder-worker, and that he was speaking of himself as humble, human and simple, as unlike as possible to the divine warrior figure for whom so many were waiting. The one fact which makes that suggestion impossible is that it appears that in fact Son of Man was a Messianic title, and a title involved in one of the most superhuman pictures of the Messiah in all Jewish thought. If the title Son of Man had any contemporary Messianic meaning at all, it was the precise opposite of a simple, humble, human figure.

It can be seen that the attempt to connect the title Son of Man with what might be called the humanity of Jesus is not successful. Nevertheless before we leave this side of the matter, there are three passages in the Gospels at which we must look, for in them it is by no means impossible that the phrase Son of Man is used in its human sense. Let us begin by remembering that the natural meaning of *bar nasha* in Aramaic and of *ben adam* in Hebrew is a man, a human being.

(a) The second chapter of Mark tells of the conflict between Jesus and the orthodox Jewish religious leaders on the question of the Sabbath law. The essence of the conflict was that the orthodox leaders believed that the Sabbath regulations must be rigidly observed, whereas Jesus believed that works of mercy and help were right on any day, and that human need must always take precedence of any ritual rules and regulations. The chapter ends:

> And Jesus said to them: The Sabbath was made for man, not man for the Sabbath; so the Son of Man is lord even of the Sabbath (Mark 2.27,28; cp. Matt. 12.8; Luke 6.5).

It is to be noted that in Mark the two statements are connected with a *so* or *therefore*. The obvious sense of the passage, and the sense which entirely suits the context, is: 'The Sabbath was made for man, not man for the Sabbath; therefore, man himself can and must decide what he is going to do with the Sabbath, and he must not be shackled by legalistic and compassionless rules and regulations which forbid the exercise of mercy.' In that passage it is at least possible that the phrase *son of man* should not be spelled with a capital letter, but should be taken in its normal Aramaic sense of man in the human sense of the term. If it is taken in that sense, it means, not so much that Jesus is in control of the Sabbath, but that the Sabbath was made for the sake of man, and must never become a tyranny in which compassion for man is impossible to exercise.

(b) In the same chapter we have the story of the paralysed man who was let down through the roof to Jesus' presence by his four friends. Jesus began his cure of the man, to the shocked astonishment of the orthodox, by conveying to that man the forgiveness of his sins by God. This he does that they may know that 'the Son of Man has authority on earth to forgive sins' (Mark 2.10; Luke 5.24; Matt. 9.6). But

Matthew ends this story with a very extraordinary statement:

> When the crowds saw it, they were afraid, and they glorified God, *who had given such authority to men* (Matt. 9.8).

To the bystanders the whole incident seemed to show in the most extraordinary way that God had acted through a human intermediary to convey to the man forgiveness for his sins, and consequent restoration of his health. It will make excellent sense, if we take it that here Jesus used the expression son of man in its human meaning. He will then be saying: 'I am here in my humanity; I am here a man among men; I am here a son of man; and in that state I am bringing from God to this man the forgiveness of his sins; and the proof of it is that he can rise and walk.' Herein there lies the tremendous truth that there are times when there is given to men the greatest of all privileges, not the privilege of *forgiving* sin, but the privilege of conveying God's forgiveness of sins to some tortured soul.

(c) There are no more puzzling passages in the Gospels than the passages which speak of the unforgivable sin, the sin against the Holy Spirit; and it is just possible that light may be thrown on them if we study the use of the expression son of man in them. The Gospel writers all report the saying of Jesus in different ways. Matthew (12.31,32) has:

> Therefore I tell you, every sin and blasphemy will be forgiven men, but the blasphemy against the Spirit will not be forgiven. And whoever says a word against the Son of Man will be forgiven; but whoever speaks against the Holy Spirit will not be forgiven, either in this age or in the age to come.

Luke (12.10) has:

> And every one who speaks a word against the Son of Man will be forgiven, but he who blasphemes against the Holy Spirit will not be forgiven.

Mark (3.28,29) has:

> Truly, I say to you, all sins will be forgiven the sons of
> men, and whatever blasphemies they utter; but whoever
> blasphemes against the Holy Spirit never has forgiveness,
> but is guilty of an eternal sin.

Two things are to be noted. First, it is very strange to find
it stated that a sin against Jesus Christ is not in fact the
most serious of all sins, and that there are sins more serious
than sins against him. Second, Mark completely omits the
reference to the sin against the Son of Man. It will make
the teaching of these puzzling passages much more intelligible,
if we take it that in the first instance Jesus used the term
son of man in the sense of a human being, and if we take
the meaning to be: 'It is forgivable to refuse and to insult
the guidance given to you by *a man*, a human being; but it
is never forgivable to refuse and to insult the guidance given
to you by the Holy Spirit of God.' It is one thing contemptuously to turn down the advice given to us by a fellow-
man; it is quite another thing contemptuously to disregard
the promptings of the Holy Spirit. It will make the meaning
of this passage very much clearer, if we read it in terms of
the contrast between refusing human and divine guidance,
and if we take the expression 'son of man' in its normal
sense.

It is not claimed that it is a fact established beyond all
doubt that in these three passages the expression 'son of man'
is to be taken in its human sense; but it can be seen that
that interpretation is a possibility which cannot be disregarded.

There is one other preliminary matter at which we must
look. It has sometimes been argued that, when Jesus spoke
of the Son of Man, he was speaking not of himself, but of
some one else whom he expected to come and for whom he
conceived of himself as preparing the way. This suggestion
is based on two facts. First, it is a fact that Jesus always

did speak of the Son of Man in the third person. There are two passages in the Gospels which might be taken as lending some support to this view. Matt. 10.23 reads:

> When they persecute you in one town, flee to the next; for truly, I say to you, you will not have gone through all the towns of Israel, before the Son of Man comes.

Luke (12.8,9) reports Jesus as saying:

> And I tell you, everyone who acknowledges me before men, the Son of Man will also acknowledge before the angels of God; but he who denies me before men will be denied before the angels of God.

It is quite true that, if these were the only passages we possessed which mentioned the Son of Man, we might well take it that Jesus was speaking of some one else, but there are compelling facts on the other side. Matthew (10.32,33) has a close parallel to Luke's version of the saying of Jesus:

> So everyone who acknowledges me before men, I will acknowledge before my Father who is in heaven; but whoever denies me before men, I will also deny before my Father who is in heaven.

This is clearly the same saying as is related in Luke, and in this case there is no question that the reference is to Jesus himself. Furthermore, there are passages in the sayings of Jesus in which 'Son of Man' and 'I' are interchangeable. Luke (6.22) has:

> Blessed are you when men hate you, and when they exclude you and revile you, and cast out your name as evil, *on account of the Son of Man!*

Matthew's version (5.11) of the same saying is:

> Blessed are you when men revile you and persecute you and utter all kinds of evil against you falsely *on my account.*

The fact is that against the two passages which we have quoted and which might be used to argue that the Son of Man was some one other than Jesus there are in fact more than 70 passages in which the identity of the Son of Man with Jesus is clear and obvious; and it is only reasonable to interpret these two passages in the light of all the others. We may take it that the point of view which distinguishes between Jesus and the Son of Man can be regarded as no more than an eccentricity of criticism.

Let us now turn to the origin of the title Son of Man and to Jesus' use of it. It will help, if we try to understand the problem which faced Jesus and the solutions which he might have adopted. Jesus' problem was the problem of communication; but what he desired to communicate was not so much a body of truth or doctrine as it was *himself.* For this purpose nothing could be more useful to him than a title which would be kind of brief summary of himself and his mission. In his search for such a title more than one course was open to Jesus. He might invent a title that was completely new. That he did not do, because the title Son of Man already existed. He might take a colourless, indefinite title and fill it with meaning of his own choosing until it became vivid and significant. That he did not do because Son of Man was by no means a colourless title. There was still one other possibility open to Jesus. He might take a title which was known and recognisable and at least to some extent familiar and use it in a way which was so new and so strange and so startling that his use of it would shock people into listening. We believe that it was this last course which Jesus adopted. Let us then begin by examining the origin of this title.

There is no doubt that the ultimate origin of the title Son of Man is in the Book of Daniel. In Daniel 7 the seer has a vision of the great empires which up until then had held world sway. He sees these empires under the symbolism of beasts; they are so callous, so cruel, so bestial that they cannot be typified in any other way. There was the lion with eagle's wings (v. 4) which stood for Babylonia. There was the bear with three ribs in its mouth (v. 5) which stood for Assyria. There was the leopard with four wings and four heads (v. 6) which stood for Persia. There was the fourth nameless beast with iron teeth, dreadful, terrible, irresistibly strong (v. 7), which stood for the all-conquering empire of Macedonia and Alexander the Great. These stood for the empires which up to that time had held sway, all of them of such savagery that beasts were the only picture of them. But their days was ended and their power was broken. So the seer goes on (Dan. 7.13,14):

> I saw in the night visions, and behold with the clouds of heaven there came one like a son of man, and he came to the Ancient of Days and was presented before him. And to him was given dominion and glory and kingdom, that all peoples, nations, and languages should serve him; his dominion is an everlasting dominion, which shall not pass away, and his kingdom one that shall not be destroyed.

So then the world power is given by God into the hands of a power which is not bestial and savage but which is gentle and humane and which can be typified and symbolised in the figure of a man. What then is this new power? We find the answer in (v. 18):

> But the saints of the Most High shall receive the kingdom, and possess the kingdom for ever, for ever and ever.

Now to say that the saints shall possess the kingdom is to say that at last the dream of Israel will be realised. She has gone through terrible things. She has been savagely and brutally treated. But now the Chosen People, Israel, the saints of the Most High, will enter into their kingdom. In other words, the long-awaited Messianic age is about to dawn.

Once Daniel 7.1-13 was interpreted messianically the next step was bound to follow. The previous kingdom had been in the power of beasts; the new power is like a son of man; it was quite inevitable that the Messiah should be thought of as this Son of Man, and so Son of Man becomes a title for the Messiah.

Had there been no other strand to add to the pattern and no other feature to add to the picture, then the picture of the Son of Man based on Daniel would have recognisably fitted Jesus like a portrait, for here was one whose main characteristic was humane gentleness, and whose empire was a direct contrast to the empires which had been founded on force and administered in mercilessness. But into this situation there enters another element. This new element was at least in part due to the historical situation. The consciousness of the Jews that they were the chosen people never wavered, but their history seemed to be a flat contradiction of their chosenness. So far from being in honour they were in humiliation; so far from being great among the nations they were in continual subjection to one power after another. It became clear to them that they would never fulfil their destiny, as they saw that destiny, by any human means; and it also became clear that a Messiah whose great characteristic was humane gentleness could never rid them of their bonds and lead them to the greatness of which they dreamed. What was needed, as the popular dreams saw it, was power and might to launch in destruction against the enemies of Israel who were the enemies of God.

Between the Testaments there emerged a book which may have assumed its final form about 70 BC. It was the Book of Enoch, and in it there is a series of pictures of *that Son of Man* in terms of this irresistible might. Let us collect its references to that Son of Man in full in the translation of R. H. Charles. There are five main passages.

In the Book of Enoch that Son of Man is always a divine pre-existent figure waiting in the heavenly places to be unleashed in vengeance and in judgment upon the world.

> And there I saw One who had a head of days,
> And His head was white like wool,
> And with Him there was another whose countenance had the appearance of a man,
> And his face was full of graciousness, like one of the holy angels.
> And I asked the angel who went with me and showed me all the hidden things, concerning that Son of Man, who he was, and whence he was, and why he went with the Head of Days? And he answered and said unto me:
> This is the Son of Man who hath righteousness,
> With whom dwelleth righteousness,
> And who revealeth all the treasures of that which is hidden,
> Because the Lord of Spirits hath chosen him,
> And whose lot hath the pre-eminence before the Lord of Spirits in uprightness for ever.
> And this Son of Man whom thou hast seen
> Shall put down the kings and mighty from their seats,
> And the strong from their thrones,
> And shall loosen the reins of the strong
> And break the teeth of sinners.
> And he shall put down the kings from their thrones and kingdoms
> Because they do not extol and praise Him,
> Nor humbly acknowledge whence the kingdom was bestowed upon them.
> And he shall put down the countenance of the strong,
> And shall fill them with shame.
> And darkness shall be their dwelling,
> And worms shall be their bed,
> And they shall have no hope of rising from their beds,
> Because they do not extol the name of the Lord of Spirits.

> (Enoch 46.1-6)

And at that hour that Son of Man was named
In the presence of the Lord of Spirits,
And his name before the Head of Days.
Yea, before the sun and the signs were created,
Before the stars of the heaven were made,
His name was named before the Lord of Spirits.
He shall be a staff to the righteous whereon to stay
    themselves and not fall,
And he shall be the light of the Gentiles,
And the hope of those who are troubled in heart.
All who dwell on earth shall fall down and worship
    before him,
And will praise and bless and celebrate with song the
    the Lord of Spirits
And for this reason hath he been chosen and hidden
    before Him,
Before the creation of the world and for evermore.
And the wisdom of the Lord of Spirits hath revealed to
    him the holy and righteous;
For he hath preserved the lot of the righteous,
Because they have hated and despised this world of
    unrighteousness,
And have hated all its works and ways in the name of
    Lord of Spirits;
For in his name they are saved,
And according to his good pleasure hath it been in regard
    to their life.
In these days downcast in countenance shall the kings
    of earth have become,
And the strong who possess the land because of the work
    of their hands,
For on the day of their anguish and affliction they shall
    not be able to save themselves,
And I will give them over into the hands of Mine elect:
As straw in the fire so shall they burn before the face of
    the holy:
As lead in the water shall they sink before the face of
    the righteous.
And no trace of them shall any more be found.
And on the day of their affliction there shall be rest on
    the earth,
And before them they shall fall and not rise again:

And there shall be no one to take them with his hands
    and raise them;
For they have denied the Lord of Spirits and His
    Anointed.
The name of the Lord of Spirits be blessed.

(Enoch 48.2-10)

And one portion of them shall look on the other,
And they shall be terrified,
And they shall be downcast of countenance,
And pain shall seize them,
When they see that Son of Man
Sitting on the throne of his glory.
And the kings and the mighty and all who possess the
    earth shall bless and glorify and extol him who rules
    over all, who was hidden.
For from the beginning the Son of Man was hidden,
And the Most High preserved him in the presence of
    His might,
And revealed him to the elect.
And the congregation of the elect and holy shall be
    sown,
And all the elect shall stand before him on that day.
And all the kings and the mighty and the exalted and
    those who rule the earth
Shall fall down before him on their faces,
And worship and set their hope upon that Son of Man,
And petition him and supplicate him for mercy at his
    hands.
Nevertheless the Lord of Spirits will so press them
That they shall hastily go forth from His presence,
And their faces shall be filled with shame,
And darkness grow deeper on their faces.
And He will deliver them to the angels for punishment,
To execute vengeance on them because they have op-
    pressed His children and His elect;
And they shall be a spectacle for the righteous and for
    His elect:
They shall rejoice over them,
Because the wrath of the Lord of Spirits resteth upon
    them,
And His sword is drunk with their blood.

And the righteous and elect shall be saved on that day,
And they shall never thenceforward see the face of the
  sinners and unrighteous.
And the Lord of Spirits will abide over them,
And with the Son of Man shall they eat
And lie down and rise up for ever and ever.
And the righteous and elect shall have risen from the
  earth,
And ceased to be of downcast countenance.
And they shall have been clothed with garments of glory,
And these shall be the garments of life from the Lord of
  Spirits;
And your garments shall not grow old,
Nor your glory pass away before the Lord of Spirits.
                                      (Enoch 62.5-16)

And after that their faces shall be filled with darkness
And shame before that Son of Man,
And they shall be driven from his presence,
And the swo. ɪl shall abide before his face in their midst.
                                      (Enoch 63.11)

And there wa.ɟ great joy among them,
And they blessed and gloried and extolled
Because the name of that Son of Man had been revealed
  unto them.
And he sat on the throne of his glory,
And the sum of judgement was given unto the Son of
  Man,
And he caused the sinners to pass away and be destroyed
  from off the face of the earth,
And those who have led the world astray.
With chains shall they be bound,
And in their assemblage-place of destruction shall they
  be imprisoned,
And all their works vanish from the face of the earth.
And from henceforth there shall be nothing corruptible;
For that Son of Man has appeared,
And has seated himself on the throne of his glory,
And all evil shall pass away before his face,
And the word of that Son of Man shall go forth
And be strong before the Lord of Spirits.
                                      (Enoch 69.26-29)

Finally, of the translation of Enoch it is said:

> And it came to pass after this that his name during his
> lifetime was raised aloft to that Son of Man and to the
> Lord of Spirits from amongst those who dwell on the
> earth (70.1).

We may briefly sum up the Enoch picture of that Son of
Man. He is pre-existent from all eternity. He is specially
related to God, in that he both shares the heavenly glory of
God and is God's special agent of vengeance and judgment.
The day is coming when he will be launched upon the earth
for the merciless judgment and destruction of sinners and
of all those who are against God's holy people. He will be the
stay, the comfort, and the guide and the support of God's
faithful people. He will triumph over his enemies and that
triumph will involve their eternal punishment. But the faithful will share in his glory and his triumph when all the earth
is at last subject to him and when the last enemy of God
and of the people of God is finally destroyed.

Here is a picture which is connected with the Book of
Daniel by the use of the title Son of Man, but which is very
different. The Book of Daniel has the picture of a power
gentle and humane; Enoch has the picture of a power with
no other object than the destruction of sinners, the triumph
of the Son of Man, and the sharing of the faithful in that
triumph. The Son of Man had become a figure before whom
the world must cower in abject terror—and that is the picture
which was in the minds of men.

We began this investigation by suggesting that in his use
of the title Son of Man Jesus took a known title and used it
in a way which was startlingly and even shockingly new.
Let us then examine Jesus' actual use of this title.

(i)   He uses it as *a substitute for 'I'*. Instead of using
the first person singular he uses the title Son of Man.

> Foxes have holes, and birds of the air have nests; but the Son of Man has nowhere to lay his head (Luke 9.58).

> The Son of Man came eating and drinking, and they say, Behold, a glutton and a drunkard, a friend of tax-collectors and sinners! (Matt. 11.19; Luke 7.34).

> Who do men say that the Son of Man is? (Matt. 16.13).

In Mark 8.27 this is given in the form: Who do men say that I am? (cp. Luke 9.20). In Matt. 16.15 the question is repeated in the form: But who do you say that I am? The various forms of this saying show the interchangeability of the pronoun 'I' and the title 'Son of Man'. It also indicates the possibility that there may well be places in the Gospel story where 'Son of Man' has been introduced by the Gospel-writers in place of 'I', because it was so natural to think of Jesus using that term in relation to himself.

> Blessed are you when men hate you, and when they exclude you and revile you, and cast out your name as evil, on account of the Son of Man! (Luke 6.22).

The Matthew parallel (5.11) once again demonstrates the equivalence of 'Son of Man' and 'I' on the lips of Jesus:

> Blessed are you when men revile you and persecute you and utter all kinds of evil against you falsely on my account.

The evidence of the Gospels is that Jesus did use the title 'Son of Man' as a substitute for 'I', although it may be that there are occasions when the title has been inserted by the Gospelwriters when it may not have actually been used.

(ii) Jesus used this title on certain occasions *when he was making his greatest claims and declarations*.

> The Son of Man came to seek and to save the lost (Luke 19.10).

The Son of Man also came not to be served but to serve, and to give his life as a ransom for many (Mark 10.45; Matt. 20.28).

For as Jonah became a sign to the men of Nineveh, so will the Son of Man be to this generation (Luke 11.30).

The Son of Man came not to destroy men's lives but to save them (Luke 9.56). (The manuscript evidence for this last passage is not strong, and it is omitted in most of the newer translations).

The evidence of the Gospels is that at least sometimes Son of Man is the title of the great occasion.

(iii) At least once the title is used *of the Resurrection,* apart from the sufferings which preceded Jesus' rising from the dead. Jesus' instruction to his disciples after the events of the Mount of Transfiguration was:

Tell no one the vision, until the Son of Man is raised from the dead (Matt. 17.9; cp. Mark 9.9).

(iv) Jesus used the title in connection with *the glory into which he* would enter.

Truly, I say to you, in the new world, when the Son of Man shall sit on his glorious throne, you who have followed me will also sit on twelve thrones, judging the twelve tribes of Israel (Matt. 19.28).

Then will appear the sign of the Son of Man in heaven, and then all the tribes of the earth will mourn, and they will see the Son of Man coming on the clouds of heaven with power and great glory (Matt. 24.30; Mark 13.26; Luke 17.26,30).

Hereafter you will see the Son of Man seated at the right hand of Power, and coming on the clouds of heaven (Matt. 26.64; cp. Mark 14.62; Luke 22.69).

(v) This is to say that the term is often found on Jesus' lips in sayings which have to do with *his Coming Again.*

For as the lightning comes from the east and shines as far as the west, so will be the coming of the Son of Man (Matt. 24.27; cp. Luke 17.24).

> Then will appear the sign of the Son of Man in heaven, and then all the tribes of the earth will mourn, and they will see the Son of Man coming on the clouds of heaven with power and great glory (Matt. 24.30)

> For the Son of Man is to come with his angels in the glory of his Father, and then he will repay every man for what he has done. Truly, I say to you, there are some standing here who will not taste death before they see the Son of Man coming in his kingdom (Matt. 16.27,28).

> The Son of Man is coming at an hour you do not expect (Matt. 24.44; Luke 12.40).

> When the Son of Man comes will he find faith on earth? (Luke 18.8).

(vi)   The term is frequently found on Jesus' lips in *sayings which have to do with judgment.*

> The Son of Man will send his angels, and they will gather out of his kingdom all causes of sin and all evil-doers (Matt. 13.41).

> When the Son of Man comes in his glory, and all the angels with him, then he will sit on his glorious throne. Before him will be gathered all the nations, and he will separate them one from another as a shepherd separates the sheep from the goats (Matt. 25.31,32).

> Whoever is ashamed of me and of my words, of him will the Son of Man be ashamed when he comes in his glory and the glory of the Father and of the holy angels (Luke 9.56).

> But watch at all times, praying that you may have strength to escape all these things that will take place, and to stand before the Son of Man (Luke 21.36).

It is not claimed that all the sayings quoted are necessarily the *ipsissima verba* of Jesus; but what is claimed is that the Gospel writers felt it right and proper to show Jesus speaking in these terms in these connections, and that it is therefore reasonable to assume that he did so speak.

If we were to stop here, if the evidence which we have collected was the only evidence, if these were the only connections in which Jesus spoke of himself as the Son of Man, then it is quite clear that Jesus' use of the term Son of Man would well fit into the Enoch picture. Here is the majestic glory, the stern and inevitable judgment, the final triumph, the terror of the entry of the divine majesty into the world of sinning and rebellious men. Anyone who thought of the Son of Man in terms of the Book of Enoch would recognise in these sayings accents with which he was perfectly familiar. From section three onwards there is nothing here that was not readily intelligible to popular Jewish thought.

But now there comes the thing which is absolutely new. Jesus repeatedly used the term Son of Man *in connection with his sufferings and death*. In fact he uses the term oftener in this than in any other connection.

I tell you that Elijah has already come, and they did not know him, but did to him whatever they pleased. So also the Son of Man will suffer at their hands (Matt. 17.12).

The Son of Man is to be delivered into the hands of men, and they will kill him and he will be raised on the third day (Matt. 17.22: Mark 9.31).

And he began to teach them that the Son of Man must suffer many things, and be rejected by the elders and chief priests and the scribes, and be killed, and after three days rise again (Mark 8.31; Matt. 16.21; Mark 10.33; Matt. 20.18; Luke 9.44; 18.31,32).

You know that after two days the Passover is coming, and the Son of Man will be delivered up to be crucified (Matt. 26.2).

The Son of Man goes as it is written of him, but woe to that man by whom the Son of Man is betrayed (Matt. 26.24 Mark 14.21; Luke 22.22).

The Son of Man is betrayed into the hands of sinners (Matt. 26. 45; Mark 14.41).

It is written of the Son of Man that he should suffer many things and he treated with contempt (Mark 9.12).

Judas, would you betray the Son of Man with a kiss? (Luke 22.48)

The angelic messenger in the empty tomb on the first Easter morning reminds the women that Jesus had said: The Son of Man must be delivered into the hands of sinful men, and be crucified and on the third day rise (Luke 24.7).

Here is the new thing. To anyone who knew the orthodox, conventional and traditional idea and picture of the Son of Man such sayings were bound to appear incredible and intolerable, impossible contradictions in terms. What had the majestic, divine glory of the Son of Man to do with humiliation and rejection? What had the irresistible might and triumph of the Son of Man to do with death on a cross? Statements like these about the Son of Man would leave the hearers shocked, incredulous, and quite unable to understand.

Once we have grasped the startlingly new idea of the Son of Man which Jesus introduced we are in possession of a key which unlocks many doors. Let us in light of all this turn to the incident of Peter's confession at Caesarea Philippi.

Let us look first at *the incomprehension of Peter*. In all the Synoptic Gospels the sequence of events is the same. Jesus asked his question; Peter made his discovery and his confession of faith. Then there comes the sentence: 'From that time Jesus began to show his disciples that he must go to Jerusalem and suffer many things from the elders and chief priests and scribes, and be killed, and on the third day be raised' (Matt. 16.21; Mark 8.31; Luke 9.22). Thereafter both Mark and Matthew tell of the violent reaction of Peter: 'God forbid, Lord! This shall never happen to you' (Matt. 16.22; Mark 8.32). (Luke omits the Peter episode.) Peter's reaction was due to more than one feeling. Of course, it was due to horror at the suggestion that such a fate awaited the Master whom he loved. But it was also due to the fact that he was totally incapable of effecting any possible kind of connection between the Son of Man and suffering and death. The two ideas belonged to different worlds. To Peter the statement of Jesus was not only heart-breaking; it was completely incredible and utterly impossible. In that moment he was confronted with teaching which his mind was quite unable to grasp and his reaction was shocked and even violent incredulity.

But now let us go further. Let us look at *the reaction of Jesus*. The reaction of Jesus was unexpectedly fierce. 'Get behind me, Satan! You are a hindrance to me; for you are not on the side of God, but of men' (Matt. 16.23; Mark 8.33). In the words of Peter the Devil spoke to Jesus again. Why? There is no doubt that Jesus knew the Enoch idea of the Son of Man. And the whole point of the temptations which he underwent at the beginning of his ministry was that *he was tempted to be the Enoch Son of Man*. He was tempted to take the way of power and might and physical force and earthly blessings. Was not this the dream that thousands of his fellow-countrymen cherished? Was not this the picture that the Book of Enoch had drawn? Was not this the conventional and orthodox expectation? In the temptations Jesus once and for all turned his back on that way and took the way of sacrificial love. But in that moment at Caesarea Philippi Peter was presenting him all over again with the very temptation with which he had been confronted in the wilderness. In the words of Peter, in the shocked love of Peter, in the blank incredulity of Peter, all unknown to Peter, the Devil was speaking to Jesus again. In that moment Jesus was again being tempted to be the Son of Man men dreamed of and not the Son of Man God purposed.

Still further, this situation will give us the clue to understanding one of the most puzzling features of the Gospel story. After Caesarea Philippi it is clear that one of the main elements in Jesus' teaching of his disciples was the teaching about his coming suffering and death. Why then were his disciples so utterly unprepared for his death? Why did his death come to them with such a shock that it disintegrated their whole universe? Again, Jesus hardly ever foretold his death without also foretelling his resurrection. Why did the resurrection come to the disciples as a complete surprise? If we accept the Gospel story at all, Jesus perfectly clearly foretold the events which would end his life, and yet the disciples were completely unprepared for them. Why? The reason can only be that to the end of the day the disciples never at any time succeeded in effecting any kind of connection in their thoughts between the idea of the Son of Man and the idea of suffering, humiliation and death. It is characteristic of the human mind that it simply refuses to assimilate an idea which is strange and alien and objectionable to it. The human mind can and does shut itself against that which it does not wish to see and to accept and to understand. An idea can be so new and so revolutionary, so contradictory of all that the mind already thinks it knows, that the mind cannot and will not cope with it. That is what happened to the disciples. They regarded Jesus as the Son of Man; they connected the Son of Man with majesty, power and glory, visible victory and earthly triumph. And they never, in spite of the teaching of Jesus, escaped from that conventional idea. That is why they were quite unprepared for the Cross, and because they had never even looked at the Cross, they were unable to see beyond the Cross, and to grasp the fact of the Resurrection.

But still further, here we have one of the reasons for the paramount importance of the Resurrection in the faith of the early Church. It has been said that the Resurrection is the star in the firmament of the early Church. *It was the Resurrection which vindicated Jesus as Son of Man.* If the

life of Jesus had come to an end in final suffering and death
with nothing beyond them, then it would have been impossible
to see in him the fulfilment of the picture of the Son of Man.
But the Resurrection brought the glory and the triumph which
were necessary for the completing of the picture.

There remains one more extremely important question to
ask. Into the idea of the term Son of Man Jesus imported
something quite new. When did he do so? If we take the
pattern of events in Mark's Gospel as representing at least in
outline the course of Jesus' life, we find that, with the doubtful
exceptions of Mark 2.10,28, Jesus did not even begin to
use the term Son of Man until after Peter's confession at
Caesarea Philippi, and, therefore, after his first foretelling of
the Cross. Now it has been suggested that Jesus began his
ministry in the hope and in the confidence that men would
receive him and accept him, that there was what has been
called 'a Galilaean spring-time' in which his hopes were
high; and that it was only under the pressure of events that
he began to see that the end was the Cross. On any such
view Jesus was compelled to think in terms of the Cross by
the events of his ministry. The Cross would then be, not
something which Jesus chose, but something which events and
circumstances forced upon him.

To answer this question we must go back to Jesus' baptism.
At the baptism the voice of God came to him personally:
'Thou art my beloved Son; in thee I am well pleased'
(Mark 1.11). That saying is composed of two Old Testament texts. *Thou art my beloved Son* is a quotation of Ps. 2.7,
which is a royal coronation psalm and which was always
accepted as a description of the Messiah. This would fit well
with the accepted ideas of the Messiah and of the Son of
Man, for the Psalm goes on: 'Ask of me, and I will make
the nations your heritage, and the ends of the earth your
possession. You shall break them with a rod of iron, and

dash them in pieces like a potter's vessel' (Ps. 2.8,9). That exactly fits the majestic conquests and the universal triumph of the Son of Man seen in terms of the pictures of Enoch.

In whom I am well pleased is a quotation of Isa. 42.1: 'Behold my servant . . . my chosen, in whom my soul delights.' That is part of the picture of the Servant whose portrait culminates in Isaiah 53 with the picture of one who was despised and rejected, who was wounded for our transgressions and bruised for our iniquities, on whom the chastisement of our peace fell, and with whose stripes we are healed.

This is to say that from the very beginning Jesus knew himself to be confronted with a double destiny. He was the Messiah whose ultimate triumph and glory were as sure as God is sure; he was the Messiah who must first be the Suffering Servant, and who must pass through the Cross on the way to the glory. To Jesus this was no afterthought; it was not a conclusion reached under the compulsion of circumstances; it was the conviction in which his work was begun, continued and ended.

So then Jesus took this title Son of Man and reminted it, in such a way that his use of it shocked those who heard it. He intended all who heard him use it to listen, to be startled and to think. He knew himself the divine Son of Man whose triumph was sure; he knew himself the Suffering Servant for whom the Cross was the only and the chosen way. As the Servant of the Lord he was to suffer for men; as the Son of Man he must in the end be the King of men. The Son of Man is the title which contains within itself the shame and the glory of Jesus Christ.

MESSIAH

THE word Messiah comes from the Hebrew verb *mashach* which means *to anoint*, and therefore 'the Messiah' is 'the Anointed One.' In Hebrew practice anointing was particularly connected with three kinds of people.

It was connected with the office of *prophet*. Elijah was instructed to anoint Elisha as prophet in his place (I Kings 19.16). It is the prophet's claim that the Spirit of the Lord is upon him, because God has anointed him to preach good tidings (Isa. 61.1).

It was connected with the office of *priest*. God's command was that the priests should be anointed and consecrated and sanctified that they should minister to him (Ex. 28.41). Anointing oil was to be taken and poured on the head of the priest (Ex. 29.7).

Above all, it was connected with the office of *king*. In Jotham's parable it is told how the trees went forth to anoint a king (Judg. 9.8). When Samuel saw the young David, the Lord said to him: 'Arise, anoint him, for this is he.' Then Samuel took the horn of oil, and anointed him in the midst of his brothers (I Sam. 16.12, 13). God says of David: 'With my holy oil I have anointed him' (Ps. 89.20). Zadok the priest and Nathan the prophet anointed Solomon king in Gihon (I Kings 1.45). Jehoiada made Joash king and anointed him (II Kings 11.12).

It is a fact of interest and importance that from the beginning the Messiah, the Anointed One, was Prophet, Priest and King, which are the three great offices of Jesus.

The word Messiah occurs very seldom in the New Testament. It occurs only twice, both times in the Fourth Gospel, and on both occasions it is translated and interpreted by the word Christ. When Andrew met Jesus, he rushed to find Peter his brother with the claim: 'We have found the Messiah' (John 1.41). The Samaritan woman told Jesus that when the Messiah came he would tell them all things (John 4.25).

As we have seen, the Fourth Gospel states that the word 'Christ' is the Greek translation of the word 'Messiah', and 'Christ' is the Greek for 'the Anointed One' just as 'Messiah' is the Hebrew word. From this there emerges a very important fact. As time went on, men began to speak of Jesus Christ, and to use the word Christ, as if Christ was no more than a proper name. It is in fact in this way that the word Christ is most commonly used today. But it must be remembered that Christ is properly not a proper name but a title, and it would be more correct to speak, not of Jesus Christ, but of Jesus the Christ.

The word Christ is not as common in the Synoptic Gospels as we might expect it to be. It is used of Jesus 13 times in Matthew, 6 times in Mark, and 2 times in Luke. Very often in the Synoptic Gospels it is clear that the word is a title. On the emergence of John the Baptizer the people wonder if he was the Christ (Luke 3.15). At Caesarea Philippi it was Peter's discovery that Jesus was the Christ (Matt. 16.16; Mark 8.29; Luke 9.20). The demand of the High Priest at the trial of Jesus was that Jesus should say whether he was the Christ (Matt. 26.63; Mark 14.61; Luke 22.67). To call Jesus the Christ is to give him the title of Messiah.

There is no doubt that in the New Testament preaching Jesus is presented as the Messiah. As we have seen, it was that discovery which Peter made, and it was for that claim that Jesus was condemned to death. It is clear that this was the substance of Paul's preaching, especially when he was preaching to Jews. Immediately after his conversion on the road to Damascus, he amazed the Jews by proving in their synagogues that Jesus was the Christ (Acts 9.22). His message in Thessalonica was that the Jesus whom he proclaimed was the Christ (Acts 17.3). In Corinth he testified to the Jews that the Christ was Jesus (Acts 18.5). Apollos in Ephesus convinced the Jews of the truth of Christianity by proving from the Scriptures that Christ was Jesus (Acts 18.28). There is abundant and unmistakable evidence that the early preaching presented Jesus as the Messiah.

The idea of the Messiah was deeply ingrained into Jewish thought. It was for the Messiah that the Jews were hoping and praying and waiting—and yet when the Messiah came they rejected him and crucified him. It is therefore essential that we should investigate the Jewish idea of the Messiah, that we may see where Jesus, as far as the Jews were concerned, failed to fit it into it. That conception has a long and varied history, and it will take us some considerable time to trace it through Jewish thought and belief.

The origin of the idea of the Messiah is closely related to the idea of the covenant relationship between God and Israel. It was the Jewish conviction that the Jewish nation was specially chosen and specially related to God. Of his own gracious free choice and initiative God had entered into a relationship with Israel in which he took them in a unique way for his people, and in which he offered to be in a unique way their God, and in which the Jewish people pledged themselves to keep and to obey his laws (Ex. 24.1-8). To the Jew the covenant relationship conveyed the idea of special privilege and special honour. They were convinced, as Stanton puts it, that 'the condition of the nation which would adequately correspond to God's covenant with them must at length be realised.' Because they were God's covenant people, the Jews believed that some day their nation must enter into the visible honour and glory and supremacy which, as at least in popular thought they saw it, were the right of the covenant people. It was to bring about that consummation that the Messiah was to come. The Messiah was to be the agent of God through whom the destiny of the nation was to be fulfilled.

At first the dream was very simple. It was nothing more than a dream of peace and of prosperity to be realised under a king of David's line. It is to be noted that sometimes the Messianic ideal centred, not so much in any single individual, but rather in a succession of kings of the line of David. In the later days the Messianic ideal was to take much more complicated and superhuman and transcendental forms, but the idea of the Davidic kingship and the idea of the Messiah as the Son of David were never totally lost, and indeed remained the popular idea.

In II Samuel the story is told of how David purposed to build a house for God. Nathan told David that that privilege was not for him but was reserved for his son Solomon, but at the same time he also brought the promise of God to David:

> Your house and your kingdom shall be made sure for ever before me; your throne shall be established for ever (I Sam. 7.16).

Prophet after prophet repeats this promise and interprets the Messianic ideal in light of it.

> There shall come forth a shoot from the stump of Jesse, and a branch shall grow out of his roots ... In that day the root of Jesse shall stand as an ensign to the peoples; him shall the nations seek, and his dwellings shall be glorious (Isa. 11.1,10).

> Behold, the days are coming, says the Lord, when I will raise up for David a righteous Branch, and he shall

reign as king and deal wisely, and shall execute justice and righteousness in the land (Jer. 23.5).

They shall serve the Lord their God and David their king, whom I will raise up for them (Jer. 30.9).

In those days and at that time I will cause a righteous Branch to spring forth for David ... For thus says the Lord, David shall never lack a man to sit on the throne of the house of Israel ... As the host of heaven cannot be numbered and the sands of the sea cannot be measured, so I will multiply the descendants of David my servant (Jer. 33.15,17,22).

And I will set up over them one shepherd, my servant David, and he shall feed them, and be their shepherd (Ezek. 34.23).

My servant David shall be king over them; and they shall all have one shepherd (Ezek. 37.24).

Afterward the children of Israel shall return and seek the Lord their God and David their king; and they shall come in fear to the Lord, and to his goodness in the latter days (Hos. 3.5).

In that day I will raise up the booth of David that is fallen and repair its breaches and raise up its ruins, and rebuild it as in the days of old (Amos 9.11).

But you, O Bethlehem Ephratha, who are little to be among the clans of Judah, from you shall come forth for me one who is to be ruler in Israel, whose origin is from old, from ancient days ... And he shall stand and feed his flock in the strength of the Lord, in the majesty of the name of the Lord his God. And they shall dwell secure, for now he shall be great to the ends of the earth (Micah 5.2-5).

On that day the Lord will put a shield about the inhabitants of Jerusalem so that the feeblest among them on that day shall be like David, and the house of David shall be like God (Zech. 12.8).

The dream of the Davidic Messiah never died. It is there in II (4) Esdras which dates to the first half of the second century AD. The seer sees the lion of Judah rebuke the eagle of Rome. 'This is the Messiah who shall spring from the seed of David' (II [4] Esd. 12.32). It is there in the Psalms of Solomon, which date to the first century BC, and which therefore come near to being the immediate background of the Messianic ideal in the very time when Jesus came into the world. The great passage is in the seventeenth of these Psalms. It is long, but it is so comprehensive a picture of the dream of the Davidic Messiah in the time of Jesus that it is worth quoting in full:

> Behold, O Lord, and raise up unto them their king, the son of David,
>> At the time in the which thou seest, O God, that he may reign over Israel thy servant.
> And gird him with strength that he may shatter unrighteous rulers,
>> And that he may purge Jerusalem from nations that trample her down to destruction.
> Wisely, righteously he shall thrust out sinners from the inheritance.
> He shall destroy the pride of the sinner as a potter's vessel.
> With a rod of iron he shall break in pieces of their substance,
>> He shall destroy the godless nations with the word of his mouth;
> At his rebuke nations shall flee before him,
> And he shall reprove sinners for the thoughts of their heart.
>
> And he shall gather together a holy people, whom he shall lead in righteousness,
>> And he shall judge the tribes of the people that have been sanctified by the Lord his God.
> And he shall not suffer unrighteousness to lodge any more in their midst.
>> Nor shall there dwell with them any man that knoweth wickedness,
> For he shall know them, that they are all sons of their God.
> And he shall divide them according to their tribes upon the land,

And neither sojourner nor alien shall sojourn with
    them any more.
He shall judge peoples and nations in the wisdom of his
    righteousness.

And he shall have the heathen nations to serve him
    under his yoke;
    And he shall glorify the Lord in a place to be seen of
        all the earth;
    And he shall purge Jerusalem, making it holy as of old;
So that nations shall come from the ends of the earth to
                  see his glory,
    Bringing as gifts her sons who had fainted,
    And to see the glory of the Lord, wherewith God hath
        glorified her.
And he shall be a righteous king, taught of God over them,
And there shall be no unrighteousness in his days in
    their midst,
    For all shall be holy, and their king the anointed of
        the Lord.
For he shall not put his trust in horse and rider and bow,
Nor shall he multiply for himself gold and silver for war,
    Nor shall he gather confidence from a multitude for
        the day of battle.
The Lord himself is his king, the hope of him that is
    mighty through his hope in God.

All nations shall be in fear before him,
For he will smite the earth with the word of his mouth
    for ever.
He will bless the people of the Lord with wisdom and
    gladness,
    And he himself will be pure from sin, so that he may
        rule a great people.
He will rebuke rulers, and remove sinners by the might
    of his word;
    And relying upon his God throughout his days he
    will not stumble;
For God will make him mighty by means of his holy Spirit.
    And wise by means of the spirit of understanding,
        with strength and righteousness.

And the blessing of the Lord will be with him; he will
    be strong and stumble not;
His hope will be in the Lord; who then can prevail
    against him?
He will be mighty in his works, and strong in the fear
    of God,
    He will be shepherding the flock of the Lord faith-
        fully and righteously,
    And will suffer none among them to stumble in their
        pasture.
He will lead them all aright,
    And there will be no pride among them that any
        among them should be oppressed.

This will be the majesty of the king of Israel whom God
    knoweth;
    He will raise him up over the house of Israel
        to correct him.
His words shall be more refined than costly gold,
        the choicest;
    In the assemblies he will judge the peoples, the tribes
        of the sanctified.
His words shall be like the words of the holy ones in the
    midst of sanctified peoples.
Blessed be they that shall be in those days,
    In that they shall see the good fortune of Israel which
        God shall bring to pass in the gathering of the tribes.
May the Lord hasten his mercy upon Israel!
    May he deliver us from the uncleanness of unholy
        enemies!
The Lord himself is our king for ever and ever.
                    (Psalms of Solomon 17.23-51)

There is the full-length picture of the Davidic Messiah, a
picture which Jesus must have known, and which must have
been the picture pondered over in many minds and cherished
in many hearts in the days of Jesus. Certain things stand out
about it. For all its beauty it is a picture whose horizon is
limited. It draws the picture of a majestic Messiah, son of
David, king in power and in glory. It is basically a nation-

alistic picture. The Gentiles have no part in it other than
their defeat and subjugation. It is the nation of Israel which
is to become the holy nation of God. The Messiah is to be a
king wise and righteous and powerful, the true shepherd of
his people, but it is Israel of whom he is going to be king, and
the whole dream is for the sake of Israel, and not for the sake
of the world.

The dream of the Davidic Messiah was a dream that never
died. It has not died yet. Still the great Shemoneh 'Esreh
prayer, the Eighteen Benedictions, is prayed in the Synagogue,
and the fourteenth and the fifteenth sections still run:

> And to Jerusalem thy city return with compassion, and
> dwell therein as thou hast promised; and rebuild her
> speedily in our days, a structure everlasting; and the
> throne of David speedily establish therein. Blessed be
> thou, O Lord, the builder of Jerusalem.

> The offspring of David thy servant speedily cause to
> flourish, and let his horn be exalted in thy salvation.
> For salvation do we hope daily. Blessed art thou, O God,
> who causest the horn of salvation to flourish.

In its early forms this dream of the Davidic king was very
simple. It was the dream of a time of freedom and security,
of peace and prosperity, of justice and goodness, under a king
who combined righteousness and kindliness and wisdom and
power. There are certain passages in the prophecies of Isaiah
where this dream appears at its loveliest.

> The people who walked in darkness
>   have seen a great light;
> and those who dwelt in a land of deep darkness,
>   on them has the light shined.
> Thou hast multiplied the nation,
>   thou hast increased its joy;
> they rejoice before thee
>   as with joy at the harvest,
>   as men rejoice when they divide the spoil.

For the yoke of his burden,
  and the staff for his shoulder,
  the rod of the oppressor,
  thou hast broken as on the day of Midian.
For every boot of the tramping warrior in battle tumult
  and every garment rolled in blood
  will be burned as fuel for the fire.
For to us a child is born,
  to us a son is given;
and the government will be upon his shoulder,
  and his name will be called
Wonderful Counsellor, Mighty God,
  Everlasting Father, Prince of Peace.
Of the increase of his government and of peace
  there will be no end,
upon the throne of David and over his kingdom,
  to establish it and uphold it
with justice and with·righteousness
  from this time forth and for evermore.
The zeal of the Lord of hosts will do this.

(Isa. 9.2-7)

There shall come forth a shoot from the stump of Jesse,
  and a branch shall grow forth out of his roots.
And the Spirit of the Lord shall rest upon him,
  the spirit of wisdom and understanding,
  the spirit of counsel and might,
  the spirit of knowledge and the fear of the Lord.
And his delight shall be in the fear of the Lord.
He shall not judge by what his eyes see,
  or decide by what his ears hear;
but with righteousness shall he judge the poor,
  and decide with equity for the meek of the earth;
and he shall smite the earth with the rod of his mouth,
  and with the breath of his lips he shall slay the wicked.
Righteousness shall be the girdle of his waist,
  and faithfulness the girdle of his loins.

(Isa. 11.1-5)

Behold a king will reign in righteousness,
  and princes will rule in justice.
Each will be like a hiding-place from the wind,

a covert from the tempest,
like streams of water in a dry place,
like the shade of a great rock in a weary land.
Then the eyes of those who see will not be closed,
and the ears of those who hear will hearken.
The mind of the rash will have good judgment,
and the tongue of the stammerers will speak readily and
distinctly.
The fool will no more be called noble,
nor the knave said to be honourable.

(Isa. 32.1-5)

In that day the Branch of the Lord shall be beautiful and glorious, and the fruit of the land shall be the pride and glory of the survivors of Israel. And he who is left in Zion and remains in Jerusalem will be called holy, everyone who has been recorded for life in Jerusalem, when the Lord shall have washed away the filth of the daughters of Zion and cleansed the bloodstains of Jerusalem from its midst by a spirit of burning. Then the Lord will create over the whole site of mount Zion and over her assemblies a cloud by day, and smoke and the shining of a flaming fire by night; for over all the glory there will be a canopy and pavilion. It will be for a shade by day from the heat, and for a refuge and a shelter from the storm and rain.

(Isa. 3.2-6)

It is quite true that Isaiah was writing in an historical situation, when the very existence of Israel was threatened by the world empires of Assyria and Egypt, and it may well be that he had the hope of some actual historical prince in mind. It may well be that he was thinking in terms which were immediate and not in terms which were generations or centuries in the distant future; but what he wrote remained true for all time, for it is also true that a prophet always says more than he knows that he is saying.

Here then is the picture of the king of David's line, a mighty warrior to rescue his people from their distresses and to subdue their enemies, a wise ruler and a judge because he has a wisdom which is more than the wisdom of men, a king who will purify Jerusalem until it is truly holy, a king whose reign will have an everlasting peace such as the world has never known.

Here we must stop to note another form of the dream of the future. There is one line of thought in regard to the Messianic age in which there is, so to speak, no Messianic figure. The action is the action of God himself without any agent or intermediary. That is the picture of Isaiah 24-27, of the whole of Haggai and Joel, and of such a passage as Zephaniah 3.

> The Lord, your God, is in your midst,
>   a warrior who gives victory;
> he will rejoice over you with gladness,
>   he will renew you in his love.
>
>   (Zeph. 3.17)

This is a form of the Messianic dream which is common in the inter-testamental literature. We get it in Baruch 4.21-25:

> Take courage, my children, cry to God,
>   and he will deliver you from the power and hand of the
>   enemy.
> For I have put my hope in the Everlasting to save you,
>   and joy has come to me from the Holy One,
> because of the mercy which soon will come to you
>   from your everlasting Saviour.
> For I sent you out with sorrow and weeping,
>   but God will give you back to me with joy and gladness
>   for ever.
> For as the neighbours of Zion have now seen your capture
>   so they soon shall see your salvation by God,
> which will come to you with great glory
>   and with the splendour of the Everlasting.
> My children, endure with patience the wrath that has come
>   upon you from God.
>   Your enemy has overtaken you,
>   but you will soon see their destruction,
>   and will tread upon their necks.

We get the same picture in Tobit 13.10-14:

> Give thanks worthily to the Lord,
>   and praise the King of the ages,
>   that his tent may be raised again for you with joy.
> May he cheer those within you who are captives,
>   and love those within you who are distressed,
>   to all generations for ever.
> Many nations will come from afar
>   to the name of the Lord God,
> bringing gifts in their hands, gifts for the king of heaven.
> Generations of generations will give you joyful praise.
> Cursed are all those who hate you;
>   blessed for ever will be all who love you.
> Rejoice and be glad for the sons of the righteous;
>   for they will be gathered together,
>   and will praise the Lord of the righteous.
> How blessed are those who love you!
>   They will rejoice in your peace.
> Blessed are those who grieved over all your afflictions;
>   for they will rejoice for you upon seeing all your glory,
>   and they will be made glad for ever.

We get the same picture in the *Assumption of Moses* 10.1-10:

> And then his kingdom shall appear throughout all his
>   creation,
> And then Satan shall be no more,
> And sorrow shall depart with him.
> Then the hands of the angel shall be filled
> Who has been appointed chief,
> And he shall forthwith avenge them of their enemies.
> For the Heavenly One shall arise from his royal throne,
> and he will go forth from his holy habitation,
> With indignation and wrath on account of his sons.
>
> . . . . . .
> For the Most High will arise, the Eternal God alone,
> And he will appear to punish the Gentiles,
> And he will destroy all their idols.
> Then thou, O Israel, shalt be happy,
> And thou shalt go up against the eagle,
> And its necks and wings shall be destroyed.

> And God will exalt thee,
> And he will cause thee to approach to the heaven
>   of the stars,
> And thou shalt look from afar, and shalt see thy enemies
>   in Gehenna.
> And thou shall recognise them and rejoice,
> And thou shalt give thanks and confess thy Creator.

We get the same picture in the Book of Jubilees 23.30,31:

> And at that time the Lord will heal his servants,
> And they shall rise up and see great peace,
> And drive out their adversaries.
> And the righteous shall see and be thankful,
> And rejoice with joy for ever and ever,
> And shall see their judgments and all their curses on their
>   enemies.
> And their bones shall rest in the earth.
> And their spirits shall have much joy,
> And they shall know that it is the Lord who executes
>   judgment,
> And shows mercy to hundreds and thousands and to all
>   that love him.

In passages like these there is the picture of the Messianic age, but the only actor in the drama is God himself; it is the inbreak of God himself into history that is expected and pictured.

This leads us very naturally to the next part of the pattern. As we have seen, the dream of a Messiah of David's line never died, and to a very great extent it remained the popular conception of the Messiah; but into the situation there came another element. The dream of the Messianic days remained as vivid and as persistent as ever; but the possibility of their coming seemed more remote as each year passed. Freedom and liberty seemed as distant as ever; even in the brief days of liberty anything even remotely approaching world empire was clearly not even a credible possibility; moral and spiritual degeneration spread more and more into the national life.

The consequence of all this was that at least some thinkers were driven to the conclusion that the situation was beyond mending by any human means, even by the emergence of a king of David's line. Therefore there entered into men's minds the dream, not of a king of David's line, but of a divine, superhuman Messiah, who would break into history clad with the might of heaven, and who by superhuman means would do what human means were unavailing to do. So the picture of the Messiah became ever more unearthly and superhuman.

We may look at this idea in two books, first, in the Book of Enoch, which belongs to the first century BC and, second, in II (4) Esdras which belongs to the second century AD.

In Enoch there are four main titles by which the coming Champion of God is called.

(a) There is the title *Son of Man,* and we have already seen that that title described a divine, superhuman, pre-existent figure waiting behind the throne of God to be despatched in irresistible might and majesty and power and judgment upon the world.

(b) There is the title *Christ,* the Anointed One. It is of interest to note that, although this title had previously been attached to many definite anointed kings, it is in the Book of Enoch that it first becomes a title of the Messiah in the technical sense of the term. The condemnation of sinners is that they 'have denied the Lord of Spirits and his Anointed, his Christ' (Enoch 48.10). The Anointed is to be potent and mighty upon earth (Enoch 52.4). Here is the picture of the conquering Christ.

(c) There is the title *The Righteous One.*

When the congregation of the righteous shall appear,
And sinners shall be judged for their sins,
And shall be driven from the face of the earth;

> And when the Righteous One shall appear before the eyes
>   of the righteous,
> Whose elect works hang upon the Lord of Spirits,
> And light shall appear to the righteous and the elect who
>   dwell upon the earth,
> Where then shall be the dwelling-place of sinners,
> And where the resting place of those who have denied the
>   Lord of Spirits?
> It had been good for them if they had not been born.
>
> > (Enoch 38.1, 2)

When the Righteous One appears the righteous shall be vindicated and the mountains shall collapse and the hills shall be as a fountain of water (Enoch 53.6,7). The Righteous One will come with holy and destructive might.

(*d*)   There is the title *The Elect*.

> On that day Mine Elect One shall sit on the throne of glory
> And shall try their works,
> And their places of rest shall be innumerable,
> And their souls shall grow strong within them when they
>   see mine elect ones,
> And those who have called upon My glorious name;
> Then will I cause Mine Elect One to dwell among them.
> And I will transform the heaven and make it an eternal
>   blessing and light;
> And I will transform the earth and make it a blessing.
>
> > (Enoch 45.3, 4)

> For he is mighty in all the secrets of righteousness,
> And unrighteousness shall disappear as a shadow,
> And have no continuance;
> Because the Elect One standeth before the Lord of Spirits,
> And his glory is for ever and ever,
> And his might unto all generations.
> And in him dwells the spirit of wisdom,
> And the spirit which gives insight,
> And the spirit of understanding and of might,
> And the spirit of those who have fallen asleep in
>   righteousness.
> And he shall judge the secret things,

And none shall be able to utter a lying word before him;
For he is the Elect One before the Lord of Spirits
 according to his good pleasure.
(Enoch 49.2, 4)

Here then is the Messianic picture in Enoch. The Messiah
has become a completely otherworldly figure of divine and
majestic and superhuman power, destined to conquer and to
judge all, to obliterate the sinners and to exalt the righteous.

We now turn to II (4) Esdras. In it there are two pictures.
One combines the picture of the Davidic Messiah with the
divine pre-existent figure. The two figures coalesce into one.
There is the picture of the lion, who is the Lion of Judah, who
destroys the eagle, which is Rome.

And as for the lion which thou didst see, roused from
the wood and roaring, and speaking to the eagle and
reproving him for his unrighteousness and all his deeds,
as thou hast heard: This is the Messiah whom the Most
High hath kept unto the end of the days, who shall
spring from the seed of David, and shall come and speak
unto them;

He shall reprove them for their ungodliness,
 rebuke them for their unrighteousness,
 reproach them to their faces with their treacheries.
For at the first he shall set them alive for judgment; and
when he hath rebuked them he shall destroy them (II [4]
Esd. 12.30-32).

The other picture is the picture of the Messiah in terms of
the Man from the sea. He comes with the clouds of heaven;
wherever he turns his countenance to look everything seen by
him trembles; when he opens his mouth to speak everything
melts away as wax melts in the fire. The Most High has been
keeping him for many ages, and, when he comes, he needs
neither spear nor weapon; his opponents are obliterated by
the power of his word (II [4] Esd. 13.3,4,25,26).

Here then we see in Enoch and in II (4) Ezra the picture

of the divine, pre-existent, all-conquering Messiah of destruction—and even at this stage we can already see the gap between this vision and the figure of Jesus of Nazareth.

Before we go on to examine in detail the pattern of the Messianic events we may look briefly at the Jewish ideas as to *the time of the coming of the Messiah.* Since these ideas depended on close and detailed study of the prophets and deductions from their sayings, we shall naturally expect to find them in the rabbinic and the scribal writings. They too believed in a pre-existent and divine Messiah who would come to earth and then return to his glory. He was to be a conqueror 'who was to destroy many people and silence many kings.' He would work a delivery for God's people comparable only to the delivery from slavery in Egypt. When he came he would bring a new law which would far transcend the old law. 'The law which a man learns in this world is nothing in comparison with the law of the Messiah.'

There were different ideas about the time of his coming. It was held that the world would last for six thousand years as it is now. The six thousand years correspond to the six days of creation, for a thousand years is in the sight of the Lord as a day (Ps. 90.4). Some thought that the Messiah would come at the end of the six thousand years; some divided time into three sections, two thousand years without the law, two thousand years with the law, and two thousand years of the reign of the Messiah.

In the time of Jesus there were two interconnected ideas. First, some held that the time for the coming of the Messiah was already past, that the tale of the years was accomplished, but that the Messiah could not come because of the sins of the people. 'If all Israel,' they said, 'would together repent for one whole day, the redemption by the Messiah would follow.' If Israel would only keep two Sabbaths as perfectly as they should be kept, then the Messiah would come. This explains the

passionate and even fanatical devotion of the devout Jews to
the law, and it also explains with what horror they regarded
Jesus because he did not keep the strict demands of the law.
So far from being the Messiah, he seemed to them a barrier
to the coming of the Messiah. Second, some held that the
Messiah had actually been born as a child in Bethlehem, and
that he was waiting in concealment, no man knew where,
because of the sins of the people. The belief was that he
would suddenly emerge full-grown to take upon himself the
government of his kingdom. That is what was in the minds of
the Jews, when they argued that Jesus could not be the
Messiah, because, when the Christ appears, no man will know
where he will have come from, whereas they knew that Jesus
came from Nazareth (John 7.27). It was common belief in the
time of Jesus that the coming of the Messiah was overdue because
it was hindered by the sin and the disobedience of the people.

It can be seen that in the time of Jesus the picture and the
idea of the Messiah were fluid and not fixed and stereotyped.
Some still looked for the king of David's line; some looked
for the divine, superhuman, majestic Messiah. Some believed
that the time for the coming of the Messiah was still to come;
others believed that the time had come, but that the Messiah
had been unable to come because of the sins of the people.

Basic to all this was the Jewish idea of time. The Jews
divided all time into two ages. There was this present age
which is wholly bad, wholly evil, wholly under the domination
of the Devil, and beyond all remedy; there was the age which
is to come which was the golden age of God. Increasingly
the conviction grew that the one could never turn into the
other by any natural growth or by any human means; and
that the change could only come about by the direct intervention of God. The time at which God was going to inter-
vene was called the Day of the Lord, and on that shattering
day the present scheme of things would be completely de-

stroyed and the new heavens and the new earth would be divinely created. It is clear that this too ties up with the idea and the events of the Messianic kingdom.

So then we go on to examine in detail the events of the Messianic kingdom. Two things are to be remembered all through this lengthy study. First, there is no consistent and unvarying, cut and dried scheme. In no one writer and in no one book do all the events occur. But when we do set down all the pieces in the pattern, a pattern does begin to emerge with certain discernible lines running through it. Second, this study is of paramount importance for the understanding of Jesus and for the reaction of the Jewish nation to him. These were the Messianic beliefs, these were the pictures in men's minds and the dreams in men's hearts when Jesus came to this world. It was against them that he would be evaluated, and it was against them that his message and his ideas would be judged, and it was against them that his own Messianic claims would be assessed. Let us then set out the pieces in the pattern.

(i) It was believed that *Elijah would return to be the herald and the forerunner of the Messiah*. That indeed is the statement of the Old Testament itself.

> Behold, I will send you Elijah the prophet before the great and terrible day of the Lord comes. And he will turn the hearts of fathers to their children, and the hearts of children to their fathers, lest I come and smite the land with a curse (Mal. 4.5,6).

This belief had a consistent place in all Jewish Messianic expectations, and it still has, for to this day at the Passover Feast a vacant place is left for the prophet Elijah. Elijah was to stand upon the hills of Israel, and announce to the world that the Messianic age had come, and so loud would be his voice that his announcement would be heard from one end of the world to the other. Sometimes it was held that it was Elijah who would anoint the Messiah, and thus, as it were, ordain him to his office. On the basis of the Malachi passage we have quoted it was held that Elijah would settle all disputes and exercise a ministry of reconciliation among men. In the Mishnah it is laid down that any disputed cases about money or property, or any case in which the owner cannot be found, must wait 'until Elijah comes'. It was held that when Elijah came he would first present himself to the Sanhedrin. It was no doubt because of that that an official deputation came from the Jews to ask John the Baptizer: 'Who are you?' (John 1.19). It was held that when Elijah came he would lead the people to that great act of repentance without which the Messiah could not come. 'Israel,' it was said, 'will not bring forth the great repentance before Elijah comes.'

In the New Testament story John the Baptizer is repeatedly identified with the returned Elijah. 'If you are willing to accept it,' Jesus said of John, 'he is Elijah who is to come' (Matt. 11.14; cp. Matt. 16.14; 17.10-12; Mark 6.15; 8.28; 9.11-13; Luke 9.18,19; John 1.19-21). And indeed John does perfectly fit the picture of Elijah. It was with the message of one to follow him, one for whom he was the herald and the forerunner, that he came. It was with the summons to repentance that he confronted the people. It may be that his baptism of Jesus was a symbolic anointing. We may well hold that the consistent Jewish expectation of the return of Elijah was actually fulfilled in John the Baptizer.

(ii) The Messianic age was to begin with what was called *the travail of the Messiah*. There would be a period of agony like the birthpangs of a new age, and out of distress and terror and destruction the new age would be born. This idea is found in the New Testament also. Of the events before the end, as the

RSV has it, Jesus said: 'All this is but the beginning of the sufferings' (Matt. 24.8; Mark 13.8). The Greek phrase is *archē ōdinōn*. *Odinai* is the Greek for the pains of birth, and the NEB vividly and correctly translates: 'With all these things the birthpangs of the new age begin.' Life always begins in agony, and there is to be a time of travail before the life of the age of God is born into the recreated world.

(iii)   The coming of the new age will be *a time of terror*. Amos has it:

> Woe unto you who desire the day of the Lord!
>   Why would you have the day of the Lord?
> It is darkness, and not light,
>   as if a man fled from a lion,
>   and a bear met him;
> or went into the house and leaned with his hand against the
>   wall, and a serpent bit him.
> Is not the day of the Lord darkness and not light,
>   and gloom with no brightness in it?
>
> (Amos 5.18-20)

Isaiah has it:

> Wail, for the day of the Lord is near;
>   as destruction from the Almighty it will come!
> Therefore all hands will be feeble,
>   and every man's heart will melt,
>   and they will be dismayed,
> Pangs and agony will seize them;
>   they will be in anguish like a woman in travail.
> They will look aghast at one another;
>   their faces will be aflame.   (Isa. 13.6-8)

The inhabitant of the land will tremble (Joel 2.1). The sound of the day of the Lord will be bitter and even the mighty man will cry aloud (Zeph. 1.14). When God launches his word against men will they not be affrighted and fear?

> They shall seek to hide themselves from the presence of
>   the Great Glory,
> And the children of earth shall tremble and quake.
>
> (Enoch 102. 1-3)

The terror of God will strike the earth.

(iv) It will be a time of *cosmic upheaval*. It will be

A day of darkness and gloom,
a day of clouds and thick darkness (Joel 2.2).

A day of wrath is that day,
 a day of distress and anguish,
a day of ruin and devastation,
 a day of darkness and gloom,
a day of clouds and thick darkness (Zeph. 1.14, 15).

Horror is piled on horror.

The stars of the heaven and their constellations
 will not give their light;
the sun will be dark at its rising
 and the moon will not shed its light (Isa. 13.10).

There will be

blood and fire and columns of smoke. The sun shall be
turned to darkness and the moon to blood.

The sun and the moon are darkened,
 and the stars withdraw their shining (Joel 2.30, 31; 3.15).

In the inter-testamental literature the visions become wilder
and wilder. The sun and the moon and the stars will depart
from their order (Enoch 80.4-6).

The whole firmament in its varied forms shall fall on the
divine earth and on the sea, and the firmament of heaven
and the stars and creation itself it shall cast into one
molten mass and clean dissolve. Then no more shall be
the luminaries' twinkling orbs, no night, no dawn, no
constant days of care, no spring, no summer, no autumn,
no winter (*Sibylline Oracles* 3.83-89).

The rocks are being rent,
and the sun quenched and the waters dried up,
and the fire cowering and all creation troubled
                          (*Testament of Levi* 4.1).

And the earth shall tremble: to its confines shall it be
    shaken:
And the high mountains shall be made low
And the hills shall be shaken and fall.
And the horns of the sun shall be broken and he shall
    be turned into darkness,
And the moon shall not give her light, and be turned
    wholly into blood.
And the circle of the stars shall be disturbed.
And the sea shall retire into the abyss,
And the fountains of waters shall fail,
And the rivers shall dry up.

(Assumption of Moses 10.4-6)

At that time the cosmos will become a chaos.

(v) It will be a time of *complete disintegration*. The
normal accepted standards will be gone; the normal relationships will be reversed and destroyed; the order of nature will
become disorder.

And straighway a stress of ungodliness shall fall upon
them, and male shall draw near to male, and they shall
set their children in ill-famed houses, and there shall be
in those days great tribulation among men, and it shall
set all things wrong (*Sibylline Oracles* 3.184-187).

Then shall the sun suddenly shine forth by night
    and the moon by day;
and blood shall trickle forth from wood,
    and the stone shall utter its voice;
the peoples shall be in commotion,
    the outgoings of the stars shall change.

And one whom the dwellers on the earth do not look for
    shall wield sovereignty, and the birds shall take to
    general flight,
    and the sea shall cast forth its fish . . .
    And the earth over wide regions shall open,
    and fire burst forth for a long period.
The wild beasts shall desert their haunts, and women
    shall bear monsters.

> And one-year-old children shall speak with their voices;
> pregnant women shall bring forth untimely births at
> three or four months, and these shall live and dance.
> And suddenly shall the sown places appear unsown,
> and the full store-houses shall suddenly be found
> empty.
> Salt waters shall be found in the sweet; friends shall
> attack one another suddenly (II [4] Esd. 5.4-9).

The last sentence of the last passage leads us directly towards
another element in the pattern.

The grimmest and the most terrible element in this picture
is that the prelude to the Messianic kingdom involved not
only a physical disintegration of the material universe; it also
involved a disintegration of personal relationships, which was
to produce a world of universal enmity and hatred in which
friendship, loyalty and love were destroyed and obliterated.
That picture appears in the Old Testament itself.

> And on that day a great panic from the Lord shall fall
> on them, so that each will lay hold on the hand of his
> fellow, and the hand of the one will be raised against
> the hand of the other; even Judah will fight against
> Jerusalem (Zech. 14.13,14).

In the inter-testamental literature this picture of a time in
which every personal relationship is shattered becomes
sharper and more terrible. It is there in Enoch:

> And in those days in one place the fathers together with
> their sons shall be smitten,
> And brothers one with another shall fall in death
> Till the streams flow with their blood.
> For a man shall not withhold his hand from slaying his
> sons and his sons' sons,
> And the sinner shall not withhold his hand from his
> honoured brother:
> From dawn to sunset they shall slay one another.
> (Enoch 100.1, 2)

It is there in the Testaments of the Twelve Patriarchs:

And the Lord shall bring upon them divisions one against
another.
And there shall be continual wars in Israel.

(Testament of Judah 22.1, 2)

It is there in II (4) Esdras. Friends shall attack one another
suddenly (5.9). Friends shall war against friends like enemies
(6.24). There shall appear

Quakings of places,
Tumult of people,
Schemings of nations,
Confusion of leaders,
Disquietude of princes (9.3).

The grimmest pictures of all are in II Baruch:

And they shall hate one another,
And provoke one another to fight,
And the mean shall rule over the honourable,
And those of low degree shall be extolled among
the famous
. . . .
And the wise shall be silent,
And the foolish shall speak
. . . .
Then shall confusion fall upon all men,
And some of them shall fall in battle,
And some of them shall perish in anguish,
And some of them shall be destroyed by their own.
. . . .
And it shall come to pass that whosoever gets safe out of
the war shall die in the earthquake,
And whosoever gets out of the earthquake shall be burned
by the fire,
And whosoever gets out of the fire shall be destroyed by
famine.

(II Baruch 70.2-8)

And honour shall be turned into shame,
And strength humiliated into contempt,
And understanding will become foolishness,

And beauty shall become ugliness.
. . . .
And passion shall seize him that is peaceful,
And many shall be stirred up in anger to injure many,
And they shall rouse up armies in order to shed blood,
And in the end they shall all perish together with them.
(II Baruch 48.35-37).

This picture has left its mark even upon the Mishnah *(Sotah* 9.15):

It is a sign of the approach of the Messiah that arrogance increases, ambition shoots up, the vine yields fruit yet wine is dear. The government turns to heresy. There is no instruction. The Synagogue is given over to lewdness ... The inhabitants of a district go from city to city without finding compassion. The wisdom of the learned is hated, the godly despised, trust is absent. Boys insult old men, old men stand in the presence of children. The son depreciates his father, the daughter rebels against her mother, the daughter-in-law against her mother-in-law. A man's enemies are his house-fellows.

The picture is the picture of a disintegrated universe. The physical universe is to be shattered, and all personal relationships are to be destroyed. Even in the New Testament there are echoes of this. There are to be wars and rumours of wars (Matt. 24.6,7). Families will be rent in twain and a man's foes will be those of his own household (Matt. 10.34-36).

(vi) It is only to be expected that the beginning of the Messianic age will be *a time of judgment.* The Lord will come like a refiner's fire and who can endure the day of his coming and who can stand when he appears? (Mal. 3.1-3). The Lord is coming as a witness against his own people, and because of the transgression of Jacob and the sins of the house of Israel

the mountain will melt under him
    and the valleys will be cleft,
like wax before the fire,
    like waters poured down a steep place.
(Micah. 1.15)

Behold, the day of the Lord comes,
  cruel, with wrath and fierce anger,
to make the earth a desolation
  and to destroy sinners from it
. . . .
I will punish the world for its evil,
  and the wicked for their iniquity;
I will put an end to the pride of the arrogant
  and lay low the haughtiness of the ruthless.
                              (Isa. 13.9-11)

On that day the Lord will punish
  the host of heaven in heaven,
  and the kings of the earth on the earth.
They will be gathered together
  as prisoners in a pit;
they will be shut up in a prison,
  and after many days they will be punished.
                              (Isa. 24.21, 22)

For behold, the Lord will come in fire,
  and his chariots like the storm-wind,
to render his anger in fury,
  and his rebuke with flames of fire.
For by fire will the Lord execute judgment,
  and by his sword upon all flesh;
  and those slain by the Lord will be many.
                              (Isa. 66.15, 16)

In the inter-testamental literature the picture becomes ever more terrible. It is there in Enoch:

And behold! he cometh with ten thousand of his holy ones
To execute judgment upon all,
And to destroy all the ungodly;
And to convict all flesh
Of all the works of their ungodliness which they have
        ungodly committed,
And of all the hard things which ungodly sinners have
        spoken against him.
                              (Enoch 1.9)

The Book of Jubilees describes the fate of the sinner, especially of the man who devises evil against his brother:

> On the day of turbulence and execration and indignation and anger, with flaming, devouring fire as he burned Sodom, so likewise shall he burn his land and his city and all that is his, and he (the sinner) shall be blotted out of the book of the discipline of the children of men, and not be recorded in the book of life, but in that which is appointed to destruction, and he shall depart into eternal execration; so that their condemnation may be always renewed in hate and in execration and in wrath and in torment and in indignation and plagues and in disease for ever (Book of Jubilees 36.10).

In a vivid phrase the Sibylline Oracles (3.60) speaks of the coming day 'when the odour of brimstone pervades all mankind'. The day will come when the Lord will require from the doers of iniquity the penalty of their iniquity (II [4] Esd. 6.18-20).

> Sinners shall perish for ever in the day of God's judgment,
>   When God visiteth the earth with his judgment,
> But they that fear the Lord shall find mercy therein,
> And shall live by the compassion of their God;
>   But sinners shall perish for ever
>   (Psalms of Solomon 15.12, 13).

We may finally note one passage in the Ascension of Isaiah (4.18) which seems to look forward, not only to the judgment, but even to the final and total extinction of the wicked: 'The Beloved will cause fire to go forth from him, and it will consume all the godless, and they will be as though they had not been created.'

The terror of judgment is an integral part of the Messianic picture.

(vii). One of the most interesting and important questions in regard to the Messianic age is *the place of the Gentiles* in it. In the earliest dreams of the Messianic age the Gentiles do not figure prominently, apart from the fact that Israel is to have peace and security from her enemies; but as time went on the Gentiles began more and more to enter into the visions of the days to come. There were no doubt various causes for this. The nation of Israel would have been more than human, if after her days of slavery and subjugation she had not dreamed of vindication and even of revenge. The emergence of the great world empires of Babylon, Assyria, Persia and Macedonia and Rome almost compelled men to think in terms of one world in a new way. As men's ideas of God developed, God became less and less a tribal deity and more and more the God of all nations and of all the world. All these things combined to bring the Gentiles within the picture. In connection with the Gentiles there are three lines of thought.

(a) There is the particularist attitude which thinks of the Gentiles as being reduced to slavery to Israel or even as being wiped out. Isa. 13.19-22 is typical of the visions of what will happen to the nations which have oppressed and subjugated Israel:

> And Babylon, the glory of kingdoms,
>> the splendour and pride of the Chaldeans,
> will be like Sodom and Gomorrah
>> when God overthrew them.
> It will never be inhabited
>> or dwelt in for all generations;
> no Arab will pitch his tent there,
>> no shepherds will make their flocks lie down there.
> But wild beasts will lie down there,
>> and its houses will be full of howling creatures;
> there ostriches will dwell,
>> and there satyrs will dance.
> Hyenas will cry in its towers,
>> and jackals in the pleasant palaces;
> its time is close at hand
>> and its days will not be prolonged.

There are times when there appears to be nothing but doom for the nations other than Israel.

> For the Lord is enraged against all nations,
>   and furious against all their host,
>   he has doomed them, given them over for the slaughter.
> Their slain shall be cast out,
>   and the stench of their corpses shall rise;
>   the mountains shall flow with their blood.
>
> (Isa. 34.2, 3)

> I trod down the peoples in my anger,
>   I made them drunk in my wrath,
>   and I poured out their lifeblood on the earth.
>
> (Isa. 63.6)

> My decision is to gather nations,
>   to assemble kingdoms,
> to pour out upon them my indignation,
>   all the heat of my anger;
> for in the fire of my jealous wrath
>   all the earth shall be consumed.
>
> (Zeph. 3.8)

Sometimes it is as if the nations, if they continued to exist at all, were to exist for the sake of Israel.

> Thus says the Lord,
> The wealth of Egypt and the merchandise of Ethiopia,
>   and the Sabeans, men of stature,
> shall come over to you and be yours,
>   they shall follow you;
>   they shall come over in chains and bow down to you.
>
> (Isa. 15.14)

The same note sounds in the inter-testamental literature.

> For the Most High will arise, the Eternal God alone,
> And he will appear in order to punish the Gentiles,
> And he will destroy all their idols,
> And thou, O Israel, shalt be happy;
> And thou shalt mount upon the necks and wings of the eagle,
> And they shall be ended.
>
> (*Assumption of Moses* 10.7, 8)

> After the signs have come, of which thou wast told before, when the nations become turbulent and the time of my Messiah has come, he shall both summon all the nations, and some of them he shall spare and some of them he shall slay ... Every nation which knows not Israel and which has not trodden down the seed of Jacob shall indeed be spared. And this because some out of every nation shall be subjected to thy people. But all those who have ruled over you, or have known you, shall be given up to the sword (II Baruch 72.2-6).

There is this particularist attitude which could culminate in the later saying that God made the Gentiles only to be fuel for the fires of hell.

(*b*) But there is quite another side to the thought about the place of the Gentiles. There is a universalist attitude to the Gentiles which thinks in terms of a world for God, and which at times even sees the duty and the destiny of Israel in terms of an obligation to bring men to the true God. This side of the matter is seldom set out as fully as it ought to be, and there is often a complete failure to recognise how universalist prophetic and inter-testamental Judaism can be. It will therefore be worthwhile to set out the evidence for this line of thought fairly fully.

It appears frequently in the Book of Isaiah.

> It shall come to pass in the latter days
>   that the mountain of the house of the Lord
> shall be established on the highest of the mountains
>   and shall be raised above the hills;
> and all nations shall flow to it,
>   and many peoples shall come and say:
> Come, let us go up to the mountain of the Lord,
>   to the house of the God of Jacob;
> that he may teach us his ways
>   and that we may walk in his paths.
> For out of Zion shall go forth the law,
>   and the word of the Lord from Jerusalem.
>
> (Isa. 2.2, 3)

On this mountain the Lord of hosts will make for all peoples
a feast of fat things, a feast of wine on the lees, of fat things
full of marrow, of wine on the lees well refined (Isa. 25.6).

Assemble yourselves and come,
    draw near together,
    you survivors of the nations!
. . . .
Turn to me and be saved,
all the ends of the earth!
for I am God and there is no other.
By myself I have sworn,
    from my mouth has gone forth in righteousness
    a word that shall not return;
To me every knee shall bow,
    every tongue shall swear.
                                        (Isa. 45.20-23)

I will give you as a light to the nations,
    that my salvation may reach to the end of the earth.
                                        (Isa. 49.6)

My deliverance draws near speedily,
    my salvation has gone forth.
    and my arms will rule the peoples;
the coastlands wait for me,
    amd for my arm they hope.
                                        (Isa. 51.5)

Behold, you shall call nations that you know not,
    and nations that knew you not shall run to you,
because of the Lord your God, and of the Holy One
            of Israel,
    for he has glorified you.
                                        (Isa. 55.5)

And the foreigners who join themselves to the Lord,
    to minister to him, to love the name of the Lord,
    and to be his servants,
everyone who keeps the Sabbath and does not profane it,
    and holds fast my covenant —
these I will bring to my holy mountain,
    and make them joyful in my house of prayer;

> their burnt-offerings and their sacrifices
>   will be accepted on my altar,
> for my house shall be called a house of prayer
>   for all peoples.

(Isa. 56.6, 7)

> I am coming to gather all nations and all tongues; and
> they shall come and shall see my glory, and I will set a
> sign among them. And from them I will send survivors
> to the nations, to Tarshish, to Put and Lud, who draw
> the bow, to Tubal and Javan, to the coastlands afar off,
> that have not heard my fame or seen my glory; and they
> shall declare my glory among the nations . . . And some
> of them also I will take for priests and Levites, says the
> Lord (Isa. 66.18-21).

Jeremia has the same vision.

> At that time Jerusalem shall be called the throne of the
> Lord, and all nations shall gather to it, to the presence
> of the Lord in Jerusalem, and they shall no more stub-
> bornly follow their own evil heart (Jer. 3.17).

If the heathen nations will learn God's name and will become
obedient to him they too, as it were, will be built into the
family of Israel (Jer. 12.15,16).

> O Lord, my strength and my stronghold,
>   my refuge in the day of trouble,
> to thee shall the nations come
>   from the ends of the earth and say,
> Our fathers have inherited nought but lies,
>   worthless things in which there is no profit.
> Can man make for himself gods?
>   Such are no gods!

> Therefore behold I will make them know, this once I
> will make them know my power and my might, and they
> shall know that my name is the Lord (Jer. 16.19-21).

In the vision of Zephaniah God says:

> Yea, at that time I will change the speech of the peoples
> to a pure speech,

that all of them may call on the name of the Lord
and serve him with one accord.

(Zeph. 3.9)

One of the greatest of the pictures is in Zechariah:

Thus saith the Lord of hosts: Peoples shall yet come,
even the inhabitants of many cities; the inhabitants of
one city shall go to another, saying, Let us go at once to
entreat the favour of the Lord, and to seek the Lord of
hosts I am going. Many peoples and strong nations shall
come to seek the Lord of hosts in Jerusalem, and to
entreat the favour of the Lord. Thus says the Lord of
hosts: In those days ten men from the nations of every
tongue shall take hold of the robe of a Jew, saying, Let
us go with you, for we have heard that God is with
you (Zech. 8.20-23).

And the Lord will become king over all the earth; on
that day the Lord will be one and his name one
(Zech. 14.9).

Without any doubt there is in the Old Testament a strong
strain of universalism; there is many a vision of God as the
God of every nation; and sometimes there is even an awareness that it is the destiny of Israel to bring the heathen to
God. And, even if Israel is not to go out, then quite certainly
the door is not shut against the Gentiles when they seek to
come in.

This strain of universalism is just as strongly represented
in the inter-testamental literature. In Enoch it is said of that
Son of Man

He shall be a staff to the righteous whereon to stay
themselves and not fall,
And he shall be the light of the Gentiles,
And the hope of those who are troubled in heart.
All who dwell on earth shall fall down and worship
before him,
And will praise and bless and celebrate with song the
Lord of Spirits.
(Enoch 48.4, 5)

In the *Testament of Levi* (18.9) it is said of the priestly Messiah:

> And in his priesthood the Gentiles shall be multiplied in
> knowledge upon the earth,
> and enlightened through the grace of the Lord.

In the *Testament of Naphtali* (8.3) it is said that God will appear

> To gather together the righteous from amongst the Gentiles.

In Enoch it is said:

> All the children of men shall become righteous, and all
> nations shall offer adoration and praise me, and all shall
> worship me (Enoch 10.21).

In the *Testament of Benjamin* (9.2) it is said:

> And the twelve tribes shall be gathered there (to the
> Temple) and all the Gentiles.

In the *Testament of Simeon* (7.2) it is said:

> For the Lord shall raise up from Levi, as it were, a High
> Priest, and from Judah, as it were, a king. He shall save
> all the Gentiles and the race of Israel.

In the Psalms of Solomon (17.34) it is said:

> Nations shall come from the ends of the earth to see his
> glory.

One of the great universalist pictures is in the *Sibylline
Oracles* (3.710-723):

> Then all the isles and the cities shall say, How doth the
> Eternal love these men!... Come, let us all fall upon
> the earth and supplicate the eternal king, the mighty
> everlasting God. Let us make procession to his Temple,
> for he is the sole potentate. And let us all ponder the
> law of the Most High God, who is the most righteous of
> all on earth.

It is very easy, and it is also very unjust, to remember only
the particularist strain in Jewish thought; there is also a uni-

versalist strain, which thinks in terms of nothing less than a world for God, and it is to be noted that even in the books in which the most particularist sayings occur often the most universalist sayings occur almost side by side with them.

(c) There remains one other dramatic picture in connection with the Gentiles. Sometimes both in the Old Testament and in the inter-testamental literature we have the picture of the Gentiles massing to mount one last tremendous attack against Jerusalem in one final struggle, a struggle the end of which is their own destruction and the ultimate triumph of God.

That picture occurs in the Gog and Magog section of Ezekiel (38.14-39.16), in Daniel 11, and Zech. 14.1-11. It occurs in symbolic language in Enoch. The eagles, the vultures and the ravens gather together to break the horn of the ram; but the Lord of the sheep comes with the staff of wrath in his hand, and the attackers are swallowed up and covered in the earth (Enoch 90.13-19). One of the most vivid pictures of this final struggle is in the *Sibylline Oracles* (3.663—672):

> But again the kings of the nations shall throw themselves against this land in troops, bringing retribution upon themselves. For the shrine of the mighty God and the noblest of men they shall seek to ravage whensoever they come to the land. In a ring round the city the accursed kings shall place each one his throne with his infidel people by him. And then with a mighty voice God shall speak unto all the undisciplined, empty-minded people, and judgment shall come upon them from the mighty God, and all shall perish at the hand of the Eternal.

In one way or another the Gentiles are brought into the picture of the Messianic days. It is quite true that there are visions of their subjugation or destruction, but there are also visions in which the enemies of God are destroyed by being made his friends.

It must never be forgotten that, although we may find in Judaism a narrow and an exclusive particularism, we can also find passages like the vision of the future in Tobit (14.6,7):

> Then all the Gentiles shall turn to fear the Lord God in truth, and will bury their idols. All the Gentiles will praise the Lord, and his people will give thanks to God, and the Lord will exalt his people. And all who love the Lord God in truth and righteousness will rejoice, showing mercy to our brethren.

(viii)   A consistent feature in the dreams of the Messianic times is *the ingathering of Israel*. Throughout the centuries the Jews had been dispersed throughout the world. Sometimes they had been forcibly removed from their own land; sometimes they had gone out of their own choice to the new opportunities which new lands provided; but in the days of the Messianic time all would be gathered back to Jerusalem. This return to Israel is a feature of the prophecies and the visions in the Book of Isaiah.

> In that day the Lord will extend his hand yet a second time to recover the remnant which is left of his people, from Assyria, from Egypt, from Pathros, from Ethiopia, from Elam, from Shinar, from Hamath, and from the coastlands of the sea.
>
> He will raise an ensign for the nations,
>   and will assemble the outcasts of Israel,
> and gather the dispersed of Judah
>   from the four corners of the earth.
>   (Isa. 11.11,12)

> In that day from the river Euphrates to the Brook of Egypt the Lord will thresh out the grain, and you will be gathered one by one, O people of Israel. And in that day a great trumpet will be blown, and those who were lost in the land of Assyria and those who were driven out to the land of Egypt will come and worship the Lord on the holy mountain at Jerusalem (Isa. 27.12,13).

> The ransomed of the Lord shall return
> and come to Zion with singing,
> with everlasting joy upon their heads.
>
> (Isa. 35.10)

From Assyria to Egypt, from Egypt to the river, from sea to sea and from mountain to mountain they will come back, and they will feed in Bashan and Gilead as in the days of old (Micah 7.12-14).

In Isaiah one of the special features of this dream is that the Gentiles and even nature itself will do everything to help the people on their journey back to their own land.

> Thus says the Lord God:
> Behold, I will lift up my hand to the nations,
> and raise my signal to the peoples;
> and they shall bring your sons in their bosom,
> and your daughters shall be carried on their shoulders.
> Kings shall be your foster fathers,
> and their queens your nursing mothers.
>
> (Isa. 49.22,23)

> Your sons shall come from afar,
> and your daughters shall be carried in the arms.
>
> (Isa. 60.4)

And they shall bring all your brethren from all the nations as an offering to the Lord, upon horses, and in chariots, and in litters, and upon mules, and upon dromedaries to my holy mountain Jerusalem, says the Lord, just as the Israelites bring their cereal offering in a clean vessel to the house of the Lord (Isa. 66.20).

Zechariah has the same vision (10.6-10):

> I will bring them back because I have compassion on them,
> and they shall be as though I had not rejected them.
> I will signal for them and gather them in,
> for I have redeemed them,
> and they shall be as many as of old.
> Though I scattered them among the nations,
> yet in far countries they shall remember me,

> and with their children they shall live and return.
> I will bring them home from the land of Egypt,
>   and gather them from Assyria;
> and I will bring them to the land of Gilead and to Lebanon,
>   till there is no room for them.

The vision of the return provides some of the loveliest passages in the inter-testamental literature. There are two such passages in Baruch: in the first of them even nature co-operates to bring God's people back:

> Arise, O Jerusalem, stand upon the height
>   and look toward the east,
> and see your children gathered from west and east,
>   at the word of the Holy One,
>   rejoicing that God has remembered them.
> For they went forth from you on foot,
>   led away by their enemies;
> but God will bring them back to you,
>   carried in glory, as on a royal throne,
> For God has ordered that every high mountain and the
>   everlasting hills be made low
> and the valleys filled up, to make level ground,
>   so that Israel may walk safely in the glory of God.
> The woods and every fragrant tree
>   have shaded Israel at God's command,
> for God will lead Israel with joy,
>   in the light of his glory,
>   with the mercy and righteousness that come from him.
>   (Baruch 5.5-9)

The second thrills with the joy of the return to the city which no Jew could ever forget:

> Look toward the east, O Jerusalem,
>   and see the joy that is coming to you from God!
> Behold your sons are coming, whom you sent away,
>   they are coming, gathered from east and west,
> at the word of the Holy One,
>   rejoicing in the glory of God.
>   (Baruch 4.36, 37)

The most beautiful of all these passages is in the Psalms of Solomon 11:

> Blow ye in Zion on the trumpet to summon the saints,
>   Cause ye to be heard in Jerusalem the voice of him
>   that bringeth good tidings;
>   For God hath had pity on Israel in visiting them.
> Stand on the height, O Jerusalem, and behold thy children,
>   From the east and west gathered together by the Lord;
> From the north they come in the gladness of their God,
>   From the isles afar off God hath gathered them.
> High mountains hath he abased into a plain for them;
>   The hills fled at their entrance.
> The woods gave them shelter as they passed by;
>   Every sweet-smelling tree God caused to spring up for
>   for them,
>   That Israel might pass by in the visitation of the glory
>   of their God.
> Put on, O Jerusalem, thy glorious garments;
>   Make ready thy holy robe;
>   For God hath spoken good for Israel, for ever and ever.
> Let the Lord do what he hath spoken concerning Israel
>   and Jerusalem;
>   Let the Lord raise up Israel by his glorious name
> The mercy of the Lord be upon Israel for ever and ever.

It is the same belief which to this day finds its place in the tenth prayer in the Shemoneh 'Esreh which is still prayed in every synagogue:

> Sound with a great trumpet to announce our freedom; and set up a standard to collect our captives, and gather us together from the four corners of the earth. Blessed art thou, O Lord, who gatherest the outcasts of thy people Israel.

At every Passover Feast the Jews are still praying and longing, 'This year, here; next year, in Jerusalem.'

The most interesting occurrence of this dream is in II (4) Esd. 13.39-48. As we have already seen, in this book there is the figure of the Messiah as the Man coming up from

the sea. Part of his function is to destroy the nations who
have been hostile to Israel and to God; but the most interesting thing about him is that he is to gather to himself the
lost ten tribes. The passage tells the story of the lost ten
tribes, and then envisages their return.

> These are the ten tribes which were led away captive
> out of their own land in the days of Josiah (an error for
> Hosea) the king, which tribes Salmanassar the king of
> the Assyrians led away captive; he carried them across
> the River, and thus they were transported into another
> land. But they took this counsel among themselves, that
> they would leave the multitude of the heathen, and go
> forth into a land further distant, where the human race
> had never dwelt, there at least to keep their statutes
> which they had not kept in their own land. And they
> entered by the narrow passages of the river Euphrates.
> For the Most High then wrought wonders for them, and
> stayed the springs of the River till they were passed over.
> And through that country there was a great way to go, a
> journey of a year and a half; and that region was called
> Arzareth. There they have dwelt until the last times;
> and now, when they are about to come again, the Most
> High will again stay the springs of the River, that they
> may be able to pass over. Therefore thou didst see a
> multitude gathered together in peace.

So then in the Messianic days all the exiles of Israel will be
brought back to Jerusalem and even the lost ten tribes shall
return.

(ix) When we remember the place that the Holy City
held in the mind and the heart of every Jew we will not
be surprised to find that an integral part of the dream of the
Messianic times was the vision of *a restored and renewed
Jerusalem*.

Jerusalem was to be beautified with the most precious things
and with gifts which all the world would bring to it.

I will make your pinnacles of agate,
 your gates of carbuncles,
 and all your wall of precious stones.

(Isa. 54.12)

Isaiah 60 is one long lyrical description of the beauties and the glories of the restored Jerusalem.

Your gates shall be open continually;
 day and night they shall not be shut,
that men may bring to you the wealth of the nations.

The glory of Lebanon shall come to you,
 the cypress, the plane and the pine
to beautify the place of my sanctuary,
 and I will make the place of my feet glorious.

Instead of bronze I will bring gold,
 and instcad of iron I will bring silver;
instead of wood bronze,
 instead of stones, iron.

(Isa. 60.11,13,17)

Haggai has his vision of the splendour of the rebuilt and restored Temple:

And I will shake all the nations, so that the treasures of all the nations shall come in, and I will fill this house with splendour, says the Lord of hosts. The silver is mine, and the gold is mine, says the Lord of hosts. The latter splendour of this house shall be greater than the former, says the Lord of hosts (Hag. 2.7-9).

Tobit has a magnificent description of the beauties of the new Jerusalem:

For Jerusalem shall be built with sapphires and emeralds,
 her walls with precious stones,
 and her towers and battlements with pure gold.
The streets of Jerusalem shall be paved with beryl, and
     ruby and stones of Ophir;
All her lanes will cry Hallelujah! and will give praise,

> saying, Blessed is God, who has exalted you for ever.
> (Tob. 13.16-18)

There is no beauty in the world which is too beautiful and too costly for the restored Jerusalem.

Jerusalem is to be purified. The Davidic king is to purge Jerusalem from nations that trample her down to destruction (Psalms of Solomon 17.25).

Jerusalem is to become everlasting. It is to be renewed in glory and perfected for evermore (II Baruch 32.4).

> And in the new Jerusalem shall the righteous rejoice,
> And it shall be unto the glory of God for ever,
> And no longer shall Jerusalem endure desolation,
> Nor Israel be led captive.
> (*Testament of Dan* 5.12, 13)

Most interesting of all, there entered into the thought of men the idea of a Jerusalem, divine, pre-existent, prepared by God in the heavenly places, there from all time, and prepared some day to come down among men. The old house is folded up and taken away, and a wonderful new house which the Lord has built comes and takes its place (Enoch 90.28,29). The pre-existent Jerusalem was shown to Adam before he sinned.

> And after these things I showed it to my servant Abraham by night among the portions of the victims [Gen. 15.9-21]. And again also I showed it to Moses on Mount Sinai when I showed to him the likeness of the tabernacle and all its vessels. And now, behold, it is preserved with me, as also is Paradise (II Baruch 4.2-6).

In the Messianic days, then shall the city which is now invisible appear (II [4] Esd. 7.26). The seer is summond to see the brilliance of the glory of the heavenly Jerusalem, and her majestic beauty.

> Therefore be not afraid, and let not thy heart be terrified;
> but go in and see the brightness and vastness of the

building, as far as it is possible for thee with the sight of thine eyes to see! Then shalt thou hear as much as the hearing of thine ears can hear (10.44-59).

The heavenly Jerusalem is too wonderful for human eyes to comprehend.

This is an idea which emerges in the New Testament. Paul speaks of the Jerusalem which is above (Gal. 4.26). It is the city of the living God, the heavenly Jerusalem of the writer to the Hebrews (Heb. 12.22). It is the new Jerusalem of the Revelation, the holy city which is to come down from heaven (Rev. 3.12; 21.2,10). It is the city for which in the Shemoneh 'Esreh the Jews still pray:

> And to Jerusalem thy city return with compassion, and dwell therein as thou hast promised; and rebuild her speedily in our days, a structure everlasting; and the throne of David speedily establish there. Blessed art thou, O Lord, the builder of Jerusalem.

The new Jerusalem is not only beautiful beyond words, it is divine, the city whose architect and builder is God.

(x) *The resurrection of the dead* is a regular hope and expectation of the Messianic age. The hope has already emerged in the Old Testament. Isa. 26.19 should read (RSV):

> The dead shall live, their bodies shall rise.
> O dwellers in the dust, awake and sing for joy!
> For thy dew is a dew of light,
>   and on the land of the shades thou wilt let it fall.

Even more definitely and unequivocally the hope is stated in Daniel (12.2):

> And many of those who sleep in the dust of the earth shall awake, some to everlasting life, and some to shame and everlasting contempt.

The hope of the resurrection of the dead grew steadily in intensity. The less God was seen in terms of a tribal or

national deity, and the more he was seen in terms of the
God of all the universe, the more certain men became that
there was nothing in life or in death that could separate them
from him. Further, the more men suffered and agonised for
their faith, and the further there receded the possibility of the
vindication of God's chosen people in this world and in the
time-scheme of history, the more firm became the conviction
that a new world was required to redress the balance of the
old, if God's love and justice were not to be frustrated and
defeated.

The hope is not always the same. Sometimes it is particularly concentrated on the resurrection of those who had been
righteous and faithful in this life, while apparently others,
sinners and Gentiles, would have no life to come. This form
of the belief is particularly characteristic of two books. It is
characteristic of the Psalms of Solomon.

> The destruction of the sinner is for ever
> and he shall not be remembered, when the righteous
>   is visited.
> This is the portion of sinners for ever.
> But they that fear the Lord shall rise to life eternal,
>   and their life shall be in the light of the Lord, and
>   shall come to an end no more (3.16).

> The Lord spareth his pious ones,
>   and blotteth out their errors by his chastening,
> for the life of the righteous shall be for ever;
>   but sinners shall be taken away into destruction,
>   and their memorial shall be found no more,
> but upon the pious is the mercy of the Lord,
>   and upon them that fear him his mercy (13.9-11).

The fourteenth of the Psalms of Solomon states this belief
most fully:

> Faithful is the Lord to them that love him in truth,
>   To them that endure his chastening,
> To them that walk in the righteousness of his
>   commandments,

In the law which he commanded us that we might live.
The pious of the Lord shall live by it for ever;
The Paradise of the Lord, the trees of life, are his
pious ones.
Their planting is rooted for ever;
They shall not be plucked up all the days of heaven:
For the portion and the inheritance of God is Israel.
But not so are the sinners and transgressors,
Who love the brief day spent in companionship with sin;
Their delight is in fleeting corruption,
And they remember not God.
For the ways of men are known before him at all times.
And he knoweth the secrets of the heart before they
come to pass.
Therefore their inheritance is Sheol and darkness and
destruction,
And they shall not be found in the day when the
righteous obtain mercy,
But the pious of the Lord shall inherit life in gladness.

Sinners shall perish for ever in the day of the Lord's
judgment,
When God visiteth the earth with his judgment.
But they that fear the Lord shall find mercy therein,
And shall live by the compassion of their God;
But sinners shall perish for ever (14.13-15).

In the Psalms of Solomon there is life for ever for the righteous, but death for ever for the sinners.

The other book in which the resurrection of the righteous is specially prominent is II Maccabees. It was only natural that in that killing time, when the righteous chose to die for their faith, the conviction of a life to come should be specially precious.

In the story of the seven brothers who chose to die in the most terrible tortures rather than eat swine's flesh this confidence is specially strong. As the second brother died, he said to his torturer:

Thou dost despatch us from this life, but the King of the

world shall raise us up, who have died for his laws, and revive us to life everlasting (II Macc. 7.9).

In the midst of his tortures the fourth brother said:

It is meet for those who perish at men's hands to cherish hope divine that they shall be raised up by God again; but thou—thou shalt have no resurrection to life (II Macc. 7.14).

In the midst of their agonies the mother of the seven sons comforted them:

It was the Creator of the world who fashioneth men and deviseth the generating of all things, and he it is who in mercy will restore to you the breath of life even as you now count yourselves naught for his law's sake (II Macc. 7.23).

In the *Testament of Judah* it is the hope that Abraham, Isaac and Jacob and all the patriarchs will rise to life.

They who have died in grief shall rise in joy,
And they who were poor for the Lord's sake shall be
    made rich,
And those who were put to death for the Lord's sake
    shall awake to life.
(*Testament of Judah* 25.1-4)

In this line of thought there is a strong element of compensation. Whatever life may have been like in this world, when this world is done, it will be well with the righteous and ill with the sinner.

In certain other inter-testamental books the expectation is that all men will be raised, the good to blessedness, the wicked to destruction. That is the belief in Enoch (51.1):

And in those days shall the earth also give back that
    which has been entrusted to it,
And Sheol also shall give back that which it has received,
And hell shall give back that which it owes.

It is the same in II (4) Esdras (13.32,37):

The earth shall restore those that sleep in her,
  and the dust those that are at rest therein,
and the chambers shall restore them that were committed
  unto them.
And then shall the Most High say to the nations that
  have been raised from the dead,
Look now and consider who ye have denied, whom ye
have not served, whose commandments ye have despised.

The *Testament of Benjamin* is very definite (10.8):

Then also shall all men rise, some unto glory, and some
unto shame.

In II Baruch the fate of the righteous and of the wicked is
compared.

Then all that have fallen asleep in hope of him shall
rise again ... But the souls of the wicked, when they
behold all these things, shall then waste away the more,
for they shall know that their torment has come and
their perdition has arrived (30.1-5).

In II Baruch 50.1-51.6 there is a vision of earth restoring
its dead exactly as they were, but then there comes the
transformation in which the righteous are changed into the
splendour and glory of the angels, and the wicked see it
and depart to be tormented.

In one form or another the expectation of the resurrection
of the dead is an essential element in the picture.

Before we leave this part of the pattern there are certain
beliefs connected with it at which we may look.

In II Macc. 12.32-45 we come upon a passage which is the
basis of prayer and sacrifice for the dead. In a battle with
Gorgias the governor of Idumaea certain Jews were killed.
When their fellow-countrymen went to the battlefield to
collect their bodies for burial, they found that all who had
fallen were wearing certain heathen amulets which, of course,
Jewish faith and religion completely forbade. It was believed

that the wearing of these amulets was the reason why these men had been killed in the battle, and the incident was used as a warning against such impiety. But Judas Maccabaeus was not content to leave the matter there; something had to be done for the men who had perished in their sin.

> He also took a collection man by man to the amount of two thousand drachmae of silver, and sent it to Jerusalem to provide for a sin offering. In doing this he acted very well and honourably, taking account of the resurrection. For if he were not expecting that those who had fallen would rise again, it would have been superfluous and foolish to pray for the dead. But if he was looking to the splendid reward that is laid up for those who fall asleep in godliness, it was a holy and pious thought. Therefore he made atonement for the dead, that they might be delivered for their sin.

The very way and tone in which the historian recounts the incident shows that he felt that the action of Judas required explanation and justification. This is a passage of quite exceptional interest because it is the foundation of prayers and masses and sacrifices for the dead.

There was one very curious rabbinic belief in connection with the resurrection of the dead. Scripture, so they argued, uses the phrase 'to inherit the land' as equivalent to 'to rise from the dead'. From this they argued that, 'Jerusalem alone is the city of which the dead shall blossom as the grass.' They therefore had the strange belief that those who were buried in other parts of the world would have to creep and crawl through underground cavities and channels until they reached the land of Palestine; and only then would they rise.

They further held that the Messiah would descend to Sheol, and that there he would lead forth the righteous dead, if they possessed the sign of circumcision, a belief which clearly has some connection with the later developments in Christian thought regarding the descent of Jesus into Hades. Later it was the rabbinic belief that all men would be raised by God, who alone possessed the key which would unlock the tombs.

(xi) One of the matters around which speculation gathered was *the duration of the Messianic kingdom*. In regard to this there were two kinds of belief.

The natural way to think of it was to think of the Messianic kingdom as lasting for ever, and that is one line of thought. This is especially true when the Messianic age is thought of in terms of the Davidic kingdom. So Jeremiah has it:

> David shall never lack a man to sit on the throne of the house of Israel ... for ever ... If you can break my covenant with the day and my covenant with the night, so that day and night will not come at their appointed time, then also my covenant with David my servant may be broken, so that he shall not have a son to reign on his throne (Jer. 33.17-21).

It is so in Ezekiel:

> They shall dwell in the land where your fathers dwelt that I gave to my servant Jacob; they and their children and their children's children shall dwell there for ever; and David my servant shall be their prince for ever (Ezek. 37.25).

In Daniel the kingdom is to be an everlasting kingdom (7.27). It is the message of Joel that

> Judah shall be inhabited for ever, and Jerusalem to all generations (Joel 3.20).

There is the same picture in the inter-testamental literature. It is said in Enoch

> The Lord of Spirits will abide over them,
> And with that Son of Man shall they eat,
> And lie down and rise up for ever and ever (Enoch 62.14).

In the Sibylline Oracles the kingdom will be for all ages

(3.767). 'A holy prince shall come to wield the sceptre over all the world unto all ages of hurrying time' (3.49,50). In the Psalms of Solomon (17.4).

> The might of our God is for ever with mercy,
>   and the kingdom of our God is for ever over the
>   nations in judgment.

But there are occasions on which we come upon a line of thought which thinks of the Messianic kingdom being of limited duration. In II Baruch the Messiah comes, completes his reign, and then returns to his glory (30.1). His principate will stand for ever until this world of corruption is at an end (40.3).

> And it shall come to pass, when he has brought low
>   everything that is in the world,
> And has sat down in peace for the age on the throne of
>   his kingdom,
> That joy shall then be revealed
> And rest shall appear (73.1).

The idea seems to be of a Messianic reign in which everything evil is destroyed and in which righteousness becomes supreme, and then the age of God.

The strangest of all thoughts is in II (4) Esd. 7.27-31. There we find that after a limited reign the Messiah will die.

> My Son the Messiah shall be revealed together with those who are with him, and shall rejoice the survivors four hundred years. And it shall be, after these years, that my Son the Messiah shall die, and all in whom there is human breath. Then shall the world be turned into the primaeval silence seven days, like as at the first beginnings, so that no man is left. And it shall be after seven days that the age which is not yet awake shall be aroused and that which is corruptible shall perish.

The four hundred years is arrived at by the combination of two Old Testament texts.

> The Lord said to Abram: Know of a surety that your
> descendants will be sojourners in a land that is not theirs,
> and will be slaves there, *and they will be oppressed for
> four hundred years* (Gen. 15.13).

> Make us glad as many days as thou has afflicted us,
>   and as many years as we have seen evil.
>   (Ps. 90.15)

The period of affliction was four hundred years, and, if the
period of joy is to be the same, it must also be four hundred
years; so, it can be argued, the Messianic kingdom will last
for four hundred years.

The difference may be due to this. We have already seen
that it was basic to all Jewish thought of the future that
all time is divided into two ages, this present age, and the
age which is to come, that this present age is doomed to
ultimate destruction, and that the age to come is the golden
age of God. Now, if the Messianic age is thought of as
the end of this present age, then it is necessarily temporary,
even if during it all evil is conquered and righteousness is
exalted. If on the other hand the Messianic age is looked
on as *the beginning of the age to come*, then it will last for
ever.

It may be that in the New Testament we have two reper-
cussions of these beliefs in a limited Messianic time. It may
be that this lies at the back of the idea of the Millennium
in the Revelation. During the Millennium the martyrs are to
be resurrected, they will reign with Christ for a thousand
years, then Satan will be released and there will come the
final battle and the ultimate triumph (Rev. 20.4-6). In a
book as Jewish as the Revelation it would not be unnatural
to find a development of what is in fact a Jewish idea. In I
Cor. 15.24-28 we find a passage with at least something of
the same thought:

> Then comes the end, when he delivers the kingdom to

> God the Father after destroying every rule and every
> authority and power. For he must reign until he has put
> all his enemies under his feet ... When all things are
> subject to him, then the Son himself will also be subjected
> to him who put all things under him, that God may be
> everything to everyone.

Here too we have the idea of a Messianic time which is the
prelude to the complete sovereignty of God. Quite certainly
Paul would know the rabbinic ideas and it is by no means
impossible that he developed them in this way.

So then the Messianic age was sometimes looked on as
lasting for ever, and sometimes as lasting for a limited
period. It would seem that here we have two points of view.
In the one the Messianic age is itself the ultimate end of
things; in the other the Messianic age is the prelude to the
kingdom in which God alone is King.

We must now turn to a very important part of this investigation. We must look at the blessings which were popu-
larly expected to come with the coming of the Messianic
age, for it is obviously of the first importance to compare
what men expected with what Jesus offered. It is only in the
light of their expectations that their refusal to accept him
and their rejection of him become intelligible.

(i) A very early and a very simple element in the
Messianic hope was *the expectation that the divided kingdom
would be reunited,* and that once again the nation would become one. 'In those days the house of Judah shall join the
house of Israel' (Jer. 3.18).

> Ephraim shall not be jealous of Judah,
>   and Judah shall not harass Ephraim.
> (Isa. 11.13)

> The people of Judah and the people of Israel shall be
> gathered together, and they shall appoint for themselves
> one head (Hos. 1.11).

In connection with this Ezekiel was commanded to perform one of the symbolic actions of which his ministry was full. He was to take two sticks, marked with the names of the two kingdoms, and join them into one stick, so that they should become one in his hand, to show that the separated kingdoms were to return to their original unity again. It was God's saying:

> I will make them one nation in the land, upon the mountains of Israel; and one king shall be king over them all; and they shall be no longer two nations, and no longer divided into two kingdoms (Ezek. 37.15-23).

It was only natural that the dream of the golden time should include the hope of the healing of the breaches which divided the two kingdoms.

(ii) A consistent element in the Messianic hope was the expectation of *a time of amazing and miraculous fertility*. Amos (9.13) has that picture:

> Behold the days are coming, says the Lord,
>   when the ploughman shall overtake the reaper
> and the treader of grapes him that sows the seed;
>   the mountains shall drip sweet wine,
> and they shall make gardens and eat their fruit.

The wilderness is to become a fruitful field, and the fruitful field is to become a forest (Isa. 32.13; 29.17).

> The wilderness and the dry land shall be glad,
>   the desert shall rejoice and blossom.
> (Isa. 35.1)

> Then God shall give great joy to men. For the earth and the trees and the innumerable flocks of sheep shall give their true fruit to mankind, of wine and sweet honey and white milk, and corn which is to men the most excellent gift of all.

> Earth the universal mother shall give to mortals her best fruit in countless store of corn, wine and oil. Yea,

from heaven shall come a sweet draught of luscious honey; the trees shall yield their proper fruits, and rich flocks and kine and lambs of sheep and kids of goats. He will cause sweet fountains of white milk to burst forth. And the cities shall be full of good things and the fields rich (*Sibylline Oracles* 3.619-623, 744-750).

The most famous passage is in II Baruch 29.5-8, a passage which Irenaeus (5.23) tells us that Papias gives as a saying of Jesus:

The earth shall also yield its fruit ten thousandfold, and on each vine there shall be a thousand branches, and each branch shall produce a thousand clusters, and each cluster produce a thousand grapes, and each grape a cor (120 gallons) of wine. And those who have hungered shall rejoice; moreover, also, they shall behold marvels every day. For winds shall go forth from before Me every morning to bring the fragrance of aromatic fruits, and at the close of the day clouds distilling the dew of health.

The manna is to descend to again, and the monsters Leviathan and Behemoth are to become food for the people.

It is easy contemptuously to write off this kind of dream as sensuous materialism, but it must be remembered that it is the dream of a people who had starved and thirsted in the desert and who lived in an age when hunger was the constant companion of men. The circumstances of a primitive community and the circumstances of a welfare state are very different.

(iii) Another consistent part, of the dream of the Messianic age is *the end of all war and strife*, a world in which peace reigns supreme.

> They shall beat their swords into ploughshares,
>   and their spears into pruning hooks,
> nation shall not lift up sword against nation,
>   neither shall they learn war any more.
>
>   (Isa. 2.4)

> They shall not hurt or destroy
> in all my holy mountain.
>
> (Isa. 11.9)

> I will cut off the chariot from Ephraim
> and the war horse from Jerusalem;
> and the battle bow shall be cut off,
> and he shall command peace to the nations.
>
> (Zech. 9.10)

There is the same dream of peace in the inter-testamental literature.

> The good law shall come forth in its fulness from the starry heaven upon men, and good justice, and with it the best of all gifts to men, sober concord and affection, faithfulness, friendship from strangers and fellow-citizens too. And lawlessness, murmuring, envy, wrath, and folly shall flee from men; penury too shall flee, and distress, and murder, and destructive strifes, and baleful feuds, and thefts by night and every evil in those days.

> The cities shall be full of good things and the fields rich; neither shall there be any sword throughout the land or battle din; nor shall the earth be convulsed any more with deep-drawn groans. No war shall there be any more nor drought throughout the land, no famine, nor hail to work havoc on the crops. But there shall be a great peace throughout all the earth, and king shall be friendly with king till the end of the age, and a common law for men throughout all the earth shall the Eternal perfect in the starry heaven, for all those things which have been wrought by miserable mortals.

> (*Sibylline Oracles* 3.373-380,750-759)

There never has been a time when the world was not weary of war.

(iv) One of the loveliest pictures of the Messianic age is the picture of *the new friendship between man and the animals,* in which the ancient enmity is taken away.

> The wolf shall dwell with the lamb,
>   and the leopard shall lie down with the kid,
> and the calf and the lion and the fatling together,
>   and a little child shall lead them.
> The cow and the bear shall feed,
>   their young shall lie down together,
>   and the lion shall eat straw like the ox.
> The sucking child shall play over the hole of the asp,
> and the weaned child shall put his hand on the adder's den.
> They shall not hurt or destroy
>   in all my holy mountain.
>
> (Isa. 11.6-9; cp. 65.25)

Hosea (2.18) has the idea of a covenant with the beasts.

> And I will make for you a covenant on that day with the
> beasts of the field, the birds of the air, and the creeping
> things of the ground; and I will abolish the bow, the
> sword, and war from the land; and I will make you lie
> down in safety.

II Baruch (73.6) has the picture of the wild beasts offering
their service to men.

> And the wild beasts shall come from the forest and
>   minister unto men,
> And asps and dragons shall come forth from their holes
>   to submit themselves to a little child.

This is a picture which is also in Philo (*Concerning Rewards
and Punishments* 15).

> Bears, lions, panthers, Indian elephants, tigers and all
> kinds of beasts of uncontrollable strength and power
> will turn from their solitary ways of life to one according
> to law, and from intercourse with few, after the manner
> of gregarious animals, will accustom themselves to the
> sight of man, who will not as formerly be attacked by
> them, but feared as their master, and they will respect
> him as their natural lord. Some, even, emulating the
> tame animals, will offer him their homage by wagging
> their tails like lap-dogs. The race, too, of scorpions,
> snakes and reptiles will then no longer have any harmful
> poison.

It is just barely possible that there is a reference to this line of thought in the gospel story. In Mark 1.13 it is said of Jesus: 'And he was in the wilderness forty days, tempted by Satan; and he was with the wild beasts; and the angels ministered to him.' It is just possible that the reference to the wild beasts is not a touch of terror, but an indication that they gave him their help and their sympathy, as in the dream of the Messianic age.

(v) It was the dream that in the Messianic age *all sorrow, all pain, all weariness, and even death itself would be gone for ever.*

> Their life shall be like a watered garden,
>   and they shall languish no more (Jer. 31.12).
> They shall obtain joy and gladness,
>   and sorrow and sighing shall flee away (Isa. 35.10).

> No more shall be heard in it (Jerusalem) the sound of
>   weeping
>   and the cry of distress.
> No more shall there be in it
>   an infant that lives but a few days,
>   or an old man who does not fill out his days,
> for the child shall die a hundred years old.
> . . . .

> They shall not build and another inhabit;
>   they shall not plant and another eat;
> for like the days of a tree shall the days of my people be.
>   (Isa. 65.20-22).

> No inhabitant will say, I am sick (Isa. 33.24).

> He will swallow up death for ever, and the Lord God
> will wipe away tears from all faces (Isa. 25.8).

The loveliest picture of all is in II Baruch 73.2-74.4:

> Then healing shall descend in dew,
> And disease shall withdraw,
> And anxiety and anguish and lamentation pass from
>   amongst men,

And gladness proceed through the whole earth.
And no one shall die untimely,
Nor shall any adversity suddenly befall

. . . .

And women shall no longer have pain when they bear,
Nor shall they suffer torment when they yield the fruit
of the womb.
And it shall come to pass in those days that the reapers
shall not grow weary,
Nor those that build be toilworn;
For the works of themselves shall speedily advance
Together with those who do them in much tranquillity

. . . .

This is the bright lightning which comes after the last
dark water.

The Messianic age will be a time when what Virgil called
'the tears of things' will be no more.

(vi)   It remains only to say that in the Messianic age there
will be *a holiness and a righteousness, divine and God-given.*
This is a picture specially beautiful in the Psalms of Solomon.

And he [the Davidic King] shall gather together a holy
people, whom he shall lead in righteousness,
And he shall judge the tribes of the people that has
been sanctified by the Lord his God.
And he shall not suffer unrighteousness to lodge any
more in their midst,
Nor shall there dwell with them any man that knoweth
wickedness,
For he shall know them that they are all sons of their God.

. . . .

And there shall be no unrighteousness in his days in
their midst
For all shall be holy and their king the anointed of
the Lord (Psalms of Solomon 17.28,29,36,37).

Blessed shall they be that shall be in those days,
  In that they shall see the goodness of the Lord which he
      shall perform for the generation that is to come,
Under the rod of chastening of the Lord's anointed in
    the fear of his God,
  In the spirit of wisdom and righteousness and strength;
That he may direct every man in the works of righteous-
    ness by the fear of God,
  That he may establish them all before the Lord,
A good generation living in the fear of God in the days
    of mercy.
                        (Psalms of Solomon 18.7-10).

At last the holy people will be holy indeed.

This then is the vision of the Messianic age, the vision of
a recreated world with a recreated people to live in it.

We have now set before ourselves a comprehensive picture
of the Messiah whom the Jews expected and of the blessings
which they expected the Messianic age to bring. We have
now to ask if Jesus fits into this picture, and if it can be
regarded as in any way a description of him and of the
blessings which he offered to men. And we have to answer
at once that Jesus does not fit into this picture at all. As
Bultmann has rightly said: 'The Synoptic tradition leaves no
doubt at all that Jesus' life and work, measured by tradional
Messianic ideas, was not Messianic.' Let us see the broad
lines in which Jesus differed from the traditional and orthodox
Messianic picture.

To the end of the day the Jewish Messianic idea remained
essentially *national*. It was centred in the Jewish nation; it
was even centred in Jerusalem. It is true that the Gentiles
entered more and more into it, sometimes as those who must
be eliminated, sometimes as those who must be subjugated,
and sometimes as those who must be enlightened. But the
fact remains that the Messianic age was for the benefit of
the Jewish nation and the Jewish nation is the centre-piece

of it. Chosenness for privilege never really ceases to be the essence of the picture. To put that in another way, the Jewish Messianic idea remained essentially *selfish*. It was in effect a rearrangement, and even a recreation, of the world and of history and of the entire scheme of things in interests of the covenant nation. The Messianic idea never escaped from the idea of a most favoured nation clause in the economy of God. This is not a picture into which Jesus can easily be fitted. It is perfectly true that his first aim was the finding and the saving of the lost sheep of the house of Israel. But from the beginning there are symbolic hints and forecasts that Jesus is the Saviour of all men. He is certainly not interested in the national exaltation of Israel. His treatment of a Gentile centurion, his attitude to a Samaritan woman and a Samaritan leper, his gentleness to a Syro-Phoenician woman even in an incident when he did stress the place of Israel, his brief time in the Decapolis are all symbolic foretastes of the universality of the gospel. The last interpretation of which the portrait of Jesus in the Gospels is susceptible is its interpretation as a nationalistic Jewish Messiah.

Further, the Jewish Messianic idea was essentially *material*. It is quite true that it involves spiritual blessings and a nation made holy to God and by God; it is quite true that it involves the restoration of a perfect worship and a perfect priesthood. But the fact remains that the pictures which are most lovingly painted, the passages which sing with the most heartfelt and lyrical poetry, are pictures and passages of a recreated world of prosperity and fertility. Whatever be the details in the scheme and the parts in the pattern which may be cited, the over-all impression it that of a material kingdom; and even passages which stress the holiness of the Messianic nation will go on, as in the Psalms of Solomon, to speak of the obliteration of the enemies of Israel. To this it may be added that the Jewish picture is basically *otherworldly,* or at least it was so by the time of Jesus. It is perfectly true that it began with a picture of a restored nation and a restored world under a Davidic king; but it went on more and more to think in terms of the total destruction of this present age and the total inauguration of a new age which was a totally new creation. It is difficult to fit Jesus into this. One of the most significant things that Jesus ever did was to teach his disciples to pray: 'Thy will be done *in earth as it is in heaven.*' It may well be that there are other sayings of Jesus which may be interpreted as pointing in other directions, but the over-all impression of the message of Jesus is that the Kingdom of God is to come in this world. Further, the Jewish picture of the Messianic age is one which involves *cosmic upheaval and shattering and sudden disaster.* In the technical word, it is an *apocalyptic* picture. Of course, there are sayings in the New Testament which can be interpreted along these lines, but Jesus spoke far too much in terms of the kind of growth by which nature grows to be classed as an apocalyptist. This is not to deny that Jesus thought in terms of a consummation, but it is to deny that he can be explained in terms of Jewish apocalyptic thought.

In the Jewish Messianic picture one of the great functions of the Messiah is *utterly and absolutely and completely to destroy sinners.* The last thing that the Jewish Messiah could be called was the Saviour of sinners; it is little wonder that the Jews stood aghast when Messianic claims were made for one who was regarded as the friend of tax-collectors and sinners. The Jewish idea was that the Messiah would obliterate sinners; Jesus came to rescue, to ransom and to redeem sinners. Lastly, in the Jewish picture the Messiah is always a figure of splendour and majesty, of power and of glory. There is no faintest hint in the Jewish picture of a suffering Messiah whose throne would be a cross; in it such a Messiah was an incredible impossibility, a contradiction in terms.

The more we examine this, the more we are forced to the conclusion that Jesus was well nigh the exact opposite of the picture of the Jewish Messiah. Are we then to say that Jesus never claimed to be Messiah and that there is no connection at all between him and the Messianic idea and ideal? This is precisely the point of view that was put forward in a very influential book by W. Wrede, *Das Messiasgeheimnis, The Messianic Secret*.[1]

What then was Wrede's argument? Wrede begins his argument from the fact that it is a characteristic of Mark's Gospel that again and again in it Jesus enjoins silence regarding his Messiahship, in particular upon those who were demon-possessed, and upon those for whom miracles had been wrought, and upon his own disciples after they had discovered who he was. The demon-possessed man who in the synagogue at Capernaum addressed him as the Holy One of God is met with the command to be silent (Mark 1.23-25). When the sick came to him and were brought to him at evening Mark's narrative says: 'And he healed many who were sick with various diseases, and cast out many demons, and he would not permit the demons to speak, because they knew him' (Mark 1.32-34). We are told that whenever the unclean spirits saw him they recognised him as the Son of God, 'and he strictly ordered them not to make him known' (Mark 3.11,12). The story of the healing of Jairus' daughter ends: 'And he strictly charged them that no one should know this' (Mark 5.43). After the healing of the deaf and stammering man, it is said: 'And he charged them to tell no one' (Mark 7.36). After the healing of the blind man at Bethsaida, the man is told not even to enter the village (Mark 8.22-26). After Peter's discovery of Jesus' Messiahship

---

1 Although published as long ago as 1901, the book has never been translated into English, but there is a full account of it in an article by Vincent Taylor in the *Expository Times* vol. 65, 1953/4, pp. 246 ff.

at Caesarea Philippi the incident ends with the statement:
'And he charged them to tell no one about him' (Mark
8.30).

Wrede finds a clue to this situation in the saying reported
in Mark 9.9, where after the narrative of the Transfiguration
it is said: 'And as they were coming down the mountain,
Jesus charged them to tell no one what they had seen, until
the Son of Man should have risen from the dead.' Wrede's
contention is that no one ever connected Jesus with Messiahship and no one ever regarded him as Messiah, *until after
the Resurrection.* During his life on earth Jesus, as Wrede
sees it, made no claim to be Messiah, and no one ever
supposed he was. The Resurrection then changed the whole
situation; he was seen to be Messiah; and these incidents
and sayings were all, to put it bluntly, invented to indicate
that all through his earthly days the Messiahship of Jesus
had been kept a close secret. Through them an attempt is
made to make it appear that Jesus was not accepted as
Messiah because his Messiahship was kept a secret. That
secret was in fact the secret of the kingdom which was given
to the disciples alone (Mark 4.2), in the Wrede recon-
struction. But in fact and as things actually happened no
one ever regarded Jesus as Messiah during his earthly life
time and Jesus never claimed to be the Messiah.

If Wrede is right, if Jesus never claimed to be Messiah,
and if all the injunctions to secrecy are simply inventions
made to push back the claim to Messiahship into the lifetime
of Jesus on earth, although no such claim was ever made
until after the Resurrection, then, whatever be the value of
the details of Mark's narrative, the whole pattern of the
narrative is nothing more than fiction. If Jesus never at any
time claimed to be Messiah, and if no one ever thought of
him as such, then we must remove from the narrative as
fiction the confession of Peter at Caesarea Philippi (9.27-30);

the story of the Triumphal Entry (2.1-10); the very essence of the examination before the High Priest (14.61-64); and the title on the Cross (15.26). The crucifixion of Jesus becomes almost unintelligible, because it is clear that, as Mark tells the story, Jesus was crucified as a Messianic pretender.

But in point of fact Wrede's argument does not make sense. It is not really conceivable that Jesus would have been acknowledged as Messiah *after* the Resurrection, if he had not claimed to be Messiah *before* the Resurrection, for not even the Resurrection could have explained a *crucified* Messiah. The message of the disciples was in fact that Jesus was the crucified Messiah, and the message itself and the reception of it only become intelligible against a situation in which the Messianic claim of Jesus was in fact universally known and universally derided because of the Cross. The whole tenor of the message is precisely that the Resurrection now validated a claim which had been made and which had been contemptuously rejected. The whole New Testament story becomes unintelligible if during his earthly life no Messianic claims had been made by Jesus.

It is in fact exactly from the injuctions to silence that we shall get the clue to the whole situation. We may begin from two basic assumptions. First, Jesus did think of himself as the Anointed One of God, as the Messiah. Second, if we are to place any reliance on the Gospel record at all, then we must believe that Jesus did insist that his Messiahship should be kept a secret. So, then, the first question is the reason for this secrecy.

The reason is in the light of history very simple. If it had been widely spread around that Jesus was the Messiah, quite certainly the populace would have read their own meaning into that term; and quite certainly that would have been a nationalistic meaning. John tells the story of the attempt to come and to compel Jesus to be king (John 6.15). If that had happened, the consequences would have been disastrous. There would quite certainly have been a rebellion and an uprising on the spot, and it would have been mercilessly crushed. It is the simple historical fact that in the thirty years from 67 to 37 BC before the emergence of Herod the Great no fewer than one hundred and fifty thousand men perished in Palestine in revolutionary uprisings. There was no more explosive and inflammable country in the world than Palestine. If Jesus had publicly claimed to be Messiah, nothing could have stopped a useless flood tide of slaughter. Before Jesus could openly make any claim to Messiahship it was absolutely necessary that he should lead men to see what Messiahship meant. He must teach them a Messiahship whose only power was sacrificial love; he must show them a picture of a Messiah whose reign was in the hearts of men, a Messiah who reigned from a cross.

The truth is that Jesus did with the conception of Messiahship what he did with the conception of the Son of Man. He accepted it, because the Messiah was the Anointed One, the Champion, the Redeemer of the people, sent by God; but he filled it with a new meaning in which the way to ultimate triumph was the way of the immediate Cross; and we must now go on to look at the conception and the picture which coloured all the thought of Jesus.

8

THE SERVANT OF GOD

IT might well be held that the title Servant is the title in the light of which all the other titles of Jesus must be seen.

The title Servant of God is a title with a great history. In the Old Testament it is the greatest and the proudest title which can be given to any man. It is the title of men whose lives are mountain peaks in the history of Israel, and who were essential actors and agents in the master-plan of God.

Abraham is the servant of the Lord (Ps. 105.42). Moses, the great leader, liberator and law-giver is called the servant of God oftener than anyone else in the Old Testament (Ex. 14.31; Num. 12.7; Deut. 34.5; Josh. 1.1,15; 8.21,23; 18.7; I Chron. 6.49; II Chron. 1.3; 24.6; Neh. 1.7; 10.29). The gallant Caleb, who believed that with God all things are possible, is called the servant of God (Num. 12.24). Joshua who inherited the leadership of the nation from Moses is called the servant of God (Josh. 24.9; Judg. 2.8). David comes second only to Moses in the number of times that he is called the servant of God (II Sam. 7.5-8; I Kings 8.66; 11.36; II Kings 19.34; II Chron. 17.4; Ps. 18 in the title of the Psalm). Elijah, the first of the great national prophets, is called the servant of God (II Kings 10.10). Job, who suffered and never lost his faith, is called the servant of God (Job 1.8; 42.7). Isaiah is called the servant of God (Isa. 20.3; 49.5). The prophets as a body are called the servants of God (II Kings 21.10; Amos 3.7). In the Old Testament the greatest title of honour that any man can have is the servant of God.

The title servant of God was not only given to individual Israelites, it was also given to the nation as a whole. So important is the part that Israel had to play in the master-plan of God that the nation is peculiarly the servant of God. This is commonest in Isaiah.

> But you, Israel, my servant,
>   Jacob whom I have chosen,
>   the offspring of Abraham, my friend;
> you whom I took from the ends of the earth,
>   and called from the farthest corners,
> saying to you, You are my servant,
>   I have chosen you and not cast you off;
> fear not, for I am with you,
>   be not dismayed for I am your God.
>
> (Isa. 41.8-10)

> Remember these things, O Jacob,
>   and Israel, for you are my servant;
> I formed you, you are my servant;
>   O Israel, you will not be forgotten by me.
>
> (Isa. 44.21)

> Go forth from Babylon, flee from Chaldea,
>   declare with a shout of joy, proclaim it,
> send it forth to the end of the earth;
>   say, The Lord has redeemed his servant Jacob!
>
> (Isa. 48.20)

> And he said to me, You are my servant,
>   Israel in whom I will be glorified.
>
> (Isa. 49.3)

Amidst all the nations and the peoples Israel is distinctively and peculiarly the servant of God.

It is easy to see that the title servant of God has a long history, that it is woven into the religious heritage of Israel, and that, therefore, it is a title which it is fitting that Jesus should inherit and possess. Even at this stage we can see that this title has certain very important significances when it is applied to Jesus.

(i)   To call Jesus the Servant of God connects him with the heroes of the nation of Israel, and with the makers of Israel's history. It connects him with the men in and through whom God acted in past generations. As we have seen, the title specially attaches to Moses. It was through Moses, the servant of God, that God's people were redeemed and liberated from slavery in Egypt, and it is through Jesus the Servant of God that all mankind are liberated and redeemed from sin. It was through Moses that the people entered into the old covenant with God; it was through Jesus that the new covenant came.

(ii)   To call Jesus the Servant of God connects him with the prophets, with those who were specially the bearers to men of the voice of God. It was through the mouth of the prophets that God made known his will to men, and supremely in Jesus Christ God sends his light and his truth and his will and his word to men. Jesus came not only to *tell* men the will of God but also to do the will of God in every moment and every action of his life.

(iii)   It follows that this title is specially fitting for Jesus because the key-note and essence of his life was obedience to the will of God. 'My food,' he said, 'is to do the will of him who sent me' (John 4.34). 'I have come down from heaven, not to do my own will, but the will of him who sent me' (John 6.38). The great essential of a good servant is obedience. In Jesus the title Servant of God finds its perfect and unsurpassable application.

(iv)   To call Jesus the Servant of God is to say that in him the history and the destiny of the nation of Israel found its completion and its consummation. It was to be his servant that God created the nation of Israel and moulded it to his will and purpose; all the experiences of Israel were designed to equip her and prepare her to be the servant of God. Out of that chosen nation there was to come in God's good time God's Chosen One, the One who uniquely embodied, realised and fulfilled God's purpose. Out of the nation which was the servant of God there came the one, who is above all others the Servant of God. The nation of Israel was created and moulded for no other reason than that out of it Jesus, THE SERVANT, should come.

There is no title which so connects Jesus with the history of Israel and the plan of God as Servant of God does.

The conception of Jesus as the Servant of God finds its peak in the conception of him as the Suffering Servant. And it seems to us that there is no doubt that this picture goes back to none other than Jesus himself, and that it indeed dominated his whole thought. The Suffering Servant is the figure the picture of whom finds its highest point in Isaiah 53. No interpretation of Jesus has been more precious to, and more influential on, Christian thought than the conception of Jesus as the Suffering Servant, and we must go on to study it in some detail.

The Suffering Servant is a strange and mysterious figure whose portrait is drawn in the pages of Isaiah. The picture is the picture of one who suffered terribly and undeservedly, of one whose contemporaries regarded him as outcast by man and God alike, of one whose sufferings came to be seen to have in some way a redemptive value for his fellowmen, and of one who in the end was vindicated by God. The picture is drawn in what are known as the four Servant Songs in Isaiah. The four songs are in Isa. 42.1-4; 49.1-6; 50.4-9: 52.13-53.12. We must begin by looking at these passages, and since the Hebrew text is difficult and in some places corrupt, and since the translation of the AV is inevitably imperfect, it will be well to begin by setting them out in the translation of the RSV.

(i)   The first song is in Isa. 42.1-4:

> Behold my servant, whom I uphold,
>> my chosen in whom my soul delights;
> I have put my spirit upon him,
>> he will bring forth justice to the nations.
> He will not cry nor lift up his voice,
>> or make it heard in the street;
> a bruised reed he will not break,
>> and a dimly burning wick he will not quench;
>> he will faithfully bring forth justice.
> He will not fail or be discouraged
>> till he has established justice in the earth;
>> and the coastlands wait for his law.

Here is the picture of one who was chosen and elected, equipped and upheld by God for a special task. That task, as it has been put, is 'the diffusion of true religion throughout the whole world'. In that task God delights in him and the nations waits for him. He will be gentle, tender, unobtrusive. He will not break the bruised reed, and he will not quench the dimly burning wick. That is to say, even when goodness is weak, and even when its flame is almost dead, he will not crush it, but will gently and tenderly nurture it. Yet for all his gentleness and tenderness there is in him a fixity of purpose and a strength of character in which he will never be discouraged and will never own defeat.

(ii)   The second song is in Isa. 49.1-6:

> Listen to me, O coastlands, and hearken you peoples
>> from afar.
> The Lord called me from the womb,
>> from the body of my mother he named my name.
> He made my mouth like a sharp sword,
>> in the shadow of his hand he hid me;
> he made me a polished arrow,
>> in his quiver he hid me away.
> And he said to me, You are my servant,

Israel, in whom I will be glorified.
But I said, I have laboured in vain,
I have spent my strength for nothing and vanity;
Yet surely my right is with the Lord,
　and my recompense with my God.
And now the Lord says,
　who formed me from the womb to be his servant,
to bring back Jacob to him,
　and that Israel might be gathered to him,
for I am honoured in the eyes of the Lord,
　and my God has become my strength—
he says:
　It is too light a thing that you should be my servant
　　to raise up the tribes of Jacob
　　and to restore the preserved of Israel;
　I will give you as a light to the nations,
　　that my salvation may reach to the end of the earth.

This song is clearly later in the Servant's life than the first
song, for by this time he has toiled and laboured, and
apparently all for nothing. He is aware that God has chosen
him for his task even before he was born into the world. He
is deeply conscious of his divine appointment. He sees himself as a weapon prepared by God and in the hand of God.
Even if humanly speaking he seems to have failed, God is
his strength and God is his honour. Nothing could be greater
or more universal than his task. Part of that task is to bring
Israel his own nation back to God and to obedience to God;
but that indeed is the lesser part of his task, for he is to be
a light to the nations, and he is to bring God's salvation
to the end of the earth. Here is a vision which far outreaches
all nationalism and which thinks in terms of a world for
God. Here, then, the Servant, speaking in his own person,
remembers his election and his equipment, realises his
apparent failure, sets out on his illimitable task, and affirms
his unshakable faith and confidence in God.

(iii)   The third song is in Isa. 50.4-9:

>The Lord God has given me
>   the tongue of those who are taught,
>that I may know how to sustain with a word
>   him that is weary.
>Morning by morning he wakens,
>   he wakens my ear
>   to hear as those who are taught.
>The Lord God has opened my ear,
>   and I was not rebellious,
>   I turned not backward.
>I gave my cheek to the smiters,
>   and my cheeks to those who pulled out my beard;
>I hid not my face
>   from shame and spitting.
>For the Lord God helps me;
>   therefore I have not been confounded;
>therefore I have set my face like a flint,
>   and I know that I shall not be put to shame;
>   he who vindicates me is near.
>Who will contend with me?
>   Let us stand up together.
>Who is my adversary?
>   Let him come near to me.
>Behold the Lord God helps me;
>   Who will declare me guilty?
>Behold all of them will wear out like a garment;
>   the moth will eat them up.

C. R. North finely says that this is the description of the Gethsemane of the Servant, and J. Skinner equally finely says that here we see the Servant made perfect through suffering. The Servant is deeply conscious that he is taught by God, and that that teaching has given him what Skinner calls 'the ministry of consolation'. His word sustains the weary, which is a contrast to the prophetic word which is like a hammer that breaks the rocks in pieces (Jer. 23.29). He has been insulted, injured, cruelly humiliated. He has been lashed and spat upon. The beard is the symbol of age and dignity, and there is no more humiliating insult in the East than to pull out the hairs of a man's beard. Yet in spite of it all he has gone steadily on with his God-given task. God is with him; nothing that men can do to him will break him; and he is certain that in the end he will be vindicated and his adversaries will vanish away.

(iv) The fourth of the songs, the best loved, best known, most read, and the most deeply mysterious of them all, is in Isa. 52.13-53.12:

> Behold, my servant shall prosper,
>   he shall be exalted and lifted up,
>   and shall be very high.
> As many were astonished at him—
> his appearance was so marred, beyond human semblance,
>   and his form beyond the sons of men—
> so shall he startle many nations;
>   kings shall shut their mouths because of him;
> for that which has not been told them they shall see,
>   and that which they have not heard they shall understand.
>
> Who has believed what we have heard?
>   And to whom has the arm of the Lord been revealed?
> For he grew up before him like a young plant,
>   and like a root out of dry ground;
> he had no form or comeliness that we should look at him,
>   and no beauty that we should desire him.
> He was despised and rejected of men;
>   a man of sorrows and acquainted with grief;
> and as one from whom men hide their faces
>   he was despised, and we esteemed him not.
> Surely he has borne our griefs
>   and carried our sorrows,
> yet we esteemed him stricken,
>   smitten by God and afflicted.
> But he was wounded for our transgressions,
>   he was bruised for our iniquities,
> upon him was the chastisement that made us whole,
>   and with his stripes we are healed.
> All we like sheep have gone astray,

we have turned everyone to his own way;
And the Lord had laid on him
  the iniquity of us all.
He was oppressed, and he was afflicted,
  yet he opened not his mouth;
like a lamb that is led to the slaughter,
    and like a sheep that before its shearers is dumb,
  so he opened not his mouth.
By oppression and judgment he was taken away;
  and for his generation, who considered
that he was cut off out of the land of the living,
  stricken for the transgressions of my people?
And they made his grave with the wicked
  and with a rich man in his death,
although he had done no violence,
  and there was no deceit in his mouth.

Yet it was the will of the Lord to bruise him;
  he has put him to grief;
when he makes himself an offering for sin,
  he shall see his offspring, he shall prolong his days;
the will of the Lord shall prosper in his hand;
  he shall see the fruit of the travail of his soul
      and be satisfied;
by his knowledge shall the righteous one, my servant,
  make many to be accounted righteous;
  and he shall bear their iniquities.
Therefore I will divide him a portion with the great,
  and he shall divide the spoil with the strong;
because he poured out his soul to death,
  and was numbered with the transgressors;
yet he bore the sin of many,
  and made intercession for transgressors.

Here then is the portrait of the Suffering Servant. Although
there is tragedy to follow, it begins with the affirmation of
triumph, and the certainty that the nations will be startled
and kings silenced at the sight of truth and wonder which
they had never seen or heard or experienced before.

The Servant is physically unprepossessing and even loathsome.
He has suffered from some illness which has left him scarcely

recognisable as a man. It is entirely probable that the writer of
the the song means us to think of the Servant as a victim of
leprosy, that terrible disease which slowly ate a man's body
away. In v. 4 the word used for *stricken* is the regular word used
for being stricken with leprosy (cp. II Kings 15.5). It was thus
that the early Jewish rabbis interpreted the passage; and the
Vulgate, the Latin translation of the Bible, actually has: *et nos
putavimus eum quasi leprosum et percussum a Deo et humilia-
tum*, 'and we thought of him as a leper and smitten by God and
afflicted'. Men regarded the Servant as a sinner, stricken by
God, just as Job was regarded by his friends. Hence the Servant
was isolated, alone, despised, rejected, loathed by all men. It may
well be that we are to think that in the end he was executed as a
sinner and made no protest.

Then slowly men came to see something. Slowly it began
to dawn on them that this suffering was undeserved, and the
sight of it did more to move their hearts than any words could
do. They came to see that somehow the suffering was for
them, that in it the Servant had borne what they should have
borne. He made himself, men began to see, a sin-offering for
his fellowmen. But the matter did not end there. It may be
that we are to go on to think of the Servant as rising from
the dead; we are to think of him as seeing the effect on
others of all his suffering; we are to think of him as enabling many to enter into righteousness who could never
have entered any other way. In his very bearing of the sins,
the sorrows and the diseases of men he enabled them to
enter into spiritual health. And in the end he was vindicated
by God, and the reason of his vindication was that he
had been one in fellowship with sinning men, that he had
borne the sins of sinners, that he had made intercession
for them.

Ever since men have studied Scripture at all this passage
has laid a fascination upon them; they have always been

fascinated with the attempt to identify the Servant of the songs and especially the Suffering Servant. Long before the time of Christianity the Jewish Rabbis pored over this passage, and made their identifications, although they never at any time connected it with the Messiah. Eichorn called this passage a *locus vexatissimus,* a most vexed passage. In his book *The Suffering Servant in Deutero-Isaiah,* C. R. North tells us that S. R. Driver, one of the most famous of all Old Testament scholars, planned to write a commentary on Isaiah, and abandoned the task in despair, when he sought to disentangle the many and varied interpretations of this passage.

There are many who without hesitation would simply say that the passage is a prophecy and a foretelling of Jesus Christ. But there is one fact which must give us cause to think. Every verb in Isa. 53.1-9 is in the *past* tense, and not one in the future. It is quite true that there is in the Hebrew of the Old Testament a kind of prophetic past tense, in which a prophet is so sure that what he is saying will happen that he speaks of it as if it had already happened. But, if we are to take this passage at its face value and in the most natural way, we must say that it describes the experience of some person whom the prophet has already seen, or at least about whom he knows, and not some person who is still to come. It is true that after v. 10 the verbs become future, and describe the future consequences of the work of the Servant; but quite certainly the passage begins as if it were describing the undeserved, sacrificial, vicarious suffering of one who had already suffered and sorrowed by his own diseases and by the injustice and the blindness of men. We must then look at some of the figures in Jewish history who have been suggested as the originals of this portrait in Isaiah 53.

It has been suggested that the portrait of the Suffering Servant was drawn from Hezekiah. Hezekiah was a good king, but he suffered from some terrible illness. It has been suggested that his illness was some form of cancer, and his suffering has been taken as the prototype of the suffering of the Servant. It is quite true that Hezekiah suffered, and suffered underservedly, but the whole point of the Hezekiah story is that Hezekiah in fact recovered and was restored to health again. The portrait therefore does not fit him at all.

It has been suggested that the picture is of Isaiah himself. In the song in Isa. 49.1-6 it is in fact the first person singular which is used, and the prophet does seem to be speaking of himself as the Servant. There is a Jewish tradition that Isaiah was of royal birth, that he was martyred in the days of Manasseh, and that he was afterwards buried near the sepulchre of the kings and so was with the rich in his death (Isa. 53.9). The idea is that he died a criminal's death, that he was buried in a felon's grave, and that then his innocence was realised, and by way of making some kind of amends, those who had once been his enemies realised their tragic error and buried him with the kings. There is no need to doubt the tradition that Isaiah died a martyr's death. It is of interest to remember that when the Ethiopian eunuch read this chapter without knowing anything about it he thought it possible that it might refer to the prophet himself. He said to Philip: 'About whom, pray, does the prophet say this, about himself or about some one else?' (Acts 8.34). But, apart from anything else, this would necessitate that we should suppose that Isaiah wrote an account of his own death!

It has been suggested that the picture is based on Uzziah. Uzziah was a leper as the Servant was (II Chron. 26.21). His leprosy came to him because he had been rash enough to burn incense in the Temple, a privilege which belonged only to the priests, and which no layman should have dared to take to himself (II Chron. 26.16-21). The idea is that the punishment of Uzziah was, humanly speaking, out of all proportion to the crime that he had committed, and that it came to be regarded as a punishment borne by the king for the sins of the people.

It has been suggested that Jeremiah is the original of the portrait. Jeremiah says of himself: 'I was like a gentle lamb led to the slaughter' (Jer. 11.19; cp. Isa. 53.7). The idea is that the prophet's undeserved sufferings were for the redemption of his people.

It is suggested that the picture of the Suffering Servant goes back to Job, the great undeserving sufferer. But terrible as Job's suffering was, and innocent as Job was, there is never any suggestion that his sufferings were for the sake of others.

One fantastic Jewish interpretation of this passage identifies the Suffering Servant with Moses. It is true that Moses offered to be blotted out of the Book of Life, if by giving his own life he could save the lives of the people who had sinned so grievously (Ex. 32.30-32). But this theory goes even further. It suggests that Moses was murdered in the desert after the apostasy at Baal-peor, that the story was suppressed by the priests, that it lingered on in the circle of the prophets, and that it is at the back of the story of the slain shepherd of the people in Zech. 11.4-13.9, and that the expectation that Moses would return to life again was for a time even more widely held than the belief in the coming of the Messiah. It can only be said that there is not a shred of evidence for any such flight of fancy.

If we are to seek the original of the portrait of the Suffering Servant in any historical person, there remain two suggestions which have more to commend them than any of the others.

It is suggested that the picture of the Suffering Servant is based on Jehoiachin the king of Judah (II Kings 24.8-20). Jehoiachin came to the throne very young. Soon after he became king Nebuchnezzar invaded Jerusalem. Jehoiachin came out of the city with his mother, his princes and his officials and voluntarily surrendered. He was taken to Babylon and he was a captive for thirty-seven years before he was released. This is the bare story, but Josephus, the Jewish historian, twice retells the story with very significant additions. Jehoiachin, he says, was of a gentle and tender disposition, and he deliberately made this act of surrender of himself and of his family to save the city of Jerusalem from fire and plunder and to save the people of Jerusalem from being put to the sword. He selflessly sacrificed himself to a long captivity for the sake of his city and his people.[1] Josephus himself used Jehoiachin as an example in the last terrible days of the siege of Jerusalem. During the last days of the siege by Titus in AD 70 John was holding the upper part of the city with a band of desperate and fanatical men. It was inevitable that in the end they should be destroyed, and it was clear that the longer they resisted, the more infuriated the Romans would become, and the more terrible would be the last slaughter. Josephus himself saw this clearly and he appealed to John by the example of Jehoiachin to lay down his arms, to surrender, and to sacrifice himself in order to save the city from destruction and the people from massacre, an appeal which John refused in his fanaticism even to consider.[2] From this it is clear that Jehoiachin was in fact regarded as a king who had sacrificed himself and his liberty, and who was ready to sacrifice his life, for the sake of his people. The one thing which militates against this theory is the historical fact that in the end Jehoiachin did not die, but after his long captivity was released in honour.

The last suggestion at which we shall look is the suggestion that the Suffering Servant is to be identified with king Zerubbabel. Zerubbabel is an enigmatic figure. He certainly returned with the first Jewish exiles from Persia under Ezra (Ezra 2.2; 3.2; Neh. 7.7). He certainly had a great deal to do

[1] *Antiquities of the Jews* 10.7.1.   [2] *Wars of the Jews* 6.2.1

with the rebuilding of the Temple, and the supposition is that Haggai and Zechariah saw in him nothing less than the Messianic king promised by God (Hag. 1.1,12,14; 2.22,23; Zech. 4.6-10). That he did return there is no doubt and that he did play a leading part in the rebuilding of the Temple and that Haggai and Zechariah regarded him with the highest hopes there is equally no doubt. But the strange thing is that he suddenly completely vanishes from history and he is not there at the rededication of the Temple. He simply disappears from the scene. Jewish tradition declares that what happened was that the Persians regarded Zerubbabel as a possible focus of trouble and rebellion, that they took him back to Persia as a hostage for the good conduct of the whole people, and that there he was finally killed. Here is the picture of a royal figure who suffered and died for his people and his country.

These then are the main suggestions as to the identity of the Suffering Servant. It remains to add that there were Jewish Rabbis who thought that behind this portrait there was an anonymous teacher of the Law, a pastor and a preacher and a teacher who was cruelly martyred because of his fidelity to God, and whose undeserved suffering moved men to wonder. But it does seem to us that none of these figures really fits Isaiah 53. In almost every case there is something which will not fit into the pattern; and, apart from that, none of them seems big enough to match the divine tragedy and triumph of that chapter. They are in a sense too ordinary to fit this extraordinary portrait. It is necessary to seek some other identification. If then no single individual fits into this portrait, where shall we look for the original of it?

(i) One of the oldest of all interpretations is that the Servant is none other than the nation of Israel. Israel is peculiarly the Chosen People, the people designed to be the

Servant of God. Israel as a nation suffered terribly and there were worse sufferings yet to come. Israel was despised and rejected by men, and yet it is by the sufferings of Israel that redemption comes into the world. It is beyond doubt from here that we must start because, apart from these general likenesses, the one definite identification of the Servant is in fact with the nation of Israel.

> But now hear, O Jacob my servant,
>   Israel whom I have chosen!
> Thus says the Lord who made you,
>   who formed you from the womb and will help you:
> Fear not, O Jacob, my servant,
>   Jeshurun whom I have chosen.
>
> (Isa. 44.1,2)

> Remember these things, O Jacob,
>   and Israel, for you are my servant;
> I formed you, you are my servant,
>   O Israel, you will not be forgotten by me.
>
> (Isa. 44.21)

> Go forth from Babylon, flee from Chaldea,
>   declare this with a shout of joy, proclaim it,
> send it forth to the end of the earth;
>   say, The Lord has redeemed his servant Jacob!
>
> (Isa. 48.20)

> And he said to me, You are my servant,
>   Israel, in whom I will be glorified.
>
> (Isa. 49.3)

Amidst all the uncertainties it is certain that at least on some occasions Israel is addressed as the Servant of God.

H. Wheeler Robinson says that the Servant represents Israel the nation and that Isaiah 53 is 'a philosophy of the sufferings of the nation, in themselves so perplexing to national pride and religious faith.' The whole picture of Isaiah 53 has been called 'an allegory of the fortunes of Israel.'

Here is something which makes good sense. Israel is the Chosen People, and yet no nation ever had so tragic a history. Defeat, exile, slavery, death, hatred among the nations—why should God's Chosen People have to suffer those things? The only explanation must be that through that suffering the knowledge and the salvation of God went out from Israel to the world, and that in the end Israel will be vindicated as the Servant of God. This then would be the explanation of the sufferings of Israel in the plan of God.

(ii) But at once a difficulty emerges. It is quite clear that by no means all the nation of Israel can be called the Servant of God. There are those who, so far from serving God, have wandered away, turned their backs upon God, rebelled against him and disobeyed him. There are those who have worshipped idols, who have gone after strange gods, and who have broken the law of God. There are those who are no better than the reed which is almost broken and the wick whose flame is almost dead (Isa. 42.3). The appeal of the Servant is to the blind and the deaf. In fact the servant himself is blind and deaf.

> Hear, you deaf;
>> and look, you blind, that you may see!
> Who is blind but my servant,
>> or deaf as my messenger whom I send?
> He sees many things, but does not observe them;
>> his ears are open, but he does not hear.
>> (Isa. 42.18-20)

Often all that the servant can say is:

> I have laboured in vain,
> I have spent my strength for nothing and vanity.
>> (Isa. 49.4)

In his preaching the Servant has been cruelly hurt and humiliated (Isa. 50.6). How can this be true, if the nation of Israel is really the Servant of God? There are two ways out of this difficulty.

(iii)   It might be said that the Servant of God is *the ideal Israel* and not the actual Israel, Israel as God sees her, Israel as she was meant to be, Israel, as A. B. Davidson put it, 'according to its true idea'. A. B. Davidson draws an illuminating parallel from the idea of the Church. We believe that the Church is God's instrument of reconciliation in the world. That is the ideal of the Church. It is easy to point at the imperfections of the Church; it is still easier to point at branches, sections, congregations of the Church, which are utterly false to their task, and which are failing tragically in it. But that does not affect the fact that we can still speak of the Church in its true form and in its idea as the instrument of God, the body of Christ. Just so, the Servant could well be the ideal Israel, suffering in the divine purposes of God to bring redemption to the world.[1]

(iv)   It is possible to put this a different way. The ideal Israel must actualise itself in something. Therefore, the servant may be, not the whole nation, which is a mixture of good and bad, disobedient and obedient, faithful and unfaithful, but the good and the true and the faithful and the loyal and the obedient within the nation: as George Adam Smith puts it, 'Israel within Israel'.[2] However far the nation as a whole may have strayed there are always those in it who are utterly faithful to God. They are the Servant of God. And when they are involved in the terrible sufferings of the nation as a whole, or when their loyalty and their fidelity bring suffering to them, somehow their sufferings are for others, and were the means whereby God's redeeming power came to men. This would mean that ideally the Servant of God is the whole nation; but in point of actual fact the true servant of God is that part of the nation of Israel which remained for ever true to God. If this is so, we can go one step

---

[1] See the chapter on 'The Servant of the Lord' in Davidson's *Old Testament Prophecy*.
[2] See his commentary on *Isaiah*, Vol. II, p. 278.

further and ask in what part of the nation this true conception of the Servant is actually realised?

(v)   We may begin with the less likely of the answers. It has been suggested that the section of the nation in which the true Israel is to be found is the *priesthood*. It is true that in the days of exile the fate of the priests was hardest of all. Their function was to offer sacrifice; sacrifice could only be offered in the Temple in Jerusalem; and therefore in a foreign land their work and their very life was gone. There was no avenue of service left for them; the reason for their existence had ceased to exist. In the exile they had to encounter the death of their life and the extinction of their hopes. And yet the fact remains, the exile compelled them to bring the knowledge of God to other nations. It was through their personal tragedy, through the extinction of all that they held dear and precious, that the knowledge of God did go out to people who had never known it. Of course, there is truth there, but, so far as we know, this was an opportunity which the priests never in fact took.

(vi)   There is a much more likely answer than that. It may well be that the true Israel is to be found in the succession of the *prophets*. The prophets were in a unique sense the servants of God and were acknowledged to be such.

> Surely the Lord God does nothing
> without revealing his secret
> to his servants the prophets.
>
> (Amos 3.7)

The prophets were indeed God's martyrs and had suffered terribly to bring the knowledge of God to men. Jerusalem, as Jesus said, was the city which had murdered the prophets and had stoned to death the messengers God sent to it (Matt. 23.27). 'Which of the prophets did your fathers not persecute?' demanded Stephen (Acts 7.52). We may well say that the prophets embodied the Servant of God in their sufferings and their sorrows and their deaths in bringing the message of God to men.

It may well be that all this was in the mind of the man who wrote Isaiah 53; it may well be that he was making a composite picture which included the lineaments of all those who had in their sufferings borne the sins of others, and who had brought God and God's word to men at the cost of their own agonies, and at the cost of life itself.

And now let us see where this argument is inevitably leading us. We began with the idea of the Servant as the nation of Israel. That idea was narrowed into the picture of those within Israel who had remained responsive, true and faithful to God, even when the rest of the nation was rebellious and disobedient. That small company of faithful people is further identified with the succession of the prophets, who in their toil, their sufferings and their deaths were the true servants of God. The next step is inevitable; the narrowing process must go on. What was the one great reason why God chose the nation of Israel at all? In order that out of it there might come his Son. Wherein does the prophetic order find its goal, its peak, its consummation? Of whom did the prophets speak? Who is at one and the same time the supreme representative of the prophets and the essence and burden of the message of the prophets? Surely once again, the Mesiah, the Son of God, Jesus Christ. He is in truth the Servant of God.

So now we see that we have every reason to take Isaiah 53 as a picture of Jesus Christ. We need not think that Isaiah was thinking of the flesh and blood Jesus of Nazareth who was born in a certain place and at a certain time in history. A man with a vision is always saying more than he knows; he is always saying things in a temporary situation of which history alone can in due time expound and reveal the full significance. Isaiah may well have been thinking of the sufferings of the nation of Israel as the nation chosen to be the

Servant of God, of the sufferings of God's people in that nation, and above all of the sufferings of the prophets in their bringing God's word to men; but inevitably and certainly his picture pointed forward to, and found its consummation in Jesus of Nazareth in whom this picture was perfectly fulfilled and embodied.

There is no doubt that the early Church thought of Jesus in terms of the Suffering Servant.

The picture is there in Acts. When Philip met up with the Ethiopian eunuch on the road to Gaza, the Ethiopian was reading Isaiah 53:

> As a sheep led to the slaughter
> or as a lamb before its shearers is dumb,
> so he opens not his mouth.
> In his humiliation justice was denied him.
> Who can describe his generation?
> For his life is taken up from the earth.

Philip asked the Ethiopian if he understood what he was reading, and the Ethiopian asked in return how could he understand, unless he had someone to guide him. He wondered if the prophet was speaking of himself or of someone else. 'Then Philip opened his mouth, and beginning with this scripture, he told him the good news of Jesus' (Acts 8.26-35). Philip had no doubt that Isaiah's picture was the picture of Jesus.

Four times in Acts Jesus is called the Servant, but in the AV the reference is obscured. The four instances are all in speeches of Peter. The first two are in Acts 3. 'The God of our fathers hath glorified his *Son* Jesus whom ye delivered up (Acts 3.13). 'God having raised up his *Son* Jesus, sent him to bless you' (Acts 3.26). The other two are in Peter's speech to the Sanhedrin in Acts 4. 'Thy holy *child* Jesus, whom thou hast anointed' (Acts 4.27). 'That signs and wonders may be done by the name of thy holy *child* Jesus' (Acts 4.30). In each case the newer translations (e.g. Moffatt, RSV, NEB) have *Servant* in all the four cases.

The reason for the obscurity is this. In all four cases the Greek word is *pais*. *Pais* is the Greek word for both 'child' and 'servant'. It can be used like the English 'boy' or the French *garçon* for either 'son' or 'servant'. But in the Acts passages it is to all intents and purposes certain that 'servant' is the correct translation. This is proved by two facts. The Hebrew word for 'servant' is *ebedh*. In the Septuagint *ebedh* is often translated *doulos* which is the most usual Greek word for servant, but it is just as often translated *pais*. Second, the Hebrew word for 'son' is *ben,* and in the Septuagint *ben* is translated by the word *huios,* which is the usual Greek word for 'son', more than four thousand times, and by the word *pais* only once. This is to say that by far the more natural translation for *pais* is 'servant'. We may take it for certain that in these four passages in Acts Jesus is being called, not the Son or the child of God, but the Servant of God. Unquestionably, in Acts Jesus is regarded as the Servant of God.

More than once in the Gospels incidents in the life of Jesus are seen as fulfilments of the Servant picture. Matthew tells how in the evening in Capernaum they brought the sick to Jesus and he healed them. Then he goes on: 'This was to fulfil what was spoken by the prophet Isaiah, "He took our infirmities and bore our diseases" ' (Matt. 8.14-17); Isa. 53.4). When Jesus withdrew in the face of the opposition of the Pharisees and when he refused to spread abroad the news of his Messiahship, Matthew saw in this a fulfilment of the prophecy of Isaiah. 'This was to fulfil what was spoken by the prophet Isaiah:

Behold, my servant whom I have chosen,
  my beloved with whom my soul is well pleased.
I will put my Spirit upon him,
  and he shall proclaim justice to the Gentiles.

He will not wrangle or cry aloud,
>   nor will anyone hear his voice in the streets;
he will not break a bruised reed
>   or quench a smouldering wick
till he brings justice to victory;
>   and in his name will the Gentiles hope.'
>   (Matt. 12.14-21; Isa. 42.1-4)

As Luke tells the story, when Jesus was foretelling his own sufferings and death, he said: 'For I tell you that this scripture must be fulfilled in me, And he was reckoned with transgressors; for what is written about me has its fulfilment' (Luke 23.37; Isa. 53.12). The Gospels too see in Jesus the Suffering Servant.

Paul too sees in Jesus the Servant. In II Cor. 5.21 he says about Jesus: 'For our sake God made him to be sin who knew no sin, so that in him we might become the righteousness of God,' which is a reminiscence of Isa. 53.6,9.

The picture is clearest of all in I Peter. Peter speaks of Jesus as a lamb without blemish or spot, remembering that Isaiah speaks of the Servant as being like a lamb that is led to the slaughter (I Peter 1.19; Isa. 53.7). He pleads with his people to follow the example of Jesus. 'He committed no sin; no guile was found on his lips. When he was reviled, he did not revile in return; when he suffered, he did not threaten; but he trusted to him who judges justly. He himself bore our sins in his body on the tree, that we might die to sin and live to righteousness. By his wounds you have been healed. For you were straying like sheep, but have now returned to the Shepherd and Guardian of your souls' (I Peter 2.22-25; Isa. 53.6,7). Peter's whole picture is based on the picture of the Servant in Isaiah 53. The early Church believed that the sufferings of Jesus Christ had been foretold by the prophets and it is Isaiah 53 of which the preachers and writers were thinking. As Peter has it: 'But what God foretold by the mouth of all the prophets, that his Christ should suffer, he thus fulfilled' (Acts 3.18). In Thessalonica Paul preached 'explaining and proving that it was necessary for the Christ to suffer' (Acts 17.3).

There is no doubt at all that the early Church saw in Isaiah 53 the picture which Jesus fulfilled. But, clearly, a much more important question is, Did Jesus think of himself in terms of the Suffering Servant? Is the interpretation of Jesus as the Suffering Servant an interpretation of the Church, read into the life of Jesus, when men thought about it with their minds and meditated upon it with their hearts, or does it go back directly to Jesus himself?

If we accept the record of the Gospels at all, we are bound to believe that the idea of the Servant coloured all Jesus' thinking from beginning to end. As we have already seen, the voice that came to Jesus at his baptism, 'Thou art my beloved Son; with thee I am well pleased' (Mark 1.11), is partly from a Messianic Psalm (Ps. 2.7), and partly from one of the Servant songs (Isa. 42.1). This can only mean that the religious experience which Jesus had in that decisive moment was an experience which launched him on his task in the conviction that the picture of the Servant was the picture of his own destiny. It can only mean that from the beginning the Servant idea was the dominant conception in the thought of Jesus.

Repeatedly Jesus foretold his sufferings and his death in Jerusalem (Mark 9.31; 10.33; Matt. 17.22; 20.18,19); and one of the most significant facts is the way in which the word *must* enters into these predictions. 'He began to teach them that the Son of Man *must* suffer many things and be rejected by the elders and the chief priests and the scribes, and be killed and after three days rise again' (Mark 8.31; Matt. 16.21: Luke 9.22). 'First he *must* suffer many things and be rejected by this generation' (Luke 17.25). Luke tells the story of the two sorrowful travellers on the road to

Emmaus, and of the saying of Jesus to them: 'O foolish men, and slow of heart to believe all that the prophets have spoken! Was it not necessary that the Christ should suffer these things, and enter into his glory? And beginning with Moses and all the prophets, he interpreted to them in all the scriptures the things concerning himself' (Luke 24.25-27). Now the fact is that the only passage in Scripture which could really be thought to give ground for expecting a Messiah who *must* suffer is that which paints the picture of the Suffering Servant. If we are to believe that from the Gospel record it is possible to gain any insight at all into the mind of Jesus, then we must believe that there is no passage in Scripture which was more influential on his thinking about himself than Isaiah 53. And, if that is so, certain things immediately emerge.

(i) It means that Jesus *chose* the Cross. The Cross was neither something which was inflicted upon him, nor was it something to which he was finally driven when all other ways had failed. Jesus was neither the victim of men nor of circumstances. From the beginning Jesus saw the end in both its shame and its glory, its tragedy and its triumph.

(ii) It marks both the *obedience* and the *courage* of Jesus. The very word servant involves the idea of obedience. This was God's chosen way for Jesus and he never drew back from it. It requires far greater courage to go steadily forward to an agonising situation which can be seen a long way ahead than it does to react heroically in some sudden emergency. Jesus had that highest kind of obedience which accepts unquestioningly the will of God, and that highest kind of courage which refuses to turn back, although it well knows the consequences of going on.

(iii) It shows that once and for all Jesus *refused the way of force*. With the fascination of words which he possessed he could have fired his followers and set the country ablaze. With the powers he possessed he could have blasted his enemies. No man was ever better equipped to use irresistible force than Jesus was. But he absolutely refused to do so. He knew that God's work can never be done, and God's interests can never be protected, by force. He knew that in the long run the greatest force in the world is sacrificial suffering borne in voluntary and spontaneous love. It is sometimes argued that there are certain values which in certain situations have to be defended by force when there is no other way to defend them. Jesus might well have said: 'The only way to defend my work is by force.' In point of fact he said: 'The only way to preserve my work is to die on a cross.' Jesus was quite clear that the highest values in life can never be defended by that which in the defending of them destroys them.

(iv) If Jesus thought of himself in terms of the Suffering Servant, it clearly means that *he thought of his life and his death in terms of sacrifice*. His life was a ransom for many (Mark 10.45). Sentence after sentence in Isaiah 53 stresses the sacrificial quality of the Servant's sufferings.

> Surely he has borne our griefs
>   and carried our sorrows.

> He was wounded for our transgressions,
>   he was bruised for our iniquities;
> upon him was the chastisement that made us whole,
>   and with his stripes we are healed.
> All we like sheep have gone astray;
>   we have turned every one to his own way;
> and the Lord has laid on him
>   the iniquity of us all.

>   Who considered
> that he was cut off out of the land of the living,
>   stricken for the transgression of my people?

> When he makes himself an offering for sin,
>   he shall see his offspring, he shall prolong his days.

> By his knowledge shall the righteous one, my servant,
>   make many to be accounted righteous;
>   and he shall bear their iniquities.
>
> He poured out his soul to death,
>   and was numbered with the transgressors;
> yet he bore the sins of many.
>   (Isa. 53.4,5,6,8,10,11,12)

The one thing that we can say of Jesus, quite apart from any theory of how it was done, is that he was utterly convinced that it required his life and his death to restore the lost relationship between man and God, and that the cost of the restoration of that relationship was the Cross.

(v) Finally, if Jesus thought of himself in terms of the Suffering Servant, then he was certain of his final vindication and triumph.

> He shall see of the fruit of the travail of his soul
>   and be satisfied (Isa. 53.11).

The picture of the Servant does not end in tragedy; it ends in triumph, in vindication by God and in recognition by men. Without a doubt Jesus saw life beyond death, and the crown beyond the cross, and the glory beyond the shame, and the triumph beyond the tragedy, and the enthronement beyond the rejection.

In the Old Testament the picture of the Suffering Servant is the supreme picture of one who suffered and died in obedience to the will of God and for the sake of men, and who in the end was vindicated by God. Jesus is the perfect fulfilment of that picture—and he knew it.

9

THE GOOD SHEPHERD

WE will now go on to look at what we might call certain of
the self-interpretations of Jesus, pictures in which according
to the story of the Gospels Jesus spoke and thought of himself, and it is clear that these pictures must give us a special
insight into the mind and the intention of Jesus. We begin
with the picture of Jesus as the Good Shepherd.

The picture of Jesus as the Good Shepherd is one of the
first pictures of Jesus presented to any child. We tend to
think of it as a picture so clear and so simple that any child
can immediately understand it. No doubt that was true in
Palestine when Jesus first used the picture, but it is far from
being so true today. In any agricultural civilisation and
society the picture is vivid and clear; but it has to be remembered that there are children in an industrial civilisation
who have never seen a shepherd, and there are countries in
which the picture of the shepherd and the sheep is altogether
strange. The nineteenth-century traveller H. B. Tristram
tells how he discovered how strange the picture can be. 'I
felt this last year,' he writes, 'when, addressing through an
interpreter a large congregation of native Christians one
Sunday in Ceylon, I unfortunately chose the subject of the
Good Shepherd. My interpreter told me afterwards that not
one of my hearers had even seen a sheep or knew what it was.
"How then," I asked, "did you explain what I said?" "Oh,"
he replied, 'I turned it into a buffalo that had lost its calf,
and went into a jungle to find it." ' We do well to remember
that even in our own country there are times and places
when the picture of the Good Shepherd needs all the infor-

187

mation with which we can clothe it to make it meaningful and intelligible to a modern city-dweller in a highly industrialised society.

When Jesus used the picture of the shepherd and the sheep, he used a picture which was woven into the thought and the language of the Jewish people. Again and again in the Old Testament God is pictured as the Shepherd of his people. 'The Lord is my Shepherd,' the shepherd psalm begins (Ps. 23.1). 'Thou leadest thy people like a flock, by the hand of Moses and Aaron' (Ps. 77.20).

> We thy people, the flock of thy pasture,
>   will give thanks to thee for ever.
>
>   (Ps. 79.13)

> Give ear, O Shepherd of Israel,
>   thou who leadest Joseph like a flock!
>
>   (Ps. 80.1)

> For he is our God,
>   and we are the people of his pasture,
>   and the sheep of his hand.
>
>   (Ps. 95.7)

'We are his people and the sheep of his pasture' (Ps. 100. 3). In Isaiah's picture God is the gentle and the loving shepherd (Isa. 40.11).

> He will feed his flock like a shepherd,
>   he will gather the lambs in his arms,
> He will carry them in his bosom,
>   and gently lead those that are with young.

In Ezekiel the Messianic king will be the shepherd of the people. 'I will set over them one shepherd, my servant David, and he shall feed them; he shall feed them and be their shepherd' (Ezek. 34.23). 'My servant David shall be king over them, and they shall have one shepherd' (Ezek. 37.24).

The picture of the Good Shepherd continued into the inter-testamental literature. In the Zadokite Fragment (16.2) it is said of the Censor of the people: 'As a shepherd with his flock he shall loose the bonds of their knots.' In II Baruch 77.13-15 the lament is that the shepherds have perished but the confidence is that true shepherds come from the law which can never perish:

> For the shepherds of Israel have perished,
> And the lamps which gave light are extinguished,
> And the fountains have withheld their stream where we
>   used to drink.
> And we are left in the darkness,
> And amid the trees of the forest,
> And the thirst of the wilderness.
> And I answered and said unto them:
> Shepherds and lamps and fountains come from the law,
> And, though we depart, yet the law abideth.

In the Psalms of Solomon (17.45) it is part of the vision of the Messianic king that

> He will be shepherding the flock of the Lord faithfully
>   and righteously,
>   And will suffer none among them to stumble in their
>   pasture.

The dream of God is that the shepherds will be faithful and true, and great is the condemnation of the shepherds who fail in their task:

> Woe to the shepherds who destroy and scatter the sheep of my pasture! says the Lord. Therefore thus says the Lord, the God of Israel, concerning the shepherds who care for my people: You have scattered my flock and have driven them away, and you have not attended to them. Before I will attend to you for your evil doings, says the Lord ... I will set shepherds over them who will care for them, and they shall fear no more, nor be dismayed, neither shall any be missing, says the Lord (Jer. 23.1-4).

Ezekiel has a grim picture of the shepherds who have been feeding themselves and not the flock. 'The weak you have not strengthened, the sick you have not healed, the crippled you have not bound up, the strayed you have not brought back, the lost you have not sought, and with force and harshness you have ruled them.' God is against such shepherds and they will receive their judgment (Ezek. 34.1-10). And then the prophet goes on to draw a picture of God himself as the shepherd of his people. 'I myself' says God, 'will be the shepherd of my sheep' (Ezek. 34.11-16).

The Old Testament is full of the picture of the shepherd and the sheep.

Jesus took over the picture of the shepherd and made it the picture of himself. He is the shepherd who goes out to the mountains and the hills, the valleys and the ravines, the cliffs and the crags to seek and to find the sheep which is lost (Matt. 18.12; Luke 15.4). He is moved with compassion for the people, because they are like sheep without a shepherd (Matt. 9.36; Mark 6.34). His disciples are his own little flock (Luke 12.32). When the shepherd is smitten the flock are leaderless and scattered (Mark 14.27; Matt. 26.31). The picture reaches its completest form in John 10.1-14, where Jesus is the Good Shepherd, who knows each of his sheep by name, whom the sheep will follow, who is for them a door of protection from danger and entrance into safety, who, unlike the hireling who flees at the first threat of danger, is ready and willing to give his life for the sheep.

This picture passed into the language and the thought of the early Church. Jesus is the Shepherd and Watchman of the souls of men (I Peter 2.25). He is the great Shepherd of the sheep (Heb. 13.20).

In the New Testament the leaders of Christ's people are likened to shepherds. The Christian leader must shepherd

the flock of God, not as a matter or constraint, not for
pay or prestige, but as an example to the flock (I Peter
5.2,3). Paul urges the elders of Ephesus faithfully to dis-
charge their duty to all the flock of whom the Holy Spirit
had made them the guardians and the watchmen (Acts. 20.
28). It is Jesus' commission to Peter that Peter should feed
his lambs and his sheep (John 21.15-19). The Church has
its pastors (Eph. 4.11), and *pastor* is nothing other than the
Latin word for shepherd.

Let us then see the picture behind this description of Jesus
as the Shepherd.

The shepherd's equipment was simple. He had his *scrip*,
which was a bag, made of the skin of an animal, and in it
he carried his simple food—bread, dried fruit, olives, cheese.
He had his *sling*. In Palestine men were skilled in the use of
the sling, so that 'they could sling a stone at a hair and
not miss' (Judg. 20.16). The Palestinian shepherd had no dog
to send after a straying sheep. So often he would take his
sling and send a stone to drop just in front of the nose of
the sheep, so that the sheep was warned to take notice and
to turn back. He had his *rod* and his *staff* (Ps. 23.4). The
staff was a long crooked stick. Always the shepherd walked
with it in his hand, and, when a sheep showed signs of
straying, he would stretch out and pull it back with the
crook. He carried the rod at his belt. It was a stout piece
of wood, perhaps three feet long, with a lump of wood the
size of an orange at one end of it. With this the shepherd
fought the battles of the flock, using it to drive off wild
beasts and to defend the flock against the robbers who would
steal the sheep. The regular dress of the shepherd was a
sheepskin robe with the fleece worn on the inside for the
sake of warmth.

It is not without interest to note that commonly the
shepherds were despised by the strictly orthodox. By the very

nature of his calling, by the very demands that the continuous care of the flock made upon him, the shepherd could not observe all the complicated rules of handwashing and ceremonial cleansing. There were times when he could not even observe the stated hours of prayer. So the pious orthodox looked down on the shepherd. But, again in the very nature of his work, the shepherd lived in the wide open spaces, beneath the silent stars at night, close to the elements, in the midst of life and death and birth and peril, and therefore inevitably the shepherd lived close to God. Orthodox ceremonial may have been impossible, but the awareness of God was never far away.

Almost everything in the shepherd's life and work illustrates the words of Jesus.

In the East the relationship between the shepherd and the sheep is different from anything which obtains in the West. In the West the sheep are mainly kept for killing; in the East they are kept for their milk and for their wool. The consequence was that in the East shepherd and sheep were together for as long as eight or nine years. The shepherd literally had a name for every sheep, and the sheep came to know their names. Often the names were descriptive like Brown Leg or Black Ears. So the Good Shepherd calls his own sheep by name (John 10.3).

In Palestine the shepherd did not drive the sheep before him; he went in front of them and they followed him. 'He goes before them and the sheep follow him' (John 10.4). Often the shepherd had to lead his flock through the narrow dark defiles, which were excellent lurking places for wild beasts and for thieves and robbers. At such a time the shepherd would go first to make sure that it was safe for the sheep to follow. As the shepherd Psalm has it (Ps. 23.4):

> Even though I walk through the valley of deep darkness,
> I fear no evil;

For thou art with me;
 Thy rod and thy staff,
 They comfort me.

Sometimes in the East a shepherd plays with his flock. In *Eastern Customs in Bible Lands* H. B. Tristram writes: 'I once watched a shepherd playing with his flock. He pretended to run away; the sheep pursued and surrounded him. Then he pretended to climb the rocks; the goats ran after him; and finally all the flock formed a circle, gambolling round him.'

The sheep, says Jesus, hear and recognise and know the voice of their shepherd (John 10.3,4). Each shepherd has a peculiar call or cry; the sheep know that call and will answer to no other. This is something which traveller after traveller has noted. H. B. Tristram writes: ' "A stranger will they not follow." Let any passing traveller try, as I have done, to imitate the shepherd's voice. At once the sheep will pause, toss up their heads, and then scamper off to huddle close to their guardian.' The voice of a stranger alarms the flock; the voice of their shepherd they recognise and know. W. M. Thomson writes in *The Land and the Book:* 'The shepherd calls sharply from time to time to remind the sheep of his presence. They know his voice and follow on; but if a stranger call, they stop short, because they know not the voice of a stranger. This is not the fanciful costume of a parable; it is a simple fact. I have made the experiment repeatedly.' An eighteenth-century traveller in Palestine tells how sheep in Palestine can actually be made to dance quick or slow, to the peculiar whistle, or the peculiar tune on the flute, of their own shepherd.

Usually in one flock sheep and goats are mixed. H. V. Morton in *In the Steps of the Master* has a description of how the shepherd literally talks to his flock. 'Sometimes he talks to them in a loud singsong voice, using a weird language unlike anything I have ever heard in my life. The first time

I heard this sheep and goat language I was in the hills at the back of Jericho. A goatherd had descended into the valley and was mounting the slope of an opposite hill, when turning round he saw that his goats had remained behind to devour a rich patch of scrub. Lifting his voice, he spoke to the goats in a language that Pan must have spoken on the mountains of Greece. It was uncanny because there was nothing human about it. The words were animal sounds arranged in a kind of order. No sooner had he spoken than answering bleat shivered over the herd, and one or two of the animals turned their heads in his direction. But they did not obey him. The goatherd then called one word, and gave a laughing whinny. Immediately a goat with a bell round his neck stopped eating, and, leaving the herd, trotted down the hill, across the valley, and up the opposite slope. The man, accompanied by the animal, walked on and disappeared round a ledge of rock. Very soon a panic spread among the herd. They forgot to eat. They looked up for their shepherd. They became consious that the leader with the bell at his neck was no longer with them. From the distance came the strange laughing call of the shepherd, and at the sound of it the whole herd stampeded into the hollow and leapt up the hill after him.' The shepherd literally talks to his herd in a voice and a language that they can understand.

H. V. Morton tells how near Bethlehem he saw two flocks of sheep put into one communal fold in a cave for the night. He wondered how in the morning the two flocks could possibly be disentangled. It was very simple. In the morning one of the shepherds stood some distance away and gave his own peculiar call, and immediately his flock ran to him, because they knew his voice. In Palestine the sheep knew the shepherd's voice and would answer it, although they would answer no other voice.

Even in modern times the shepherd has to face perils and

dangers for the sake of his flock, and that was even more so in the time of Jesus. The wolf and the hyaena are still ready to spring on the unwary sheep. Tristram tells of meeting a little shepherd boy with his little flock of half a dozen sheep. The lad was weeping bitterly, because a wolf had pounced on a lamb and he had not had the strength to drive it away. In the time of Jesus the leopard and the panther and the lion were still in Palestine. The lion vanished from Palestine after the time of the Crusades, but David the shepherd boy had with his bare hands killed the lion and the bear who had attacked the flock and stolen a lamb (I Sam. 17.34). There were sheep-stealers always ready to steal the lamb. Tristram describes the scene: 'The hill-sides on either side of the valley break out into various little mullahs or wadys, which form a puzzling labyrinth for the stranger and a convenient lurking-place for the wolf, the jackal and the thief.' Sometimes the shepherd did lay down his life for the sheep. Thomson writes: 'When the thief and the robber come (and come they do), the faithful shepherd has often to put his life in his hand to defend his flock. I have known more than one case in which he had literally to lay it down in the contest. A poor faithful fellow last spring, between Tiberias and Tabor, instead of fleeing actually fought three Bedawin robbers until he was hacked to pieces with their khanjars, and died among the sheep he was defending.' The good shepherd did in fact give his life for the sheep (John 10.10).

Jesus draws the distinction between the courageous shepherd and the cowardly hireling (John 10.12,13). Often in Palestine the shepherd owned the flock, or he was the son of the owner. In that case the sheep were really and truly his. If that was not the case, very often the shepherd was not paid in money, but was given a share in the produce of the flock. So much of the wool and of the cheese made from the milk of the sheep and so many of the lambs fell to him.

Again in such a case the shepherd had a very real interest in the welfare and the safety of the flock. But sometimes shepherds were 'hirelings'. They were paid so much per day. Such hireling shepherds came and went; they had no interest in the flock; they never came to know the sheep, nor the sheep them. They were only in the business at all for the little money that they could make out of it. In the hour of danger such hirelings were apt to flee for safety, whereas the shepherd who had been with the flock for years, and to whom the sheep and the lambs really belonged, was ready to lay down his life for his flock. No danger was too great for him to defend the sheep whom he had come to love and who had come to love him.

The shepherd's love and care for his flock had certain aspects which are specially significant when we think of Jesus in terms of this picture.

'He will feed his flock like a shepherd,' Isaiah said of the Servant of God (Isa. 40.11). Pasture was scanty and wells were few, and the shepherd had to know where to lead the flock that they might find food and drink. In the winter time, when even in Palestine there was snow on the high ground, the shepherd had to find food for his flock or they would die. Thomson writes of the Lebanon district: 'In the vast oak woods along the eastern side of Lebanon, between Baalbek and the cedars, there are gathered (in the late autumn and the winter) innumerable flocks, and the shepherds are all day long in the bushy trees, cutting down the branches, upon whose green leaves and tender twigs the sheep and goats are entirely supported.' Knowledge, skill, unremitting toil—the shepherd needed them all to feed his flock.

The shepherd's care of the flock was necessarily continuous. Often he had to carry the little lambs who had not the strength to keep up with the flock. 'I had often,' writes Tristram, 'seen a shepherd carrying a lamb under each arm,

and two or three more in the hood of his *a'beih* or cloak.'
The shepherd had to know just how far the sheep could
travel without being exhausted, especially when the ewes were
with young. 'He will gather the lambs in his arms, he will
carry them in his bosom, and gently lead those that are
with young' (Isa. 40.11). Jacob said to Esau: 'My lord knows
that the children are frail, and that the flocks and herds
giving suck are a care to me; and if they are overdriven for
one day all the flocks will die' (Gen. 33.13). The shepherd
must demand from the flock no more than their strength
could give.

The shepherd had one specially interesting custom. As we
have seen, he carried his long crook-handled staff, nearly as tall
as himself. At evening the flock entered the fold through a
narrow entrance, one at a time. When they were entering, the
shepherd held his rod across the entrance, close to the ground.
Each sheep had, therefore, to pass *under the rod*. And, as the
sheep passed under the rod, the shepherd gave it a quick examination to see that it had suffered no injury in the course of the
day. That is the picture in Ezekiel, when the prophet hears God
say: 'I will make you pass under the rod' (Ezek. 20.37). It is a
picture of God's loving care for his people.

The vigilance of the shepherd had to be unceasing and
unsleeping day and night. The very configuration of the
ground made Judaea a dangerous place for sheep flocks.
Judaea consists of a central plateau rather more than thirty
miles long from north to south. On either side danger and
death awaited the straying sheep. On the west the ground
fell away into the Shephelah, which dipped down to the
shore of the Mediteranean Sea. It was a place of deserted
hills and valleys and gullies and dips in the ground. On the
east there were the terrible cliffs and crags which plunged
two thousand feet down to the Dea Sea. That wilderness of
limestone rocks and stones was called Jeshimmon, which

means The Desolation, and no sheep could ever have survived there. Pasture was scanty and there were no surrounding
walls; and the sheep were always ready to stray away. Sheep
are very like human beings. Some were docile and obedient
and never wished to stray far from the company of the
shepherd; some were adventurous and wandered off alone;
some were foolish and strayed thoughtlessly away or lingered
behind. All this meant that the vigilance of the shepherd could
never be relaxed.

The shepherd was entirely responsible for the flock. If
a sheep was sick, he must tend it. If a sheep strayed, he must
follow it. The shepherds were expert trackers, and often the
shepherd would find the sheep in a place which he had to
risk his life to reach. If a sheep died, the shepherd must
produce the fleece of the sheep to show how it had died.

Even when the flock was gathered for the night within
the fold the shepherd's responsibility was not ended and his
watchfulness could not be relaxed. The fold might be a cave
on the hillside. It might be an enclosure walled around with
stones. On the higher slopes of the hills it might be no more
than a space enclosed by a roughly made palisade of branches
and thorn bushes. Whatever it was like, the fold had one
constant characteristic—it had an opening, but it had no
gate or door of any kind. At night the shepherd lay down
across the opening, and thus no sheep could get out and no
foe could get in except over the shepherd's body. That is
what Jesus was thinking of when he said: 'I am the door'
(John 10.9). The body of the shepherd was literally the
protecting door which kept the sheep safe.

Sir George Adam Smith in his *Historical Geography of
the Holy Land* sums up the character of the shepherd: 'With
us sheep are often left to themselves; but I do not remember
ever to have seen in the East a flock of sheep without a
shepherd. In such a landscape as Judaea, where a day's pasture

is thinly scattered over an unfenced tract of country, covered with delusive paths, still frequented by wild beasts, and rolling off into the desert, the man and his character are indispensable. One some high moor, across which at night the hyaenas howl, when you meet him, sleepless, far-sighted, weather-beaten, armed, leaning on his staff, and looking out over his scattered sheep, everyone of them on his heart, you understand why the shepherd of Judaea sprang to the forefront of his people's history; why they gave his name to their king, and made him the symbol of providence; why Christ took him as the type of self-sacrifice.'

It is not difficult to set down the great qualities of the shepherd, and it is not difficult to see how these qualities reach their divine consummation in Jesus Christ.

(i) The shepherd had to have strength and courage, or he could never have carried out his task.

(ii) He had to have ceaseless and unsleeping vigilance, or he could never have protected his flock.

(iii He had to have infinite patience with the wayward foolishness of his sheep. Unless he had loved his sheep and loved his task, he could not have set his hand to it at all. He had to have an infinite, unwearied kindness, born of love for the sheep in his charge.

(iv) He had to have the spirit of self-sacrifice, in which, if necessary, he would risk, and even give, his life for the sake of the sheep who had strayed away.

The Jews have a lovely legend to explain why Moses was chosen as the leader of the people of God. 'When Moses was feeding the sheep of his father-in-law in the wilderness, a young kid ran away. Moses followed it until it reached a ravine, where it found a well from which to drink. When Moses came up to it, he said: "I did not know that you ran away because you were thirsty. Now you must be weary." So he took the kid on his shoulders and carried it back.

Then God said: "Because you have shown pity in leading back one of a flock belonging to a man, you shall lead my flock, Israel." ' In the shepherd's patient love God saw the quality in man which above all he could use.

Jesus is the Good Shepherd. He came in strength and courage to lead men back to God. Unceasingly he watches over his people, with them, as he promised, even to the end of the world. With gentle kindness he heals their diseases and comforts their sorrows and finds for them the food which is the living bread. With unwearied patience he bears with all their follies, their mistakes and their sins. And in the end he sacrificed his life that they might be safe.

> Souls of men, why will ye scatter
>   Like a crowd of frightened sheep?
> Foolish hearts! why will ye wander
>   From a love so true and deep?
>
> Was there ever kindest shepherd
>   Half so gentle, half so sweet,
> As the Saviour who would have us
>   Come and gather round his feet?

10

THE DIVINE PHYSICIAN

THAT he was the Divine Physician is something which Jesus claimed for himself. After Jesus had called Matthew to follow him, Matthew invited his fellow-outcasts to a meal in his house. At that meal Jesus was present. The Scribes and Pharisees were openly shocked that he should sit at a meal with tax-collectors and sinners. Jesus' answer was: 'Those who are well have no need of a physician, but those who are sick . . . I came not to call the righteous, but sinners' (Matt. 9.9-13; Mark 2.14-17; Luke 5.27-32). There Jesus states his claim to be the Divine Physician who came into the world to cure the ills of men.

The physician of the soul is a common picture in ancient thought. 'Is there no balm in Gilead?' Jeremiah asks. 'Is there no physician there?' (Jer. 8.22). Epictetus called his lecture-room 'the hospital for the sick soul'. Epicurus called his teachings 'the medicines of salvation'. The world was searching for some one who could heal the sickness of the soul.

It is true that sometimes the New Testament quotes jibes which were commonly flung at physicians. Jesus says that the people of Nazareth are likely to say to him what they might say to any doctor who claimed to give health: 'Heal yourself' (Luke 4.23). The woman with the hemorrhage had spent all she had on doctors and the only result was that she was worse instead of better (Mark 5.26; Luke 8.43). But in the ancient world the doctor had his special honour. The great Jewish tribute to him is in the Apocrypha, in Ecclus 38.1-8.

> Honour the physician with the honour due to him,
>   according to your need of him,

for the Lord created him;
for healing comes from the Most High,
   and he will receive a gift from the king.
The skill of the physician lifts up his head,
   and in the presence of great men he is admired.
The Lord created medicines from the earth,
   and a sensible man will not despise them.
Was not water made sweet with a tree
   in order that his power might be known?
And he gave skill to men
   that he might be glorified in his marvellous works.
By them he heals and takes away pain;
   the pharmacist makes of them a compound.
His works will never be finished;
   and from him health is upon the face of the earth.

Then Jesus ben-Sirach, who wrote Ecclesiasticus, with his customary combination of piety and common sense sets out the duty of the sufferer and of the doctor; the sufferer must turn to God, make his sacrifice and then turn to the physician; and the physician will ever pray that God will give him skill to discover and to treat the diseases of men:

My son, when you are sick, do not be negligent,
   but pray to the Lord and he will heal you.
Give up your faults and direct your hands aright,
   and cleanse your heart from all sin.
Offer a sweet-smelling sacrifice and a memorial portion
     of fine flour,
   and pour oil on your offering, as much as you can afford.
And give the physican his place, for the Lord created him,
   let him not leave you, for there is need of him.
There is a time when success lies in the hands of physicians,
   for they too will pray to the Lord
that he should grant them success in diagnosis
   and in healing, for the sake of preserving life.
He who sins before his Maker,
   may he fall into the care of a physician.
                        (Ecclus 38.9-15).

Thus prayer and skill combine to heal.

It is of interest to note that in the ancient Jewish world two things militated against the work of the physician. First, to all Jews dead bodies were unclean and to touch one was to contract uncleanness (Num. 19.11). The result was that it was very difficult for Jewish doctors to acquire any skill in anatomy, for they could not dissect dead bodies without breaking the ceremonial law. There is a grim record of the body of a criminal being boiled until the flesh came away from the bones, so that the bones could be examined and counted. Only thus could the would-be student of anatomy get at them. Second, it was a basic tenet of Jewish theology that all suffering was due to sin, and to the personal sin of the sufferer. It was, therefore, sometimes argued that the physician who sought to cure the disease and to ease suffering was interfering with the action and the decree of God. As Schechter puts it, rigid orthodox Judaism sometimes regarded the physician as 'a man counteracting the decrees of God'. But the rabbis found in Scripture a way round this difficulty. Ex. 21.19 says that, if in any fight or brawl a man injures another man, he shall pay compensation to the injured man for the time lost when he was injured, 'and shall have him thoroughly healed'. Here Scripture itself lays down the necessity of healing and so from this passage the rabbis argued that 'the law gives permission to the physician to practise his art'.

In the Graeco-Roman world the doctor was held in high esteem. Luke himself was a doctor (Col. 4.14), and he may well have learned his art in the university of Tarsus, which was the most famous medical university of its day. It is from Greece that there comes the famous Hippocratic oath, the oath taken by Greek doctors before they entered upon the practice of medicine and the oath which to this day governs medical ethics and practice: in it the doctor begins by swearing always to care for the man who taught him his art, and always to pass on the healing art to his own sons and to the sons of all other physicians without fee or charge. Then the oath goes on:

> The regimen I adopt shall be for the benefit of the
> patients to the best of my power and judgment, not for
> their injury or for any wrongful purpose. I will not give
> a deadly drug to anyone, though it be asked of me, nor
> will I lead the way in such counsel; and likewise I will
> not give a woman a pessary to procure abortion. But I
> will keep my life and art in purity and holiness. Whatso-
> ever house I enter, I will enter for the benefit of the sick,
> refraining from all voluntary wrong-doing and corrup-
> tion, especially seduction of male or female, bond or
> free. Whatsoever things I see or hear concerning the
> life of men in my attendance on the sick, or even apart
> from my attendance, which ought not be be blabbed
> abroad, I will keep silence on them, counting such things
> to be religious secrets.

By that ancient and splendid oath the ethics of the doctor are
still governed.

In the ancient world medicine and religion were very
closely connected. When a man was ill, it was rather to God,
and to the priest of God, and to the house of God that he
would turn than to the doctor and his surgery or consulting
room. The Chronicler blames Asa the king for what he thought
a foolish course of action. 'In the thirty-ninth year of his
reign Asa was diseased in his feet, and his disease became
severe; yet even in his disease he did not seek the Lord, but
sought help from physicians' (II Chron. 16.12). The Chronicler thought that Asa should have turned to God before he
turned to the physician. Amongst the Jews it was the priest
and not the physician who examined a man to see that a cure
from leprosy was genuine (Matt. 8.4; Lev. 14).

What was true of the Jewish world was equally true of
the Graeco-Roman world. If a person was ill, it was to the
temple of Aesculapius that he would go. There he underwent
the process called *incubatio*. That is to say, he spent a night
in the temple in the hope that in the darkness the god would

come to him and touch him and heal him. There are many inscriptions which record a cure after this *incubatio*. One of them runs: 'A man had an abdominal abscess. He saw a vision, and thought that the God ordered the slaves who accompanied him to lift him up and hold him so that his abdomen could be cut open. The man tried to get away, but the slaves caught him and bound him. So Aesculapius cut him open, rid him of the abscess, stitched him up again, and then released him from his bonds. Straightway he departed cured, and the floor of the Abaton was covered with blood.' In those days there were no hospitals and it was to the temple of Aesculapius that the sufferer went, and such is the power of hope and prayer and faith and expectation that beyond a doubt men were healed and cures happened.

If then Jesus regarded healing as an essential part of his work, he was fully in line with the religious thought of his day. And he certainly did so. He regularly connected the kingdom of God and the healing of the bodies of men. 'He went about all Galilee, teaching in their synagogues and preaching the gospel of the kingdom and healing every disease and every infirmity among the people' (Matt. 4.23). When he sent out apostles on their mission, his instructions to them were that they were to preach that the Kingdom of Heaven was at hand, and, as they preached, they were to heal the sick, raise the dead, cleanse the lepers and cast out demons (Matt. 10.7,8). In Jesus' mind there was clearly the closest connection between the coming of the Kingdom and the conquest of suffering and the defeat of disease and pain and death. If Jesus was the bringer of the Kingdom then he was necessarily the healer of men, both in body and soul.

In the New Testament *sōtēria* is the word for salvation, and it is interesting and significant to remember that *sōtēria* was not originally a theological or specially religious word, but meant health, safety, security in general. In the private letters of the papyri we constantly find people writing to enquire about the *sōtēria*, the health and the welfare, of their friends and their loved ones. We find Epicurus using the word *sōtēria* of welfare and security quite generally. 'The first measure of *sōtēria*,' he says, 'is to watch over one's youth and to guard against what makes havoc of all by means of pestering desires.' The history of the word *sōtēria* makes it clear that the supreme bringer of it must be physician both of the bodies and the souls of men. Herophilus, one of the great Greek physicians, says: 'Science and art have equally nothing to show, strength is incapable of effort, wealth is useless, and eloquence is powerless, if health is wanting.' True Christian salvation is salvation of body and soul alike.

Finally, let us ask what the picture of Jesus as the Divine Physician reveals about Jesus. What are the characteristics of the doctor and the physician?

(i) It has been said that a lawyer sees men at their worst, a minister sees men at their best, and *a doctor sees men as they are*. A doctor necessarily sees men stripped of the accidental externals of life. The doctor sees a man, not as a prince or a pauper, not as a labourer, a stockbroker, a professor, a teacher, an engineer, a clerk, a shopkeeper, but as a human being in need of help and healing. The very word physician comes from the Greek word *phusikos,* which is connected with *phusis,* which means 'nature'. A physician is a man whose study is nature, the very essence and bedrock of life. A physician is a man who sees and accepts men as they are—and so does Jesus Christ.

(ii) The physician is the man with the mind and the eye trained to diagnose what is wrong. He sees signs that the layman cannot see, and interprets them in a way not possible for the layman. The physician is the man who sees what is wrong, for no cure can follow until the cause of the trouble is diagnosed. Jesus Christ can diagnose the sickness of sin, and can reveal just where that sickness attacks each individual life.

(iii)   Having seen the man as he is, and having diagnosed the cause of the trouble, the one desire of the physician is to help and to heal. The physician never regards the sufferer with repulsion or loathing or contempt. It is easy, it is almost inevitable, for the layman to regard an illness or a wound or an injury as something ugly and disgusting, something from which he shudders away in horror; that the doctor never does. Missionaries tell us that primitive peoples often regard illness as defilement. Even after the coming of Christianity there are tribesmen who will not come to take the Sacrament in illness, because they believe that illness is the sign that they have been spurned by God. But, as Paul Tournier puts it, the doctor is clear that his duty is sometimes to heal, often to relieve, and always to comfort.

The fact that Jesus took to himself the title of physician is the sure sign that he never turns in loathing and repulsion from the sinner, never regards the sinner with disgusted and nauseated contempt, never looks on the sinner as someone to be annihilated and obliterated, but always looks on the sinner as a sufferer needing above all things the healing power of grace.

(iv)   The physician is the man who will often risk his life for the man who is ill. The physician will not hesitate to attend a man suffering from a dangerously infectious illness. He will take all wise and reasonable precautions, but having taken them, as a matter of course, he will risk his own life to help and heal. A doctor, for instance, will not refuse to attend a man suffering from smallpox, although well aware of the danger of contact with such a case. Many and many a doctor has laid down his life in the service of the healing of his fellowmen. So too Jesus did not hesitate to die to find a cure for men.

(v) When the doctor has seen the essential man, when he has diagnosed the trouble, when his sympathy has gone out to the sufferer, he is characteristically and in virtue of his art the man who knows what to do. He knows the treatment which is required. It is true that there are ills which still defy the doctor's skill, but nonetheless, when we are ill, when the doctor enters the room, our instinctive reaction is that the man who can deal with this has come.

Jesus Christ is the one who has the cure for sin. Sometime ago I had to visit a friend who was psychologically unbalanced. I talked to his psychiatrist. I said: 'I suppose that when he comes out of this hospital he will be quite cured, repressions, inhibitions, complexes gone, a new man.' The psychiatrist looked at me thoughtfully. 'So,' he said, 'you are another man who believes in psychiatrists?' I said that I had been led so to believe. 'Let me tell you something,' said the psychiatrist. 'We can only strip a man naked until we see him as he is; and if, when we have done that, he is bad stuff, we can't do a thing about it. *That's where you come in.*' So even the doctor saw in Christ the healer whose power can operate even when the power of men is baffled, for Christ can not only cure, he can recreate.

Jesus the Divine Physician has the cure for the sickness of the soul in face of which the wisest man is helpless.

11

SAVIOUR

No title of Jesus is more dear and precious to the Christian than the title Saviour. We must begin our study of this title by remembering that Jesus came into a world in which salvation was the universal and the deepest desire of the hearts of men. The world, as Seneca put it, *ad salutem spectat*; the world was looking towards salvation.

There were many reasons for that deep longing of the human heart. Samuel Angus, in his book *The Mystery Religion and Christianity*, said: 'The two centuries preceding the Christian era had been a period of uninterrupted misery', and the centuries immediately succeeding the beginning of the Christian era were such as to strike terror into the mind and heart of any thinking man who could read the human situation. Many years were to pass before the collapse of the Roman Empire, but the pressure on the frontiers had begun, and the first faint warnings of the end were there for those who could hear them. There can seldom have been any time of such political insecurity. It was the time of tyrannical and capricious rulers, who boasted, as Galba did, that they could do what they liked and do it to anyone. It was the age of the *delator*, the informer, who would lay information against his dearest friend for what he could get out of it, and there was no career which led more quickly to a fortune than the career of informer. It was the age when the affairs of the Roman Empire were directed by the imperial secretaries who were freedmen who had once been slaves and who had the mentality of slaves. The ancient gods were on the way out. It was not a case of men becoming so depraved that they abandoned their gods; it was a case of the gods becoming so depraved that they were abandoned by men. Men could no longer believe in beings of whom the stories were that they plotted and fought, grew drunken and intrigued and committed adultery. The old gods were going and there was nothing to take their place, and, as has been truly said, 'No nation has ever survived the loss of its gods.' There was the terrifying superstition which haunted the minds of men. There was the universal belief in the demons lurking everywhere to injure men. There was the almost universal belief in astralism. Men believed in the power of the stars. They believed that their fate was settled by the stars under which they were born and that there was no escape from that rigid and iron determinism. There was the consciousness of moral failure and moral helplessness. Men, as Seneca said, hated their sins but could not leave them. They were desperately and despairingly conscious of 'their weakness in necessary things'. They knew that they were sinners, but they knew no cure for sin. Perhaps even more than anything else, there was the fear of death. There is no man, said Seneca, young or old or middle-aged, who, if you get him off his guard, is not afraid of death. Long ago in the *Odyssey* Achilles had said that he would rather be the servant of a poor man upon earth than the king of all the dead.

In an age like that it is small wonder that men were searching for salvation. One of the signs of that search is the quite extraordinary prevalence of the word Saviour as a title. Any ruler who could bring to life any kind of peace and safety and security, or even any ruler who, men hoped, might bring such things, received the title Saviour. It was a regular title of the kings of Egypt. So a document is dated, 'in the reign of Ptolemy, the son of Ptolemy, the Saviour.' In Asia Minor we read of Antiochus-Apollo, the Saviour. An Athenian inscription describes Julius Caesar as Saviour and Benefactor. An Ephesian inscription describes him as God manifest and universal Saviour of human life. An inscription from Halicarnassus, dating from 2 BC, describes Augustus as 'protecting God and Saviour of the whole human race', because 'land and sea enjoy peace, and the cities flourish under your good government'. Propertius the poet described the same Augustus as *mundi salvator,* the Saviour of the world. Even an Emperor like Claudius was described as, 'God manifest, our god Caesar Saviour of the world.' An inscription of AD 67 describes Nero as 'god, the Saviour for ever.' The title Saviour was given even to local officials who ruled well, who kept the peace and who dispensed justice. In Egypt a suppliant turns to the magistrate: 'I turn to you, my saviour, to obtain my just rights.' The populace greet a good governor: 'Prosperous prefect! Saviour of honest men, our ruler!' The title 'Saviour' was given in hope to anyone who seemed likely to bring some kind of security and justice into a life whose foundations had been shaken. 'Men', says Samuel Angus, 'were in search of salvation from whatever quarter.'

All this is even truer of the religions to which men gave their hearts in the Graeco-Roman world into which Christ and Christianity came. Men were desperately seeking some kind of peace and security amidst the uncertainty of life and living and the terror of dying. It was, says Samuel Angus, 'a world crying out for saviour gods.' 'The cry for *sōtēria* became persistent, and only saviour gods could command a hearing.' The title Saviour became especially attached to two kinds of gods.

It became particularly attached to Aesculapius, the god of healing, whose temple at Epidaurus became the Lourdes of the ancient world. Men crowded to the temple to spend a night in its precincts, so that in the darkness the god might touch and they might be healed. Men called Aesculapius 'Saviour of the World', 'the great joy of all mortals', 'the Lord', 'the Healer', 'the Gentle One'. Aristides, the Athenian orator called Aesculapius 'Saviour of all and Guardian of the immortals'. Julian the Emperor, who made the last effort to re-establish the ancient gods, spoke of Helios begetting Aesculapius 'to be the Saviour of all'. And there is no doubt that in the temple of Aesculapius healing happened, for it is always unto men according to their faith, even when the faith is only a dim and distant glimpse of the truth, the groping of a wistful heart which knows no better.

This was even more the case with what are known as the Mystery Religions. These Mystery Religions were unquestionably the most vital religious forces in the world into which Christianity came. They were all in the nature of passion plays. They were all founded on the story of some god who lived and suffered and died and finally rose again to live for evermore. The initiate underwent a long course of preparation in which he was instructed in the inner meaning of the story, and in which he underwent severe ascetic discipline, and in which he was moved to the highest pitch of expectation. The story was then played out in his presence with subtle lighting, sensuous incense, moving music and often a splendid and noble liturgy. The aim was that the worshipper should be so moved that he entered into complete identity with the god. The aim was that he might say: 'I am thou, and thou art I.' In this identity he was meant to share in the life, the sufferings, the death, the resurrection of the god, and, therefore, in the final triumph of the god over all the malign and destructive forces of the world, a triumph which extended beyond life and conquered death. Again, there is no doubt that things happened; there is no doubt that many an initiate had a mystical experience of the divine. To all these gods of the Mystery Religions the name Saviour was given, for it was Saviour that they all claimed to be.

Lucius in *The Golden Ass* prays to Isis who was one of them:
'Thou bestowest a mother's sweet love on miserable
mortals . . . Thou dispellest the storms of life, and stretchest
out the right hand of salvation to struggling men.'[1] The
Mystery Religions were partly competitors and partly preparations for Christianity.

It may truly be said that the true Saviour of the world came
into a world which was passionately hoping and searching for
salvation.

Closer to the heart of the Christian message there lies
the thought of the Old Testament. We, therefore, turn to the
Septuagint to see what light it throws upon the idea of a
Saviour and of salvation.

(i) In the Septuagint we find that the word *sōtēr* is sometimes applied to men. Othniel and Ehud are said to be
saviours whom God raised up for Israel (Judg. 3.9,15). In
the time of Nehemiah the people amid their difficulties look
back and remember how in time past God gave his people
saviours who saved them from their enemies (Neh. 9.27).
Those who rescued Israel in the nation's evil day were saviours.

(ii) We frequently find the word saviour applied directly
to God. Isaiah prays to the God of Israel the Saviour (45.15),
and addresses God as a righteous God and a Saviour (45.21).
It is the lament of Moses that Jeshurun, that is, Israel,
forsook God his Saviour (Deut. 32.15). Israel's demand for
a human king meant that they had rejected God their Saviour
(I Sam. 10.19). In the Septuagint, the Greek Old Testament,
the word *sōtēr* as applied to God is much commoner than
in the English of the AV. Very often where the AV speaks
of 'the God of our salvation' the Greek is simply 'God our
Saviour' (Ps. 24.5; 27.9; 65.5; 79.9; Micah 7.7; Hab. 3.18).
And very often where the AV speaks of God as 'my salvation',
or as 'the rock of our salvation' the Greek is also simply

[1] Apuleius, *Metamorphoses* 11.25.

'Saviour' (Pss. 27.1; 62.2; Isa. 12.2; 17.10; 62.11). The Old Testament glories in calling God Saviour.

Let us now turn to the word *sōtēria*, salvation, in the Greek Old Testament.

(i) *Sōtēria* can mean simply *peace* or *welfare*. Abimelech and Isaac part in *sōtēria*, in peace (Gen. 26.31). It is Job's lament that terrors are turned upon him, and that his *sōtēria*, his welfare, has passed away like a cloud (Job 30.15).

(ii) *Sōtēria* can mean *preservation in safety*. 'God is my salvation,' says Isaiah, 'I will trust and not be afraid' (Isa. 12.2). It is Jacob's vow that the Lord will be his God, if he returns to his father's house again in *sōtēria*, in peace, that is to say, if his life is spared in the exile and the dangers which face him (Gen. 28.21). Salvation is preservation when dangers threaten and when life is difficult.

(iii) *Sōtēria* can mean *deliverance from an unhappy situation*. When Hannah's childlessness was at last blessed with a child, she rejoices in her salvation (I Sam. 2.1). It is deliverance from a hurting and humiliating situation in life.

(iv) *Sōtēria* can mean *help and assisance and deliverance* in a dangerous and threatening situation. It is Saul's message to the people of Jabesh-Gilead in their peril that tomorrow they shall have *sōtēria* (I Sam. 11.9). It is the hand powerfully stretched out to help when danger threatens.

(v) *Sōtēri*a can mean *deliverance and victory combined*. For David the death of Absalom turns the *sōtēria* into mourning (II Sam. 19.2). When Eleazar smote the Philistines in the field of barley, the Lord wrought a great *sōtēria* that day (I Sam. 23.10; I Chron. 11.14). It is more than simply rescue; it is rescue plus victory.

(vi) By far the commonest meaning of *sōtēria* is *rescue in danger*. It is rescue, liberation and release from some situation which is bound to result in disaster and death. The crossing of the Red Sea was the salvation of the Lord (Ex. 14.13;

15.2). Samson calls his defeat of the Philistines with no greater weapon than the jawbone of an ass a great *deliverance* from God (Judg. 15.18). After the defeat of the Ammonites the saying is: 'Today the Lord has wrought *salvation* in Israel (I Sam. 11.13). The victories of Jonathan and David are called a great *salvation* for Israel (I Sam. 14.45; 19.4). Before entering the battle Joab and Abishai come to an agreement that, if the enemy is too strong for either of them, the other will immediately come *eis sōtērian,* for the salvation, to the rescue of the one in trouble (II Sam. 10.11). It is David's lament that he must flee, for otherwise there is no *sōtēria,* no escape, no rescue, from the advance of Absalom (II Sam. 15.14). God has given David the shield of salvation and has been his tower of salvation (II Sam. 22.36,51). In the face of the threat of Shishak, Rehoboam and the people humbled themselves, and God said that he would not destroy them, but that he would grant them *sōtēria,* he would come to their rescue (II Chron. 12.7).

In almost all these cases which we have cited the reference is to rescue in battle, or in time of some physical peril and threat; but later the word comes to denote rescue from every kind of peril which can threaten life.

It is the Psalmist's complaint that people say of him: 'There is no *sōtēria* for him in God,' God will not come to his rescue (Ps. 3.2). God has given the king great *salvation* (Ps. 18.50). The *salvation* of the righteous is of the Lord (Ps. 36.39). Vain is the help, the *sōtēria* of man; there are situations in life from which no human power can ever rescue a man (Ps. 60.11; 108.12). It is God who gives *salvation* to kings, and delivers his servant David from the sword that would wound him (Ps. 144.10). God goes forth for the *salvation,* the rescue, of his people (Obad. 3.13). It is Israel's trust that God is our arm every morning and our *salvation* in time of trouble (Isa. 33.2). All other hopes are vain, for truly in the Lord our God is the *salvation* of Israel (Jer. 3.23).

In all these cases the idea is that of God rescuing his people from some situation in which they are powerless to rescue themselves and in which without his help they are doomed to destruction.

(vii) Almost inevitably the idea of *sōtēria* becomes even wider yet, and comes to include not only rescue from the perils of life, but also *rescue from sin.* 'Deliver me from blood-guiltiness, O God,' prays the Psalmist, 'thou God of my salvation' (Ps. 51.14). Here the rescue is from sin and the consequences of sin.

(viii) Finally, in the Greek Old Testament, the word *sōtēria* comes to describe *eschatological deliverance*, that is to say, deliverance in the day when this present age comes to an end, and when the wrath and the judgment of God break in upon the world. In that day Israel will be able to say: 'Lo! this is our God . . . We have waited for him; we will be glad and rejoice in his salvation' (Isa. 25.9). Israel shall be saved in the Lord with an everlasting salvation (Isa. 45.17). God will place salvation in Zion for Israel his glory (Isa. 46.13). In that end time Israel is to be God's salvation to the ends of the earth (Isa. 49.6; 52.10).

We may say that salvation, *sōtēria*, is equivalent to the state when God will enter into his kingdom and reign. The message of the one who comes to announce salvation is: 'Thy God reigneth' (Isa. 52.7).

Here then is the idea of *sōtēria* in the Greek Old Testament, and of the dominant idea of it there is no question. Always at the back of the word there is the idea of rescue, rescue from a situation in which nothing but the action of God can be effective. Salvation is God's rescuing power in this life and in the age to come.

Having seen the desire for salvation in the pagan world into which Christ came, and having examined the word in the Greek

Old Testament, we now turn to the New Testament itself.

(i) It is to be noted in the first place that in the New Testament on no fewer than eight occasions *it is God who is called Saviour*. It is Mary's song: 'My spirit rejoices in God my Saviour' (Luke 1.47). Paul is an apostle by the command of God our Saviour (I Tim. 1.1). His preaching has been entrusted to him by the command of God our Saviour (Titus 1.3). God our Saviour desires all men to be saved (I Tim. 2.3). The living God is the Saviour of all men, especially of those who believe (I Tim. 4.10). Everything is to be done in such a way as to adorn the teaching of God our Saviour (Titus 2.10). In Christ there appeared the goodness and the loving kindness of God our Saviour (Titus 3.4). In Jude the ascription of praise is to the only God our Saviour (Jude 25).

This is important. It once and for all forbids any setting in contrast the love of Jesus and the stern wrath of God. It forbids any view of the work of Christ which implies or suggests that Jesus did something to alter the attitude of God to men, to turn the wrath of God into the love of God, to persuade God to withold a hand stretched out to destroy. God is the Saviour God; Jesus Christ did not live and die to change the attitude of God to men; he lived and died to demonstrate what that attitude is.

(ii) Of the fact that the New Testament calls Jesus Saviour and of the fact that the early Christians experienced Jesus as Saviour there is no doubt. The message of the angel was that his name was to be called Jesus, which is the Greek form of Joshua, which means 'Jehovah is salvation', because 'he will save his people from their sins' (Matt. 1.21). It was the conviction of the writer to the Hebrews that 'he is able for all time to save those who draw near to God through him' (Heb. 7.25). It is nonetheless only on the rarest occasions that the Gospels call Jesus Saviour. In

Matthew and Mark that title does not appear at all. In Luke it occurs only once, in the message of the angels to the shepherds: 'To you is born this day in the city of David a Saviour who is Christ the Lord' (Luke 2.11). In John also the title Saviour occurs only once. The people of Samaria, after they have heard and seen Jesus, say that they no longer need to take the woman's word for it; they know that this 'is indeed the Saviour of the world' (John 4.42).

In Acts the name Saviour occurs only twice. Peter says of Jesus that God has exalted him to his right hand as Leader and Saviour, to give repentance to Israel and forgiveness of sins (Acts 5.31). Paul at Antioch in Pisidia says that of David's posterity God has brought to Israel a Saviour, Jesus, as he promised (Acts 13.23).

In the unquestioned letters of Paul the title occurs only once. Paul writes to the Philippians: 'Our commonwealth is in heaven and from it we await a Saviour, the Lord Jesus Christ' (Phil. 3.20).

In the questioned letters of Paul the name Saviour occurs five times. In Ephesians Christ is the Head of the Church, his Body, and is himself its Saviour (Eph. 5.23). In the Pastoral Epistles it is said that the purpose of God is manifested through the appearance of our Saviour Christ (II Tim. 1.10). The Letter to Titus begins with the prayer for grace and peace from God and Christ Jesus our Saviour (Titus 1.4). The same letter speaks of the appearing of the glory of our great God and Saviour Jesus Christ (Titus 2.13). The same letter says that God poured out his Spirit through Jesus Christ our Saviour (Titus 3.6).

The title Saviour does not occur in James or First Peter al all. In the little letter of Second Peter Jesus is called Saviour no fewer than five times. The greeting is to the Gentiles who have been granted a faith equal to that of the chosen people through the righteousness of our God and

Saviour Jesus Christ (II Peter 1.1). II Peter 1.11 speaks of the Kingdom of our Lord and Saviour Jesus Christ. The knowledge of our Lord and Saviour Jesus Christ protects a man from the defilements of this world (II Peter 2.20). The recipients of the letter are bidden not to forget the commandment of our Lord and Saviour which they received through the apostles (II Peter 3.2). They are bidden to grow in the grace and knowledge of our Lord and Saviour Jesus Christ (II Peter 3.18).

The New Testament contains only one more instance of the title Saviour. In I John we read that the Father sent his Son as Saviour of the world (I John 4.14).

At first sight the number of occasions on which Jesus is called Saviour in the New Testament is surprisingly small, twice in the four Gospels, twice in Acts, once in the un-doubted letters of Paul, five times in the disputed letters, once in First John, and five times in Second Peter. It is significant that the greater number of these times is in the later books of the New Testament, and the greatest number of all is in Second Peter, the latest book of all. This means that the more men thought about Jesus, and the more they experienced him, the more they were convinced that he was their Saviour and the Saviour of the world. But although the title Saviour occurs so seldom in the New Testament, there is no lack of reference to his saving work. That material occurs in connection with the word *sōzein,* which means *to save*; and it is to an examination of that word that we must now turn to see what the New Testament content of salvation is.

(i) *Sōzein* is used of *rescue in danger*. In the storm at sea the cry of the terrified disciples is: 'Save, Lord; we are perishing' (Matt. 8.35). As Peter sinks in the waves which he has recklessly set out to cross, his appeal is: 'Lord, save me' (Matt. 14.30). Jesus demands of the Scribes and

Pharisees: 'Is it lawful on the Sabbath day to save life or to kill?' (Mark 3.4; Luke 6.9). In the great storm on the Mediterranean sea on his way to Rome, it is Paul's insistence that unless all stay in the ship none can be saved (Acts 27.20,31). Peter's invitation to the crowds in Jerusalem is: 'Save yourselves from this crooked generation' (Acts 2.40). Jesus asks himself if he is to pray: 'Father, save me from this hour' (John 12.27). The onlookers at the crucifixion say to Jesus: 'You who would destroy the Temple and build it in three days, save yourself' (Matt. 27.40; Mark 15.30; Luke 23.35). Their taunt is: 'He saved others; himself he cannot save' (Matt. 27.42; Mark 15.31; Luke 25.37). They tell another to stand back to see if Elijah will come and save him (Matt. 27.49). The impenitent thief says: 'Are you the Christ? Save yourself and us' (Luke 23.39). The Son of Man is come to seek and to save the lost (Luke 19.10). In all these cases the idea is that of rescue from some terrible situation in which the one who appeals is unable to save himself.

(ii) It is used of *preservation in safety*. He who endures to the end will be saved (Matt. 10.22; 24.13; Mark 13.13). Whoever seeks to save his life, that is, to keep it safe, to preserve it in safety, will lose it (Matt. 16.25; Mark 8.35; Luke 9.24). In the last days, so terrible will be the tribulation that, if the days had not been shortened, no human being would have been saved, that is, would survive (Matt. 24.22; Mark 13.20). Here the idea is not so much that of rescue *from* a situation as of preservation *within* a situation.

(iii) It is repeatedly used of *healing in sickness*. It is the belief of the woman who touched the fringe of Jesus' garment that, if she could only touch it, she would be *made well* (*sōzein*); and it is Jesus' word to her: 'Your faith has *made you well*' (Matt. 9.12,22; Mark 5.28,34; Luke 8.48). It is the appeal of Jairus that Jesus should come and lay his hand on his daughter that she may be *made well;* and

it is Jesus' response: 'Only believe and she shall *be well*'
(Mark 5.23; Luke 8.50). It is Jesus' word to the blind
man: 'Your faith has *made you well*' (Mark 10.52; Luke
18.42). Those who had seen the cure of the Gerasene demoniac went and told how the man *was healed* (Luke 8.36).
It is Jesus' word to the leper: 'Rise and go; your faith has
made you well' (Luke 17.19). When Jesus said that Lazarus
was asleep, the reaction of the disciples is to say that, if
he is sleeping, he *will recover* (John 11.12). Peter speaks of
the means whereby the lame man at the gate of the Temple
was healed (Acts 4.9). Paul sees that the lame man at
Lystra has faith to be *made well* (Acts 14.9). James holds
that the prayer of faith will *heal* a sick man (James 5.15).

Quite often the English translation necessarily obscures
the fact that it is the verb *sōzein* which is being used in
these cases. It is very significant that the word which is the
word for salvation should so often be used of the healing of
the bodies of men.

(iv) It is used of *saving from death*. Jesus prayed with
loud cries and tears to him who was able to save him from
death (Heb. 5.7). Whoever brings back a sinner from the
error of his ways will save his soul from death and will
cover a multitude of sins (James 5.20). The connection of
salvation with salvation from death is very natural in that
our Saviour Jesus Christ abolished death and brought life
and immortality to light through the Gospel (II Tim. 1.10).

(v) It is used of preserving a man in *the dangers and
temptations of life and living*. In Second Timothy it is the
writer's confidence that the Lord will rescue him from every
evil and will *save* him for his heavenly kingdom (II Tim.
4.18). Salvation is the keeping power which keeps a man in the
way everlasting, and brings him in safety to his journey's end.

(vi) On one occasion *to be saved and to enter the kingdom are equated*. Jesus says that it is easier for a camel to

go through the eye of a needle than for a rich man to enter the kingdom of heaven. The reaction of the disciples is: 'Who then can be saved?' (Matt. 19.23-25; Mark 10.23-26; Luke 18.24-26). To be saved and to be a member of the kingdom are the same thing.

(vii)   Very commonly *sōzein* is used in connection with *being saved from judgment*. Salvation becomes eschatological; it passes beyond the limits of this world and enters into the presence of God.

(a)   *To be a Christian and to be saved are the same thing.* The Christians are described as those who were being saved (Acts 2.47; II Cor. 2.15). Peter is to tell Cornelius the message by which he and his household will be saved (Acts 11.14). The Judaisers claim that, unless converts are circumcised after the custom of Moses, they cannot be saved (Acts 15.1). Salvation and Christianity are synonymous terms.

(b)   *The offer of this salvation is very wide.* It was to save sinners that Christ Jesus came into the world (I Tim. 1.15). God our Saviour will have all men to be saved (I Tim. 2.4). The offer of salvation is neither selective nor exclusive; it is as wide as the world.

(c)   *This whole matter of salvation is bound up with Jesus Christ.* There is no other name by which we must be saved (Acts 4.12). It is he who calls on the name of the Lord who will be saved (Acts 2.21; Rom. 10.13). It was that through him the world might be saved that God sent his Son into the world (John 3.17). 'I say this,' said Jesus, 'that you may be saved' (John 5.34). Jesus is the door, through which, if any man enter in, he will be saved (John 10.9). Jesus did not come into the world to condemn the world, but to save the world (John 12.47). The process of salvation is bound up with Jesus Christ. It is through him, and through him alone, that salvation becomes available for man.

(d)   *Salvation comes through grace.* It is the conviction

of the early Church that through the grace of the Lord
Jesus Christ we shall be saved (Acts 15.11). It is by grace
that we have been saved (Eph. 2.5,8). God saved us, not
in virtue of our works, but in virtue of his own purpose and
grace (II Tim. 1.9). He saved us, not because of deeds done
by us in righteousness, but in virtue of his own mercy, by
the washing of regeneration and renewal in the Holy Spirit
(Titus 3.5). The New Testament is clear beyond any doubt that
man does not deserve and cannot win salvation. Salvation depends on the grace of God. It is God's free gift to men, given
in mercy, and totally undeserved.

(e) Although salvation is the absolute gift of God, man
must bring something to it. *He must bring the response of
faith.* 'By grace,' writes Paul, 'you have been saved through
faith' (Eph. 2.8). It is those who believe that it pleases God
to save (I Cor. 1.21). It was the faith of the woman who
was a sinner which saved her (Luke 7.50). It is the devil's
aim to take away the good seed of the word, 'that they
may not believe and be saved' (Luke 8.12). Paul's answer to
the enquiry of the Philippian gaoler as to what he must do
is: 'Believe in the Lord Jesus Christ, and you will be saved'
(Acts 16.30). It is those who refuse to accept and to love
the truth who are shutting themselves off from salvation
(II Thess. 2.10).

There is in man that which can say yes and that which
can say no. There is in man an inviolable core of personality
or self or whatever we may care to call it, which has to
submit or to refuse to submit to the claim of God, and
which has to accept or to refuse to accept the offer of God.
Not even God can compel a man to be saved.

This faith has two sides to it. Inwardly, it means accepting
Jesus Christ at his word, believing absolutely that what he
says and offers is true, believing that what he tells us about
God is the eternal and unchangeable truth, and committing

one's life to that belief. Outwardly, it is the translation of
that belief into action which befits it and which carries it
out in life, for, as James so clearly saw, a faith which has
no deeds to match is not a saving faith (James 2.14).

(f) In this salvation we are *saved from the wrath of God*
(Rom. 5.9). It is not so much that the hand of God raised
to obliterate is stayed. It is rather that we enter into a new
relationship with God. If we believe that what Jesus says of
God is true, then, trusting in the mercy of God and relying
on the grace of God, we can go to God no longer in fear
and in trembling but in childlike confidence and boldness.
Jesus came to put us into a new relationship with God, not
by changing God's relationship to us, but by changing our
relationship to God.

(g) We are not only saved by the death of Christ; *we
are saved by the life of Christ*. We are reconciled by his
death and saved by his life (Rom. 5.10). The idea here is
that we do not need only forgiveness for past sin; we need
constant help and strength and guidance for present life.
And in the death of Christ we have that which acts upon
our past sin; in the earthly life of Christ we have that
which is a pattern and an example to us; and in the presence
of the resurrected and ever-living Christ we have the strength
to live the life we ought to live.

(h) Salvation includes *the salvation of the body*. It is in
the hope of the redemption of the body that we are saved
(Rom. 8.24). He will change our lowly body to be like his
glorious body (Phil. 3.21).

There are two ideas behind this. First, it means that in
any life which is, or is to come, our personality remains.
We never lose our individuality; we are not absorbed and
lost in the divine, or mystically swallowed up in God.
Neither Greek nor Hebrew had any word for *personality;*
and indeed it is very difficult to conceive of personality at

all without some kind of body in and through which the personality can act and be expressed. So, then, to say that the body can be saved and must be saved means, in modern terms, that personality and individuality survive any change in any life. Second, it means that the Christian believes in the salvation of the total personality. There have been many religions which have seen their own particular brand of salvation in release and liberation from the body, which they considered an unmitigated evil and the seat of temptation and sin. But Christianity teaches the salvation of every part of the man. It will be true that the body that a man wears in glory will be very different from that which he wears now, as the golden daffodil is very different from the shrivelled bulb from which it springs; but it remains true that Christianity refuses to regard the body as evil and insists that it can be consecrated in time and saved in eternity.

(*i*) Salvation involves the confession that *Jesus is Lord,* and *the unshakable belief in the resurrection* (Rom. 10.9). Salvation demands that a man should take his stand for Christ unashamedly, and that he should be quite sure that Jesus is not a figure in a book, but a living and an abiding presence. As it has been said: 'No apostle ever *remembered* Jesus.' He did not remember him; he daily lived with him.

(*j*) Amazing as it may seem to be, this salvation is *mediated through men,* for Jesus Christ has chosen men to be his messengers and ambassadors. Paul acts as he does that he may save least some of his fellow-Jews (Rom. 11.14). He has become all things to all men that he may by all means save some (I Cor. 9.22). He seeks to give no offence to Jew or to Greek; he seeks not his own advantage, but the advantage of all, that all may be saved (I Cor. 10.23). If in a marriage one partner is a pagan and one a Christian, they are not to separate, for—who knows?—the believer may be the means of saving the unbeliever (I Cor. 7.16). The true teacher who takes thought for himself and his teaching will save both himself and his hearers (I Tim. 4.16). Just as a man can aid the purposes of salvation, so he can hinder them. It is the sin of the Jews that they have tried to hinder Paul from preaching to the Gentiles that they might be saved (I Thess. 2.16). It is part of the glory of the gospel that it is given to men to convey it to their fellow-men.

(k) The experience of salvation comes *through the implanted word* (James 1.21). The picture is that of the word being sown into a man's heart (cp. Matt. 13.1-9). The word is a gospel, it is good news (I Cor. 15.2). The message of salvation is brought to men in the message of the saving word, even if that word seems folly and foolishness to those who refuse to believe (I Cor. 1.21).

(i) It sometimes happens that *the experience of salvation is not easy*. There are those who have to be delivered to Satan for the destruction of their flesh that their spirit may be saved (I Cor. 5.5). This probably means that there are those who have to be temporarily excommunicated, banished from the fellowship of their fellow-Christians, in order that their pride and stubbornness may be destroyed, so that their souls may be saved. If the righteous man is scarcely saved, what will happen to the sinner? (I Peter 4.18). Some have to be saved like brands plucked from the burning (Jude 23). A man may come to God, as it were, spontaneously and of his own free-will, or he may have to be disciplined and chastened into the acceptance of the offer of God.

This idea is in line with the whole Jewish idea of history. The Jews did not believe that suffering was purposeless, nor did they believe that it came simply from the will of men. There is a passage in Second Maccabees (6.12-16), which is worth quoting in full, for it has in it the whole Jewish philosophy of history, which in turn affected the Christian idea of the action of God in salvation. The Second Maccabees passage refers to the terrible and agonising sufferings which came upon the Jewish nation in the days when Antiochus Epiphanes by the most brutal and savage methods attempted to obliterate Judaism completely:

> Now I urge those who read this book not to be depressed by such calamities, but to recognise that these punishments were designed, not to destroy but to discipline our people. In fact not to let the impious alone for long, but to punish them immediately is a sign of great kindness. For in the case of the other nations the Lord waits patiently to punish them until they have reached the full measure of their sins; but he does not deal in this way with us, in order that he may not take vengeance on us afterward when our sins have reached their height. Therefore he never withdraws his mercy from us. Though he disciplines us with calamities, he does not forsake his own people.

An agonising situation may well be the sign of the mercy of God. God will not leave a man alone to destroy himself; and therefore salvation may come at the cost of fiery trial, and of punishment which is not vengeance but discipline.

(m) In the later parts of the New Testament salvation is *sacramentally mediated and received*. In the longer ending of Mark, which is not part of the original Gospel, it is said that he who believes and is baptised will be saved (Mark 16.16). Baptism now saves us through the appeal of a clear conscience to God and the work of the risen Christ (I Peter 2.21). It is the washing of regeneration and the renewal of the Spirit which bring salvation (Titus 3.5).

Here then is the meaning of the title Saviour when it is applied to Jesus. And no matter from what angle it may be approached the basic and essential idea is the idea of *rescue*, rescue from a situation in which a man is quite unable to rescue himself.

It is *rescue from the past*. Through the work of Jesus

Christ the penalty which man's sin deserves no longer hangs threateningly over him. The estrangment between man and God need no longer exist. The power and slavery of past sin are broken and man is no longer shackled by the chains which his own sin forged.

It is *rescue for the future*. Through Jesus Christ, the living and ever-present Christ, man is no longer a slave to his own sin. He can break the habits which have been his fetters, and conquer the sins which conquered him. He is no longer frustrated and defeated; he has found the way to victorious living. He is no longer the victim of temptation; he is victorious over temptation.

Salvation does not deal only with a man's past; it makes him a new man and gives him a new future. It is not merely negative escape; it is positive victory.

Jesus is indeed the Saviour for whom men were desperately searching, and for whom a world was waiting, and whom the world still needs.

12

PROPHET

THERE is nothing more certain than that Jesus was regarded as a prophet when in the days of his flesh he lived and taught in Palestine. The conception of him as prophet comes from two directions.

(i) It comes from those who clearly saw his greatness, but who were unaware of his uniqueness, from those who thought him a man of God, but who did nor realize that he was the Son of God.

After he had raised the son of the widow of Nain, as Luke tells the story, the reaction of the people was: 'A great prophet has arisen among us' (Luke 7.16). The report of Jesus that was brought to Herod was that John the Baptist had arisen from the dead, or that one of the old prophets such as Elijah or Jeremiah had returned to life (Luke 9.8; Mark 6.15). When Jesus asked his disciples what people were saying about him, their answer was that they were saying that he was Elijah or Jeremiah or one of the prophets (Matt. 16.14; Mark 8.28; Luke 9.19). The verdict of the people at the Triumphal Entry was: 'This is Jesus, the prophet of Nazareth of Galilee' (Matt. 21.11). When the two travellers on the Emmaus road were remembering Jesus with sorrow and regret, they spoke of him as Jesus of Nazareth, a prophet mighty in deed and word (Luke 24.19). There is abundant evidence that it was a popular verdict that Jesus was a prophet.

In the Fourth Gospel—and it may well be deliberately —there are two stories in which the discovery that Jesus is a prophet is the prelude to the greater discovery that he is the Messiah. In the story of the woman of Samaria the

woman's first reaction is: 'Sir, I perceive that you are a
prophet.' But her final reaction is: 'Can this be the Christ?'
(John 4.19,29). In the story of the healing of the man
blind from his birth, the man's first reaction is: 'He is a
prophet.' But he ends by expressing his belief that Jesus is
none other than the Son of God (John 9.17,35-38). It may
well be that John intends us to see that belief in Jesus as a
prophet is a stage on the way to full belief in Jesus as the
Messiah and the Son of God.

(ii) The second series of passages which think of Jesus
in terms of a prophet come from Jesus himself. When
he was rejected at Nazareth, he said: 'Truly, I say to you,
no prophet is acceptable is his own country' (Luke 4.24;
Matt. 13.57; Mark 6.4; John 4.44). When he was warned of
the danger of going to Jerusalem, his answer was: 'It cannot
be that a prophet should perish away from Jerusalem' (Luke
13.33). His description of Jerusalem was that that city was
the killer of the prophets and the stoner of the messengers
of God (Matt. 23.37; Luke 13.34). And in every one of
these cases the reference is unmistakably to Jesus himself.
It is quite clear that the title prophet is a title which Jesus
would certainly not have refused or rejected.

We must now bring into our study a famous Old Testament
passage which is more than once echoed and quoted and
applied to Jesus. It was God's promise to Moses: 'I will
raise up for them (the people of Israel) a prophet like you
from among their brethren, and I will put my words in 'his
mouth, and he will speak to them all that I command him'
(Deut. 18.18). The AV alters the meaning of that passage
by spelling the word *prophet* with a capital P, therby at
once making it refer to an individual. This is a mistake
corrected as early as the Revised Version, and thereafter in
all new translations. If we read the whole passage in Deut.

18.15-22, it begins with the statement: 'The Lord your God
will raise up for you a prophet among you like me from
among your brethren—him shall you heed.' But as the passage goes on it becomes quite clear that the reference is not
to any one individual but to a series of God-sent men who
throughout the ages to come will be the messengers of God
to men. It is in effect a promise that God will never leave
himself without a witness.

The individualising of this passage was helped by two
things. First, in Deut. 34.10 we read: 'and there has not
arisen since a prophet in Israel like Moses, whom the Lord
knew face to face.' If this is taken very closely with Deut.
18.15, it could mean that men were still waiting for the
prophet like Moses to emerge, and that the great figure is
still to come; but quite certainly the original meaning of the
passage was that all through history the God-given line of
the prophets would never fail. Second, the Samaritans definitely did take this as a promise of the reincarnation of Moses.
There were two reasons for this. The Samaritans did not
accept any of the Old Testament except the Pentateuch, the
first five books of it, the Law. They therefore in point of
fact did not have any of the books of the prophets. The
prophets for them did not exist. Since therefore they acknowledged no prophets in the past they earnestly looked forward
for the great prophet still to come. Second, the Samaritans
had a different reading in Deut. 34.10. Their version ran:
'There *will not arise* a prophet in Israel like Moses.' They
therefore had their own special belief that Moses would come
back as the *Taheb,* the restorer of all things. In view of
all this the passage in Deut. 18.15 was at least sometimes
individualised, and was regarded as the foretelling of the
coming of the supreme prophet, who would be to the people
a second Moses.

That belief is referred to more than once in the New

Testament. The question put to John the Baptist was: 'Are you that prophet?' (John 1.21). Twice, according to the Fourth Gospel, that belief was connected with Jesus. After the feeding of the five thousand there were some who said: 'This is indeed the prophet who is to come into the world' (John 6.14). After the events of the Feast of Tabernacles there were those who said: 'This is really the prophet' (John 7.40). Even in the days of his flesh there were those who saw in Jesus the promised prophet.

It was inevitable that in the early Church the Deuteronomy promise should be applied to Jesus. It was so applied by Peter. He quoted the promise of Moses and then claimed that that promise had been fulfilled in Jesus (Acts 3.22-26). Even more directly Stephen declared that Jesus was the promised prophet (Acts 7.37). And by the second century it had become part of accepted Christian belief that Jesus was the prophet promised by Moses.

It may well be that in the days of his flesh the most popular and widespread view of Jesus was that he was a prophet. Some certainly saw him in terms of Elijah who was to be the forerunner and the herald of the Messiah (Mal. 4.5). Some saw him, as it were, as a prophet in his own right. And it must be noted that this in itself was a remarkable thing, for in the time of Jesus the Jews sadly believed that for the last three hundred years the voice of prophecy had been silent. To believe that Jesus was a prophet was, if nothing else, to believe that God was speaking in him as he had not spoken for three centuries. It is quite true that the view of Jesus as prophet is not adequate, but it was capable of becoming the gateway to a larger belief and the starting point for a wider vision.

Since Jesus was regarded as a prophet, and since that was a title which Jesus would certainly have accepted, we must go on to see what the function of a prophet really was. In

popular thought a prophet had two functions. First, he foretold the future; and, second, he thundered doom and denunci-
ation against mankind in general. Popular thought sees the
prophet as the predicter of the future and the messenger of
doom. This is a very inadequate idea of what a prophet really
was.

Let us begin by looking at the word *prophet*. In I Sam 9.9
there is a note which says that a prophet was formerly called
a *seer*. There are three words for *prophet*, two of which are
commonly translated *seer*.

There is the word *roch*. This is a word which is very commonly applied to Samuel, who is repeatedly called Samuel the
roeh, Samuel the seer (I Chron. 9.22; 26.28; 29.29). We also
read of Hanan the seer (I Chron. 16.7,10), and the word is
used generally of the prophets (Isa. 9.9; 30.10).

There is the word *chozeh*. We read of Gad, David's *chozeh*,
David's seer (II Sam. 24.11; I Chron. 21.9). Heman (I Chron.
25.5), Iddo (II Chron. 9.29; 12.15), Asaph (II Chron. 29.30),
Amos (Amos 7.12) are all called by this title.

There is the commonest word of all, the standard word for
a prophet, *nabi*. There is no general agreement as to what
the root of this word means, but Kirkpatrick approves the
suggestion that its root has something to do with *bubbling
over*, and therefore with *ecstasy*. The word *nabi* is itself
passive in form, and it may well mean a man who is controlled by the divine Spirit, a man in whom, as it were, this
Spirit bubbles over, so that he becomes the inspired bearer of
the word of God to men. As for *roeh* and *chozeh*, Kirkpatrick
suggests that they may have some connection with the means
whereby the Spirit of God communicates the message to the
prophet, by word, by dream, and by vision. So, then, the
basic Old Testament belief about a prophet is that he is a
man controlled and inspired by God, and entrusted with the
message of God to men. Let us go on to see what the Old

Testament tells us of the prophet and his function.

There is no doubt at all of the place of the prophet in the life of Israel. If Israel was a theocracy, that is, a kingdom whose only real king was God, then quite clearly the prophet is the most important person in the community, because the prophet is the mouthpiece of God, the intermediary between God and man, the messenger and the voice of God. Moses was the deliverer of Israel and nothing less than the maker of the nation. Samuel was the maker and the unmaker of kings. Nathan was the man who dared to rebuke David to his face (II Sam. 12). Elijah was the man who said 'Thus far and no farther' to Jezebel and Ahab (I Kings 18). The place of the prophet in the life of Israel is clear for all to see.

Just because of that the Jewish law was clear that there can be no greater danger to a community than a false prophet. Deut. 13.1-5 lays down the penalty which a false prophet must pay and that penalty is death. It was in fact one of the duties of the Sanhedrin to test those who claimed to be prophets, and to deal with the false prophet. The Old Testament is full of the threat of the false prophet. There is the prophet in whose mouth there is a lying spirit (I Kings 22.22, 23); the prophet who teaches lies, and that in the name of God (Isa. 9.15; Jer. 14.14); the prophet who prophesies falsely (Jer. 5.31); the prophet and the priest who are ungodly (Jer. 23.11); the prophets of the deceit of their own hearts (Jer. 23.26); the prophets who see false and deceptive visions (Lam. 2.14); the prophets who see delusive visions and give lying divinations (Ezek. 13.9); the prophets who lead God's people astray (Micah 3.5); the prophets who are wanton and faithless (Zeph. 3.4). The very fact that the prophets possessed such influence made the false prophets a very serious danger in the life of the community. But let us piece together the description of the true prophet as we find it in the Old Testament.

(i) The prophet is a man *sent by God*. The Lord sent a

prophet to the children of Israel (Judg. 6.8; II Kings 24.19). Jeremiah is ordained by God the prophet to the nations (Jer. 1.5; 26.5). The prophet is not a man who has chosen his task, but who is chosen for it. Often the prophet realised his own utter inadequacy for the task, but he also knew that there was no escape from it.

(ii) The prophet is a man *spoken to by God*. Again and again in every prophet we read that the word of the Lord came to the prophet (Isa. 38.4; Jer. 18.1; Ezek. 20.2; Hos. 1.1; Joel 1.1; Micah 1.1; Zeph. 1.1; Hag. 1.1). The characteristic phrase of the prophet is: 'Thus says the Lord.' The prophet is not venturing to express an opinion; he is not even witnessing to his own conviction; he is nothing less than the mouthpiece and the messenger of God.

(iii) The prophet is, therefore, a man who *belongs to God*. 'Touch not my anointed ones,' says God, 'do my prophets no harm' (I Chron. 16.22; Ps. 105.15). The prophet is in a peculiar sense the property of God. He is possessed by God in a double sense of the term. He is possessed by the Spirit of God, and he is the possession of God. His life is not his own; he belongs to God.

(iv) The prophet is not only a man to whom God speaks, he is the man *through whom God speaks*. God speaks through his servants the prophets (II Kings 21.10). The Lord spoke by Jeremiah the prophet (Jer. 50.1). Daniel speaks of the prophets who spoke in the name of God (Dan. 9.6). 'I have spoken through the prophets, God said to Hosea (Hos. 12.10). The word of God comes by the prophet (Hag. 2.1). 'The Lord,' says Zechariah, 'cried by his former prophets' (Zech. 7.7, AV).

This is not to say that the prophet has no more to do with the message than an instrument has to do with the music it produces or a typewriter with the material it writes. There is nothing mechanical in this. The whole matter moves in the

world of persons and is the outcome of a personal relationship between the prophet and God. The prophet fits himself
through God's grace and guidance to be the messenger of
God; he accepts the message of God; he interprets it and
passes it through his own mind; he must have courage and
winsomeness to deliver it in a way that is challenging and
effective. Certainly God speaks through the prophet, but the
prophet must be such that God can speak through him.

(v) The prophet is pre-eminently *the servant of God*.
This is the commonest title of all for the prophet (I Kings
14.18; II Kings 9.7; 24.2; Jer. 26.5; 29.19). He therefore
takes his orders from no one but God and is answerable to no
one other than God. It could be said of the prophet as it
was said of John Knox: 'He feared God so much that he never
feared the face of man.'

(vi) The prophet is the man who has been *given a vision
by God*. We read of the vision of Isaiah the prophet
(II Chron. 32.32). Isaiah 6 tells us of such a vision. We read
of the prophets who obtain no vision from the Lord
(Lam. 2.9). It is the vision of God which gives the prophet
his plan for the new world.

Next, we must look at the function of the prophet, for in
the Old Testament there are certain things which the prophet
is characteristically said to do.

(i) The prophet *brings God's commandments to men*.
We read of the commandments of the Lord by his prophets
(II Chron. 29.25). It is not advice which the prophet brings;
it is commands.

(ii) The prophet is the man who is *in the confidence of
God*. 'Surely,' said Amos, 'the Lord does nothing without
revealing his secret to his servants the prophets' (Amos 3.7).
This is not to say that the prophet is able to predict everything
to the day and the hour and the month and the year. What it
is to say is that the prophet has *the insight to see where any*

course of action is going. Percy Gardner writes in *The Ephesian Gospel:* 'Through all history the prophets who have tried to detail future history have failed; but the great ones among them, who have seen into the heart of things and declared in what direction they were moving, have succeeded.' The prophet is the man who sees the end of every road in its beginning, because he sees things with the eyes of God. He sees whether any course of action is moving to blessedness or to disaster, because he knows whether or not it is in accordance with the will of God.

(iii) The prophet is the man who *testifies against sin.* The disobedient people slew the prophets who testified against them (Neh. 9.26). It was in his forbearance that God testified against the people through his Spirit in his prophets to make them turn back from their self-chosen disasters (Neh. 9.30). The prophet is the witness of God.

(iv) But in spite of that the prophet is the man whose supreme function is *to turn men back to God.* His aim is not to scarify their souls, not to achieve their total condemnation; his aim is not their destruction and their obliteration; his aim is their return to God (Neh. 9.26). God sent his prophets to bring the people back again to the Lord (II Chron. 24.19). 'Turn now every one of you from his evil way,' is the summons of Jeremiah (Jer. 35.15). Daniel speaks of the laws which God set before us by his servants the prophets (Dan. 9.10). The prophet is not essentially a messenger of doom; he is essentially the reclaimer and the recaller of men. In order to reclaim he may have to threaten with disaster; but his one aim is to recall men to a penitence and to a new way of life through which the disaster will be averted and the doom escaped.

Before we leave the prophets, we must note two of the methods which they particularly used.

(i) Of course, the prophets were primarily preachers, and

they were masters of eloquence, of oratory and of poetry. But there were times when words were useless, when the spoken word would not penetrate the refusal of men to listen and to understand. It was then that the prophets resorted to symbolic, dramatic action in the assurance that eye-gate could be opened when ear-gate was closed, and as if to say: 'If you will not listen, you must see.' When Ahijah wished to say vividly that ten of the tribes were going to revolt to Jeroboam and that only two were going to remain faithful to Rehoboam, he did so by taking his robe and tearing it into twelve pieces, and by handing ten of the pieces to Jeroboam and keeping two (I Kings 11.26-35). When Jeremiah wished to demonstrate his certainty that Nebuchadnezzar would conquer Israel, he did so by wearing a yoke, and by sending yokes to the kings who were under threat (Jer. 27.1-11); and when Hananiah wished to show that in his opinion Jeremiah's message was false he did so by breaking the yokes (Jer. 28.10, 11). Ezekiel was a master of the symbolic action (Ezek. 4 and 5). This was something which Jesus also used, for the Last Supper was a dramatic action, with its symbolism of the bread and wine, of what Jesus had come to do for men, and of the cost of it.

(ii) The other great prophetic method was the use of the parable. Isaiah told the parable of the vineyard (Isa. 5.1-7), and Nathan told the parable of the one ewe-lamb to bring David suddenly to his senses (II Sam. 12.1-6). In his use of parables Jesus was within the prophetic tradition.

To all this there remains one thing to add: *the prophets were characteristically martyrs*. Jezebel slew the prophets (I Kings 18.13; II Kings 9.7). It happened again and again, as Jeremiah said that 'your own sword has devoured your own prophets' (Jer. 2.30). The prophet was the man who was always ready to lay down his life for the truth, and to seal his message with the scarlet seal of his own blood.

It is easy to see how aptly the title Prophet fits Jesus. Jesus came forth from God. He was sent into the world because God loved the world (John 3.16). He came with a message from God; not only did he bring a word, he was the Word. He came with the supreme and complete revelation. God had spoken in many and various ways, but in Jesus he spoke in one who was a Son, and in whom the revelation was no longer fragmentary and temporary but complete and eternal (Heb. 1.1). Jesus was supremely the Servant of God. It was his meat and drink to do the will of his Father (John 4.34). It was in obedience that he came and it was in obedience that he went to the Cross. Jesus brought the commandments of God to men; he was God's witness against the sin of man. And above all it was his great aim and task to persuade men to return to God. He even used the prophetic methods of symbolic action and of parable to press home his message upon the dull, closed minds of men. There is nothing which the prophets were or did which is not perfected and completed in Jesus Christ.

And yet it remains true that the title prophet is not a full and complete description of Jesus Christ. He was not only in the line and in the succession of the prophets; he was also the One to whom all the prophets pointed and of whom all the prophets spoke. He was at one and the same time the crown and the peak of the prophetic succession and the One to tell of whom the whole prophetic succession came into being and existed.

It is right to call Jesus prophet, but it would be wrong to call him only a prophet, or even to call him The Prophet. It may be that prophet is the highest human term by which he can be described, but the fact is that no human term adequately describes him. He was a prophet and more than a prophet, for, while there are many prophets, there is only one Christ.

13

KING

JESU, *rex admirabilis*, began the prayer of Bernard of Clairvaux, or, as the hymn translates it: 'O Jesus, King most wonderful.' There is a sense in which the interpretation of Jesus as king comes most inevitably of all to the mind and the heart and the lips. Theology has often thought of Jesus in terms of the three great offices—Prophet, Priest and King. Jesus came to earth to be the complete revelation of God to men, and in the Old Testament there is no commoner title for God than king. 'The Lord is king for ever and ever,' says the Psalmist (Ps. 10.16). He is the king of glory (Ps. 24.7-10). He is the king of all the earth (Ps. 47.7). 'The Holy One of Israel is our king,' comes very near to being a one sentence statement of the faith of Israel (Ps. 89.18). 'My king and my God' is the instinctive language of love and devotion (Ps. 84.3).

When we come to the New Testament there is a certain inevitability about this title. The centre of Jesus' message was the kingdom, and how can there be a kingdom without a king? It is significant that in certain of the greatest parables the relationship involved is that of subject and king. It is so in the parable of the marriage feast (Matt. 22.2); in the parable of the unforgiving servant (Matt. 18.23); and in the parable of the great judgment (Matt. 25.34). In these parables there is implicit Jesus' own relationship with men.

In the gospel story Jesus is set forth as king very specially at the beginning and at the end. The Magi come with the question: 'Where is he who has been born king of the Jews?' (Matt. 2.2). The message to Mary about the son she will bear is: 'The Lord will give to him the throne of his father

240

David, and he will reign over the house of Jacob for ever'
(Luke 1.32,33).

But it is at the end of the story that again and again Jesus
is presented as king. When he entered Jerusalem for the last
time, men saw in that entry the fulfilment of the ancient
prophecy of Zechariah: 'Behold, your king is coming' (Zech.
9.9; Matt. 21.5; John 12.15). It was then that the crowds
greeted him with the shout: 'Blessed be the king who comes
in the name of the Lord' (Ps. 118.26; Luke 19.38; John
12.13). It was on the charge that he claimed to be king that
the Jews brought Jesus before Pilate. 'We found this man
perverting our nation,' they said, 'and forbidding us to give
tribute to Caesar, and saying that he himself is Christ, a king'
(Luke 23.2). 'If you release this man,' they said to Pilate,
'you are not Caesar's friend. Everyone who makes himself a
king sets himself against Caesar' (John 19.12). It was a
charge which in the days to come the Jews were to use against
the followers of Jesus, for in Thessalonica their charge
against Paul and his friends was: 'They are all acting against
the decrees of Caesar, saying that there is another king,
Jesus' (Acts 17.7). Pilate's first question to Jesus was: 'Are
you the king of the Jews?' And Jesus answered: 'You have
said so' (Matt. 27.11; Mark 15.2; Luke 23.13; cp. John 18.23).
Jesus' answer is very revealing. It is the answer to a question
which does not admit of an unconditional yes or no. 'You
say so.' The implication is that the man who gives it will not
deny it, but that he himself might have expressed the matter
differently, or might have given his own interpretation of its
meaning. As A. H. McNeile puts it,[1] it is as if Jesus said that
it was verbally correct to call him a king, but that at the
same time neither Pilate nor the Jews had even begun to
understand what that kingship meant.

When Jesus was handed over to the soldiers part of their

[1] In his *Gospel according to St Matthew*.

mocking horseplay was to dress him in a parody and carica-
ture of a royal robe and to say to him: 'Hail, king of the
Jews!' (Matt. 27.29; Mark 15.18; Luke 23.27; John 19.3).
When a condemned criminal was led out to be crucified, he
was set in the midst of a hollow square of four Roman
soldiers, and another soldier walked in front with a placard
on which was written the charge on which the criminal was
to be executed, and the placard was later attached to the
cross. In the case of Jesus the inscription on the placard read:
'This is Jesus, the king of the Jews' (Matt. 27.37; Mark 15.26;
Luke 23.38; John 19.19).

It was with this title that Pilate mockingly presented Jesus
to the mob. He offered them their choice between Barabbas
and Jesus. 'Do you want me,' he asked them, 'to release for
you the king of the Jews?' (Mark 15.9,12; John 18.39).
'Here is your king,' he said to the people. 'Shall I crucify
your king?' (John 19.14,15).

When Jesus was on his Cross it was as a broken and dis-
credited king that the crowd jeered at him. 'He is the king of
the Jews,' they said. 'Let him come down from the cross and
we will believe on him' (Matt. 27.42; Mark 15.32). It is
extraordinary how the king-motif runs through these last
hours.

But if there were those on whose lips the word king was a
jest and a mockery, there were also those on whose lips it was
a confession of faith. Nathanael, for all his unwillingness to
believe, when he was confronted with Jesus, was compelled to
say: 'Rabbi, you are the Son of God! You are the king of
Israel!' (John 1.49). When his ministry was reaching its
climax, James and John came with the request that they
might occupy the principal places when he came into his
kingdom (Matt. 20.21). And even on the Cross the cry of the
penitent thief was: 'Jesus, remember me when you come in
your kingdom' Luke 23.42). And the day was to come when

the confession of the Church was that Jesus is King of kings and Lord of lords (Rev. 17.14; 19.16).

We may say three things about Jesus and the idea of kingship.

(i) There is a very real sense in which the idea of kingship was a temptation to Jesus. Jesus well knew that the Messiah for whom men were waiting was to be a warrior prince and king, who would smash his enemies and the enemies of Israel and who would mount the throne of power. It was precisely with that temptation that the tempter faced Jesus when he offered him all the kingdoms of the world, if he would enter into a compromise with him (Matt. 3.8-10; Luke 3.5-8). The temptation returned when, after the feeding of the five thousand, there were those who wished to take him and make him a king whether he liked it or not (John 6.15). There is no doubt that Jesus was tempted to be the kind of king for whom the nation was waiting.

(ii) It is in John's story of Jesus' encounter with Pilate that we see Jesus laying down the 'differentness' of his kingdom. Whether or not the words are the *ipsissima verba* of Jesus they certainly represent his mind. 'My kingship is not of this world,' Jesus said. 'If my kingship were of this world, my servants would fight that I might not be handed over to the Jews, but my kingship is not from the world' (John 18.36). The kingship of Jesus was based on the royalty of sacrificial love and on nothing else. The only throne he could ever occupy was a throne in men's hearts.

> I saw the conquerors riding by,
>   With cruel lips and faces wan;
> Musing on kingdom sacked and burned,
>   There rode the Mongol, Genghis Khan.
>
> And Alexander, like a god,
>   Who sought to weld the world in one,
> And Caesar with his laurel wreath,
>   And like a thing from hell, the Hun.

And leading like a star the van,
  Heedless of outstretched arm and groan,
Inscrutable Napoleon went,
  Dreaming of empire and alone.

Then all they perished from the earth,
  As fleeting shadows from a glass,
And conquering down the centuries
  Came Christ the swordless on an ass.

Jesus was the swordless king. He knew the temptation to found
his kingdom on power; but his kingdom is immortal for the
very reason that he founded it on love. The crowds shouted:
'Come down from the cross and we will believe on you.' General
Booth commented: 'It is precisely because he did *not* come
down that we believe on him.' It is the fact that he died for us
and for all mankind that gives Jesus his place within our hearts.

(iii) One thing remains to say, and in the last analysis
it is the most important thing of all. For Jesus the real and
only king is God, and it is to God that the kingdom belongs.
'Thy kingdom,' Jesus taught men to pray, not, 'My kingdom
come' (Matt. 6.10). We well know that the ascription of
praise at the end of the Lord's prayer, 'Thine is the kingdom
and the power and the glory' (Matt. 6.13), is not part of the
original text, but for all that it is quite certainly a correct
interpretation of the mind of Jesus. Paul knew the mind of
Christ when he spoke of Christ subduing all things and then
delivering the kingdom to God (I Cor. 15.24). Jesus was
never the rival to God, but always the servant of God. Though
it was his task to announce the kingdom, in the end the
kingdom is the kingdom of God. It was the one aim of Jesus
to persuade men to respond to the love of God, incarnate in
himself, and to enthrone God as king within their hearts and
over all the earth.

14

THE STONE

THERE is no doubt that in the early Church 'the Stone' became one of the titles of Jesus. In the *Dialogue with Trypho* ch. 34 Justin Martyr undertakes to prove from the Scriptures that Christ is 'King and Priest and God and Lord and Angel and Man and Captain and Stone.' 'It was foretold,' he says in the same work, 'that Christ would suffer and be called a Stone' (ch. 36). This may seem a strange way in which to describe Jesus, but in the New Testament there is a whole series of passages in which the idea occurs.

In the parable of the wicked husbandmen Jesus told how the husbandmen wounded and maltreated the servants whom the master sent to them, and how in the end they killed the master's son. In this parable Jesus is clearly foretelling what he knew would happen to himself, and the end of the parable is the destruction of the evildoers. The parable then ends with the saying of Jesus that all this would be a fulfilment of the prophecy: 'The very stone which the builders rejected has become the head of the corner; this was the Lord's doing and it is marvellous in our eyes' (Mark 12.10,11; Matt. 21.42). It is clear that Jesus was taking that quotation from the Old Testament and was applying it to himself.

In one of his sermons in Acts Peter takes this same text and applies it to Jesus. He tells the Jews that they crucified Jesus and that God raised him from the dead, and then he goes on to say: 'This is the stone which was rejected by you builders, but which has become the head of the corner' (Acts 4.11).

Luke in his version of the Parable of the Wicked Husbandmen adds still another Old Testament text. He tells the same parable, makes the same quotation about the rejected and honoured stone, and then adds: 'Everyone who falls on that stone will be broken to pieces; but when it falls on anyone it will crush him' (Luke 20.17,18). It may be that Luke has the same Old Testament passage in mind when he tells how, when the aged Simeon saw the infant Jesus in the Temple, he said: 'Behold, this child is set for the fall and the rising of many in Israel' (Luke 2.34).

Paul makes use of the same picture. When he is writing of the tragic Jewish rejection of Jesus, he says: 'They have stumbled over the stumblingstone, as it is written, Behold, I am laying in Zion a stone that will make men stumble, a rock that will make them fall; and he who believes in him will not be put to shame' (Rom. 9.32,33). In Ephesians also Paul uses the stone idea in a different way. He is speaking about the new status of his converts: 'So then you are no longer strangers and sojourners, but you are fellow-citizens with the saints and members of the household of God, built upon the foundation of the apostles and prophets, Christ Jesus himself being the chief cornerstone' (Eph. 2.20).

The idea occurs in First Peter where all the stone pictures are, as it were, assembled into one. 'It stands in scripture,' Peter writes, 'Behold, I am laying in Zion a stone, a corner-stone chosen and precious, and he who believes in him will not be put to shame. To you, therefore, who believe, he is precious, but for those who do not believe, the very stone which the builders rejected has become the head of the corner, and a stone that will make men stumble, a rock that will make them fall' (I Peter 2.6-8).

The idea of Jesus as the stone is spread all over the New Testament and has become an integral part of the picture of Jesus and of the material of early preaching. All these stone references go back to the Old Testament, and we must now turn to the Old Testament passages from which they come. There are four Old Testament passages involved.

(i) There is Ps. 118.22: 'The stone which the builders has rejected has become the head stone of the corner.' This is the simplest passage. The Jews themselves applied it to Abraham and to David and even to the Messiah. But the main reference is clearly to the nation of Israel. Israel was small and despised; it was subject to power after power; it was treated with hatred and contempt; and yet the Jews were completely confident that some day God would give his people the position in the world which, as they saw it, the covenant nation was bound to enjoy. The stone, that is, Israel, which the builders rejected, that is, which the nations despised, would become the head stone of the corner, that is, would occupy the place of greatest honour. This is the prophecy of the ultimate honour of the nation which the world despised.

(ii) There is Isa. 8.14: 'He [that is, the Lord of hosts] will become a sanctuary, and a stone of offence, and a rock of stumbling to both houses of Israel, a trap and a snare to the inhabitants of Jerusalem.' This is a very difficult saying, for it seems to say two quite contradictory things. It seems to say, first, that God will be a sanctuary, and, second, that God will be a stumbling-stone. How can these things both be true? Sir George Adam Smith explains it in this way. Suppose a man to be fleeing in trouble and in terror across the country, and suppose him to come to an altar of God. If he is a man who believes in God, and who loves God, and who trusts God, then that altar for him will be a sanctuary where he meets God and finds the presence of God. But, if he is an unbeliever, who has neither use nor time for God, then the altar is simply a heap of stones over which he may stumble, and nothing better than a barrier and a hindrance in his way. God is a precious possession to those who love him and a nuisance to those who have no use for him.

(iii)   There is Isa. 28.16: 'Therefore, thus says the Lord, Behold I am laying in Zion for a foundation a stone, a tested stone, a precious cornerstone, of a sure foundation.' This comes from a passage which speaks of people who have made lies their refuge and who have taken falsehood as their shelter (Isa. 28.15). It means that those who have disbelieved and disobeyed, and who have turned their backs on God, are seeking their shelter and their foundation in things which are false and futile, but God is offering to those who believe in him and trust him a sure foundation for their lives.

(iv)   There is the passage in Dan. 2.31-35. This strange passage tells of Nebuchadnezzar's dream. In it he sees a great, marvellous, composite image. It has legs of iron, and feet partly of iron and partly of clay. Then there comes a stone, 'cut by no human hands', and the stone smites the great image and smashes it to pieces. Then 'the stone that struck the image became a great mountain and filled the whole earth.' The symbolism is that the day is coming when God will set up his kingdom, which will destroy the greatest kingdoms of the earth, and which itself will cover the whole world, and will never be destroyed. Here the stone stands for the power of God invading the world and conquering until God's last enemy is destroyed.

Here then in the Old Testament we have four stone ideas. There is the idea of the stone first rejected and then honoured, the idea of the stone which can either be a sanctuary or a hindrance, the idea of the stone which is the sure foundation, and the idea of the stone which invades the earth, destroys the enemies of God and finally fills the world. Let us then take these four ideas and see how they apply to Jesus.

(i)   Jesus is pictured as the stone which the builders rejected and which has become the head stone of the corner (Ps. 118.22). There are two ideas here.

(a)   There is the conviction that Jesus might be reviled

and insulted, rejected and crucified, but that in spite of that the ultimate victory and glory belong to him. There is in Jesus what can only be called an indestructible quality. During his lifetime on earth and all through history there have been those who have been trying to eliminate him, but still he stands supreme. It is significant that, if we trust the New Testament records at all, Jesus never prophesied his own rejection and death without at the same time prophesying his resurrection and his triumph. The bleakest forecasts of the future always end with the confidence that he will rise again on the third day (Mark 8.31; 9.31; 10.33; Matt. 17.22,23). Jesus always regarded himself as victor and victim in one.

The most famous attempt to wipe out Christ and Christianity was made by the Roman Emperor Julian, known as the Apostate. Constantine had made Christianity the religion of the Empire, but Julian was determined to put the clock back and to bring back the ancient gods. He tried to annihilate the Christian Church. During that time a pagan asked a Christian what the Galilaean carpenter was doing now. Back came the answer: 'Making a coffin for your Emperor.'[1] In his campaigns Julian was fighting in far-off Persia, and he received a fatal wound. Men told how he took a handful of his own blood as it ebbed away, and flung it into the air, as if he was flinging it in the face of Christ, and said, as if acknowledging defeat: 'Thou hast conquered, O Galilaean.'[2] As Ibsen made him say in his play: 'To shoulder Christ from out the topmost niche of fame was not for me.' The rejected Christ had triumphed. The saying that the rejected one has become the honoured one has been historically true.

(b) Jesus is called 'the head stone of the corner', and in the Ephesians passage, 'the chief cornerstone'. This may

---

[1] Sozomen, *Ecclesiastical History* 6.2.9; Theodoret, *Ecclesiastical History* 3.23 (18).
[2] Sozomen, *Eccl. Hist.* 6.2.10–12; Theodoret, *Eccl. Hist.* 3.25 (20).7.

mean either of two things. It may refer to the centre stone
of the arch, the keystone on which the arch depends. Or, it
may mean the cornerstone which literally holds the building
and the foundation together, and on which the weight of the
whole edifice rests. Whatever be the precise meaning, the
significance is that, if the centre stone of the arch or the
cornerstone of the building is removed, the whole building
will disintegrate and collapse. So it is Jesus Christ and Jesus
Christ alone who holds the Church together. Peter likens the
Church to a spiritual house built up of the living stones of all
its members (I Peter 2.5); and the foundation of the whole is
Christ. Creeds may divide; forms of ecclesiastical government
may keep men apart; the Church can only be united in Jesus
Christ. We do well to remember that the Church is not built on
bishops or presbyters or on anything or anyone else. It is built
on Christ and can only hold together when it is founded and
united in him.

(ii) Jesus is pictured as the stone which is at once a
sanctuary, and the rock over which men stumble, or which
crushes them (Isa. 8.14). We have seen that the picture
comes from the fact that a holy altar can be a blessed refuge
or a heap of stones standing in the way. How can this be true
of Jesus? The answer to this is found especially in the way in
which the Fourth Gospel thinks of Jesus Christ. God sent
Jesus Christ into this world in love and only for the redemption of men. Therefore, the most important thing in life
is a man's reaction to this Christ. If, when a man is confronted with Jesus, he feels in his heart the outrush of love,
then all is well. But if, when a man is confronted with Jesus,
he remains coldly indifferent or actively hostile, then he has
passed a judgment on himself. Jesus is the touchstone of God.
If in his presence a man feels the tug on his heart, the desire
to worship and adore, then, however inadequate his life may
be, he is still in the way of salvation. If in the presence of

Christ a man feels nothing or feels anger, then that man has judged himself. Confrontation with Christ is in itself judgment. That is why Jesus Christ can be the refuge of the heart or the stone over which a man stumbles to disaster. Jesus is in the nature of things Saviour and Judge, and as a man reacts to him, he is judged or saved.

(iii) Jesus is pictured as the tested stone, the precious stone, the stone which is the sure foundation (Isa. 28.16). The significance for this is that Jesus Christ is the only sure foundation for life. This is exactly the picture that Jesus worked out in the parable of the wise and foolish builders (Matt. 7.24-27; Luke 6.47-49). It means that we can and must take Jesus Christ at his word, and build life on that. Within a year of his death David Livingstone amidst his trials wrote in his diary: 'He will keep his word, the gracious one full of grace and truth—no doubt of it. He said, "Him that cometh unto me I will in no wise cast out," and, "Whatsoever ye shall ask in my name, I will do it." He *will* keep his word; then I can come and humbly present my petition. Doubt is here inadmissible surely.' To think of Jesus as this sure foundation is to think of him as the one person in the world on whom we can absolutely and without doubt depend to keep his word, and that, therefore, we can accept his commands, relying on his promises.

(iv) Jesus is pictured in terms of the stone which shattered the great image, which set up the kingdom of God, and which became a mountain which filled the earth (Dan. 2.31-35). Here the idea is that Jesus is the inbreak of God into the world, the invasion of time by eternity, the founder of the kingdom which will put an end to all other kingdoms and which itself will have no end. The meaning of this is that with the coming of Jesus something happened, and that that something will never cease happening. That something is the coming of the kingdom of God in which the will of God will be supreme and the purposes of God will be achieved. It means that with and in Jesus a seed has been planted whose growth nothing can stop, a dynamic has entered life which nothing can resist, power has come into the universe which in the end is undefeatable.

So in the end this strange idea of the Stone has become infinitely meaningful. Jesus is the one who was rejected, but to whom belongs the final glory. Jesus is the one who alone can hold the living body of the Church together in union. Jesus is the one who in confronting men presents men with a refuge or a stumbling-block, Saviour and Judge in one. Jesus is the one in whom the power of God entered the world, a power which will work unceasingly and undefeatably until the kingdoms of the world become the kingdom of God.

15

THE BRIDEGROOM

It may be said that the Bridegroom is one of Jesus' self-chosen titles for himself. The disciples of John the Baptist came to Jesus with a question about a matter which to them was a problem. It was their practice to fast, as it was the practice of the Pharisees to fast, and they wished to know why Jesus and his disciples did not do so. Jesus' answer was that the wedding-guests could not fast so long as the bridegroom was with them. But, he went on, the days would came when the bridgroom would be taken away, and then they would fast (Matt. 9.14, 15; Mark 2.18-20; Luke 5.33-35). There the reference is unmistakably to Jesus himself. We have the same implication in the parable of the wise and foolish virgins (Matt. 25.1-13). The fault of the foolish ones was that they were unprepared for the coming of the bridegroom, and their punishment was that they were shut out from his presence. There too the reference is to Jesus.

The same thought meets us in the picture of the Church as the Bride of Christ. The Revelation speaks of the Bride, the Lamb's wife, and the meaning is the Church, the community of the saints (Rev. 21.9). We read of the marriage of the Lamb, by which is meant the intimate and indissoluble union between Christ and his own, between Christ and the Church (Rev. 19.7).

Paul speaks of his aim for the church at Corinth: 'I feel a divine jealousy for you, for I betrothed you to Christ to present you as a pure bride to her one husband' (II Cor. 11.2). Behind this picture there is a Jewish marriage custom. Edersheim writes: 'In Judaea there were at every marriage two groomsmen or friends of the bridegroom, one for the bridegroom and the other for the bride. Before marriage, they acted as a kind of intermediaries between the couple; at the wedding they offered gifts, waited upon the bride and bridegroom, and attended them to the bridal chamber, being also, as it were, guarantors of the bride's virgin chastity.' Paul thought of himself as the intermediary for the marriage between the church at Corinth and Jesus Christ. He knew that his task was to present that church in virgin purity and fidelity to Jesus Christ the Bridegroom. In Eph. 5.22,23 Paul likens the marriage relationship to the relationship which must exist between Christ and the Church.

The idea of Jesus as the Bridegroom goes back to a whole circle of ideas which are part of Old Testament thought. In the Old Testament we frequently meet with the idea of the nation of Israel as the bride of God. God is the divine lover who has chosen Israel for himself. Hosea hears God say to Israel: 'I will betroth you to me for ever; I will betroth you to me in righteousness, in justice, in steadfast love' (Hos. 2.19,20). Isaiah says: 'Your Maker is your husband; the Lord of hosts is his name' (Isa. 54.5). 'As the bridegroom rejoices over the bride, so shall your God rejoice over you' (Isa. 62.5). Jeremiah hears the appeal of God to his people: 'Return, O faithless children, for I am your master (husband)' (Jer. 3.14).

It is from this thought that there come certain Old Testament pictures which are strange to us. This is why the nation of Israel may be said to go a-whoring after strange gods (RSV; play the harlot after strange gods) (Ex. 34.15; Deut. 31.16; Judg. 2.17; 8.27,33). When the nation of Israel was disobedient and unfaithful, when she flirted with the worship of other gods, when she gave her love and loyalty to the false gods, she was guilty of infidelity to the marriage bond which existed between her and Yahweh and which never ought to be broken.

This is why a heathen city, or an unfaithful Jewish city, can be called a harlot. When Nahum writes of Nineveh, he writes:

Woe to the bloody city,
all full of lies and booty—
. . . . . .
And all for the countless harlotries of the harlot,
    graceful and of deadly charms,
who betrays nations with her harlotries,
    and people with her charms.

(Nahum 3.1-4)

It is thus that Isaiah speaks of Tyre:

Take a harp,
    go about the city,
    O forgotten harlot!
. . . . . .

At the end of seventy years the Lord will visit Tyre, and she will return to her hire, and will play the harlot with all the kingdoms of the world upon the face of the earth (Isa. 23.16,17).

It is thus that Isaiah can mourn even over Jerusalem; 'How the faithful city has become a harlot!' (Isa. 1.21). The charge of Ezekiel is: 'You trusted in your beauty and played the harlot because of your renown, and lavished your harlotries on any passer-by' (Ezek. 16.15). Jeremiah makes the same charge: 'You have played the harlot with many lovers' (Jer. 3.1). Perhaps the passage in which the idea is most fully worked out is in Jer. 3.6-10:

The Lord said to me in the days of King Josiah: Have you seen what she did, that faithless one, Israel, how she went up on every high hill and under every green tree, and there played the harlot? And I thought: After she has done all this she will return to me; but she did not return, and her false sister Judah saw it. She saw that for all the adulteries of that faithless one, Israel, I had sent her away with a decree of divorce; yet her false sister Judah did not fear; but she too went and played the harlot. Because harlotry was so light to her, she polluted the land, committing adultery with stone and tree. Yet for all this her false sister Judah did not return to me with her whole heart, but in pretence, says the Lord.

The bond between Yahweh and Israel is like the marriage bond; to break it is to be guilty of infidelity, and to go and worship and serve another god is adultery.

It is this idea which is responsible for another New Testament phrase. More than once the generation to which Jesus spoke is called 'an evil and adulterous generation' (Matt. 12.39; 16.4; Mark 8.38; NEB 'wicked and godless''. The word 'adulterous' is not there to be taken in the sense of physical and fleshly sin, but in the sense of spiritual infidelity. The Jewish nation had been consistently unfaithful to God, and never more so than in her attitude to the Son of God, when he came.

There is in the Old Testament still another way of speaking which is closely associated with this whole circle of ideas. Not infrequently God is called 'a jealous God' (Ex. 20.5; 34.14; Deut. 4.25; 5.9; 6.15). It may be that to modern ears such a phrase sounds strange and even offensive, but behind it there is a very beautiful and lovely idea. The picture is that of God as the passionate lover of the souls of men. Love is always exclusive; no one can be totally in love with two people at the same time; no lover can bear to share his loved one with some one else. To say that God is a jealous God is to say that God is the lover of men, and that his heart can brook no rival, but that he must have the whole devotion of the hearts of the men who he loves so much.

To think of Jesus as the Bridegroom and to think of God as the lover of the souls of men sheds a flood of light upon the whole relationship between God and man. It means that the divine-human relationship is not that of king and subject, nor that of master and servant, nor that of owner and slave, nor that of judge and defendant, but that of lover and loved one, a relationship which can only be paralleled in the perfect marriage relationship between husband and wife. In any such relationship there are certain essentials.

(i) There can be no such relationship without *fidelity*. God will never be unfaithful to us, and we must never be unfaithful to God; for, if God is the lover and we are the loved ones, it means that sin is not a breach of the law but a crime against love. The sinner does not so much break God's law as he breaks God's heart.

(ii) There can be no such relationship without *intimacy*. All life must be a closer and closer communion and fellowship between us and God in Jesus Christ. There should be a oneness between us and Jesus Christ such as exists between husband and wife in a perfect marriage.

(iii) There can be no such relationship without perfect *trust*. We must trust the love of God in Christ as we trust the love of our nearest and dearest. We must be as sure of God as we are sure of those whose loyalty it would never cross our minds to doubt.

(iv) Such a relationship is of necessity *unbreakable and indissoluble*. The marriage ring, the circle which has no ending, speaks of the love which has no ending, and says in its sign and symbol that two people have taken each other for richer or for poorer, in sickness or in health, for better or for worse. And that must also be the symbol of the way in which the Christian has pledged himself to Jesus Christ who is the Bridegroom and the lover of the souls of men.

16

THE BREAD OF LIFE

In one sense the Bread of Life is one of the simplest titles of Jesus; it bears its meaning on its face. But at the same time it has roots which are very deep and implications which are very wide.

Jesus had fed the five thousand on the far side of the Sea of Galilee. He had then returned to Capernaum, and there he met the Jewish leaders. (John 6.1-14,24). The feeding of the five thousand had almost inevitably brought memories of the manna in the wilderness (6.31). It was Jesus' insistence that it was. not Moses, but God, who had given the people the manna (6.32). He then goes on to say that the true bread, the bread which gives life and defeats death, must come from God (6.32). Then there comes his great claim: 'I am the bread of life . . . I am the living bread which came down from heaven' (6.35,48,51). Here was a saying which the Jews bitterly resented; they thought that they knew who Jesus was, and they could not see how any one whom they regarded as a familiar person had the right to talk like that (6.42). Then Jesus went even further when he identified this bread of life with his own body and blood, which, he said, men must eat in order to enter into the life which in this world is life indeed, and which death cannot touch (6.52-58).

(i) We began by saying that this story has roots which go very far back. Any mention of bread from heaven would immediately turn the thoughts of a Jew to the manna which God gave them in their wilderness journeyings (Ex. 16.1-36). That story was deeply imprinted on the Jewish memory. In Nehemiah the manna is called bread from heaven (Neh. 9.15).

It is called by the same name in the Psalms (Ps. 105.40). In the Psalms it is also called *grain of heaven* and *the bread of angels* (Ps. 78.24,25). To the Jew there was something mysteriously divine about the manna, and for Jesus to claim to be the bread from heaven was in itself a claim to be divine.

(ii) The manna had other connections in Jewish thought. It was part of Jewish Messianic belief that, when the Messiah came, he would once again feed his people with the heavenly manna. It was the belief that in Solomon's temple there had been laid up the ark, with the tables of the ten commandments, the rod that budded, and a golden pot of the manna. It was said that, when the temple was destroyed, Jeremiah had hidden away the pot of manna, and that, when the Messiah came, he would produce it again, and the faithful would eat of it.

This belief appears in the New Testament itself, when in Rev. 2.17 it is promised to the faithful that they will be given the hidden manna to eat. It is common in the literature between the Testaments. In the Messianic age 'the treasury of manna shall again descend from on high' (II Baruch 29.8). Manna will be the food of the members of the Messianic community (*Sibylline Oracles* 7.149). It was rabbinic belief that whatever Moses had done the Messiah would repeat. Therefore, the Messiah will be a second Moses who will bring down the manna from heaven. 'You will not find manna in this age,' ran the rabbinic teaching, 'but you will find it in the age that is to come.' It is prepared for the righteous in the coming age, and those who are worthy will eat of it. Moses the first redeemer brought down the manna from heaven, and the Messiah the second redeemer will do so again.

Another belief belongs to the same circle of ideas. It was believed that in the Messianic age God would make a great banquet for the faithful, at which leviathan and behemoth would provide the fish and the meat. In the New Testament this belief in the Messianic banquet is echoed in the saying: 'Blessed is he who shall eat bread in the kingdom of God' (Luke 14.15).

From all this it becomes clear that for Jesus to say that he was the bread from heaven was to say that he was the Messiah, and that with him the Messianic age had begun. To the Jews that claim was clear, and it was precisely that claim that roused their anger.

(iii) But there is a still greater claim here. There is in the passage the stressing of the fact that the giver of the manna was not Moses but God (John 6.32). It was a standard part of Jewish belief that the manna was given because of the transcendent merits of Moses, and that, therefore, with his death it ceased. This Jesus denied, and insisted that the giver of the manna was no human person, *but God*. If then Jesus went on to insist that it is he who gives, and is, the living bread, then this is a claim to be nothing less than divine. He is claiming in some sense to be God, or at least to be doing what only God can do.

(iv) The qualities of the manna were even more wonderful. The manna was said to be angels' food, distilled from the upper light, 'the dew from above'. It was said to answer to every taste and to every age. It varied in itself according to the need and wish and condition of the eater. Whatever the eater needed, that the manna was. Here then is the claim of Jesus that, whatever be the need of any man, he can satisfy it.

(v) The Jews made still another identification. In Prov. 9.5 it is Wisdom's invitation: 'Come, eat of my bread, and drink of the wine I have mixed.' Here again is a reference to bread from heaven; and so in Jewish exegesis the bread from heaven was identified with the heavenly Wisdom which is from above. If then Jesus claimed to be the bread from heaven, he was claiming to be the perfect Wisdom, which alone could teach men how to live.

(vi) Bread is the staff of life, that which enables life to go on. The bread of life is the bread which gives life, and Jesus claims that that life is a life which can defeat even death. It is Jesus' claim that he is able to give life in this world and life in the world to come.

(vii) There follow the startling words of Jesus about eating his flesh (6.51-58). Without doubt this is a reference to the words of the sacrament—This is my body broken for you. The teaching of John is that this new life, which is sufficient for this life and for the life to come, enters into a man with the elements of the bread and wine at the sacrament of the Lord's Supper. It is John's belief that at the Lord's Table the Christian receives what Ignatius called 'the medicines of salvation', the heavenly food which is sufficient for victorious living and victorious dying.

Whatever be our view of the sacraments, the meaning of this is that the Christian must take Jesus Christ into his inmost being, that he must enter into us as does the food we eat and drink. There may well be something here which is as old as the most primitive religion, and yet as full of mystery as God himself. The most ancient of all religious ceremonies is a meal in a sacred place at which part of the meat which has been sacrificed is eaten by the circle of the worshippers. At such a feast the god himself was believed to be a guest. More, the god was thought of as entering into the worshipper in all his divine life and strength with the meat of the sacrifice. One thing is certain, John is sure that we can never know what life is until Jesus Christ enters into us. Matthew Arnold wrote his famous poem about meeting a preacher in the worst London slum:

> 'Twas August, and the fierce sun overhead
> Smote on the squalid streets of Bethnal Green,
> And the pale weaver, through his windows seen
> In Spitalfields, look'd thrice dispirited.
> I met a preacher there I knew, and said:

'Ill and o'erwork'd, how fare you in this scene?'
'Bravely!' said he: 'for I of late have been
Much cheered with thoughts of Christ, the living bread.'

I am the bread of life—here is at the same time one of the
greatest claims and one of the greatest offers of Jesus Christ.

17

THE LIGHT OF THE WORLD

REPEATEDLY in the Fourth Gospel Jesus speaks of himself, and is spoken of, as the light. 'I am the light of the world,' Jesus said, 'he who follows me will not walk in darkness, but will have the light of life' (John 8.12). 'As long as I am in the world, I am the light of the world' (9.5). 'I have come as light into the world, that whoever believes in me may not remain in darkness' (12.46). Repeatedly in the Prologue to the Gospel Jesus is thought of in terms of light. 'In him was life, and the life was the light of men. The light shines in the darkness, and the darkness has not overcome it' (1.4,5). John the Baptist was not himself the light, but came to bear witness to that light. 'The true light that enlightens every man was coming into the world' (1.7-9).

To describe Jesus in terms of light is to speak in a religious language which is universal. It may well be true to say that light was the first thing which men ever worshipped, for in the most primitive of all religions the sun is often the first of all the gods. For all men the light is something to love and the darkness is something to fear. But in the days of the Fourth Gospel the conception of Jesus as the light was specially relevant, for it grew out of, and appealed to, both the background from which the gospel sprang, and at which it was aimed.

(i) The conception of Jesus as the light of the world has roots in the Old Testament. The Psalmist sings: 'The Lord is my light and my salvation' (Ps. 27.1). In the last time

> The sun shall be no more
>   your light by day,

263

> nor for brightness shall the moon
> give light to you by night;
> but the Lord will be your everlasting light.
>
> (Isa. 60.19)

Religion is thought of in terms of light, for it is the divine function of Israel to be a light to the Gentiles (Isa. 42.6; 49.6). Isa. 60.1 reads: 'Arise, shine; for your light is come,' and from that verse the rabbis drew the conclusion that 'Light is the name of the Messiah'. Jewish thought closely connected God and light, though it never identified the two.

(ii) The connection between light and God was, if possible, even closer in the pagan world. Persian religion, Zoroastrianism, was founded on the belief that the whole universe is the scene of the struggle between the power of the light and the power of the dark, a struggle in which man must choose his side.

Graeco-Roman mysticism identified light and God. This is specially clear in the Hermetic literature of which a full account is given in C. H. Dodd's *The Bible and the Greeks*. That primal light which is God is there even before 'the horrible and sullen darkness' which is chaos. 'I your God am that light.' God is characteristically 'life and light', and the Logos, the Word, is the voice of light. In the act of creation, 'Mind, the father of all, being life and light, generated a man equal to himself, whom he loved as his own child.' This man became 'from life and light, soul and mind; from life soul, from light mind.' There are therefore in the world two ways, the way of light and the way of darkness, the way of life and the way of death. The one way is light (*phōs*), knowledge (*gnōsis*), truth (*alētheia*), sobriety (*nēpsis*), salvation (*sōtēria*); the other way is darkness (*skotos*), ignorance (*agnōsia*), error (*planē*), drunkenness (*methē*), and destruction (*phthora*). So life has its duty: 'The God and Father of whom man came is life and light. If, therefore, you learn that you are life and light, and believe that you are these, you will move into life again.' The same line of thought is in Philo with the difference that Philo was too good a Jew to make the complete identification of light and God. Commenting on Ps. 27.1, 'The Lord is my light and my salvation,' Philo (*On Dreams* 1.75) writes: 'First, God is light; for in the Psalms it says, "God is my illumination (the word is *phōtismos*, not *phōs*) and my Saviour." And not only light, but the archetype of every other light; or, rather, older and higher than any archetype; for it says: "God said, Let there be light", and he is himself like no created thing.' It is clear that Greek mysticism knew all about the connection of, and even the identification of, God and light.

(iii) It may be even more relevant to remember that the thought of the Dead Sea Scrolls from the Qumran community frequently moves in the same circle of ideas. The title of one of them is *The War of the Sons of Light and the Sons of Darkness*. He who undertakes to enter the community must pledge himself 'to love all the children of light . . . and to hate all the children of darkness.' If a man is false to his pledge and taints himself with idolatry, 'God shall set him apart for misfortune, and he shall be cut off from the midst of all the children of light in that through the taint of his idolatry and through the stumbling-block of his iniquity he has defected from God.' There is a Spirit of light and a Spirit of darkness. 'The origin of truth lies in the Fountain of Light, and that of perversity in the Wellspring of Darkness. All who practise righteousness are under the domination of the Prince of Lights, and walk in the ways of light; whereas all who practise perversity are under the domination of the Angel of Darkness and walk in the ways of darkness.' The Spirit of Darkness is ever seeking to make the sons of light stumble. 'All the spirits that attend upon him are bent on causing the sons of light to stumble. Howbeit the God of Israel and the

Angel of his truth are always there to help the sons of light."[1]

It is almost impossible to turn to any background of the New Testament in which the dualism of light and darkness does not appear, and in which God and the Light are not intimately connected.

So, then, with all this as a background, Jesus said: 'I am the light of the world' (John 8.12). The occasion of this saying in its Johannine setting makes it all the more vivid. Jesus had come to Jerusalem for the Feast of Tabernacles (John 7.2,10), and when he said these words he was in the part of the Temple known as the Treasury because the collecting boxes for the pilgrims' offerings stood there. The Treasury was part of the Court of the Women, and at the close of the first day of the Feast of Tabernacles a most dramatic ceremony took place within that court. Four great candelabra, each with four great golden bowls, were prepared. When evening came the people flocked to the Court of the Women until it was crowded to capacity. Then, when the darkness had come down, four high-born youths of priestly lineage at a given signal lit the great candelabra, and suddenly the darkness was pierced with such a light that it was said to illuminate every street and court and square in the city of Jerusalem. It was in that very court at that very time that Jesus claimed to be the light of the world. That Jewish ceremony of lighting the candelabra had certain connections.

(i) The Feast of Tabernacles in its historical reference commemorated the journeyings through the wilderness of the people of Israel. It was called the Feast of Tabernacles because throughout its seven days the people lived in little booths or 'tabernacles' made of branches in order to remind themselves of the days when they had no houses and when they lived in tents in the wilderness. During that time they

---

[1] These quotations are from *The Manual of Discipline* and are taken from T. H. Gaster, *The Scriptures of the Dead Sea Sect*.

had been guided by the pillar of cloud by day and the pillar of fire by night (Ex. 13.21); and the blaze of the Temple candelabra piercing the dark was to remind them of the light which had guided them in their nation's pilgrim days.

(ii) One of the great conceptions of the Jews was the conception of the Shekinah. The Shekinah was the glory of God, and at certain times it was thought to become visible in the form of a luminous, glowing, radiant cloud. That luminous cloud rested on the Tabernacle (Num. 9.15-22), and on Solomon's Temple on the day of its dedication (I Kings 8.10,11; II Chron. 5.13,14). And the light which blazed from the Temple court at the Feast of Tabernacles was to remind them of the glory of God, dwelling among them.

(iii) One other thing must have been in the mind of the people as the light blazed through the darkness. The prophet had said: 'The people who walked in darkness have seen a great light; they that dwelt in a land of deep darkness, on them has light shined' (Isa. 9.2). The light must have reminded the people of the light of God illuminating the darkness of the world.

Jesus could not possibly have chosen a more dramatic place and a more dramatic moment to make his great claim that he was the light of the world. It is a tremendous claim, for it involves the claim that he was the Messiah, the claim that he was the divine guide of God, the claim that in him the glory of God's light had come to earth, the claim that in him the glory and the splendour of God's light was piercing the shadows and the darkness of earth.

There are certain significances in this claim of Jesus.

(i) *Light is the most revealing thing in the world.* Jesus is the great revealer of men and things as they are. That is why those whose deeds are evil fear the light and hate Jesus (John 3.19-21). Before penitence can be awakened and the desire of goodness be born, the horror and ugliness of sin

must be revealed in the light of Jesus Christ, however bitter
and humiliating that revelation may be.

(ii) *Light is the greatest guide in the world.* If a man
has the light he sees the way and does not stumble. Jesus is
the light in which men see the way to God (John 11.9).

(iii) *There is always a certain limitation in light.* The
day has its hours of light but the darkness comes. There are
things which have to be done while we have the light. A
man must accept Jesus and follow him, while he still has the
opportunity to do so (John 12.35,36).

(iv) *There is the closest possible connection between light
and life. Growth* depends on light. No plant will grow, no
flower will blossom, no fruit will ripen, if it is deprived
of the light of the sun. *Health* depends on light. Health cannot flourish in darkened hovels where the light cannot come,
and the surest way to improve the health of a nation is to
tear down the ancient slums and to build homes into which
the light can shine. *Goodness* depends on light. Light is the
great destroyer of crime. A darkened street or lane or square
may be the scene of vice and immorality and crime. Let it
be brilliantly lit, and the evil things automatically disappear,
because they cannot stand the light. Light and life are inseparable. Jesus is the one in whom is life, and the life is
the light of men (John 1.4).

(v) *There is a certain unconquerable quality in light.* As it
has been put, not all the darkness in the world can extinguish
the smallest light. The light and the darkness stand for ever in
opposition, but the wonderful thing about the light is that,
though many things can put it out, the darkness by itself can
never extinguish it. Jesus is the light and the darkness cannot
overcome that light (John 1.5).

Jesus is the light of the world and only in his light can
men find the way to goodness and to God.

18

THE DOOR

THE passage in which Jesus is pictured in terms of the Door is in John 10.1-9. It is by no means an easy passage to interpret. The difficulty of interpretation springs from the fact that this is what has been described as a 'conglomerate' passage, in which there is heaped together almost everything from sheep and shepherds and sheepfolds which can be used to illuminate the work of Jesus. The result of this is that the passage is not so much one picture as it is a collection of pictures. So far as the idea of Jesus as the Door is concerned there are three pictures in it.

(i) There is first of all the idea of Jesus as the Door, taken, as it were, by itself, as a separate picture.

When men thought in terms of a firmament, when they thought of the sky as a solid dome, above and beyond which lay heaven, then it was natural to think of a door in that dome leading into heaven. So after the experience at Bethel Jacob said: 'How awesome is this place! This is none other than the house of God, and this is *the gate of heaven*' (Gen. 28.17). So the Psalmist says of God:

> Yet he commanded the skies above,
>   and opened the doors of heaven;
> and he rained down upon them manna to eat,
>   and gave them the grain of heaven.
> (Ps. 78.23, 24)

In Third Baruch we read of angels opening the three hundred and sixty-five gates of heaven (III Baruch 6.13). The idea of a gate or a door into heaven is by no means uncommon. The main use of such a door was twofold.

269

(*a*)　When it was opened, it revealed the vision of heaven. This is what was given to Jacob. The John of the Revelation begins his visions witht he statement: 'After this I looked, and, lo, in heaven an open door!' (Rev. 4.1). So then to say that Jesus is the door is to say that in him there is given the full revelation of heaven and of God.

(*b*)　When it was opened, it was through it that there came help and salvation to men. It was through the door of heaven that the manna came to men. Through the open door of heaven God either sent help to, or himself came to help of, his people. So then to call Jesus the door is to say that he is the means whereby the help and the salvation of God came to men.

(ii)　But in this passage the idea of the door is used in two ways which are connected with the shepherd and his work. First, there is the picture in John 10.1-6. The larger house in Palestine had a courtyard surrounded by a high wall, and in the country places that courtyard served as a fold for the sheep at night. The courtyard had only one door, and at that door the porter, or gate-keeper, was in constant attendance. Any honest man on any honest errand would seek admission through the door, and such a man would be immediately admitted by the porter. Only a thief and a robber with some nefarious purpose would avoid the door and seek to gain an entry by climbing over the wall. The man who really cared for the flock entered by the door; the man who was out to hurt and injure the flock sought some other way of entrance. So Jesus says: 'I am the door.'

This is to say that first of all *Jesus is the door for the shepherd*. He is the door through which the pastor of the sheep enters in to the sheep. This must mean that any man who wishes to serve as a pastor of the flock of God must come to them through the door of Jesus Christ. It is always true that no man can teach what he does not know, and no man can introduce others to some one with whom he is not acquainted. Clearly, therefore, anyone who had been given the task of being teacher or pastor or servant to the people of God must enter upon his task through Jesus Christ. A man must come to the teaching and the shepherding of the flock of God not through any selfish and self-centred motive, such as personal ambition or the desire for prestige; he must come through Jesus Christ, for only then can he serve Jesus Christ and serve the flock of Jesus Christ.

(iii) But in this passage there is a still further idea. Jesus says: 'Truly, truly, I say to you, I am the door of the sheep.' Moffatt in this verse has not '*the door* of the sheep', but '*the shepherd* of the sheep.' It is certainly true that that translation gives good sense, but is not the reading of any of the great Greek manuscripts; it occurs only in the Sahidic, which is one of the early translations of the New Testament into one of the languages of Egypt. We must keep the word *door*, for the manuscripts all point that way.

So then Jesus is not only the door of the shepherd, he is also the door of the sheep. Here we have another picture, a picture at which we have already looked when we were thinking of Jesus as the Good Shepherd. This time the picture is not of a fold which was the courtyard of a house; here we have the picture of one of the folds on the mountain-side, which was simply a ring of grass surrounded by a stone dyke or a hedge of thorns. Such a fold had no door at all. It simply had an opening, and across the opening the shepherd lay at night, so that he was literally the door, and so that no sheep could get out and no foes could get in except over the shepherd's body. This is the other part of the picture of which Jesus was thinking when he said that he was the Door. He is the means whereby his flock enter into safety and whereby they are protected from danger.

So then the picture of Jesus as the door tells us certain things about him.

(i)   It is Jesus alone who gives us entry into the presence of God. Others may guess and grope; others may search and come back with partial fragments of the truth. He alone can lead us directly into the presence of God.

(ii)   It is Jesus alone who gives us security. Through him who is the door the sheep *go in and come out. Going in and coming out* was the Hebrew phrase for going uninterruptedly upon one's business. In Deuteronomy the promise is: 'Blessed shall you be when you come in, and blessed shall you be when you go out' (Deut. 28.6). It is the promise in the Psalm: 'The Lord will keep your going out and your coming in from this time forth and for evermore' (Ps. 121.8). Here is the promise of that security in life which is still safe 'when all safety's lost', and from which no trial and tribulation or threat or danger or sorrow can take away its peace. The Christian goes out to his day's work with Christ and comes back to his home to meet Christ.

(iii)   It is Jesus alone who gives food for the soul. Through him the sheep go in and out and find pasture (John 10.9). The hunger of the human soul is satisfied alone in all that Jesus Christ can be to us and give to us.

(iv)   It is Jesus alone who gives life. Unlike the thief who comes to break in and destroy Jesus comes to give life and life more abundantly. No man knows what real life is until he has lived life with Jesus Christ.

Jesus said: 'I am the door.' He is the door to the knowledge of God; he is the door to security and peace; he is the door through which we can enter to find the fulfilment of the heart's deepest desires; he is the door to the life which is real life.

19

THE VINE

It is in John 15.1-11 that we find the picture of Jesus as the Vine. As John has it, Jesus said: 'I am the true vine ... I am the vine, you are the branches' (John 15.1,5). This picture would be full of meaning for the Jews.

We may well wonder why Jesus chose the vine as a symbol of himself. The vine is not a noble tree. Often vines were allowed simply to trail along the ground supported by little forked sticks; sometimes the vine was allowed to twine itself around another tree; sometimes it was grown on poles; and sometimes it was trained to spread on walls or trellises. In dignity it was not to be compared with the olive, the cedar or the oak.

But in spite of that in the Old Testament the vine is repeatedly the symbol of Israel. The inhabitants of Jerusalem are like a vine out of whose wood nothing can be made, and whose branches, once they are cut down, are fit for nothing but to be burned (Ezek. 15.1-8). Once Israel was like a splendid vine, but now it is like a vine transplanted to the wilderness and fit for nothing but destruction (Ezek. 19.10-14). Israel is the vineyard of the Lord which received the care of the Lord, and which has done nothing to repay it (Isa. 5.1-7). Jeremiah hears God accuse Israel:

> Yet I planted you a choice vine,
>   wholly of pure seed.
> How then have you turned degenerate
>   and become a wild vine?
>
> (Jer. 2.21)

273

Israel may be like a luxuriant vine but Israel's heart is false (Hos. 10.1,2). Israel is the vine which God brought out of Egypt, but now the boar from the forest has ravaged it (Ps. 80.8-13). II (4) Esd. 5.23-27 is a beautiful passage in which Israel is likened to God's chosen vine:

> And I said: O Lord, my Lord, out of all the woods of the earth and all the trees thereof thou hast chosen thee one vine; out of all the lands of the world thou hast chosen thee one planting-ground; out of all the flowers of the world thou hast chosen thee one lily; out of all the depths of the sea thou hast replenished for thyself one river; out of all the cities that have been built thou hast sanctified Sion unto thyself; out of all birds that have been created thou hast called for thyself one dove; out of all the cattle that have been formed thou hast provided thee one sheep; and out of all the peoples who have become so numerous thou hast gotten thee one people; and the law which thou didst approve out of all laws thou hast bestowed upon the people whom thou didst desire.

Here then is the first background of the picture of Jesus as the vine. But it must be noted that in the Old Testament the picture of Israel as the vine is repeatedly used in connection with the *degeneracy* of Israel. Israel is the vine which has gone bad, which has grown wild, which has never fulfilled the purposes of him who planted it and cared for it. On the other hand, the claim of Jesus is that he is the *true* vine, the *real* vine. That is to say, it is the people who are united with Jesus who are the real Israel, the real people of God. Jesus, as the *Didache* has it (9.2), is the true vine of David. Here is the first suggestion that the racial and the national Israel has lost its place in the purposes of God and that the Church has become the new and the real Israel (cp. Gal. 6.16).

But the picture has a further development. In the rabbinic literature the vine becomes the picture of the *restored* Israel.

There is a rabbinic saying: 'As the vine is the least of all trees, and yet is the master of all, so the people of Israel appear insignificant in the world, but in the future (that is, in the Messianic age) their sovereignty will extend from one end of the world to the other.' In Ecclesiasticus the vine is the symbol of that immortal and eternal Wisdom who was and is God's instrument in the creation and enlightenment of the world. 'As the vine,' says Wisdom, 'brought I forth pleasant savour, and my flowers are the fruit of honour and riches' (Ecclus. 24.17). In II Baruch 36-39 the seer has a vision of a vine over against a whole forest. Out of the vine there flowed a peaceful fountain, but that fountain went in great waves against the forest and destroyed it, except for one cedar. Finally that cedar is also destroyed. The explanation is that the vine stands for the Messiah, and the forest and the cedar for the enemies of God.

In view of all this it is clear that Jesus' claim to be the vine is a claim that he is the Messiah and that in him the true destiny of Israel is fulfilled and consummated. It is a claim that in him the Messianic age is inaugurated.

We must now ask where Jesus found the immediate background for this picture, for Jesus always spoke in pictures which were the product of the circumstances in which his listeners lived.

In John's narrative this claim was made immediately after the Last Supper with its bread and wine, and it may be that it was the wine of the Last Supper which sent Jesus' thoughts to the vine. It may even be, as some one has suggested, that there was a vine trained to climb its way across the wall of the house in which the Last Supper was eaten, and that its tendrils were peeping round the window opening, giving Jesus exactly the picture he required. If Jesus actually spoke this on the way to Gethsemane on the Mount of Olives, he and his disciples would pass through a vineyard on the lower slopes of the hill, and the vines were there. Even more—Jesus spoke of the useless branches being burned; and on the way to Gethsemane he and his disciples would pass by the very valley in which the refuse of Jerusalem was thrown to be burned. Vine wood and vine prunings were quite useless and could be used for no purpose, and it was there that they were destroyed.

But the vine was everywhere. Because it was the symbol of Israel it appeared on Jewish coinage as the national emblem. Over the main door of a synagogue there was usually a carving, which often represented the paschal lamb, or the pot of manna and Aaron's rod, and oftenest of all the vine and the grapes. Above all this symbol was in the Temple. Josephus describes the great doors of the Temple at Jerusalem: 'Under the crown-work was spread out a golden vine, with its branches hanging down from a great height, the largeness and the workmanship of which were an astonishing sight to the spectators.'[1] There was many a place which would provide Jesus with the symbolism for his great claim.

Jesus' picture speaks of the pruning and burning of the vine branches and of the life of the branches in the vine. We have already noted that vine wood is good for nothing. Ezekiel demands concerning the vine wood: 'Is wood taken from it to make anything? Do men take a peg from it to hang any vessel on? Lo, it is given to the fire for fuel; when the fire has consumed both ends of it, and the middle of it is charred, is it useful for anything? Behold, when it was whole it was used for nothing, how much less when the fire has consumed it and it is charred, can it ever be used for anything!' (Ezek. 15.3-5). Vine wood, cut away from the vine, was notoriously useless. So the Christian apart from Christ has no life and no usefulness in him.

As for pruning, no tree requires such savage pruning as

[1] *Antiquities of the Jews* 5.5.4.

the vine does. Tristram tells how in the vineyards in France and Germany the vine-wood is cut back to the very stump, leaving nothing but shapeless, gnarled and distorted stumps. But the great characteristic of the vine is that the branches will grow again. That is where the vine is a contrast to the cedar. Cut down the cedar and it will die; that is why the phrase 'to cut down like a cedar' is a synonym for total destruction and obliteration. Justin Martyr uses this as a parable of the persecution of the Church. However much the Church is devastated it cannot die for it is the vine planted by God.[1] Here there is the parable both of the necessity of the discipline of the Church and of the indestructibility of the Church.

Jesus said: 'I am the true vine.' In that claim he claims to be the chosen one of God in whom the new, the real, and the true Israel finds life. In that claim he tells us that the Christian can only find true life in fellowship with him, in Christ, as the branch draws its life from the vine. And in this claim he warns us that separation from him means uselessness and death.

[1] *Dialogue with Trypho* 110.

20

THE WAY, THE TRUTH AND THE LIFE

To say that Jesus is the Way, the Truth and the Life is the most comprehensive of all claims (John 14.6). Moffatt translates this: 'I am the true and living way', and it would be correct Hebrew idiom that the latter two nouns should be used adjectivally to describe the first. The NEB has: 'I am the way; I am the truth and I am life.' To a Jew every word would be full of associations and full of promise.

(i) Jesus said: 'I am the Way.' Centuries before this the Psalmist had prayed: 'Teach me, thy way, O Lord' (Ps. 27.11; 86.11). The great law-giver had laid it down that men must not turn to the right or to the left, but must walk in the way which the Lord their God had commanded them (Deut. 5.32,33). It was the fear of Moses that the people would turn aside from the way which he had taught them (Deut. 31.29). Isaiah heard God say: 'This is the way, walk in it' (Isa. 30.21). The promise was of a way of holiness in which nothing and no one unclean could exist, and which was so clear that not even a fool could miss it (Isa. 35.8). Again and again the sages spoke of the way or the path of life. 'The reproofs of discipline are the way of life' (Prov. 6.23). 'He who needs instruction is on the path to life' (Prov. 10.17). 'The wise man's path leads upward to life' (Prov. 15.24). The people have erred from the way of truth' (Wisd. 5.6). It is the claim of Tobit: 'I have walked all the days of my life in the way of truth and justice' (Tob. 1.3). And was not the first name for the Christian religion The Way? (Acts 9.2; 19.9). Philo called philosophy 'The Royal Way', and Confucius called his teaching 'Tao', the way.

278

The Letter to the Hebrews speaks of the new and living way which Jesus opened for us to the presence of the Father (Heb. 10.19); and the Letter to the Ephesians speaks of the access that both Jew and Gentile have through Jesus Christ and his Spirit into the presence of God (Eph. 2.18).

But the claim of Jesus goes beyond any of these sayings, great as they are. Jesus did not say: 'I show you the way.' He did not even say: 'I open for you the way.' He said:' I *am* the way.' Let us take a human analogy. We may direct a person to his destination in words, giving him careful and detailed instructions as to how to get there. We may supply a person with a map which gives him his route and with a careful description of it. But even with the most careful instructions and even with the best of maps a person may still get lost. Best of all is to say to the person: 'I know the way, come with me, and I myself will take you there.' Then the last possibility of losing the way is gone. For that person we then become the way. Even so Jesus did not only tell us the way; he did not only give instruction about the way; he *is* the way in whom no man can fail to find his way into the presence of God.

(ii) Jesus said: 'I am the truth.' This phrase has more than one background against which it becomes meaningful.

(*a*) It has a Hebrew background. As the AV has it, all the ways of the Lord are mercy and truth (Ps. 25.10). 'Thou hast redeemed me, O God of truth,' says the Psalmist (Ps. 31.5). God is plenteous in mercy and truth (Ps. 86.15). In all these cases, and in many others, the word for *truth* is *emeth,* and, as the RSV will show, it means *truth* in the sense of *fidelity,* reliability, trustworthiness, faithfulness. It is truth in the sense in which a lover will say: 'I will be true to you.'

If we take truth in this sense, then it means that Jesus is fidelity incarnate, that we can completely and unhesitatingly and without reservation rely on him. He is the one person in the universe whom we can trust in the certainty that we shall never be failed or disappointed.

(b)   It has a Greek background. In Greek the noun *alētheia* has a double sense. It means *truth as distinguished from false-hood*, and it means that which is *real and genuine* as opposed to that which is *unreal and counterfeit*.

If we take it in a combination of both these meanings, it means that in Jesus we come face to face with truth and reality. In him we penetrate beyond the guesses and the gropings, beyond the perhapses and the maybes, and arrive at The Truth; we pass beyond the counterfeits and the substi-tutes, the imitations and the shadows, and arrive at reality. Because Jesus is the truth, he alone can tell us about God and bring us into the things which are real. Vincent Taylor says that Jesus is the Truth because 'revelation is embodied in his person.'

(c)   There is still a third side to this. For the Fourth Gospel the truth is not simply something which is intellectual, it is also something which is moral; it is not something which is simply to be known, it is something which is also to be done. So John can speak about *doing* the truth. 'He who does what is true comes to the light' (John 3.21). 'If we say that we have fellowship with him and walk in darkness, we lie and do not the truth' (I John 1.6, AV).

This idea of truth as something to be done is characteristic of the thought of the Qumran community as we find it in the Dead Sea Scrolls. In the *Manual of Discipline* we read: 'It is only through the spiritual apprehension of God's truth that man's ways can be properly directed.' The truth is some-thing to direct a man's ways. As things are there is a conflict in the world and in man between the Spirit of Light and the Spirit of Darkness, between truth and perversity. But the Spirit of Light will in the end triumph. 'Then truth will emerge triumphant for the world, albeit now and until the

time of the final judgment it go sullying itself in the ways of
wickedness owing to the domination of perversity. Then, too,
God will purge all the acts of man in the crucible of his
truth.' 'Like waters of purification God will sprinkle upon
man the spirit of truth, to cleanse him of all the abominations
of falsehood and of all pollution through the spirit of filth.'
'The lore of the sons of heaven' is going to make men 'blameless in their ways.' 'If a man casts in his portion with truth,
he does righteously and hates perversity.' It is easy to see
how far this kind of truth is removed from intellectual truth
alone. The truth is that which enables man to live the good
life. In this line of thought truth and goodness are one. To say
that Jesus is the truth is to say that he is incarnate goodness,
the perfect pattern of life as it should be lived.

To say that Jesus is the Truth is at one and the same time
to say that Jesus is the incarnation of fidelity, the revelation
of reality, and the pattern of goodness.

(iii) Jesus said: 'I am the Life.' We shall leave much
that must be said about this claim until we come to deal with
the claim of Jesus to be the Resurrection and the Life. But there
are certain things to be said here and now.

As the Fourth Gospel sees it, this claim is to be taken in
two ways. It is to be taken of physical life. The Prologue to
the Gospel speaks of the part of the eternal Word in the
creation of the world. 'All things were made through him,
and without him was not anything made that was made. In
him was life, and the life was the light of men' (John 1.3,4).
The Word, the Son, the pre-existent Christ was the bringer
of life into the world. But even more it is to be taken of
eternal life. Jesus is the creator of life, and Jesus is the re-
creator of life. He brought life in the beginning and he came
to make life new.

Eternal life is one of the great themes of the Fourth Gospel,
and we shall do well to see what Jesus Christ is offering us

when he offers us eternal life. It is quite clear that eternal life must mean more than life which exists for ever. The mere extension of life in time could obviously be a curse and not a blessing. The infinite prolongations of a defeated, frustrated, agonised, truncated life would be much nearer a hell than a heaven. Whatever *eternal* means, it means more than *everlasting*. Quite clearly quality as well as length must enter into it.

The Greek word for *eternal* is *aiōnios*. Even in secular Greek this word has a mysterious and untranslatable quality in it. There are two passages in Plato which greatly illuminate its meaning. In the *Laws* (904a) Plato speaks of the body and the soul as being *indestructible,* but not *aiōnios,* not eternal. This means that a thing can be permanent, indestructible and everlasting without being eternal. In the *Timaeus* (37d) he speaks of the creation of the world by God. The created universe is in fact a shadow of the eternal universe. God wished to make the created universe as like the eternal universe as possible; 'but to attach eternity to the created universe was impossible; therefore the created universe can be no more than a kind of moving shadow and image of eternity.' Here again it is clear that *aiōnios* means far more than everlasting. It is clear that the word *aiōnios* is the word of eternity as opposed to time; the word of deity as opposed to humanity; the word of God as opposed to man; the word of heaven as opposed to earth. It is precisely here that we have the key to the meaning of the word *aiōnios*. The only person to whom the word *aiōnios* may properly be applied is God. And, therefore, the life which is *aiōnios,* eternal life, is nothing other than, and nothing less than, the life of God. The life that Jesus brings to men is the life of God. Westcott puts it this way: 'Jesus is the bridge by which the two worlds are united.' This is exactly what Jesus went on to say, when he said: 'No one comes to the Father but by me.' Through him men can enter into the life of God.

There is a very faint and imperfect human analogy, and yet an analogy essentially right because it moves in the world of love. It is the fact of human experience, of which anyone who has ever loved is aware, that in the presence and company of certain people life acquires a new quality, a new vividness, a new intensity, a new radiance, and a new value. What others sometimes do for us on the human level Jesus does for us on the divine level; in his presence and in his company life is lifted above the levels of earth and partakes of the life of God.

We may conclude our study of this claim of Jesus by quoting the words of two great teachers which are based upon it. Thomas Aquinas expanded this passage: 'I am the Way, the Truth, and the Life. Without the way, no journey can be taken. Without the truth, no truth can be known. Without the life, no life can be lived. I am the Way which must be followed; I am the Truth which must be believed; I am the Life for which man must hope.'

Erasmus took these words of Jesus and made of them one of the best known prayers, the prayer of the University of Glasgow, whose motto is *Via, Veritas, Vita:*

> O Lord Jesus Christ, who art the Way, the Truth, and the Life, we pray thee suffer us not to stray from thee, who art the way, nor to distrust thee, who art the Truth, nor to rest in any other thing than thee who art the Life. Teach us, by thy Holy Spirit, what to believe, what to do, and wherein to take our rest.

21

THE RESURRECTION AND THE LIFE

As John tells the story, it was to comfort Martha in her sorrow for the death of her brother Lazarus that Jesus made his claim to be the Resurrection and the Life, 'I am the Resurrection and the Life; he who believes in me, though he die, yet shall he live; and whoever lives and believes in me shall never die' (John 11.25,26). In this statement two of Jesus' great recurring claims and promises are put together.

Jesus said that he is the *Resurrection*. The hour is coming, he said, when those in the tombs will hear the voice of the Son, and when they will come forth, either to the resurrection of life or the resurrection of judgment (John 5.28,29). It is his repeated promise to the man who sees him and believes in him: 'I will raise him up at the last day' (John 6.39,40,44,54). When Paul preached at Athens, it was Jesus and the resurrection that he preached (Acts 17.9). And Bengel's comment on this promise of Jesus was: 'This is the ultimate end, beyond which no peril remains.'

Jesus said that he is the *Life*. Life and especially eternal life are the great characteristic terms of the Fourth Gospel. In it the word *life* occurs thirty-three times, and on fifteen of these occasions it is *eternal life* that is spoken of. To bring men that life is the basic purpose of the Fourth Gospel. The Gospel was written to move men to believe that Jesus is the Christ, the Son of God, that so believing they may have life in his name (John 20.31). In him was life (1.4); he came that men might have life, and have it abundantly (10.10); God granted Jesus power to give life to all whom God had given to him (17.2). If we are to see what Jesus means and offers, as the Fourth Gospel sees him, we must study this word *life*.

We must first see *in what this life consists*.

(i)   Life is *the opposite of perishing*. Jesus was sent into the world that those who believe in him should not perish but have eternal life (3.15,16). Real life is the opposite of final death. Jesus came to rescue men, not only from physical death, but from the death of the soul.

(ii)   Life is *the opposite of judgment*. He who believes in Jesus has eternal life; and such a man does not come into judgment, but he has passed from death to life (5.24). To enter into life is the precise opposite of entering into judgment. Eternal life is the life in which through Jesus Christ a man enters fearlessly, lovingly and confidently into the presence of God.

Next we must see *how this life is obtained and entered into*.

(i)   It is found by *following*. The man who follows Jesus will not walk in darkness but will have the light of life (8.12). To follow Jesus is to find life here and now and to be on the sure and certain way to life hereafter. A man does not need to understand everything in order to begin following. If he follows the light as he sees it, the life will come. *Solvitur ambulando* is one of the basic principles of the Christian life.

(ii)   It is found by *venturing*. The man who loves his life will lose it; and the man who hates his life will keep it to life eternal (12.25). Self-preservation may be the first law of man's natural life, but it is certainly not the first law of his spiritual life. As John Bunyan, faced with death, said, 'I will venture for thy name.' Life is found not in self-protection but in self-giving.

(iii)   It is found by *listening*. Jesus said: 'The words that I have spoken to you are spirit and life' (6.63). No man can find any way unless he is prepared to listen to some one who knows the way. He who would find life must listen to the

Lord of life. The energy of action must proceed from the stillness of listening.

(iv) It is found in *studying*. To search the Scriptures is to find the way to eternal life (5.39). But that search must be in the willingness to receive what Scripture says and not in the arrogance which merely uses Scripture as a source wherein to find one's own beliefs. Eternal life is to be found in the Scriptures because the Scriptures tell of Jesus Christ. Luther's one test of any book was: 'Does it speak of Jesus Christ?' 'The true touchstone for testing any book is to discover whether it emphasises the prominence of Christ or not . . . What does not teach Christ is not apostolic, not even if taught by Peter or Paul. On the other hand, what does preach Christ is apostolic, even if Judas, Annas, Pilate or Herod does it.' To study in receptive humility that which tells of Christ is the way to eternal life.

(v) It is found by *obeying*. The commandments of God are eternal life (12.50). Every commandment of God is not only an order; it is also a revelation. Obedience is the way to knowledge. Even on the human level, the more implicitly we obey a person, the more we can enter into fellowship with him, and the more he can tell us about himself. To obey God is not to enter into servitude to God, but to enter into fellowship with God, and that fellowship is eternal life.

(vi) It is found by *worshipping*. In particular the sacrament is the channel of eternal life. It is, as John vividly puts it, by eating the flesh and blood of Jesus that we find life (6.51-54). The sacrament provides a way, not only to make contact with Jesus Christ, not only to remember him, but also to enter into union with him, and union with him is eternal life.

(vii) It is found above all by *believing*. It is he who believes who has eternal life (3.36; 5.24,40; 6.33-54). To believe in Jesus Christ means to be quite certain of his unique relationship with God, and then to accept as binding every one of his commands and to accept as certain beyond all doubt his promises. A life lived in that total committal to Jesus Christ is eternal life.

Finally we must ask *what eternal life gives*.

(i) It gives *security*. 'I will give them eternal life,' said Jesus, 'and they shall never perish, and no one shall snatch them out of my hand' (10.28). Eternal life means a connection with Jesus Christ which nothing in life or in death can sever. It does not mean ease and comfort; it does not mean exemption from all the trials which witness to Christ must bring; it does not mean release from all the ills and sorrows to which the flesh is heir. But it does mean victorious living and security in the real sense of the word in any situation which death or life can bring.

(ii) It means *knowledge of God*. 'This is eternal life, to know thee the only God and Jesus Christ whom thou hast sent' (17.3). To know what God is truly like, to know the meaning of the love of God, is to enter upon a life which is a new creation.

It remains to remember that only Jesus Christ can give that life. It is only he who can give the water which will be as a spring within man welling up to eternal life (4.14). Jesus did not say: 'I *show* you the Resurrection and the Life.' He did not even say: 'I *give* you the Resurrection and the Life.' He said: 'I *am* the Resurrection and the Life.' It is therefore clear that the way to this eternal life lies not only in listening to him and learning from him; it comes through a personal relationship, a living connection, with him.

Our human life provides us with an analogy for this. The relationships of life which mean most to us and without which life could never be the same, do not come from what a person says to us, or even what he does for us, but from the person himself. In the deepest moments of life, the moments of glory and the moments of agony, our sole desire is to be *with* that person. He may be able to say very little; he may be able to do nothing. What we want is the person himself. So Jesus *is* the Resurrection and the Life. He is not some one who taught us the way of life and whom we remember; he is not even some one who proved to us that there is a Resurrection and that there is something which is called eternal life; he is the living presence in whose company and in whose presence, and in union with whom, earthly life becomes eternal life, and existence becomes superlative living.

It is quite clear both on general and on particular grounds that the life which Jesus offers is not physical life, nor is it simply life which continues indefinitely in time. On quite general grounds, it can easily be seen that life which goes on for ever could well be the greatest of curses and not the greatest of blessings. On particular grounds, there are both the whole context of this saying and the saying itself. The statement was made when, according to the story, Lazarus was lying dead in the tomb. So far as physical death goes, Lazarus had certainly died. Let us look at the saying itself again: 'I am the Resurrection and the Life; he who believes in me, though he die, yet shall he live; and whoever lives and believes in me shall never die.'

The plain fact is that in regard to physical death the man who believes in Jesus Christ dies exactly as any other man dies. Death stays his course for no man, believer or un-believer. In regard to death, as Epicurus said, all men live in an unfortified city. When Jesus said: 'Whoever lives and believes in me shall never die', he was quite certainly not promising any man immunity from physical death. What was Jesus promising? Let us look at human life as we know it and see it and experience it.

Life can be a *mental death*. The psychologists tell us that no man can learn anything new after he is forty, or at least

THE RESURRECTION AND THE LIFE

that after that age the process of learning is very much
slowed down. The ability to learn dies.

Life can be a *moral death*. Glover speaks of what he calls
'the necrosis of the soul'. Persius, the Roman satirist, bids
the guilty man look upon virtue, and mourn that he has lost
her for ever. Epictetus demands: 'When a man is hardened
like a stone, how shall we deal with him by any argument?'
If a man repeatedly chooses the lower way, if he repeatedly
turns his back on goodness, there can come into life an in-
creasing moral helplessness, the death of resistance to evil,
the paralysis of the reaching out after good, the withering of
all that is fine and lovely. A man can become the slave of the
habits which he cannot break. He can so accept evil and so
reject good that he ends in moral death.

Life can be *a spiritual death*. It can be a slow drift away
from God, a slow obliteration of the values which are the
real values of life, a slow process of degeneration, a loss of
ideals, a dull contentment with things as they are, an acceptance of defeat, a loss even of the awareness of God. Thomas
Hood wrote in his sad poem:

> I remember, I remember
>   The fir trees dark and high;
> I used to think their slender tops
>   Were close against the sky.
> It was a childish ignorance,
>   But now 'tis little joy
> To know I'm further off from heaven
>   Than when I was a boy.

Life comes threatening its many deaths—intellectual death,
moral death, spiritual death. But the plain fact is that when
life is lived with Jesus, none of these things can happen.
Eternal life, as we have seen, is God's life, and when that life
is ours in Christ life is always victorious and never defeated.

But now we have a further conclusion. Jesus is the

Resurrection. What is the meaning of this? Our relationship
with Jesus cannot be broken. He is with us always to the end
of time and beyond. The life the Christian lives is nothing
less than God's life. If this is so, then life can never come to
an end. Physical death is powerless to destroy this kind of
life. The belief in life after death is founded on a new basis.
The basis of it is not the nature of the soul or the nature of
man or the nature of anything human. The basis of it is a
personal relationship with Jesus Christ, and through him with
God. Man has become inextricably and indissolubly linked
and united with him who conquered death and with him who
is the source of all life and being, and a life such as that
cannot be ended by death.

Hoskyns in commenting on this passage lays down as a
general Christian truth that if we call Jesus the Resurrection,
then 'physical death is trivial and irrelevant'. In a sense that
is far from true. It is far from trivial and irrelevant to wake
up on a world in which the sun has set at midday, in which
life is steeped in tears, and in which in the heart there is a
loneliness which is the most terrible pain in the world. But it
is true it does mean that death is not a final event. If we are
indissolubly connected with Jesus, if eternal life is the life of
God, then death is only the gateway to a larger life. This is a
truth which men even long before Jesus glimpsed. Euripides
wrote:

> Who knoweth if to die be but to live,
> And that called life by mortals be but death?

Westcott in his exposition of this passage cites two quotations.
There is a saying in the Talmud: 'What has a man to do
that he may live? Let him die. What has a man to do that he
may die? Let him live.' The idea is that somehow it is after
death that life fully and really begins. The last words of
Edward the Confessor were: 'Weep not. I shall not die but

live; and, as I leave the land of the dying, I trust to see the blessings of the Lord in the land of the living.' It is not a case of passing from life to death, but a case of passing from living, through death, to life.

Jesus said: 'I am the Resurrection and the Life.' This is the claim which covers life and death, time and eternity, this world and the world to come. It is the claim that with Jesus the years will be characterised by surge after surge of power and not by the creeping death and paralysis which are so often characteristic of life. It is the guarantee that death is not the end, for through Jesus Christ men enter into the life of God which nothing can ultimately destroy.

22

THE JUDGE

THE conception of Jesus as Judge is one that is quite central to the Christian faith. It has found its place in the creeds. In the Apostles' Creed the death, the resurrection and the ascension of Jesus are stated. Then the creed states that Jesus has taken his place at the right hand of God, and 'from thence he shall come to judge the quick and the dead.' In the same way it has its place in the Nicene Creed: 'And he shall come again with glory to judge both the quick and the dead.' Just as this conception has found its place in the Church's creeds, so it has found its place in the hymns of the Church. Charles Wesley's hymn has it:

> Rejoice in glorious hope;
>   Jesus, the Judge, shall come,
> And take his servants up
>   To their eternal home;
> We soon shall hear the archangel's voice;
> The trump of God shall sound, 'Rejoice'.

The idea of Jesus as Judge is deeply rooted in the theology and the worship of the Church.

When we turn to the New Testament it becomes clear that the prominence of the idea of Jesus as Judge is fully justified. In the sermon to Cornelius Peter says that God commanded the followers of Jesus to preach and to testify 'that Jesus is the one ordained by God to be judge of the living and the dead' (Acts 10.42). The Pastoral Epistles use exactly the same phrase when they speak of 'Christ Jesus who is to judge the living and the dead' (II Tim. 4.1). It is the Lord, the

292

righteous judge, from whom Paul looks for the crown which he has won (II Tim. 4.8). Thinking of the imminence of the Second Coming James says: 'The judge is standing at the doors' (James 5.9). Peter encourages his people by reminding them that those who illtreat and abuse them will give account 'to him who is ready to judge the living and the dead' (I Peter 4.5).

From Hebrews we learn that the belief in Jesus as Judge was part of the elementary and basic instruction which every Christian first received. The elementary teaching, to which the recipients of the letter should not have found it necessary to return, consisted of repentance from dead works, faith towards God, 'with instructions about ablutions, the laying on of hands, the resurrection of the dead, and eternal judgment' (Heb. 5.2). Paul insists that according to his gospel the day comes when God judges the secrets of men by Christ Jesus (Rom. 2.16). 'We must all,' he writes, 'appear before the judgment seat of Christ, so that each one may receive good or evil, according to what he has done in the body' (II Cor. 5.10). The connection of Jesus with judgment is an integral part of New Testament thought.

The idea of judgment was part of religion long before the New Testament, for it is equally central to the teaching and the thought of the Old Testament. Whenever a religion becomes an ethical religion the idea of judgment is bound to enter into it. An ethical religion is based on the fact that there are certain commandments which a man is bound to keep, and it is impossible that the ultimate destinies of the man who keeps them and the man who breaks them should be the same. Judgment becomes an essential part of the picture. We shall do well, therefore, to begin with the Old Testament picture of judgment.

In the Old Testament it is, of course, God who is Judge. 'Shall not the Judge of all the earth do right?' (Gen. 18.25).

'The heavens declare his righteousness, for God is judge' (Ps. 50.6). 'Rise up, O judge of the earth,' prays the Psalmist, 'render to the proud their deserts' (Ps. 94.2). 'The Lord is our judge; the Lord is our ruler; the Lord is our king; he will save us,' is the confidence of Isaiah (Isa. 33.22).

The New Testament does not forget the idea of God as Judge. The writer of the Hebrews speaks of the Christians coming 'to a judge who is God of all' (Heb. 12.23). Peter reminds his people that the one whom they invoke as Father is the one who judges each one impartially according to his deeds (I Peter 1.17). Jesus amid all his sufferings and his rejection 'trusted to him who judges justly' (I Peter 2.23). Paul speaks of the impossibility of escaping the judgment of God (Rom. 2.1-3).

Before we go on to the New Testament, it will be useful to look at the Old Testament idea of God as Judge.

(i)　God is the Judge who in any human transaction decides who is in the right and who is in the wrong. Gideon calls upon the Lord, the Judge, to decide between the people of Israel and the people of Ammon (Judg. 11.27; cp. Gen. 16.5; 31.53; I Sam. 24.12).

(ii)　It is God who allots to each man his reward. God executes judgment, putting down one and lifting up another (Ps. 75.7; cp. Ps. 7.8).

(iii)　In particular God's judgment falls upon the arrogant, the insolent, and the oppressor. The Psalmist calls upon God to render to the proud their deserts (Ps. 94.2).

(iv)　It is a corollary of this that God is the Judge who protects the rights of the defenceless and the unjustly oppressed (Ps. 10.18).

(v)　The very idea of God as a holy God, the God who desires his people also to be holy, involves the fact that the standard of God's judgment involves an ethical test of a man's life. God will punish sinners for their ways (Ezek. 18.30;

33.20; 36.19). Infidelity to God necessarily brings judgment (Ezek. 16.38).

(vi) It is therefore not unnatural that it is the prosperous and the exalted who are in greatest danger of judgment. God judges those who are on high (Job. 21.22).

(vii) Since God is the God of all the earth, his judgment goes out in ever-widening circles.

(a) He judges his people. God stands up to judge the people (Isa. 3.13). He judges the people and in so doing gathers to himself those who have made and kept covenant with him (Ps. 50.4).

(b) He judges the heathen. In the end time the heathen will be judged from Jerusalem (Joel 3.16).

(c) His judgment is a universal judgment involving the whole earth. 'Arise, O God,' prays the Psalmist, 'judge the earth, for to thee belong all nations' (Ps. 82.8). He executes judgment among the nations (Ps. 110.16). He judges the world with righteousness (Ps. 9.8), and the peoples with equity (Ps. 96.10; cp. Ps. 7.8; 67.4; 98.9; I Chron. 16.33).

No one lies outside the judgment of God.

(viii) But the characteristic thought of the Old Testament is the connection of judgment with vindication.

(a) God's judgment will be a vindication of Israel. God's judgment will fall on the nations whom Israel has had to serve (Gen. 15.14). 'The Lord will vindicate his people and have compassion on his servants' (Ps. 135.14; cp. Ps. 110.6; 54.1; 9.4; Deut. 32.36; I Sam. 2.10; II Chron. 20.12).

(b) God's judgment will vindicate the righteous. Men will see what happens to the wicked and will say: 'Surely there is a reward for the righteous. Surely there is a God who judges on earth' (Ps. 58.11).

(c) Frequently the judgment of God is awaited as a personal vindication. 'Judge me, O Lord,' prays the Psalmist, 'according to my righteousness, and according to the integrity that is in me' (Ps. 7.8). 'Vindicate me, O Lord, for I have walked in my integrity' (Ps. 26.1; cp. Pss. 35.24; 43.1; Lam. 3.59).

It is quite true that there is always a threat in God's judgment. 'God is a righteous God, and a God who has indignation every day' (Ps. 7.11). But through much of Old Testament thought there runs a strain which eagerly awaits judgment, and which sees in judgment a vindication of the claims of Israel and of a man's personal righteousness. Judgment is not so much for condemnation as it is for justification.

We now turn to the New Testament, and we do not need to go further than the parables to see the part that judgment plays in the thought of Jesus, and to see many of the things which involve a man in judgment.

The parables of the drag net, and of the wheat and the tares make it clear that the separation of the good from the bad must come (Matt. 13.47-51, 24-30, 36-43). The parable of the unforgiving debtor shows that the unforgiving spirit brings condemnation (Matt. 18.21-35). The parable of the wedding feast and of the guest without the garment shows what happens to the man who rejects the invitation of God, or who accepts it in the wrong way (Matt. 22.1-14). The parable of the wicked husbandmen shows the consequences of the rejection of the Son of God (Matt. 21.33-46). The parable of the talents shows what happens to the man who refuses to use the gifts which God has entrusted to him (Matt. 25.14-30). The parable of the barren fig-tree shows that uselessness invites disaster (Luke 13.6-9). The parable of the rich fool shows what lies in store for the man whose eyes are never lifted beyond the horizon of the things of this world (Luke 12.16-20). The parable of the Pharisee and the tax-collector shows that self-righteousness is in itself separation from God (Luke 18.10-14). The parable of the sheep and the goats, and the parable of the rich man and Lazarus show the fate of the man who is impervious to the claims of human need (Matt. 25.31-46; Luke 16.19-31).

The New Testament connection of Jesus with judgment follows three special lines.

(i) Judgment is connected with the Second Coming of Jesus. This, as we have seen, is the connection of Jesus with judgment in the historic creeds. Jesus at his appearing is to judge the living and the dead (II Tim. 4.1). God has fixed a day when he will judge the world in righteousness by a man who he has appointed (Acts 17.31).

It is precisely this connection which the New Testament preachers use as one of the supreme dynamics of the Christian faith and life. They constantly appeal to their people to get by God's grace such a character that they will meet the returned Lord of glory with confidence and joy—a return which they expected at any moment. It is Paul's prayer that the Corinthians will be guiltless in the day of our Lord Jesus Christ (I Cor. 1.8). It is his prayer that the Philippians may be so enabled to discern between the right and the wrong that they may be pure and blameless at the coming of our Lord Jesus Christ (Phil. 1.10). It is his prayer that God may so sanctify the Thessalonians that they may be kept sound and blameless in body and soul at the coming of our Lord Jesus Christ (I Thess. 5.23). The writer of Second Peter urges his people to direct every energy to be found by Jesus Christ without spot or blemish and at peace (II Peter 3.14).

It is true that that appeal would be even more vivid and impressive when the Second Coming was expected at any moment; but in every generation it always has been used as one of the supreme moral incentives of the Christian life.

(ii) Judgment is connected with what happens after death. So Paul says that we shall all appear before the judgment seat of Christ to receive reward or punishment for the things done in the body (II Cor. 5.10). In the New Testament the two ideas, the ideas of judgment at the Second Coming and judgment after death, exist, as it were, side by side, for, as we have seen, both occur in the thought of Paul.

(iii)   In both the ideas which we have been considering the judgment of Christ is eschatological. It takes place either at the end time of the world or when, for a man, the world is finished. But when we turn to the Fourth Gospel we come to a quite different circle of ideas.

(a)   In the Fourth Gospel there is the idea that God has committed the task of judgment to Jesus. 'The Father judges no man, but has given all judgment to the Son' (John 5.22). 'The Father has given the Son authority to execute judgment' (John 5.27). The Son is, as it were, the Judge appointed by God, the Judge to whom God has delegated his authority and power.

(b)   Nonetheless, it is not his own judgment but the judgment of the Father that the Son carries out. 'I can do nothing of my own authority,' Jesus says. 'As I hear, I judge; my judgment is just, because I seek not my own will, but the will of him who sent me' (John 5.30; 8.15.16). The Son is not the rival of the Father; he has not usurped the rights of the Father; his judgment is the judgment which ultimately belongs to the Father.

(c)   It is now that we come to the paradox of the Fourth Gospel. In it Jesus says: 'For judgment am I come into the world' (John 9.39). Yet at the same time Jesus says: 'I did not come to judge the world, but to save the world' (John 12.47). The paradox of the Fourth Gospel is that Jesus came into the world both to judge and to save. What is the explanation of this?

Let us set out in full a passage which we have already quoted in part. Jesus said: 'If anyone hears my sayings and does not keep them, I do not judge him; for I did not come to judge the world, but to save the world. He who rejects me,

and does not receive my sayings, has a judge; the word that I
have spoken will be his judge at the last day' (John 12.47,48).

When we were dealing with Jesus as the Stone, we already
touched on this situation. There is no real contradiction here.
We may use a human analogy. It is possible to offer a man an
experience which is meant solely for his benefit and for his
good, and for that very experience to turn out a judgment on
the man. Let us suppose that I love noble orchestral music
and that I have a friend who has never experienced it. I take
him to a concert at which a great orchestra is playing a great
symphony under a great conductor. My whole intention is to
give this man a great and ennobling experience. Now let us
suppose that within minutes of the beginning of the symphony
this man begins to fidget, and that he is obviously bored.
Clearly, the man has no music in his soul. The experience
which I meant for the man's benefit and delight has turned
out a judgment on him.

Even so, Jesus came into this world to bring men the love
of God; he came in order that men might be saved. But if a
man, confronted with Jesus, sees in Jesus nothing lovely,
nothing great, nothing splendid, nothing to be worshipped
and adored, then that man has judged himself. He has been
confronted with incarnate love, incarnate truth, incarnate
beauty, incarnate God, and it has left him cold and unmoved,
or even hostile and resentful. That man is judged. The love of
God, the offer of God, the grace of God have become a
judgment to him. The Fourth Gospel sees Jesus as the supreme touchstone of God. A man's reaction to Jesus proves
beyond all possible doubt what that man is.

Such a judgment is not eschatological; it is immediate.
True, its consummation is still to come, but judgment has
come. A man's reaction to Jesus is the supreme test; and that
is why Jesus is supremely the Judge.

We do well to remember that Jesus is Judge and that there

is such a thing as judgment. It is easy to sentimentalise the love of God. 'God will forgive', said Heine. *'C'est son métier. It is his trade.'* Hebert Kelly, the founder of Kelham, used to say that there is a kind of theology whose party line is: 'God is nice and in him is no nastiness at all.' We do well to remember that in Jesus Christ God offers us the wonder of his love and that our reaction to that offer is a judgment. That is why Jesus is for ever Saviour and Judge.

23

THE LAMB

No name of Jesus has been dearer to Christian devotional thought and language than the Lamb. It is embedded in the liturgy of the Lord's Supper.

> Lamb of God, that takest away the sins of the world, have mercy upon us.
> Lamb of God, that takest away the sins of the world, have mercy upon us.
> Lamb of God that takest away the sins of the world, grant us thy peace.

It is a favourite name of Jesus in the great hymns of the Church:

> O Lamb of God, still keep me
> Close to thy pierced side.

Or, as Christina Rossetti has it in her great hymn;

> None other Lamb, none other Name,
> None other Hope in heaven or earth or sea,
> None other Hiding-Place from guilt and shame,
> None beside thee.

It is not that the name the Lamb is used often in the New Testament, except in the Revelation, and in that book its use is unique and must be separately considered. When John the Baptist pointed out Jesus to his disciples, he said: 'Behold, the Lamb of God who takes away the sin of the world!' (John 1.29,36). We are not, says Peter, ransomed with perishable things like silver or gold, but 'with the precious blood of Christ, like that of a lamb without blemish or spot' (I Peter 1.18,19). When Philip encountered the Ethiopian eunuch the Ethiopian was reading the passage from Isaiah (53.7,8):

> As a sheep led to the slaughter
> or a lamb before its shearers is dumb,
> so he opens not his mouth.
> In his humiliation justice was denied him.
> Who can describe his generation?
> For his life is taken up from the earth.

And it was beginning from there and in these terms that Philip expounded to him the gospel of Jesus Christ (Acts 8.32-35). Apart from the Revelation these are the only passages in the New Testament where Jesus is described as the Lamb. Before we pass on to the deeper meanings which are in this word, we may look at two significances of it which lie upon the surface.

(i) The lamb has always been the symbol of innocence, meekness, lowliness, gentleness, of a life which would never cause hurt or harm to anyone. 'Take my yoke upon you,' said Jesus, 'and learn of me, for I am gentle and lowly in heart' (Matt. 11.29). 'I entreat you,' said Paul, 'by the meekness and gentleness of Christ' (II Cor. 10.1). The word has in it all the purity and innocence and the gentleness which belonged to the life of Jesus of Nazareth, when he was a man among men upon earth.

(ii) The lamb is often the symbol of dependence. God is the Shepherd of men (Ps. 23.1). We are the people and the sheep of his pasture (Ps. 100.3). 'He will feed his flock like a shepherd, he will gather the lambs in his arms, he will carry them in his bosom' (Isa 40.11). No one is more dependent on any one than the lamb is upon the shepherd. The lamb is the symbol of utter trust and dependence. Even so, the name expresses the complete trust and dependence of Jesus on God his Father.

(iii) But there are meanings of this name which go

deeper than that. Among the Jews the lamb was uniquely the animal of sacrifice. In the old Genesis story the question of Isaac to his father Abraham is: 'Where is the lamb for a burnt offering?' (Gen. 22.7,8). There was hardly a Jewish sacrifice in which a lamb was not involved. The daily burnt offering in the Temple consisted of a whole lamb offered morning and evening (Ex. 29.38-41; Num. 28.1-8). At the beginning of the month seven lambs were offered (Num. 28. 11). This to the Jew was the most sacred of all offerings, and the greatest of all disasters was when it was impossible to offer to God the morning and the evening lamb. In the days when Antiochus Epiphanes desecrated the Temple and attempted to wipe out Jewish religion, the tragedy was that 'the daily sacrifice was taken away' (Dan. 8.11-13; 11.31; 12.11). The saddest day in Jewish history was and is the 17th day of the month Thammuz in AD 70, for it was from that day that the siege of the Roman armies made it impossible for the starving people to offer the sacrificial lamb, and it was from that day that sacrifice in the Temple ceased for ever.[1]

There were many other sacrifices with which the lamb was connected. The lamb was the trespass offering when a leper was healed (Lev. 14.10-32), as it was in the ceremonies connected with the Nazirite vow (Num. 6.1-21). A lamb and a pigeon—two pigeons if she was poor—constituted the woman's offering for purification after she had had a child (Lev. 12.6-8). The lamb was the burnt offering and the peace offering at the dedication of the altar of the Tabernacle (Num. 7.15-17). The lamb was part of the offering in the ceremonies connected with the redemption of the first-born (Ex. 34.20). All the great Jewish Feasts had agricultural as well as historical significances. In the agricultural part of the Passover the lamb was offered, and seven lambs were offered

[1] Josephus, *Wars of the Jews*, 6.2. 1.

on each day throughout the seven days of the Feast (Lev. 23.12; Numbers 28.19). At Pentecost, at the Feast of the First Fruits, at the Feast of the Trumpets, seven lambs were offered (Lev. 23.18-21; Num. 28.27; 29.2).

On every great occasion the lamb formed part of the sacrificial ceremonies. At David's preparations for the building of the Temple, which Solomon was afterwards to erect, as the Chronicler tells the story, one thousand bullocks, rams and lambs were offered (I Chron. 29.21). In the time of Hezekiah after the cleansing of the Temple seven lambs were offered for a sin offering and two hundred as a thank offering (II Chron. 29.21,32). At the time of the reformation under Josiah, Josiah gave to the people that they might keep the Passover thirty thousand lambs and kids and three thousand bullocks, as the Chronicler tells (II Chron. 35.7). We need not stop to argue about the arithmetical accuracy of these figures; the point is that they show the place of the lamb in the sacrificial system of Israel. In the sacrificial ceremonies after the return of the people from exile in the time of Ezra there were offered twelve bullocks, ninety-six rams, seventy-seven lambs, and twelve he-goats (Ezra 8.35). In Ezekiel's picture of the restored Temple the lamb is to be offered as a daily offering, and six lambs on Sabbaths and on new moons (Ezek. 46.4-15).

In the regulations of Leviticus for the sin-offering it is laid down that a female lamb without blemish is to be offered, that the offerer must lay his hands upon it, that the blood must be put upon the horns of the altar, and poured out at the bottom of the altar, and then it is said that this sacrifice is an atonement for sin (Lev. 4.32-35).

Here then is the sacrificial background of the lamb; and from it the conclusion is clear. No Jew could ever hear Jesus called the lamb without thinking of him as the sacrifice and the offering to God whereby atonement is made for the sin of man, and through whom man and God are reconciled.

(iv) There remains the sacrificial use of the lamb which was most deeply rooted of all in Jewish life: the connection of the lamb with the Passover. The story of the first Passover, and of the initiation of the Passover Feast, is told in Exodus 12. In spite of repeated appeals and in spite of repeated demonstrations of the power of God, Pharaoh had refused to let the people go from Egypt. So there came the last terrible stroke of the hand of God. The angel of the Lord was to walk throughout the land in the night, slaying the firstborn son in every Egyptian home. But before this happened every Jewish household was to take and kill a lamb; they were to dip a bunch of hyssop in the blood of the lamb, and with it they were to smear the doorposts of their houses; and, when the avenging angel saw the mark, he would pass over that house, knowing that in it there was a family of the people of God.

The word *pascha* is used to mean both the Passover Feast and the Passover Lamb. It is possible to speak of the Passover being killed in the sense of the killing of the Passover lamb (Mark 14.12; Luke 22.7,11; John 18.28). Of all the pictures of the lamb used of Jesus this is the one most definitely and distinctly applied to him. Paul writes: 'Christ, our paschal lamb, has been sacrificed' (I Cor. 5.7). Here Jesus is definitely called the Passover lamb. This would be a picture which every Jew would recognise. The Passover Feast stood at the very heart of Jewish life and religion. Every adult male Jew who lived within twenty miles of Jerusalem was bound by law to attend it, and it was the ambition of every devout Jew who lived outside Palestine to attend at least one Passover Feast in Jerusalem, even if he had to save for half a lifetime to do so. The Passover Lamb stood for two things.

(*a*) The Passover lamb was the symbol of deliverance. Nowhere in history did the Jews see the delivering power of God so clearly and definitely demonstrated as in the events which brought them out of Egypt. Here was the deliverance *par excellence,* and without parallel. And to think of Jesus as the Passover lamb is to see in him the delivering and rescuing power of God come to earth for the salvation of men. Just as the first Passover lamb was the sign of God's deliverance of his people from their slavery in Egypt, so Jesus the second Passover lamb is the symbol of their deliverance from slavery to sin.

(*b*) But there is a real sense in which the Passover lamb was more than a symbol of deliverance; it was *the means of deliverance.* It was the mark of the blood of the lamb, which the lamb had to die to provide, which was the means which kept the Jewish homes safe on that terrible night of death and destruction. The death of the lamb was essential for the deliverance of the people. Jesus therefore is the means of salvation whereby men are saved from the penalty and the power of their sins. Through his sacrifice and death that salvation came.

The Fourth Gospel very definitely and deliberately presents Jesus in terms of the Passover lamb. It is quite clear that in the Synoptic Gospels and in the Fourth Gospel the time of the crucifixion is different. In the Synoptic Gospels it is clear that the Last Supper is a Passover Feast and that Jesus was crucified *after* the Passover (Matt. 27.17-20); Mark 14.12-17; Luke 22.7-15). It is equally clear that in the Fourth Gospel Jesus was crucified before the Passover Feast, for in its narrative the Jewish leaders refuse to enter Pilate's judgment hall, lest they be defiled and so be rendered unclean, and therefore ineligible to eat the Passover (John 18.28). It is said distinctly and in so many words that it was on the preparation for the Passover, about 12 o'clock midday, that Jesus was crucified (John 19.14). And that is precisely when the Passover lamb was killed. The Passover lamb was not killed by the individual worshipper. It was killed in the

Temple. It was killed by the priests, its throat was slit, its blood was collected in a silver bowl and thrown upon the altar; then the body of the lamb was given back to the worshipper that it might be cooked and eaten at the Feast. This was all done at midday and in the early afternoon preceding the Feast. This is to say that Jesus was being crucified at exactly the time when the Passover lambs were being killed. Beyond question, the symbolism is that he *is* God's Passover lamb, sacrificed for the deliverance of God's people.

To this day the Jew keeps the Passover; and always the lamb has stood for the deliverance wrought by God and for the reminder and the memorial that God is mighty to save. To see Jesus as the lamb at all is to see him in terms of sacrifice; and to see him as the Passover lamb is to see him, not only as the symbol, but as the means of God's deliverance of his people. It is to see him as the culmination of the whole sacrificial system, to see him, as the writer to the Hebrews saw him, as the sacrifice which makes all other sacrifices unnecessary for ever.

There is still another strand to add to this picture. There are times in the Old Testament when Jewish religious thought saw great men who had lived and suffered and died for their fellowmen in terms of the sacrificial lamb. So it is said of the Servant in Isa. 53.7: 'Like a lamb that is led to the slaughter, and like a sheep that before its shearers is dumb, so he opened not his mouth.' Jeremiah says of himself: 'I was like a gentle lamb led to the slaughter' (Jer. 11.19). Here there is the idea of the sacrificial man as the lamb. So to call Jesus the lamb is not only to say that he is the culmination of the sacrificial system, it is also to say that he is the culmination and the peak of the prophets and the martyrs who died that others might live, and by whose deaths men were brought nearer to God.

From whatever direction we approach the title the Lamb as given to Jesus, we arrive at the picture of him as the means of God's deliverance of man from man's slavery to sin.

We must now turn to the special use of the title the Lamb as we find it in the Revelation. In the Revelation Jesus is caled the Lamb no fewer than twenty-nine times; it is in fact the characteristic title of that book for him. We may well begin by noting one linguistic fact. The word which the Revelation uses for *lamb* is different from the word which both John and Peter use. In John and Peter the word is *amnos*, which is the same word as the Septuagint uses in Isa. 53.7; in the Revelation the word is *arnion*, which is the same word as is used in Jer. 11.19. It may well be that the Revelation uses a different word to underline the fact that it is introducing a different idea. Let us then examine what the Revelation has to say about Jesus as the Lamb.

(i)   It does not by any means discard the old sacrificial idea, for it speaks of the Lamb which was slain, and the Lamb still retains the marks of his sacrifice (5.6,12).

(ii)   It speaks about 'the blood of the Lamb'. The white-robed saints have washed their robes and made them white in the blood of the Lamb (7.14). The white robes stand for the purity of soul and the excellence of character of the saints; and this means that their purity and their victory over sin has been won at the cost of the death and sacrifice of Jesus. It is through the blood of the Lamb that the saints and the martyrs can defy the Accuser (12.10,11). The accuser is Satan. The very word *Devil* comes from the Greek word *Diabolos* which means a *slanderer;* and the word *Satan* itself means an *adversary* or *opponent.* Jewish thought had the idea of a kind of prosecuting angel who did everything to state the case against a man, and to make that man fall, as Satan did in the case of Job (Job 1). Satan is, so to speak, the counsel for the prosecution at the trial of man before God. But because of the sacrificial death of Jesus Christ the saints and the martyrs are beyond accusation; his sacrifice has put them for ever right with God.

(iii) The gentle kindness of the Lamb is not lost in the Revelation, for it is the Lamb who leads those who have suffered for their loyalty to their Lord to the living fountains of water and feeds them with his food (7.17).

(iv) The Lamb is the Master and example of his own. The apostles are the apostles of the Lamb (21.14). Those who are pure and undefiled are those who have followed the Lamb wherever he goes, and the redeemed are the first fruits of God and the Lamb (14.4).

(v) So far there is nothing really new in all this; but now we come to a circle of new ideas. The Lamb has *power,* for the Lamb has seven horns and seven eyes, and in the Bible the horn is always the symbol of power (5.6).

(vi) The Lamb has *authority.* The Book of Life belongs to the Lamb (13.8; 21.27). In the East every king and chief had a register of the citizens who were living and loyal to him. The Book of Life is the register of the citizens of the Kingdom of God, and it belongs to the Lamb.

(vii) In a strangely paradoxical phrase the Revelation speaks of the *wrath* of the Lamb, and that wrath can be a terrible thing (6.16).

(viii) The Lamb has *victory.* The wicked will one day be tortured in the very presence of the Lamb (14.10), and the enemies of God who make war against the Lamb are utterly defeated and shattered (17.14).

(ix) The Lamb has *the control of history.* Only the Lamb can open the seals of the book which contains, as it were, the story of history written in advance (6.1). This means that the Lamb presides over history, and over the destinies of men and nations and the future of the world.

(x) The Lamb is *worshipped.* The most tremendous doxologies are sung to the Lamb (5.12,14); and the four living creatures and the twenty-four elders fall down and worship the Lamb, as do the innumerable company of the redeemed (5.8; 7.9). The Lamb stands on Mount Zion (14.1).

(xi) Worship implies *deity*. The Lamb is in the midst of the throne of God (5.6; 7.17). In the age to come there is no temple in the new Jerusalem, but the Lord God Almighty and the Lamb are its Temple (21.22), and the Lamb is its light (21.23). Here the Lamb shares in the very glory of God.

(xii) Finally, the Lamb is *closely connected with the Church*. We read of the marriage of the Lamb, and the Bride of the Lamb, and the Bride of the Lamb is the Church (19. 8,9; 21.9).

This is a circle of new ideas. The gentleness and the sacrifice remain, but now there is a background of power and strength and might and glory, a background of avenging might and majesty. At first sight this is a strangely paradoxical picture, for we seem to have entered into a sphere of ideas which are the reverse of any ideas which we would naturally connect with a lamb.

But there is an historical fact which sheds a flood of light on this. In the period between the Testaments it was not uncommon to speak of great warrior champions as horned lambs. It is so in Enoch. Here is how Enoch describes the anointing of David by Samuel and the tragic fall of Saul: 'And the Lord of the sheep (that is, God) sent the lamb (that is, Samuel) to another lamb (that is, David), and raised it to being a ram and a leader of the sheep, instead of that ram which had forsaken his glory (that is, Saul)' (I Enoch 89.45). When Enoch is describing the fate of Israel in the terrible days of Antiochus Epiphanes and the heroic role of the Maccabees, it says that the sheep (that is, the people of Israel) were torn and tormented by the dogs and the kites and the eagles (that is, Antiochus and his forces); then lambs

were born and horns grew upon the lambs; on one lamb especially there grew a great horn (that is, Judas Maccabaeus) and
the eagles and the vultures and the ravens could not hurt it
(I Enoch 90.6-17).

Here is precisely the picture of the Revelation. The great
heroes, David and Samuel, and especially that tremendous
warrior Judas Maccabaeus, those who broke the power of the
enemies of God, are horned lambs. The picture of the warrior
lamb may seem strange to us, but it is a picture which the
readers of the Revelation would readily understand. They
would know that the horned lamb is the trumphant warrior
of God.

Now we see what the John of the Revelation has done.
He has taken two pictures of the Lamb and he has welded
them into one composite picture. He has taken the old
sacrificial picture of the Old Testament of the Lamb as the
sacrificial victim, and he has shown us Jesus Christ as the
Lamb who was slain. The sacrifice is not forgotten; the
agony and the sweat and the tears are still there in the
very forefront of the picture. But to that picture he has added
the picture of the horned lamb, of the victorious warrior,
the divine champion, the God-sent, God-strengthened conqueror. To the picture of the agony and the suffering he has
added the picture of majesty and power. And he has crowned
it by setting the Lamb in the very throne of God. The Lamb
who was slain, the Lamb who is the irresistible conqueror,
and the Lamb who shares the throne of God are all one.

In one of the greatest pictures of Jesus in the New
Testament the Revelation has united the gentleness and the
majesty, the suffering and the glory, the humiliation and the
exaltation of that Jesus who is at one and the same time the
victim who died and the victor who is heaven's exalted king.

24

THE SCAPEGOAT

IT is at least possible that in one passage of the New Testament Jesus is thought of in terms of the scapegoat. The passage is in I Peter 2.24, where it is said of Jesus that 'He himself bore our sins in his body on the tree,' or 'He himself carried up our sins in his own body to the tree.' It is quite true that there are certain scholars who hold that this is not a reference to the scapegoat, but a reminiscence of Isa. 53.12, where it is said of the Suffering Servant that 'He bore the sins of many.' It might be held that this interpretation is supported by the fact that the word for *bearing* is the same in I Peter and in Isaiah (*anapherein*). But even if it is held that the words of Peter are an immediate allusion to the Isaiah passage, it may still well be held that *both* the Isaiah and the Peter passage go back to the picture of the scapegoat.

The scapegoat was involved in the ceremonies of the Day of Atonement which, the Law lays it down, must be observed once a year for ever (Lev. 16.34). The Day of Atonement came near to being the central ceremony of Jewish religion. Margolis, writing in the Jewish Encyclopaedia, says: 'No matter how much else has fallen into desuetude, so strong is the hold of the Day of Atonement on the Jewish conscience that no Jew, unless he has cut himself entirely from the Synagogue, will fail to observe the Day of Atonement by resting from his daily pursuits and attending service in the Synagogue. However much a Jew has drifted away from Judaism, however much of the Jewish Law he has abandoned, unless he has become a complete religious renegade, to this day he will keep the Day of Atonement.'

What then is this unique day? All Jewish religion centres

in the covenant relationship between God and the Jewish people. The covenant relationship is dependent on the keeping of the Law. If the Law is broken, then the covenant relationship is also broken. It was precisely to meet this situation that the whole sacrificial system came into being. Sacrifice was the thing which restored the covenant relationship when breaches of the Law had interrupted it. But a grim and terrible possibility enters into this. What if in some way of which men may well be unaware the Temple itself, the altar itself, the Holy Place itself has become tainted and infected and contaminated? Then clearly all the sacrifices are unavailing. What if there are sins of which the people and even the priesthood are guilty of which they are quite unaware? What if there are sins of which they are not conscious perhaps because of their own sinfulness? If that be so, then the sacrifices are rendered ineffective. So it is laid down for the priest: 'He shall make atonement for the sanctuary, and he shall make atonement for the tent of meeting and for the altar, and he shall make atonement for the priests and for all the people of the assembly' (Lev. 16.33). The Day of Atonement was one grand act of sacrifice in which atonement was made for sins known and unknown, for defilement of the Holy Place itself, and of the priests and of the people. It was one comprehensive act which covered all possible defilement of all possible people and places. It was one grand act of penitence covering every sin, known and unknown, deliberate and accidental, realised and unrealised.

It was an act of penitence in which every one in Israel was to take part. 'In the seventh month, on the tenth day of the month, you shall afflict yourselves, and shall do no work, either the native or the stranger who sojourns among you, for on this day shall atonement be made for you to cleanse you; from all your sins you shall be clean before the Lord' (Lev. 16.29,30). Fasting was rigorous and was obligatory on every male from twelve and every female from thirteen years upwards. Children even younger than that were encouraged to begin fasting, so that they would be ready to practise it in all its rigour when they came to be of an age when they were bound to do so.

The ritual of the Day of Atonement is described in Leviticus 16. And one of the most dramatic parts of it centred round the scapegoat. Two goats were taken. Lots were drawn, and one goat was for the Lord, and it became a sin offering; the other goat was, as the AV has it, the scapegoat, as the newer translations have it, for Azazel (Lev. 16.6-10). Originally the lots which were drawn were of box-wood, but in the time of Jesus they were of gold. To the horn of the scapegoat a tongue-shaped piece of scarlet cloth was tied.

The meaning of Azazel is uncertain, but Azazel was probably a desert demon to whom the scapegoat was to be delivered. The scapegoat was brought forward, and then the regulations go on: 'And Aaron shall lay both his hands upon the head of the live goat, and confess over him all the iniquities of the people of Israel, and all their transgressions, all their sins; and he shall put them on the head of the goat, and send him away into the wilderness by the hand of a man who is in readiness. The goat shall bear all their iniquities upon him to a solitary land' (Lev. 16.20-22). The words which the High Priest said in later days, while he rested his hands on the goat, were as follows: 'O Lord God, they have committed iniquity; they have transgressed, they have sinned— thy people, the house of Israel. O Lord God, cover over, I entreat thee, their iniquities, their transgressions and their sins, which they have wickedly committed and sinned before thee—thy people, the house of Israel. As it is written in the Law of Moses thy servant saying: "For in that day it shall be covered over for you to make you clean from all your sins; before the Lord ye shall be cleansed." '

When the goat was led away, a scarlet thread was tied to the sanctuary, and, when the goat was killed, so it was said, the thread turned to white. This may well be the origin of Isaiah's saying:

> Though your sins are like scarlet,
>   they shall be as white as snow;
> though they are red like crimson,
>   they shall become like wool.

(Isa. 1.18)

There is no doubt that the idea was that in some way the sins of the people were transferred to the goat, and that it went out to the desolate wilderness bearing the sins known and unknown of the people, and thus making forgiveness and reconciliation possible for every one who was penitent in heart.

We believe that it was this picture which Peter saw in Jesus. He saw Jesus carrying our sins in his own body to the Cross, just as the scapegoat carried the sins of Israel. He believed that if a man with a contrite and penitent heart laid his sins, as it were, on Jesus Christ, Jesus bore them in his own body in his death on the Cross, and thus restored the lost relationship between man and God. To us the ritual may be strange but to a Jew the picture of Jesus as the scapegoat would be very vivid. And this we do know—it was indeed our sins which crucified our Lord, and he in his death found the remedy and the cure for them.

25

APAUGASMA AND *CHARAKTER*

WE now move on to consider in this and in the following six chapters titles and interpretations of Jesus which are to be found in the Letter to the Hebrews.

We have left the title with which we are dealing in this chapter in the original Greek, because it is very difficult to come to a decision as to what the translation of *apaugasma* really is. When we study the renderings of *apaugasma* in the various translations we find that it oscillates between two meanings. Into the first class there fall the following translations:

> The *brightness* of God's glory and the express image of his person (AV).
>
> The *effulgence* of his glory and the very image of his substance (RV).
>
> The *radiance* of the glory of God and the very expression of his being (*Twentieth Century New Testament*).
>
> The *radiance* of the glory of God, and the very expression of his being (J. B. Phillips).
>
> The *effulgence* of God's grandeur and the representative of his essence (Ferrar Fenton).
>
> The *effulgence* of God's splendour, and the stamp of God's very being (NEB).

Into the second class there fall the following translations:

> He *reflects* the glory of God and bears the very stamp of his nature (RSV).
>
> The *reflection* of God's glory and the living image of his being (C. Kingsley Williams).
>
> He brightly *reflects* God's glory and is the exact representation of his being (Weymouth).

316

The reason for this divergence is that *apaugasma* has two closely interrelated meanings. It comes from the verb *augazein*, which means both 'to flash out', that is 'to radiate', and 'to flash back', that is, 'to reflect'. Hence the noun *apaugasma* can mean either a light emitted from some luminary, that is a 'radiance' or 'effulgence', or a light reflected from some luminary that is a 'refulgence' or 'reflection'.

It is in point of fact sometimes very difficult to decide which of the two meanings the word has. In Wisd. 7.25,26 there is a description of the divine Wisdom in a series of interrelated words:

> She is a *breath* (*atmis*) of the power of God,
> a pure *emanation* (*aporroia*) of the glory of the Almighty,
> ....
> She is an *apaugasma* of eternal light,
> a spotless *mirror* (*eisoptron*) of the working of God,
> and an *image* (*eikōn*) of his goodness.

The difficulty of that passage is that, if we take *apaugasma* with the two words which go before, *atmis*, 'breath' and *aporroia*, 'outflow' or 'emanation', then 'apaugasma must mean 'effulgence', and the picture is that of Wisdom as the light streaming from eternal light. If on the other hand we take *apaugasma* with the two words which follow, *eisoptron,* 'mirror', and *eikōn,* 'image', then *apaugasma* must mean 'reflection', the light reflected from the eternal light.

Philo uses the word *apaugasma*. As Plato saw it, there are laid up in the heavenly places the perfect patterns and forms and ideas of which everything in this world is a shadowy and imperfect copy. So Philo, basing his world view on Platonic thought, describes the universe as the *apaugasma* of sacred things and the copy of the archetype.[1] There the meaning can only be 'reflection'.

On the other hand the Nicene Creed speaks of Jesus as

---

[1] *Concerning Noah's Work as a Planter* 12.

'Light of Light'. Here the idea is that Jesus is the light, the radiance streaming from God, and thus there is laid down the completely inseparable connection between the Father and the Son. Lactantius works out this idea: 'The Father is as it were an overflowing fountain, the Son like a stream flowing from it; the Father is like the sun, the Son, as it were, a ray extended from the sun. Since he is faithful and dear to the Most High Father, he is not separated from him, any more than the stream is from the fountain, or the ray from the sun; for the water of the fountain is in the stream, and the sun's light is in the ray.'[1] Origen says: 'The Father did not beget the Son, and then, as it were, rid him of begetting, but he is continually begetting him, just as the light continually produces its own radiance.'[2] When we think of Jesus as the radiance streaming from God, then we see the essential and continuous living connection between the Father and the Son.

If we take *apaugasma* to mean 'reflection' rather than 'radiance', the essential meaning is not so very different. It may indeed be that this is rather the more likely sense of the word, for *apaugasma* is frequently used of the images in mirrors. The meaning would then be that Jesus is the reflection of the glory of God, that in him as in a mirror we see the glory of God. We might use as an analogy the way in which the roof of Chartres Cathedral can be seen. The roof is marvellously painted and carved, but it is so vast and lofty that it is impossible to see it as a whole. But there is in the centre of the Cathedral a font of still, clear water, and in the surface of the water the whole roof is reflected, and can be seen as a whole, as it can be seen in no other way. So man could never have seen the infinite God at all, unless he saw God reflected in the mirror of Jesus Christ.

To say that Jesus is the *apaugasma* of the glory of God is

[1] *The Institutes* 4.29.   [2] *Homily on Jeremiah* 9.4.

either to say that Jesus is the radiance which streams from God, or it is to say that Jesus is the reflection of God, in whom infinity and eternity are made visible to humanity and time. Either meaning stresses the unbreakable connection between Jesus and God.

The word *charaktēr* is very much easier to deal with. *Charaktēr* is the impression produced by a seal or by a diestamp in wax or in metal. Aristotle, for instance, says that the metal which was originally used for buying and selling was counted and valued simply by weight, but finally a *stamp (charaktēr)* was impressed upon it to state its value and so to do away with the clumsy method of weighing it.[1] Because of this *charaktēr* comes very easily to mean 'an exact replica', copy or reproduction. This meaning was extended so that, for instance, a man could speak of a statue as *charaktēr tēs emēs morphēs,* an exact reproduction of my shape. So then to say that Jesus is the *charaktēr* of God is to say, as it were, that Jesus is the exact reproduction of God, that in Jesus there is a clear and accurate picture of what God is.

Charaktēr went on to mean 'a distinguishing mark', a mark by which a thing or person could be clearly distinguished from other things or persons, for it is just such a distinction and identification that the mark of a seal brings about. It can mean, for instance, a linguistic dialect, a special way of speaking by which a person's country or place of origin may be known; it can mean an orator's style, the particular way of speaking by which his speeches can be recognised. Theophrastus wrote his book of *Characters* in which he set out the different characteristics which distinguish different types of people. The word can be used for the features of a man's countenance which distinguish him from other people, and which, at least to some extent, indicate his ancestry. And so the word *charaktēr* comes in the end to have very

[1] *Politics* 1267 a 40.

much the same meaning as the English word 'character' or 'characteristic', the distinguishing marks which make a person the person he is. So to call Jesus the *charaktēr* of God is very near to saying that in him we see expressly reproduced the character of God.

So now we see the great composite picture which these two words paint of Jesus Christ. If Jesus is the *apaugasma* of God, he is either the radiance which streams from God or the reflection of God. If Jesus is the *charaktēr* of God, he is the one in whom the essential character of God is with complete accuracy displayed and reproduced.

Further, these two words are complementary in the most notable way. If we were to say that Jesus is the *apaugasma* of God and stop there, it would in effect be to deny that Jesus has or can have any independent existence at all, for clearly the ray of light cannot exist apart from the light. If we were to say that Jesus is the *charaktēr* of God, it might well mean that, while in one sense he was the accurate reproduction of God, in another sense he was quite different, for the seal itself might be of gold or of a precious stone, and the substance on which it was impressed might be no better than wax or clay. But to say that Jesus is *apaugasma* and *charaktēr* is at one and the same time, is to state the essential identity of Jesus with God and the essential independence of his being; it is at one and the same time to state his deity and his humanity.

Jesus is at one and the same time the radiance of God's glory and the reflection of his majesty, and the perfect replica and reproduction of the character of God in human form. In other words, it is in Jesus that God uniquely makes himself known to men in a form which all men can see and understand.

26

APOSTLE

On only one occasion in the New Testament is Jesus called
by the title *apostle*. In Heb. 3.1 he is called the Apostle and
High Priest of the religion we profess (NEB). So unusual
is this that A. B. Bruce called it 'an example of the fresh,
creative genius of the writer, and the unconventional nature
of his style.' Apostle never became a title that was widely
used of Jesus. In later days Justin Martyr called Jesus 'the
Son and Apostle of the Father of all and of the Lord God',
and 'the Messenger and Apostle, for he announces all that
needs to be known, and is sent to tell all that is announced.'[1]
But although 'Apostle' never became a popular title for Jesus,
it is an extremely meaningful title.

The Greek word *apostolos* is really an adjective. It comes
from the verb *apostellein,* which means 'to send forth,' and it
means 'sent forth', 'despatched.' In classical Greek by far
the commonest use of it has to do with ships which are sent
out, and it often describes a naval squadron sent into action
or on foreign service. Twice Herodotus uses it to describe a
herald or envoy sent to carry proposals from one government
to another (1.21; 5.28). It later Greek it can describe a
group of people sent out for any purpose, such as, for instance, to colonise some foreign place; and it can also describe the leader of such an expedition. It can be seen that
in ordinary Greek the word is always passive; it always
describes some one despatched as agent, envoy, representative,
ambassador of some power greater than himself.

There is no difficulty in applying the word to Jesus in this

[1] *First Apology* 12, 63.

sense. Again and again in the Gospels Jesus speaks of himself as
being sent, and often the word for the sending is *apostellein*.
'He who receives me,' said Jesus, 'receives him that sent me'
(Matt. 10.40; Mark 9.37; Luke 9.48; 10.16). The parable
of the wicked husbandmen describes how the son, who is
Jesus, was sent (Matt. 21.37; Mark 12.6). This way of speaking of Jesus as *sent* is specially characteristic of the Fourth
Gospel (e.g. John 3.17,28; 5.36; 6.29,57; 8.42; 10.36; 17.3,8,
18,21,23,25). To describe Jesus as the Apostle is to describe
him as the One whom God uniquely sent into this world.

To this conclusion we could have come from the Greek
background of the word alone; but when we examine the
Jewish usage of it, it becomes even more significant when
it is applied to Jesus. Amongst the later Jews the word was
in common use in its Hebrew form *shaliach,* which also
means one 'who is sent'. In all religious matters the Sanhedrin
was the supreme governing body of all Jews not only in
Palestine but also all over the world. When the Sanhedrin
wished to despatch an instruction, a command, a warning to
Jews in any part of the world, the bearer of it was known as
a *shaliach* or *apostolos*. After Jerusalem was destroyed, and
when the leaders of Judaism were in exile, the Jewish patriarch
had around him a body of counsellors, who acted as his
advisers at home and his agents abroad, and the title of
such men was *shaliach* or *apostolos*. Saul, for instance, was
the *shaliach* or *apostolos* of the Sanhedrin when he went
to Damascus to organise a campaign of persecution against
the Christians (Acts 9. 1,2). In Acts 28.21 the Jews of Rome
say that they have received no letters from Judaea concerning
Paul. That is to say, no *shaliach* or *apostolos* had come
from the Sanhedrin with instructions as to how Paul was to
be treated.

It is here that a new and very important element enters
into the meaning of the word. To the Jew the *apostolos* or

shaliach was not only a messenger; he was a delegate who
for the time being and for the particular duty assigned to
him exercised all the power and the authority of the
Sanhedrin. Hence the rabbis said: 'The one whom a man
sends (that is, his *apostolos* or *shaliach*) is the equivalent of
the man himself.' 'A king's ambassador is as the king himself.'
An *apostolos* is more than a messenger; on him rests all the
power and the authority of the one who sent him.

In the popular Greek of the papyri we meet a very similar
use of the word *apostolos*. In the arranging of a marriage,
a divorce, or any contract an *apostolos* was very commonly
used. The *apostolos* was the chosen and delegated representative of the contracting party; he spoke and acted as such
and entered into agreements and undertakings for the person
whom he represented. The principal party acted through the
apostolos, and the *apostolos* had complete authority to act
for the person whom he represented.

We must briefly return to the Jewish world of thought. To
four great prophets the name of *Shaliach* was given, to Moses,
to Elijah, to Elisha and to Ezekiel. It was given to them
because God had in a very special way delegated his power
to them so that they were able to perform miracles and to do
the things which only the power of God could do. Moses
brought water out of the rock; Elijah brought the rain, and
restored to life one who had died; Elisha also restored one
to life, and also opened a mother's womb; and, basing on
Ezekiel 37, the rabbis said that Ezekiel would receive the
key to the graves at the resurrection of the dead. The *apostolos*
was not only the messenger of God; he exercised the power
of God which had been delegated to him. It is in fact significant that in the passage of Hebrews in which Jesus is called
apostolos the very next verse begins with a reference to
Moses. By the power of God Moses delivered the people from
Egypt; by the power of God Jesus delivered men from sin.

It is also to be noted that the writer to the Hebrews join in this same verse the two titles Apostle and High Priest. And one of the rabbinic titles for the High Priest was 'the envoy, the *shaliach*, the *apostolos*, of the Merciful.' And so the *apostolos* brings to men not only the power but also the mercy of God.

So, then, the word *apostolos* as applied to Jesus means that Jesus was uniquely sent by God, and that Jesus is delegated by God to bring to men both the power and the mercy of God.

27

FORERUNNER

THE name forerunner, *prodromos,* is only once applied to Jesus in the New Testament, but the picture in it is so vivid and dramatic that it is well worthwhile to make a study of it. The one passage in which it occurs is Heb. 6.20; the writer to the Hebrews has been speaking about the hope of the Christian, and he goes on: 'That hope we hold. It is like an anchor for our lives, an anchor safe and sure. It enters in through the veil, where Jesus has entered on our behalf as forerunner, having become a high priest for ever in the succession of Melchizedek' (NEB).

It is not common in the Greek Old Testament. The days of spring are said to be the forerunners of the grape (Num. 13.22, LXX). The early figs are said to be the forerunners of the main harvest (Isa. 28.4). It was God's threat that he would send out hornets before his people to drive out the Hivite, the Canaanite and the Hittite (Ex. 23.28), and these hornets are called the forerunners, the *prodromoi,* of the host of God (Wisd. 12.8).

It is the secular Greek background of the world which is of the greatest interest. In secular Greek *prodromos* is very largely a military word, and is is used of the troops which were sent out in advance of the main army to reconnoitre the ground and to ensure the safety of the main army which was to follow. The *prodromoi* were the scouts, the advance guard, the reconnaissance corps of the army.

Herodotus uses the word of the picked cavalry of the Scythians, sent out in advance of the main army to test the strength of the Persian forces (4.121,122). He uses it of the advance guard of the Spartans sent out to meet the invading Persians (9.14). When Thucydides is describing the siege of Athens, he tells how Pericles the Athenian leader was certain that the best policy for the Athenians was to remain within their walls and not sally out. He nevertheless constantly sent out cavalry detachments to prevent *prodromoi,* flying parties, of the enemy from raiding the fields near the city and so ravaging the crops (2.22). *Prodromoi* is the word for flying columns, swift-moving skirmishers, whose duty it was to ensure the safety of the main body of the troops.

The *prodromoi* were a most important factor in ancient warfare. In his treatise on *The Cavalry Commander* Xenophon says that they must be well equipped, well trained in the use of the javelin, and above all kept at the highest peak of efficiency, to attain which he recommends continuous competition between the *prodromoi* attached to different regiments.[1] In *The Constitution of Athens* Aristotle recommends that the *prodromoi* must be frequently and rigorously inspected and that all who are unfit must be mercilessly weeded out.[2] Alexander the Great was one of the world's great cavalry commanders, and he had a special corps of *prodromoi* to act as the scouts, the guides and the advance guard of his army.[3] There is one other relevant military use of the word. Herodotus uses it of heralds sent out in advance to announce the coming of a leader, and to invite the loyalty of the people to him (1.60).

Prodromos is also a naval word. It was used of the lightest and swiftest triremes which were sent out ahead of the fleet to scout in advance of the main squadron and to strike unexpected blows.[4]

[1] *The Cavalry Commander* 1.25,26.
[2] *The Constitution of Athens* 49.1.
[3] Arrian, *Anabasis* 1.12.7.
[4] Alciphron, *Letters of Fishermen* 1.14 (11).

There is one further use of the word which I have seen
mentioned but not documented. The great harbour of
Alexandria was difficult to enter. A pilot boat was sent out
to sail in front of the ship entering the harbour and to lead
it along the channel, and it is said that that pilot boat was
called the *prodromos*. It went first to make it safe for the
larger ship to follow.

The whole essence of the word *prodromos* is that it
describes some one whose function it is to go first in order
to make it safe for others to follow.

It is said of Jesus that he enters into the inner shrine
behind the curtain as our forerunner. Here is a picture clear
and dramatic to every Jew who knew the Temple. The
Temple consisted of a series of courts into each one of which
fewer people had the right to go. First, there was the Court
of the Gentiles into which anyone could go. Second, there
was the Court of the Women, beyond which women could
not go unless they were definitely about to make some
sacrifice. Third, there was the Court of the Israelites, beyond
which no lay person could go for any purpose. Fourth, there
was the Court of the Priests in which the sacrifices were
made and the Temple ritual carried out. At the far end there
stood the Temple proper. It was divided into two parts by
a curtain. The outer part was the Holy Place; and the inner
part was the Holy of Holies. Into the Holy of Holies only
one man might ever enter, the High Priest; and he might
only enter on one day, the Day of Atonement; and even on
that day he must not linger, 'lest he put Israel in terror'.

The whole essence of the matter is that the way to the
nearer presence of God is shut and barred to any ordinary
person, and even for the High Priest there is danger in the
approach to God. This is typical of Old Testament religion.
'No man shall see me and live,' God said to Moses (Ex.
33.20). The terrified cry of Manoah, after he had realised

who his heavenly visitor was, is: 'We shall surely die because we have seen God' (Judg. 13.22). The greatness of Jesus Christ is that he opened that way to God for every man. He is the great forerunner who goes first into the presence of God to make it possible for others to follow.

The great characteristic of sin is that it separates men from God. When Adam and Eve had broken the commandment their first instinct was to hide from God (Gen. 3.8). Jesus came to do something in his life and in his death which made men see that God is no longer the terrible Judge waiting to blast his people but the loving Father whose one desire is that they should come home to him.

In any army the *prodromoi* were the bravest of the brave; they had to take their lives in their hands, they had, if need be, to lay down their lives to make it safe for others to follow. Jesus is the great *prodromos* who gave his life to make it safe for us to enter fearlessly into the presence of God.

28

SURETY

THE word for *surety* is *egguos* and it is used of Jesus only once in the New Testament. It is used in Heb. 7.22, where, as the AV translates it, Jesus was made a surety of a better testament. The RSV says that Jesus was made the surety of a better covenant. And J. B. Phillips has it that Jesus was made *the living guarantor* of a better agreement.

Although the word *egguos* occurs only once in the New Testament, it well repays close and detailed study. Although it is the only one of them to appear in the New Testament, it belongs to a group of closely interrelated Greek words, and to get the full flavour of *egguos* we must look at the whole group. The basic meaning of the whole group is the idea of surety, guarantee, security, pledge. The idea behind them is that of a sponsor who will never break his word and of a pledge which is certain to be fulfilled.

(i) We begin with the word *egguos* itself. We find it in the Septuagint. There is a famous passage in Ecclesiasticus which tells of the obligation and the danger of being a surety, and of the obligation that is laid upon a man when some one stands surety for him:

A good man will be surety for his neighbour,
   but a man who has lost his sense of shame will fail him.
Do not forget all the kindness of your surety,
   for he has given his life for you.
A sinner will overthrow the prosperity of his surety,
   and one who does not feel grateful will abandon his
     rescuer.
Being surety has ruined many men who were prosperous,
   and has shaken them like a wave of the sea.

It has driven men of power into exile,
  and they have wandered among foreign nations.
Assist your neighbour according to your ability,
  but take heed to yourself lest you fall.

(Ecclus 29.14-20)

It is a strangely prophetic passage. Many an ungrateful man has ruined the generous man who stood surety for him. To have some one stand surety for us is not only to receive a privilege, it is also to enter into a responsibility and what is true on the human level is true on the divine level also.

The word can be used metaphorically. In II Maccabees there is the story of how the Jewish leaders prepared to face the forces of Antiochus Epiphanes: 'Just as dawn was breaking, the two armies joined battle, the one having as *pledge* of success and victory not only their valour but their reliance upon the Lord, while the other made rage their leader in the fight' (II Macc. 10.28).

Xenophon uses *egguos* in its legal sense. He suggests that it might be a good thing if the state owned public slaves and hired them out to those who required their services, in which case the hirer of the slaves would have to become the guarantor (*egguos*) for their price.[1]

The word is not uncommon in legal agreements in the papyri. So in a marriage contract a father is surety for the payment of the dowry (P.Oxy.905). A woman had no legal status and therefore could not legally adopt a child. So when she wished to do so her guardian had to stand as surety for her (P.Oxy.38). The idea of guarantee and pledge is always in *egguos*, and the guarantee must be honoured and the pledge must be kept, even at the cost of a man's whole fortune or of his life itself.

(ii) The second word in the group is *egguētēs*, which is in fact the commoner legal word. *Egguos*, although it is used

Ways and Means 3.14.

as a noun, is really an adjective meaning *reliable, under good security*. *Egguētēs* is the real noun and means a *sponsor*, a *surety*, a *guarantor*. It is very widely used. It is used of the trustees who guarantee the solvency of a bank and who are sureties that money deposited will be honoured and repaid.[1] Xenophon suggested that the state itself might own ships and hire them out to merchants as required if proper *security* was given.[2] When Socrates was discussing the penalty which should be exacted from himself, he suggested that he should be fined thirty minae, a sum which he could not himself pay, but, he said, he had friends of ample means who would stand surety for him.[3] Aristotle says that the law is the *guarantor* (*egguētēs*) of men's just claims on one another; the existence of the law guarantees that a man's just rights will be observed and protected.[4] He says that money stands as a guarantee of exchange in the future; the possession of it is a guarantee that a man will be able to meet his needs in the future, even if he does not wish not wish to spend it now.[5]

Herodotus has one of his pleasantly gossipy stories which illustrates the meaning of this word. He is dealing with marriage customs in Assyria. On a certain day in every village the marriageable girls are assembled. They are offered for sale, and for the very beautiful ones large sums are paid. By-and-by the uncomely and the ill-favoured and the actually ugly are reached. They are offered to prospective husbands along with a sum of money taken from the proceeds of the sale of the beautiful ones. But the man who undertakes to accept such a girl together with the compensating sum of money must provide a guarantee, must become an *egguētēs*,

---

[1] *Demosthenes* 33.10.   [2] *Ways and Means* 3.14.
[3] Plato, *Apology* 38c.   [4] *Politics* 1280b 11.
[5] *Nicomachean Ethics* 1133b 12.

that he will not take the money and then refuse the marriage.[1]

Once again we arrive at the same basic idea of some one who guarantees that some agreement will be kept.

(iii)   The third of our words is the related verb *egguaomai* which means *to pledge oneself,* to give security on someone's behalf. It is the word for going bail for a man, in order to save him from going to prison because he cannot pay a fine which has been imposed upon him.[2] In any sale the broker, the middleman, is security for the legality of the transaction.[3] It is used for the guarantee, the promise, the pledge between the contracting parties that a treaty will be kept.[4] The word is commonly used in the same way as we sometimes say: 'I guarantee that...' So Socrates says: I guarantee that all who do not possess knowledge will wish to possess it.[5]

Once again we are back at the same basic idea of a pledge and a guarantee.

It is into this circle of ideas that the writer to the Hebrews brings Jesus when he says that Jesus is the guarantor of a better covenant between God and man. Just what does he mean by this?

A covenant is really a relationship between two people. Jesus is, therefore, the guarantor that there is possible a new relationship between man and God. Wherein does this newness lie? The basis of the old covenant was the law (Ex. 24.1-6). The old covenant was dependent on the keeping of the law. Since God is essentially perfect and since man is essentially imperfect, this relationship always inevitably left man in default, and it necessarily thought of God in terms of law-giver and judge and of man as law-breaker and defendant. The new relationship between God and man which Jesus brought is summed up in the word Father. That is to say, the

---

[1] Herodotus 1.196.
[2] Plato, *Laws* 855b.
[3] Plato, *Laws* 953e, 954a.
[4] Xenophon, *Anabasis* 7.4.13.
[5] Plato, *Euthydemus* 274b.

new relationship is based on love and not on law. In such a relationship God is no longer thought of as the judge who must condemn; he is thought of as the Father who cannot be happy until the family circle of his children is complete.

But the almost necessary reaction to any such message is that it is too good to be true. How can I believe that? What possible guarantee have I that that is true? The guarantor of that new relationship is Jesus. He did not come only to tell in words that this is the case; he came in his own person to demonstrate that this is the case. 'He who has seen me,' he said, 'has seen the Father' (John 14.9). 'The word became flesh' (John 1.14), or, as we might paraphrase it: 'The mind of God became a person.' Jesus is the exact demonstration of what God is like, of the mind of God, of the attitude of God to man. In Jesus we see one who fed the hungry, healed the sick, comforted the sorrowing, was the friend of outcasts and sinners. And, because Jesus is one with God, he is the guarantee that God is like that. To put it at its very simplest, Jesus is the guarantor of the love of God. It is through him and him alone that we know what God is like; he lived and he died to show us the heart of God; he is the guarantor of the possibility of the new relationship with God, the relationship in which the old fear has become the new love.

29

MEDIATOR

THE idea of Jesus as Mediator is deeply embedded in Christian thought and interwoven into Christian language, especially the language of liturgy and devotion. In the New Testament the word mediator is four times applied to Jesus. In the Pastoral Epistles it is said that there is one mediator between God and men, the man Christ Jesus (I Tim. 2.5). In the Letter to the Hebrews Jesus is three times said to be the mediator of a better covenant between God and man (Heb. 6; 9.5; 12.24).

The Greek word for mediator is *mesitēs,* which is closely connected with the word *mesos,* which means *in the middle.* The *mesitēs* is literally a *middleman.* Westcott defines a *mesitēs* as 'one who standing between the contracting parties shall bring them into fellowship'. Hillard says that a *mesitēs* was anyone 'who formed the channel of communication between two others'. The word *mesitēs* is itself late; it does not appear in classical Greek and does not emerge until Hellenistic times, but the idea behind it is deeply embedded in ancient thought, and especially in the thought and the whole way of life of the Greeks. But before we come to the Greek picture we must see the idea and the use of the word in Hebrew thought.

The word occurs only once in the Greek Old Testament. It occurs in Job 9.33 where, as the AV translates it, it is the complaint of Job that there is no *daysman* between him and God. The margin gives *umpire* for daysman, and this is the translation adopted by Moffatt and the RSV. It is Job's feeling that there is no one to bring him and God together so that he may plead his innocence.

In later Hebrew thought the word *mesitēs* was most commonly applied to Moses. In the *Assumption of Moses,* one of the inter-testamental books, Moses is portrayed as saying to Joshua: 'God designed and devised me, and he prepared me before the foundation of the world, that I should be the mediator of his convenant.' The same book speaks of 'the commandments, in which Moses was the mediator to us' (1.14; 3.12). It was through Moses that God gave the covenant and the Law to Israel. Moses is therefore the mediator between God and his people.

There is one other Hebrew use of this word. Jewish thought became increasingly conscious of the transcendence of God. The result of this was a deep awareness of the unbridgeable gulf between the divine and the human, between God and man. One consequence of this was that it was sometimes felt that the prayers of men could not have direct access to this transcendent God, but that they were brought to God by angels as intermediaries. The angel who had this particular charge was Michael, and sometimes in Jewish thought Michael was called the *mesitēs,* the mediator between God and man.

The word came even into pagan religion. As Plutarch tells, in Persian religion, in Zoroastrianism, there are two great powers, Oromazes, the power of the light, and Areimanius, the power of the dark; and between the two there stands Mithras, who was called the mediator.[1]

But it is in Greek life and thought that the idea of mediation is most deeply rooted. It was the Greek aim to settle all disputes by mediation so that they would never reach the law-courts. In Athens especially this custom of mediation was an integral part of the life of the community. The word *mesitēs,* as we have seen, had not yet emerged, but the word

---

[1] Plutarch, *Concerning Isis and Osiris* 46.

diaitētēs, usually translated *arbitrator,* means almost exactly the same thing, and describes the man who had exactly the same function. Aristotle speaks of the wisdom of preferring artistration which is based on equity to law in the law-courts which is necessarily based on strict justice. Arbitrators, mediators, are appointed that equity may prevail.[1] In *The Constitution of Athens* he describes how this was done. There was a body known as The Forty; it consisted of four members from each of the ten Athenian tribes. In all cases involving sums of less than ten drachmae, about ten shillings, the decision of The Forty was final and binding. In sums greater than that The Forty appointed a *diaitētēs,* an arbitrator, a mediator. These arbitrators consisted of all Athenian citizens in their sixtieth year, and they were compelled by law to accept the duty of mediation when they were selected for it. Their sole function was to bring the disputing parties together, and so to effect an agreement, or, at least, a compromise. If they could effect no agreement, they must at least give their decision, and only if the parties refused to accept this did the matter reach a jury and the law-courts. Greek society knew all about mediation; it was almost founded upon it.

By the time we come to the papyri and to New Testament times the word *mesitēs* has actually emerged, and frequently in legal papyri we read of two disputing parties coming to the magistrate with a request to appoint a *mesitēs* in order to settle some difference between them.

What was true of individuals in Greece was equally true of states. Almost all Greek treaties contained a clause that in the event of any further difference as to the interpretation of the terms of the treaty arising, the matter should be settled by arbitration and mediation. For instance, during the Peloponnesian War we find the Athenians saying to the Spartans: 'You shall give satisfaction to us, and we to you, according to

[1] *Rhetoric* 1.13.18.

our ancestral customs, settling disputed points by arbitration without war.''

The world of the New Testament knew all about mediation both between individuals and states. Here then is the picture of Jesus. Jesus is the *mesitēs,* the mediator, the middleman, between man and God. It is his supreme function to bring together man and God. There are certain essential qualities which any mediator must possess.

(i) The *mesitēs* must be able perfectly to represent both parties in the dispute. He must fully understand and sympathise with both. Otherwise his decision is bound to be prejudiced, one-sided, unjust and inequitable. Jesus is therefore the only possible mediator between God and man, because he is perfectly God and man. Irenaeus describes Jesus thus, *hominibus ostendens Deum, Deo autem exhibens hominem,* showing God to men, and at the same time presenting men to God. There is no other person in the universe who can be the middleman between God and men.

(ii) The first duty of the mediator is to establish communication between the two parties who are in dispute. In the case of Jesus the problem was not to establish communication between God and man, for God never needed to be reconciled to man; the problem was to establish communication between man and God. God had always been knocking at the door of man's heart; but man had always been barring that door, setting out to the far countries of the soul, and turning his back on God. And even when man realised his sin, in his terror he thought of nothing but of making the futile attempt to run away from God. The task of Jesus was to bring men back to God by showing them the love of God in such a way that they would hate their sins and turn again to the God whose heart is ever yearning for them.

¹ Thucydides 4.118.8.

(iii) But the task of the mediator goes beyond merely establishing communication; he has to establish between the two conflicting parties a new relationship in which suspicion has turned to trust, enmity to friendship, and hatred to love. There lies the heart of the matter. It was the essential task of the mediator to establish, not merely a legal relationship, but a personal relationship in which love is the bond. Jesus is not the mediator who brings two legal disputants together; he is the mediator who brings together two lovers who have drifted apart and for whom life can never be complete until they are in fellowship again. God, being love, needs man. Man, being weak and sinful and helpless, needs God. And Jesus is the mediator, the middleman, who standing in the midst draws man and God together again.

30

ARCHEGOS

THE title *archēgos* is given to Jesus four times in the New Testament, and for the moment we have left it untranslated, because it has been given a veritable splendour of translations. Before we begin to study it in detail we shall look at the way in which it has been rendered in eight translations of the New Testament. In the tabulation of the renderings we shall set down the AV as a basis and then see how the other translations depart from it.

(i) It occurs first in Acts 3.15 in the speech of Peter:

> You killed the *Prince* of life.

This is also the translation of Weymouth, Kingsley Williams, and J. B. Phillips. The margin of the AV and the RSV have the *Author* of life. Moffatt has the *Pioneer* of life. The *Twentieth Century New Testament* has the *guide* to life. The NEB has *him who leads the way* to life.

(ii) It occurs second in Acts 5.31, again in a speech of Peter:

> Him hath God exalted with his right hand to be a *Prince* and Saviour.

This is also the translation of J. B. Phillips. The RSV and the NEB have *Leader* and Saviour; Moffatt has *Pioneer* and Saviour; Kingsley Williams has *Captain* and Saviour; Weymouth has *Chief Leader* and Saviour; the *Twentieth Century New Testament* has *guide* and Saviour.

(iii) It occurs in Heb. 2.10:

> It became him (that is, God) in bringing many sons unto glory, to make the *captain* of their salvation perfect through sufferings.

339

Moffatt and the RSV have *Pioneer;* Weymouth has *Prince Leader;* Kingsley Williams, J. B. Phillips and the NEB have *Leader*; the *Twentieth Century New Testament* has *author*.

(iv) It is used in Heb. 12.2 where the instruction is that the Christian should walk 'looking unto Jesus the *author* and finisher of our faith'. The AV has *beginner* in the margin; the RSV and Moffatt have *pioneer;* the *Twentieth Century New Testament* and Kingsley Williams have *leader*; Weymouth has *Prince Leader*; Phillips has the *source* of our faith; the NEB paraphrases: 'Jesus on whom faith depends from start to finish.' Ther is perhaps no word in the New Testament which has produced such magnificence of translation. Let us investigate the meaning of this word in detail.

(i) We begin with the usage of the word in the Septuagint in which it frequently occurs.

(*a*) It is used of the heads of families (Ex. 6.14; I Chron. 5.24; 8.28; I Esd. 5.1; Neh. 7.70,71). The idea here is what modern language would express by speaking of the chief of the clan.

(*b*) It is used of national leaders, apart from military commanders, both in the case of Israel and of other nations (Num. 10.4; 13.3,4; 16.2; 24.17; 25.4; Deut. 33.21; Isa. 30.4). The modern equivalent would be a minister of state.

(*c*) It is used of military leaders and captains (Judg. 9.44; I Chron. 12.20; 26.26; II Chron. 23.14; Neh. 2.9). In this use it may denote anyone from the captain of a company to the general of an army.

(*d*) It is used adjectivally meaning chief. Lam. 2.10 in the Septuagint speaks of the chief maidens or virgins of Jerusalem.

(*e*) It is used of a particular leader. The rebellious people in the desert plan to appoint an *archēgos* to lead them back to Egypt (Num. 14.4). In the day of their national trouble the people come to Jephthah with the request that he should undertake the task of being their *archēgos* (Judg. 11.6,11; cp. Isa. 3.6,7). It describes the leader chosen for a particular task.

(*f*) It is used metaphorically to describe a leader in iniquity (Micah 1.13), or the author of mischief (I Macc. 9.61).

(*g*) It is used of the originator of some course of action. In I Macc. 10.7 Alexander is said to be the *archēgos* of peaceful words. That is to say, he took the lead in making proposals for peace.

(*h*) It is once used of God in Jer. 3.4 where it is said that there were once days when Israel called God her Father and her *Guide*.

Even were we to go no further, we could see that *archēgos* is a word with a wealth of meaning in its background.

(ii) Now let us turn to the meaning of *archēgos* in secular Greek.

(*a*) As an adjective, the word has two uses. It means *that which begins or originates something*. Euripides speaks of words which are the *originators* of evil things.[1] It means *primary, leading,* or *chief*. Euripides makes Hecuba speak of the days when she enjoyed the *chief* honours in the land.[2] When Aristotle is discussing anatomy, he uses it to describe the *chief* or *principal* veins of the body.[3]

(*b*) As a noun, *archēgos* can mean *the founder of a city*. The natives of the place called Colonus claim as their founder, their tutelary hero, what we would call their patron saint, the hero called Colonus.[4] The city of Sais in Egypt claimed as its founder the goddess Neith.[5]

(*c*) It is used as *the founder or the ancestor of a family*. Apollo in inscriptions is claimed as the founder of the royal

[1] *Hippolytus* 881.　　　　　[2] *The Trojan Women* 196.
[3] *Concerning the Parts of Animals* 666b 25.
[4] Sophocles, *Oedipus at Colonus* 60.　　　[5] Plato, *Timaeus* 21e.

line of King Seleucus Nicator. Aristotle uses *archēgos* to describe the common ancestor, common descent from whom draws men into mutual friendship and fellowship.[1]

(*d*) It is used for *the founder of a school of philosophy*. Thales is said to be the *archēgos* of the school of philosophy which ascribed the origin of all things to water.[2] So Zeno is said to be the *archēgos* of the Stoic School.[3]

(*e*) It is used in the sense of *prince* or *chief*. So Zeus is said to be the *archēgos* of the gods.[4] In this sense it may well be the equivalent of king.

(*f*) It is used of an *instigator* both in a good and bad sense. In his letter to the church at Corinth Clement speaks of the *instigators* of abominable jealousy, and of the *leaders* who are tearing the Church apart.[5] Xenophon uses it to describe the instigators of a treacherous plot.[6]

(*g*) It is used of what in modern language we would call the First Cause. Plato speaks of the cause (*aitios*) and ruler (*archēgos*) of all things.[7]

(*h*) In the papyri it is used of one who is the *source* or *origin* of something. The inhabitants of a village speak of their governor as the *archēgos*, the source, of all their blessings.

(*i*) Finally, as indeed we would expect, *archēgos* becomes in the later Christian writers a description of Jesus. The writer of the work which we know as *II Clement* calls him the *archēgos,* the Prince or the Source, of immortality (20.5). The martyrs at Lugdunum acknowledge Jesus as the *archēgos* of the life of God, which may mean the Prince to whom the life of God belongs, or the Source from which the life of God comes to men.[8]

---

[1] *Nicomachean Ethics* 1162b 4.   [2] Aristotle, *Metaphysics* 983b 20.
[3] Athenaeus, *Deipnosophistae* 13.563e.   [4] Bacchylides 5.179.
[5] *I Clement* 14.1; 51.1.   [6] *Hellenica* 3.3.4.
[7] *Cratylus* 401d.   [8] Eusebius, *Ecclesiastical History* 5.2.3.

It can easily be seen that the word *archēgos* came into Christian vocabulary trailing clouds of glory. To annex it as a description of Jesus was a stroke of genius on the part of the New Testament writers. It may well be far more the language of adoration than of theology, but we must at least try to see what it says when it is used of Jesus.

(i) In the first place the word *archēgos* has in it the quality of pre-eminence; it has in it a certain princeliness; it describe the natural, born leader, the one who stands head and shoulders above all others. The very word *archēgos* sets Jesus in the foremost and the topmost place.

> The highest place that heaven afford
> Is his, is his by right,
> The King of kings, the Lord of lords,
> And heaven's eternal Light.

(ii) As we have seen in our study of it, the word *archēgos* has in it what might be called a whole series of foundational qualitites. It describes men who were the source and origin of things great in themselves, and of things which still last.

(*a*) *Archēgos* describes the founder of a city, and that turns our thoughts to Jesus the founder of the city and the kingdom of God, that kingdom whose only law is love, and whose citizens are those who in humble obedience accept the will of God.

(*b*) *Archēgos* describes the founder of a family, and that turns our thoughts to Jesus as the founder and creator of the family of God, which is the Church. Through Jesus Christ Christians are the adopted sons and daughters of God, brought into the great household and family of the faith through him.

(*c*) *Archēgos* describes the founder of a philosophy, and that turns our thoughts to Jesus who gave men the knowledge of God which without him they never could have had, and who showed men what the good life is in a way that without him they could never have known. We may say that with Jesus a new theology and a new ethic came into the world.

(*d*) But the really peculiar character of the meaning of *archēgos* is that it regularly describes some one who originates and initiates something into which others can follow. The *archēgos* is the first to do something or to discover something, but the characteristic of his action and his discovery is that it opens a way for others to enter into the same benefits and the same greatness. The *archēgos* is the person who blazes the trail for others to follow. That is why the translations Guide, Leader, and, above all, Pioneer are best of all.

The pioneer goes first that others may walk in his steps. Someone has suggested this analogy. Suppose a ship to run on the rocks; and suppose the only way to safety is for some one to take a rope and swim ashore through the surf and the rocks, so that when the line is fastened on the shore others may follow to safety. That exactly is the work of the *archēgos*. Jesus is the great pioneer who blazes the trail for others to follow in his footsteps into the presence of God. The New Testament calls him the Pioneer of three things.

(i)　He is the Pioneer of faith (Heb. 12.2). In him faith became incarnate; in him trust reached its zenith and its peak beyond which it cannot go; and through him faith becomes possible for others. He is the pioneer who opened the way of faith for others to follow.

(ii)　He is the Pioneer of salvation (Heb. 2.10). Salvation is the state of the man who is at peace with God, and who is therefore safe in this or in any other life. Jesus is the Pioneer who showed men the way to peace and friendship with God.

(iii)　He is the Pioneer of life (Acts 3.15). He came that we might have life and that we might have it more abundantly

(John 10.10), and he came to bring life and immortality to light (I Tim. 1.10). He is the Pioneer who came to open the way to real life in this world, and to make men for ever certain of the life that is beyond.

Jesus Christ is the Pioneer of faith, of salvation, of life; he blazed the trail to God for us to follow.

31

HIGH PRIEST

IN view of the unique position which the Temple held in the religious life of the Jews, and in view of the consequently unique position of the High Priest, it is surprising that in the Old Testament itself the Messiah is never thought of in terms of the priesthood. There is however one inter-testamental book in which the picture of a priestly Messiah is drawn. In the second century before Jesus a quite unusual position had arisen in the life of the Jewish community. When Antiochus Epiphanes embarked upon his deliberate and savage attempt to wipe out Judaism and to substitute Hellenism for it, the Maccabees emerged to become the saviours of their people. Through their stand for freedom and through their heroic victories against incredible odds the Maccabees achieved a unique position. They came to be at one and the same time the kings and the High Priests of the nation. It was not a situation of which all Jews approved, but at this time the kingship and the priesthood became amalgamated. At that time there was written a book called *The Testaments of the Twelve Patriarchs* in which each of the patriarchs in turn is made to give his dying testimony. And in that book there is a picture of a Messiah who was to come, not from the tribe of Judah, but from the tribe of Levi, and who was to be at once priest and king. The fullest picture of him is in *The Testament of Levi* 18:

> Then shall the Lord raise up a new priest,
> and to him the words of the Lord shall be revealed;
> and he shall execute righteous judgment upon earth for a
>   multitude of days,

and his star shall arise in the heavens, as of a king.
. . . .
He shall shine forth as the sun on the earth,
And shall remove all darkness from under heaven,
. . . .
and there shall be peace on all the earth.
And in his priesthood the Gentiles shall be multiplied in
           knowledge upon the earth,
and enlightened through the grace of the Lord;
in his priesthood sin shall come to an end,
and the lawless shall cease to do evil,
and the just shall rest in him.
And he shall open the gates of paradise
. . . .
And the Lord shall rejoice in his children,
and be well pleased in his beloved ones for ever.

This picture of the priestly Messiah did not last; it flashed on the screen and passed away. The Maccabean dynasty vanished, and the situation which gave rise to this picture disappeared, and it left very little mark, at least upon popular Jewish thought.

But in Christian thought this picture was reborn, and the picture of Jesus as High Priest is the very basis of the thought of the unknown religious genius who wrote the letter to the Hebrews.

Religion has always meant different things to different people, and to the writer to the Hebrews religion was above and beyond all else access to God. It may well be said that his whole letter is written on the text: 'Let us then with confidence draw near to the throne of grace' (Heb. 4.16). At the back of his thought there are three conceptions, two of them general and one particular.

(i) In Old Testament thought it is always dangerous to approach God. To enter into the nearer presence of God is to die, or at least to be in danger of death. Moses hears the voice of God saying: 'You cannot see my face; for man shall not see me and live' (Ex. 33,20). When Moses came down from the mountain top, the astonished exclamation of the people was: 'We have this day seen God speak with man and man still live' (Deut. 5.24). When the terrified Gideon discovers that he has been speaking to the angel of the Lord, the divine voice reassures him: 'Do not fear; you shall not die' (Judg. 6.22,23). When Manoah discovered the identity of the divine messenger with whom he had been speaking, his awestricken reaction is: 'We shall surely die, for we have seen God' (Judg. 13.22).

We have already seen that this belief had left its mark on the ritual of the Day of Atonement. Only the High Priest might enter into the Holy of Holies, and he only on the Day of Atonement. And even for him it was dangerous. He must do what he had to do as quickly as possible, and must not linger, 'lest he put Israel in terror'.

From this there emerges one conception of the function of the priest. It is the function of the priest to enter into the presence of God on behalf of the people. He is their representative to do what they cannot and must not do. In him they enter in.

(ii)   To this there must be added a characteristically Greek line of thought. Plato had worked out the theory of ideas, the belief that in heaven there were laid up a series of perfect ideas, forms, patterns, archetypes of which everything in this world is a pale, shadowy, and imperfect copy. In this world, in Cicero's phrase, there are only *umbrae et imagines,* shadows and copies.[1] If that is so, clearly the whole task of life is to penetrate beyond the shades and shadows to the realities which are beyond. What the Greek wanted was access to reality, which is only another way of saying access to God.

So with his two backgrounds the writer to the Hebrews

De Officiis 3.17.

would have said that Jesus is the High Priest who gives us access to God and access to reality, both of which are impossible without him.

(iii) Now we come to our particular background, and the particular background is the covenant relationship between God and Israel. A covenant is a special relationship; but a covenant is not to be thought of as an agreement, an arrangement, a bargain which is entered into two parties by mutual agreement. The supreme characteristic of a covenant is that in it one of the parties spontaneously offers a relationship which the other could never have acquired, and the other has only to receive and take. So in the covenant God spontaneously and of his own free will entered into a special relationship with Israel, not because of any merit which the Jewish nation possessed but simply and solely out of his undeserved and unmerited grace.

But that covenant was not without its conditions. We see it being entered into in the story in Ex. 24.1-8, and the condition is clearly laid down. The covenant relationship between Israel and God depended on Israel's acceptance of and obedience to the Law of God.

This at once opens a new line of thought. Clearly, man in his weakness and sinfulness cannot perfectly obey the law of God. He is bound to break it. If the law is broken, the covenant relationship is broken. The law quite certainly will be broken. What then is to be done? It is here that the whole sacrificial system enters in. When the law is broken, appropriate sacrifice must be made in the Temple, along with the penitent and the contrite heart, and thereby the covenant relationship can be restored. If this is so, it clearly makes the Temple the most important place, and the High Priest the most important person, in the world for Jewish religion, for in them the whole sacrificial system centres.

But the sacrificial system and the High Priest as he is are

both demonstrably inadequate for the task they have to perform. In the first place, the priest is himself a sinner and has to offer sacrifice for his own sins before he can proceed to offer sacrifice for the sins of the people (Heb. 7.27; Lev. 9.7). Obviously a sinning man cannot make atonement for a sinning people, and a sinning man the High Priest was. In the second place, the Temple offerings are clearly not doing what they are designed to do, because they have to be offered over and over again. Daily and yearly they must be endlessly remade and re-offered (Heb. 10.1).

The grim conclusion is that the covenant relationship cannot but be broken and that the available means to restore it are in fact inadequate and unavailing. The necessity is for a new covenant, a new sacrifice and a new priest.

That Jesus had brought the new covenant is exactly what the Church claimed (I Cor. 11.25). That a new covenant would be made is precisely what Jeremiah had foretold (Jer. 31.31-34). 'Behold, the days are coming, says the Lord, when I will make a new covenant with the house of Israel and the house of Judah.' The claim of the Christian Church was that in Jesus Christ that covenant had come.

The old covenant was deficient in two directions, in its sacrifices and in its priesthood; but it is the claim of the writer to the Hebrews that in the new covenant Jesus is at one and the same time the perfect sacrifice and the perfect priest.

Jesus made the perfect offering of himself and of his obedience to God; he not only *made* the perfect offering, he *is* the perfect offering. 'When he had offered for all time a single sacrifice for sins, he sat down at the right hand of God' (Heb. 10.12). His sacrifice avails for every one and for all time and never, like the Temple sacrifices, need be made again.

He is the perfect priest. The perfect priest must have three qualifications. If the perfect priest is to be the perfect bridge between man and God, if once and for all he is to secure for man access to God, he must be at one and the same time fully divine and fully human. He must, to paraphrase Irenaeus' saying, perfectly bring God to man and perfectly bring man to God.

(i) Jesus, then, is perfectly divine. No New Testament book has a more majestic view of the deity of Jesus than the letter to the Hebrews has. 'He reflects the glory of God and bears the very stamp of his nature' (1.3). His place is at the right hand of God (1.3; 10.12). The prophets were men of God but he is Son of God (1.2).

(ii) But also Jesus is perfectly human. Equally no New Testament book has such a moving picture of the manhood of Jesus. He is the partaker of the same nature as men have (2.14). Son though he was, he learned obedience by all the experiences of this mortal life (5.8). The pioneer of our salvation was made perfect through suffering (2.10). The picture of Gethsemane must have haunted the mind of the writer to the Hebrews, for he shows us Jesus praying to God with loud cries and tears (5.7). It is just because he is so perfectly human that he can deal gently with the ignorant and the wayward, since he himself is beset with weakness (5.2). We have not a high priest who is unable to sympathise with our weakness, but one who in every respect has been tempted as we are, yet without sinning (4.15). He knows the human situation because he has shared it.

(iii) So Jesus is the perfect priest because he is at one and the same time perfectly divine and perfectly human; he can bring together man and God because he is man and God. But there remains one further qualification for the priest. A priest cannot appoint himself to his sacred office; he must be appointed by God. His appointment must necessarily be not a human but a divine appointment. It is just here that the writer to the Hebrews produces his own special and peculiar interpretation of Jesus, the interpretation of him as the High Priest after the order of Melchizedek. He finds the basis of this interpretation in two Old Testament passages:

> After his return from the defeat of Chederlaomer and the kings who were with him, the king of Sodom went out to meet Abraham at the Valley of Shaveh (that is, the King's Valley). And Melchizedek king of Salem brought out bread and wine; he was priest of God Most High. And he blessed Abraham and said:
>
> Blessed be Abraham by God Most High,
>   maker of heaven and earth;
> and blessed be God Most High,
>   who has delivered your enemies into your hand!
>
> (Gen. 14.17-20)
>
> The Lord has sworn
>   and will not change his mind,
> 'You are a priest for ever
>   after the order of Melchizedek.'
>
> (Ps. 110.4)

On these two passages the writer to the Hebrews bases his interpretation of Jesus. Before we go on to study his interpretation we must note certain things. First, however odd and unconvincing the arguments may be to us, it must be remembered that the whole method of the writer to the Hebrews is a first-class example of Jewish exegesis and would be entirely convincing to those to whom it was addressed. Second, Jewish exegesis found four meanings in any passage. (a) *Peshat,* the simple meaning which lies on the surface. (b) *Remaz,* the meaning which the passage suggests. (c) *Derush,* the meaning of the passage after every resource of study and investigation has been brought to bear upon it. (d) *Sod,* the inner or the allegorical meaning. It was the most important of all. Third, for the correct understanding of the method of the writer to the Hebrews it is of the first

importance to remember that a Jewish exegete thought himself every bit as much entitled to argue from the silences of
Scripture as from the sayings of Scripture. The two passages
in which the writer to the Hebrews works out his interpretations are 5.1-10 and the whole of chapter 7, and these
two passages should be carefully read as a whole before we
embark on the detailed study of them. Let us then turn to
chapter 7 where the interpretation is fully worked out.

(i) The writer to the Hebrews begins (7.1,2) by taking the
name *Melchizedek* which can mean *King of Righteousness*.
Therefore, in the first place, the priesthood of Jesus Christ
is a royal and a righteous priesthood. Melchizedek is *King
of Salem,* and *Salem* is interpreted to mean *peace (shalom).*
So from these two names there is drawn the conclusion that
the priesthood of Jesus Christ is a royal, a righteous, and
a peaceful priesthood.

(ii)   There follow two arguments from silence.

(*a*)   Melchizedek is without father or mother or genealogy
(7.3). In the Old Testament story nothing whatever is said
about the lineage or parentage of Melchizedek; he has no
human background whatsoever. Therefore, he is said to be
without father and without mother. Now this is the very
reverse of Jewish priesthood, for no Jew could ever be or
ever become a priest unless he was able to produce an un-
broken pedigree stretching back to Aaron. That is to say,
the ordinary priest is a priest *in virtue of his descent;* Jesus
is a priest *in his own right,* or, as it is put later (7.16), 'not
according to legal requirement concerning bodily descent but
the power of an indestructible life.' It is not his lineage but his
own personality which makes him a priest.

(*b*)   Melchizedek has 'neither beginning of days nor end
of life' (7.3). This conclusion is drawn because nothing is
said in the Old Testament story of either the birth or the
death of Melchizedek. He is therefore assumed to be timeless

and eternal. So the priesthood of Jesus, unlike the temporary priesthood of the levitical priests, is for ever and ever. The other priests are born and die; Christ has neither beginning nor end.

(iii) There follows a series of proofs of the superiority of the priesthood after the order of Melchizedek, all of which are drawn or deduced from the two Old Testament passages.

(a) The ordinary levitical priests exact tithes from those who are their brethren, and they do so because the law lays it down that they have a right to do so, whereas Melchizedek took tithes from Abraham, who was a total stranger to him and a man of another race, and he did so, not because any law entitled him to do so but as a personal and unquestioned right (7.4-6). Clearly, he possessed rights and exercised an authority not possessed by the levitical priesthood.

(b) The levitical priests are men who die, but Melchizedek lives for ever (7.8).

(c) In the old story it is Melchizedek who blesses Abraham. Now it is always the superior who blesses the inferior. Therefore, Melchizedek was actually greater than Abraham, the founder of the nation (7.7).

(d) The writer to the Hebrews then uses a very curious argument. The law is that it is other men who should pay tithes to the Levites, not the Levites to other men. But in this case it was Levi who paid tithes to Melchizedek. How can that be when Levi was not yet born? Levi, although not yet born, was a descendant of Abraham, and therefore could be said to be 'in the loins of his ancestor'. Levi, being as it were in the body of Abraham, paid tithes to Melchizedek when Abraham did. (7.9,10).

(iv) There follows another series of arguments, this time based rather on Ps. 110.4.

> The Lord has sworn
> and will not change his mind,
> 'You are a priest for ever
> after the order of Melchizedek.'

The very fact that a priest is promised after the order of Melchizedek, is in itself the proof that the ordinary levitical priesthood is inadequate. If it had been adequate, no other kind of priest would have been needed (7.11).

(*b*) There follows an ingenious and a far-reaching argument. The ancient priesthood was entirely in the possession of the descendants of Aaron. To be a priest a man must be a pure-blooded descendant of Aaron, as the law unalterably laid it down. That is to say, it is from the tribe of Levi that all priests come. *But Jesus comes from the tribe of Judah.* Here is a radical change which shows that not only is there a new kind of priesthood, but that also the whole legal system is now abrogated and a new system instituted (7.12-14). The old order has passed away, and a new has come.

(*c*) Still another argument for the superiority of the priesthood after the order of Melchizedek is drawn from Ps. 110.4. The Psalm says, 'The Lord has sworn and will not change his mind.' That is to say, the everlasting character of the priesthood after the order of Melchizedek is affirmed and confirmed by nothing other and nothing less than the oath of God. And quite certainly nothing can have greater permanent validity than that to the continuance of which God has pledged himself (7.20-22).

Finally, the writer to the Hebrews reiterates three last claims for the high priesthood of Jesus.

(*a*) Unlike the levitical priests who died and who therefore could not continue in office, Jesus holds his priesthood permanently and for ever, for death cannot touch him; and that is why for all time and beyond time he is able to save those who come to him (7.23-25).

(*b*) He is the perfect High Priest who has no need to offer sacrifice for his own sins as the levitical priests are bound by law to do (7.26,27).

(*c*) The sacrifice he has made, the sacrifice of himself and his obedience, never needs to be remade, as the levitical sacrifices have to be daily repeated. It has been made once and for all and never needs to be made again (7.26,27).

There remains one further feature of the interpretation of Jesus of the writer to the Hebrews, and it is perhaps his greatest reach of thought of all. He regards the high priesthood of Jesus as something which continues for ever, and he thinks of Jesus as still exercising his priestly function. He always lives to make intercession for men (7.25). He is now appearing in the presence of God on our behalf (9.24).

There is a sense, and a very real sense, in which the life and death of Jesus on earth are an incident in time demonstrating what is always happening in eternity. It may be said that the life and death of Jesus are a window in time opening on to what is always and for ever happening in the heart of God. God is eternally seeking, eternally loving, eternally sacrificing, and eternally redeeming. What happened in Palestine and on Calvary is an episode in time allowing men a glimpse of that which is always going on in the heart of God. The writer to the Hebrews combines two great truths. He sees quite clearly the once-for-allness of the sacrifice of Jesus Christ, and he sees equally clearly that the life and death of Jesus Christ are actions in time which show what the heart of God for ever is to men. In one of his plays Ibsen makes one of his characters say: 'Where is he now? What if *that* at Golgotha, near Jerusalem, was but a wayside matter, a thing done, as it were, in the passing? What if he goes on and on, suffers and dies and conquers again and again, from world to world?' There is a sense in which that is true, for Jesus Christ showed that God is for ever suffering love and redemptive power.

It may be that the whole letter to the Hebrews moves in a world of thought that is strange to our thought. But at the back of it there is one simple and always intelligible thought. The Latin word for priest is *pontifex,* which means a bridge-builder, and Jesus is not only the bridge-builder, he is himself the bridge between the world of time and the world of reality, between man and God.

32

BELOVED, ONLY, CHOSEN

BELOVED, Only, Chosen, *agapētos, monogenēs, eklelegmenos,*
these three titles of Jesus are so closely interrelated and
interconnected that it is best to deal with them together.

The word *agapētos,* beloved, is specially applied to Jesus on
two of the greatest occasions in his life, at his Baptism and at his
Transfiguration. At the Baptism, the voice which came to
Jesus, as the AV has it, was: 'Thou art my beloved Son, in
whom I am well pleased' (Mark 1.11; cp. Matt. 3.17; Luke
3.22). But the RSV recognises in a footnote that there is
another possible translation, and it is this other translation
which is accepted by the *Twentieth Century New Testament,*
by Moffatt, and by the NEB, and which is almost certainly
right: 'Thou art my Son, my Beloved, or, the Beloved.' In
this translation *agapētos,* Beloved, becomes not so much an
adjective describing Jesus as another title for him. This translation is strongly supported by the Syriac version which was
one of the earliest translations of the New Testament and
which has: 'My Son and my Beloved.'

The situation is further complicated by the different readings
in the same saying in the Transfiguration story. In the
AV the translation given is the same as the translation of
the saying at the Baptism: 'This is my beloved Son' (Mark
9.7; Matt. 17.5). The modern translations make the same
correction, and translate the saying, 'This is my Son, the or
my Beloved.' In Luke's version of the story (Luke 9.35) the
AV has the same translation of the saying, but in that passage
the best MSS read not *agapētos* but *eklelegmenos,* which
means 'chosen', and the more modern translations (e.g.

RSV and NEB) have: 'This is my Son, my Chosen.' Here then 'chosen' is substituted for 'beloved', *eklelegmenos* for *agapētos*.

To complete the New Testament evidence, we may note that the saying at the Transfiguration is quoted in II Peter 1.17 in the form in which we find it in Matthew and Mark: 'This is my Son, my Beloved.' And finally we note that it was his beloved son that the master of the vineyard sent in last appeal to the wicked husbandmen (Mark 12.6; Luke 20.13).

In the early Church 'the Beloved' became one of the great and lovely titles for Jesus; but to be strictly accurate we must note that here it occurs in still another form. In the New Testament itself the word is *agapētos*, as we have seen, which is an adjective; in later use the word becomes *ēgapēmenos*, which is the perfect participle passive of the verb *agapan*, which means 'to love', and which therefore means also 'beloved'. This form of the title begins in the New Testament. Eph. 1.6 speaks of the glorious grace which 'God has freely bestowed upon us in the Beloved.' Ignatius begins his letter to Smyrna which greetings to the Church of God the Father, and of the Beloved Jesus Christ, The *Letter of Barnabas* speaks of the Christians as 'a people prepared in the Beloved' (3.6). It speaks of the new covenant made for us in Jesus the Beloved (4.8). The apocryphal *Acts of Paul and Thecla* speak of 'the birth and resurrection of the Beloved' (2.1).

At first sight the meaning of the title seems so obvious that it requires no explanation; but, great as it is at first sight, there is more in it than meets the eye. Let us therefore begin by studying the word *agapētos*.

(i) In classical Greek the word *agapētos* often describes that with which a man may be well content, or that for which in all the circumstances he ought to be thankful. A man must learn virtue, says Plato, and for that reason, if there is some one who excels us even a little in showing the way to virtue, it is *agapētos,* something for which we ought to be devoutly thankful.[1] Xenophon speaks of the necessity of being prepared. Wise sailors are prepared to meet a storm at sea, and, if at such a time God punishes the careless but refrains from destroying the innocent, it is *agapētos,* something for which we should be thankful.[2] Aristotle speaks of friendship. There are, alas, very few friends whom we can love entirely for their own sake and entirely for their virtue and, if we have only a few such friends, it is something for which we ought to be very thankful, it is *agapētos.*[3]

At its lowest, therefore, *agapētos* describes something for which we should be devoutly thankful to God.

(ii) *Agapētos* sometimes describes something which is highly desirable. Xenophon speaks of a beautiful, good and *lovable* (*agapētos*) character which a man has only to look upon to love and to be moved to seek as his own.[4] When the elements are well mixed in a man, then, says Plato, his life becomes *agapētos,* most admirable, most desirable and lovely. *Agapētos* describes that which moves a man to love.

(iii) *Agapētos* in secular Greek of all ages has one very illuminating and suggestive meaning. It describes an *only son,* and therefore a son very specially loved. This use goes back to Homer. When Telemachus the son of Odysseus wishes to leave home to search for his father, his mother Penelope seeks to keep him at home: 'Whither art thou minded to go over the whole earth, thou who art an only son and well beloved (*monos* and *agapētos*)?'[5] Later Penelope says that she has already lost her dear husband in his wanderings, and, 'Now my well-beloved son (*agapētos*) is gone forth in a hollow ship, a mere child, knowing naught of toils and

---

[1] *Protagoras* 328b.   [2] *Oeconomicus* 8.16.
[3] *Nicomachean Ethics* 1171b 20.   [4] *Memorabilia* 3.10.5.
[5] *Odyssey* 2.365.

gathering of men.'¹ Andromache comes to meet Hector her
husband carrying in her arms the little Astyanax, 'the tender
boy, the little child, Hector's beloved son (*agapētos*), like
unto a beatiful star.'² In one of Aristophanes' plays one
woman says to another: 'O Mica, who has robbed thee of
thy flower, and snatched away thy babe, thine only one
(*agapētos*)?'³ Alcibiades has only one cherished love (*agapētos*), even Socrates himself.⁴ Xenophon has a picture of
Gobryas telling Cyrus of the death of his son, his only son,
how he buried 'with the first down upon his cheeks, his best,
his well-beloved son' (*agaptētos*).⁵ Aristotle speaks of how the
high-minded man will spend much money on the wedding of
his only (*agapētos*) son.⁶ There is a passage in Aristotle
which clearly shows how completely *agapētos* had come to
mean 'only'. He says that the injury which a man does when
he puts out the eye of a one-eyed man is far greater than
it would have been if the man had had two eyes, for the eye
of the one-eyed man is *agapētos*.³

Even in secular Greek there is a curious quality about this
word *agapētos*. It never ceases to mean 'beloved', but there
is so often in it a certain poignancy, a certain sense of the
incalculable preciousness and of the utter irreplaceability of
the person so described. A child must always be dear, but
an only child is dearer still. The death of any child is a
tragedy, but to lose an only child is to lose all. The word
comes to Christian usage with poignant and tragic overtones.

When we turn to the Septuagint we find the situation
accentuated. There we find the word *agapētos* used to translate the Hebrew word *iachid* which means 'only'. So three
times in Genesis 22 we find Isaac described as Abraham's

---

¹ *Odyssey* 4.817.　　　　² *Iliad* 6.401.
³ *Thesmophoriazusae* 761.　　⁴ Plato, *Alcibiades* 131e.
⁵ *Cyropaedia* 4.6.5.　　　　⁶ *Eudemian Ethics* 1233b 2.
⁷ *Rhetoric* 1.7.41.

agapētos son, where the Hebrew is *iachid* and where the English translation is 'only' (Gen. 22.2,12,16). The description of Jephthah's daughter (Judg. 11.34) varies in the MSS of the Septuagint. In some she is called *agapētos* and in some *monogenēs,* which means 'only-begotten', as we shall presently see. The two words are used as equivalent. In the Septuagint of Amos and Jeremiah mourning for a son who is *agapētos,* beloved, is spoken of, where the Hebrew has 'only' (Amos 8.10; Jer. 6.26).

So then when God at the Baptism and at the Transfiguration speaks of Jesus as his *agapētos,* it means that Jesus is not only his beloved son, but also his only son. It is as if God is saying: 'In giving men Jesus Christ I am giving all I have to give because, once I have given him, I have nothing left.' The word describes vividly not only God's love for Jesus but also God's love for men.

The second of our words leads our thoughts along exactly the same line. *Monogenēs* literally means 'only-begotten' and is therefore the literal word for an only child. It is used to describe the son of the widow at Nain (Luke 7.12); the epileptic boy for whom the disciples could do nothing and whom Jesus healed (Luke 9.38); the daughter of Jairus (Luke 8.42); Isaac the son of Abraham (Heb. 11.17).

Monogenēs is quite frequently used of Jesus in the New Testament. His glory is as of the *only* Son from the Father (John 1.14). God sent his *only* Son for the saving of those who believe in him (John 3.16,18). God's love is made manifest by the fact that he sent his *only* Son into the world (I John 4.9).

It can be seen that *agapētos* and *monogenēs* go closely together. It is not enough to say that Jesus is God's *only* Son; not is it enough to say that he is God's *beloved* Son; he is God's *only and beloved Son.* The two words together describe the uniqueness of Jesus and the cost of God's gift to men. They together describe the generosity of the heart of God and the poignancy of the grief of God. They tell at one and the same time of the splendour of the love of God and the awfulness of the crime which the sin of man committed against that love.

We must now turn to a third line of thought which will lead us to our third word. The word 'beloved', in this case *ēgapēmenos* and not *agapētos,* is used in the Old Testament in a special way. It is used of Abraham (II Chron. 20.7), and it is used in particular of the nation of Israel. It is the Psalmist's prayer that God should be exalted in order that his beloved may be delivered (Ps. 60.5; 108.6). God, says the writer of Baruch, gave the way of knowledge to Jacob and to Israel his beloved (Baruch 3.36).

There is one curious feature of the Septuagint. Four times in the Hebrew and English Old Testament Israel is called by the name Jeshurun, and in each case the Septuagint substitutes 'the Beloved' for Jeshurun. Jacob ate and was filled and the beloved kicked. That is to say, the people of Israel were rebellious (Deut. 32.15). He shall be prince with the beloved one (Deut. 33.5). There is not any such God as the God of the beloved (Deut. 33.26). 'Fear not, my servant Jacob', Isaiah hears God say, 'and beloved Israel whom I have chosen' (Isa. 44.2). In all these cases the Hebrew is Jeshurun.

It is easy to see how in view of this 'The Beloved' became a title of the Messiah. It is here that we find the explanation of Luke's version of the saying at the Transfiguration. Both Matthew and Mark have: 'This is my Son, the Beloved' (Matt. 17.5; Mark 9.7). Luke has: 'This is my Son, the Chosen' (Luke 9.35). This is actually a quotation of Isaiah 42.1:

> Behold my servant, whom I uphold,
> My Chosen in whom my soul delights.

In so far as the actual wording goes it is Luke who is right; but it is clear that Matthew and Mark regarded Beloved and Chosen as meaning the same thing.

This is very significant. Both Abraham and the nation are called The Beloved. The nation is the beloved nation because it was in fact the chosen nation. Israel was chosen that out of it there might come God's Messiah, God's Chosen One, God's Beloved One, God's Anointed King. If the nation was chosen, then clearly when the Messiah came, he would be *par excellence* the Chosen One. And so to speak of Jesus as The Beloved, The Chosen One, is to say that in him the destiny of Israel was fulfilled and consummated, and that he is the Messiah. Out of the Chosen People there came the Chosen One, the Messiah.

Here then we have three great words, all closely inter-related, all to some extent interchangeable, but each with its own distinctive atmosphere and meaning.

(i)   Jesus is *agapēgos*, The Beloved One, and here is the word that tells of the poignancy of the love of God, and the un-surpassable sacrifice of God for men.

(i)   Jesus is *agapētos*, The Beloved One, and here is the word word which tells of the uniqueness of Jesus. Never before was there, and never thereafter can there be, anyone like him, the only Son of God.

(iii)   Jesus is *eklelegmenos*. He is the Chosen One. Out of the Chosen People there had come the Chosen One, the Messiah, the One born to be the King of love.

33

THE JUST ONE

THE Just One is a title of Jesus which belongs rather to the
AV than to any of the more modern translations. In Greek
the word translated 'just' in the AV is *dikaios,* and the more
modern translations tend to render it 'righteous'. Further, the
various translations of the New Testament do not agree as to
when this is simply an adjective describing Jesus and when
it is a title of Jesus. There is in fact an odd inconsistency
with regard to this word even in individual translations. So
much so in this the case that it is worth setting out the
treatment of this word as applied to Jesus in three translations, the AV, the RSV, and the NEB. The cases in which
it is applied to Jesus are as follows.

(i)   Acts 3.14:
AV: Ye denied the Holy One and the Just, and desired a
         murder to be granted to you.
RSV: You denied the Holy and Righteous One.
NEB: You repudiated the one who was holy and righteous.
The AV and RSV by using capitals makes this a title; the NEB
by using small letters makes it a description.

(ii)   Acts 7.52:
AV: The prophets showed before the coming of the Just
         One.
RSV: The prophets announced beforehand the coming of
         the Righteous One.
NEB: The prophets foretold the coming of the Righteous
         One.
Here all three translations take it as a title.

(iii)   Acts 22.14:

AV: The God of our fathers chose Paul that he should see
         the Just One.
RSV: The God of our fathers chose Paul to see the Just One.
NEB: The God of our fathers chose Paul to see the Righteous
         One.

Here again all three take it as a title, but for some reason
which is not obvious the RSV reverts to the translation 'just'.

There are certain other occasions when the word *dikaios*
is used of Jesus in the New Testament, and in them similar
variations of translation occur. The message of Pilate's wife
(Matt. 27.19) is in the AV: 'Have nothing to do with that
just man.' The RSV has 'that righteous man', and the NEB
has 'that innocent man'. In Luke 23.47 we find the verdict of
the centurion on Jesus. In the AV it is: 'Certainly this was
a righteous man'. The RSV and the NEB both have 'innocent'
for 'righteous'.

In I Peter 3.18 it is said of Jesus that in him the just
suffered for the unjust (AV), the righteous suffered for the
unrighteous (RSV), while the NEB has 'He, the just,
suffered for the unjust', where there is no capital letter, but
where the translation gives the word the flavour of a title.

Finally the word occurs in I John 2.1, where it is said that
we have an advocate to plead our cause, Jesus Christ the
righteous (AV and RSV), and where the NEB has, 'Jesus
Christ, and he is just'. In only the two passages Acts 7.52
and Acts 22.14 do all the translation unequivocally agree in
making this word a title of Jesus. It is nonetheless quite clear
that the word was regularly applied to Jesus, and the Acts
passages make it clear that in the early Church it was one
of the titles by which he was known.

Although it was not one of the common titles, there is
evidence that the Jews did use it as a title of the Messiah.
In Enoch it is said that the Righteous One will appear before

the eyes of the elect, and will reward those who were faithful to him and give sinners their deserts (Enoch 38.2). The Righteous and Elect One will cause the house of the congregation to appear (Enoch 53.6).

There were at least two Old Testament passages in which this word occurs which the Christians would inevitably apply to Jesus. In Zech. 9.9 the AV translates in agreement with the Septuagint 'Rejoice greatly, O daughter of Jerusalem... Behold, thy king cometh unto thee; he is just (*dikaios*) and having salvation.' Above all, in the description of the Suffering Servant it is said: 'By his knowledge shall the righteous one, my servant, make many to be accounted righteous' (Isa. 53. 11). On the basis of that saying alone the title was bound to be applied to Jesus.

Let us then try more nearly to define the meaning of this word. The Hebrew word which *dikaios* represents is *tsaddiq;* it occurs more than 200 times in the Old Testament, and in the AV it is 41 times translated 'just' and 164 times 'righteous.' There is ample material to define its meaning.

(i) It is the existence of the righteous which halts the avenging hand of God. It is God's promise that if there are only ten righteous men in Sodom and Gomorrah, he will spare these cities (Gen. 18.23-33). In a sense, the righteous save the world from divine destruction.

(ii) The righteous are under the particular protection of God. It is forbidden to slay the innocent and the righteous (Ex. 23.7). God never withdraws his eyes from the righteous (Job 36.7). The Lord knows the ways of the righteous (Ps. 1.6). The Lord loves the righteous (Ps. 146.8). The righteous are the concern of God.

(iii) Loyalty and fidelity are the keynote of the life of the righteous. 'The just shall live by faith,' says Habakkuk (2.4), and in the original context that means that it is because of his loyalty and fidelity to God that the righteous man shall live.

Loyalty to God is the supreme manifestation of righteousness.

(iv) It is here that Old Testament thought diverges along two opposite lines. One line of thought stresses the prosperity of the righteous. 'I have been young and now am old,' says the Psalmist, 'yet I have not seen the righteous forsaken, or his children begging bread' (Ps. 37.25). In his days may the righteous flourish (Pss. 72.7; 92.15). The Lord does not let the righteous go hungry (Prov. 10.3). The righteous is delivered from trouble (Prov. 11.8). In the house of the righteous there is much treasure (Prov. 15.6). No ill befalls the righteous (Prov. 12.21). Such sayings could be multiplied over and over again. There is a line of thought in the Old Testament in which righteousness and prosperity go hand in hand.

(v) But there is another line of thought in the Old Testament which stresses the necessary suffering of the righteous. The wicked watches the righteous and seeks to slay him (Ps. 37.32). They band together against the life of the righteous, and condemn the innocent to death (Ps. 94.21). The righteous man perishes and no one lays it to heart (Isa. 57.1). The wicked sell the righteous for silver, and afflict the righteous (Amos 2.6; 5.12). The wicked surround the righteous, so justice goes forth perverted (Hab. 1.4). Job is a just and blameless man, but he has become a laughing-stock (Job 12.4). There are those who shed the blood of the righteous (Lam. 4.13).

In the deeper parts of the Old Testament the agony of the righteous is writ large.

Greek ethical thought also was dominated by the idea of the righteous man (dikaios) and of righteousness (dikaiosunē). Both these words come from the Greek word dikē, which means 'justice'. It denotes the customs by which men live together. It is convention in the highest and best sense of the term. Righteousness, justice, is the supreme virtue of a social being. It is, as John Ferguson puts it in *Moral Values in the Ancient World*, 'the full function of man as a member of society'. 'The man who is *dikaios* is the man who refuses to break the conventions ... out of self-interest or for any other purpose. He is under obligation to his fellows which he knows and fulfils.' The Stoics were to define *dikaiosunē*, righteousness, as the quality of the man who gives both to men and to gods what is their due, the man who never fails in his duty to God or to man.

We can see how true all this is of Jesus. Indeed, it was for his sake that God spared the world. God did indeed love him and was well pleased with him. His loyalty to God went to the Cross. He knew the agony of injustice and he knew the triumph after the tragedy. And there is no one in all the universe who so perfectly fulfilled his duty to God and to man. No wonder that to Jew and Greek Jesus became *par excellence* The Righteous One.

34

HE THAT SHOULD COME

HE that should come, *ho erchomenos,* is one of the simplest titles of Jesus. Sometimes it is applied to him directly, and sometimes by implication.

It is most clearly and definitely applied to Jesus by John the Baptist. When John's courage and fidelity had brought him to the dungeons of the Castle of Machaerus, and when for the moment there were doubts and questions in his mind, he sent some of his men to ask Jesus: 'Are you he who is to come, or shall we look for another?' (Matt. 11.3; Luke 7.15). When John was baptising the penitent and the seeking people, he told them of the power and the greatness of the one who who was coming after him, the one who was coming after him, the one who was to come (Matt. 3.11; Luke 3.16). It was his testimony: 'He who comes after me, he who is to come, ranks before me' (John 1.15). It was to the greatness of the one who was to come that he looked, and he felt that for him he was not able to render even the humblest service (John 1.27).

We find the same description of Jesus on the lips of Martha. Her confession of faith is: 'I believe that you are the Christ, the Son of God, he who is coming into the world' (John 11.27).

The same picture was in the minds of the crowd on the day when Jesus entered Jerusalem: 'Blessed is he who comes in the name of the Lord' (Mark 11.9; Luke 19.38). And this is a picture which Jesus would not have rejected, for in his lament over Jerusalem he said that they would not see him again, until the day when they would say: 'Blessed

370

be he who comes in the name of the Lord' (Matt. 23.29; Luke 13.35; cp. Ps. 118.26).

In Acts again this title is applied to Jesus and it is again connected with the preaching of John the Baptist. Paul describing the message of John says: 'John baptised with the baptism of repentance, telling the people to believe in the one who was to come after him, that is, Jesus' (Acts 19.4).

We find the picture in the Letter to the Hebrews, this time with a definite Old Testament background. The writer tells his people that they have need of endurance, if they are to receive the promised reward.

> For yet a little while,
> and the coming one shall come, and shall not tarry;
> but my righteous one shall live by faith,
> and if he shrinks back,
> my soul has no pleasure in him (Heb. 10.26-28).

This is a doubly interesting passage. It is a quotation from Hab. 2.3,4, but it is a quotation from the Septuagint. In the Hebrew it is a *vision* which is to come; in the Greek it is a *person* who is to come; and the writer to the Hebrews follows the Greek instead of the Hebrew, and applies it to Jesus.

Finally in the New Testament the picture emerges in the Revelation, and there the title becomes nothing less than a title of God, for there God is the one 'who is and who was who is to come' (Rev. 1.8; 4.8).

Let us then see what this title means when it is applied to Jesus.

(i) One of the unchanging Messianic expectations of the Jews, an expectation which still exists, was and is that Elijah is to come back to announce the imminent coming of the Messiah. 'Behold,' says God to Malachi, 'I will send you Elijah the prophet before the great and terrible day of the Lord comes' (Mal. 4.5). The prophecy regarding John the

Baptist is that he is to go before the Lord to prepare his ways (Luke 1.76). It was indeed with this prophecy that Jesus connected John (Matt. 11.10; Luke 7.27; Matt. 17.9-13). It would certainly have been natural to call the returned Elijah him who was to come. If we took the phrase of Jesus in that sense, it would mean that he was not himself the Messiah, but had come to announce the coming of the Messiah.

(ii) It is however clear from the narrative of the Gospels that when this title was applied to Jesus, it was applied to him, not in the belief that he was the herald of the Messiah, but in the conviction that he was the Messiah himself. The people of Israel, in spite of the disasters of their national history, never lost their consciousness of being the Chosen People, or the confidence that one day their present condition would match their future destiny. For that reason all through their history they awaited the Messiah, the one who is to come, and it is in that sense that the title is used of Jesus. He was the one in whom the purposes and the promises of God were to be fulfilled.

This means that he was the inaugurator of the Kingdom of God. We can see this in two ways.

(a) When John sent his question to Jesus, asking if he was the one who was to come, or if they must look for some one else, Jesus did not argue in words. He said: 'Go, and tell John what you hear and see; the blind receive their sight and the lame walk; the lepers are cleansed and the deaf hear, and the dead are raised up and the poor have the good news preached to them' (Matt. 11.4,5; Luke 7.22). That claim is the claim to be the fulfilment of a whole series of Messianic prophecies. In the time of the reign of God sorrow and sighing would flee away (Jer. 31.12; Isa. 35.10); there would be no more weeping and no more untimely death (Isa. 65.20-22); the inhabitant of the land would not know what sickness was (Isa. 33.24); and even death would be finally conquered (Isa. 25.8). It was Jesus' claim that all this has happened. In him the Messianic kingdom has come, and its promised events are in actual operation. He that should come is here.

(*b*) John the Baptist saw the work of Jesus in two ways. First, he said that Jesus would bring a baptism of the Spirit and of fire. The Baptism of the Spirit must stand for full and final revelation and illumination, for in Judaism the twofold function of the Spirit was to bring to men the truth of God and to enable men to recognise that truth when they saw it. The baptism of fire must stand for full cleansing and purification (Matt. 3.11; Luke 3.16). This is exactly what Joel foretold when he said that in the Messianic times God would pour out his Spirit upon all flesh (Joel 2.28,29). It was exactly the surge of the Spirit that the Messiah was to bring, and it was exactly the surge of the Spirit that Jesus did bring (Acts 2.17-21).

Second, John saw the work of Jesus in terms of separation and of judgment in which the wheat would be separated from the chaff (Matt. 3.12; Luke 3.17). And this is exactly what Malachi foresaw when he told of the coming of the messenger of the covenant who would be like a refiner's fire, and the day of whose coming none could withstand (Mal. 3.1-3).

It is precisely in Messianic terms—revelation and illumination, purifying and cleansing, judgment and separation— that John described Jesus. These were the works of the One who was to come, and these were the works of Jesus.

It may be felt that this is to describe Jesus in purely Jewish terms. But we can go further, for these things are only symbolic of the larger truth that Jesus came to satisfy and to fulfil the dreams and the desires of all men. It may be that Jesus thought of himself as the one who was to come more than we realise, for in the Fourth Gospel there is very frequently on his lips the claim: 'I came that...' (John 9.39; 10.10; 16.28; 18.37). He came to make men's dreams into realities; he came to bring God to men and to bring men to God. In him the longed-for one who was to come had come.

35

THE AMEN

In the letters to the seven churches in the Revelation the letter to Laodicea is introduced with the words: 'The words of the Amen, the faithful and true witness, the beginning of God's creation' (Rev. 3.14). The Amen may seem to us a very strange title for Jesus. It never wove itself into the language of liturgy or devotion. It occurs only this once directly in the New Testament. There is nevertheless in it a wealth of meaning which makes it well worth studying in detail.

The word *amen* is connected with the Hebrew verb *aman*, which mean *to confirm, to establish, to support*. *Amēn* is itself an adverb and in the Old Testament it means *truly, verily*, and in the answer to a question it is the equivalent of an emphatic *yes*. In the Old Testament it has certain standard uses.

(i) It expresses full agreement with, or acceptance of, that which has been said or laid down. In the Law it is laid down that a woman suspected of infidelity is to be subjected to certain tests; she is told that, if she is innocent, she will be exonerated, and, if she is guilty, she will be cursed. As she listens, she is to say: 'Amen, Amen' (Num. 5.22). In Deuteronomy it is laid down that a whole series of curses on different kinds of evildoers is to be read to the people, and as the people listen they are to say: 'Amen, Amen' (Deut. 27.15-26). When Ezra read the Law to the people, they answered: 'Amen, Amen' (Neh. 8.1-6). Amen is the response of the man who signifies his complete agreement with what has been said. His answer is: 'So let it be.'

(ii) It sometimes expresses agreement with some plan or request which has been made. David tells how it is his will that his son should succeed him, and that even before his own death the son should be given a special place of honour, and Benaiah answers Amen (I Kings 1.36). His answer is: 'I accept and approve your plan.'

(iii) It sometimes expresses acceptance of a task which has been offered. Jeremiah is directed to go and tell the people to keep the covenant and to tell them of the blessings which will follow if they keep it and the curses which will follow if they break it, and his answer is Amen (Jer. 11.5).

(iv) It is very commonly used by a worshipping company of people to show that they share in some prayer or some ascription of praise and glory which has been offered. The officiating priest says: 'Blessed be the Lord, the God of Israel from everlasting to everlasting.' Then all the people say: 'Amen' (I Chron. 16.36; Ps. 41.13; 106.48). It is the response of the worshipping people.

We now follow the word into the New Testament.

(i) Amen is used at the close of a doxology or a prayer which is one's own. The John of the Revelation writes: 'To him who loves us and has freed us from our sins by his blood and made us a kingdom, priests to his God and Father, to him be glory and dominion for ever and ever. Amen' (Rev. 1.5,6). It guarantees the sincerity, the genuineness and the reality of the prayer.

(ii) It is used to adopt as one's own what some one else has said. All the creatures of the universe sing their praise to God, and the four living creatures respond Amen (Rev. 5.14). In this use a man aligns and identifies himself with some act of worship and praise.

(iii) Sometimes it is used at the end of a statement to mark it as a serious and solemn affirmation. So Paul uses it in Rom. 1.25 and 9.25.

In the Jewish Synagogue it was the regular practice that the congregation responded to prayers, thanksgivings, benedictions, doxologies with a united Amen, thereby making them their own.

This was a practice which from the beginning was part of Christian worship. Justin Martyr describes a Christian service. He tells how the leader conducts it, then he says: 'When he has concluded the prayers and thanksgivings, all the people present express their assent by saying Amen.' 'The president offers prayers and thanks according to his ability, and the people assent, saying, Amen.'[1]

We must now turn to certain suggestions regarding the origin of this title as applied to Jesus.

(i) In Isa. 65.16, as the AV and RSV have it, God is twice referred to as 'the God of truth'. Moffatt translates it 'the faithful God'. The Hebrew is literally 'the God of Amen'. The meaning is that God is the God of the truth and the fidelity which are established beyond question and beyond shaking. To call Jesus the Amen in that sense would mean that he is the one who is faithful and true, which is exactly what John goes on to say in Rev. 3.14.

(ii) In the narrative of the Gospels the great sayings of Jesus are often introduced, as the AV has it, by the words: 'Verily, verily'. The RSV has: 'Truly, truly'. The NEB has: 'In truth I tell you'. The Greek is: '*Amēn, amēn* (e.g. John 3.5,11). It is suggested that the title goes back to that way of speaking, and that it means that Jesus is the embodiment of the truth which he spoke. He did not only *speak* the truth; he *is* the truth. He did not only *say* Amen; he *is* Amen.

(iii) There is a passage of Paul which gives us the illuminating clue to the meaning of this title. It is so highly compressed a passage that it will be well to look at the renderings

---

[1] *First Apology* 65 and 67.

of it in a number of different translations. In the AV it runs
(II Cor. 1.20):

> For all the promises of God in him are yea, and in him
> Amen, unto the glory of God by us.

Yea translates the Greek word *nai* which means yes, just as
amēn is the Hebrew word of affirmation.

The RSV renders it:

> All the promises of God find their yes in him. That is
> why we utter the Amen through him to the glory of God.

Moffatt renders it:

> The divine 'yes' has been at last sounded in him, for in
> him is the yes that affirms all the promises of God.

The *Twentieth Century New Testament* renders it:

> Many as were the promises of God, in Christ is the yes
> that fulfils them. Therefore through Christ let the Amen
> rise through us to the glory of God.

J. B. Phillips renders it:

> He is the divine yes. Every promise of God finds its
> affirmation in him, and through him can be said the final
> Amen to the glory of God.

The NEB renders it:

> He is the yes pronounced upon God's promises, every
> one of them. That is why, when we give glory to God,
> it is through Christ Jesus that we say Amen.

Here is a tremendous thought. Jesus, as it were, says 'Yes'
to all the promises of God. How can we believe that the
promises of God are true? How can we believe that God's
magnificent offer to men is an actual fact? We can believe
because of Jesus Christ. As Paul said, if God gave us his
only Son, he will surely give us all things with him (Rom.
8.32). Jesus is the 'yes' to every promise of God. And
the second half of Paul's close-packed statement means this.

When we know that Jesus is the 'yes' to all the promises of God, then, when we hear these promises read to us, or expounded to us, because of Jesus Christ we can say: 'Amen; I know that this is true; I accept it and I appropriate it'; and, when we pray, we can say: 'Through Jesus Christ our Lord, Amen.' Jesus says 'yes' to all the promises of God, and because of that, we can say, 'Amen', to them.

To say that Jesus is the Amen is to say that he is the unshakeable affirmation and guarantor of the promises of God.

36

ALPHA AND OMEGA,
THE BEGINNING AND THE END

THREE times in the Revelation we find the title Alpha and
Omega (Rev. 1.8; 21.6; 22.13), and the astonishing fact is
that the first two of these cases unmistakably describe God,
and the last one just as unmistakably describes Jesus Christ.
The extraordinary fact is that a title which is the title of
God is given unhesitatingly and without qualification to Jesus
Christ. As John saw it, the prerogatives of God are the pre-
rogatives of Jesus Christ.

(i) Let us begin with the fact that Alpha and Omega,
the Beginning and the End, is characteristically a title of
God. It is so in Hebrew thought. Isaiah hears God say: 'I,
the Lord, the first and with the last, I am he' (Isa. 41.4).
'I am the first and I am the last, besides me there is no
God' (Isa. 44.6). 'I am the first and I am the last' (Isa. 48.12).

Josephus the Jewish historian calls God 'the beginning
and the end of all things'. The Jewish rabbis loved curious
methods of exegesis. The Hebrew word for truth is *emeth*.
Hebrew originally had no vowels, and the word *emeth* is
made up of three consonants, *aleph, mem* and *tau*. The rabbis
declared that *emeth* is the symbol and the name of God,
because they said *aleph* is the first letter of the alphabet,
mem is the middle letter, and *tau* the last letter. (In point of fact
mem is not the middle letter for it is the thirteenth letter
of a twenty-two letter alphabet.) They argued that the word
emeth stands for the beginning, the middle and the end, and
therefore for God. In *aleph*, the first letter, God says: 'I
am the first—for there is none from whom I received my

kingdom.' In *mem*, the middle letter, God says: 'I am the middle—for there is none who shares my kingdom with me.' In *tau*, the last letter, God says: 'I am the last—for there is none to whom I shall hand my kingdom over.' For a Jew, 'the Beginning and the End' was a title of God.

It was so for the Greek also. Plato speaks of 'God, who, as old tradition tells, holds the beginning, the end, and the centre of everything'.[1] The ancient Greek commentators explained that God was the beginning, because he is the creative cause of all things; he is the end, because he is the goal to which all things go; he is the middle, because he is equally present in all things.

Here then we see that Jesus Christ is being interpreted in nothing less than terms of God.

(ii) Let us go on to see still further meanings of this title. *Alpha* is the first letter of the Greek alphabet and *omega* is the last. We have already seen that *aleph* is the first letter of the Hebrew alphabet and *tau* is the last. In both languages the phrases 'from *alpha* to *omega*', and 'from *aleph* to *tau*' denote completeness and comprehensiveness. The Jewish rabbis said, for instance, that Adam transgressed the law from *aleph* to *tau* and Abraham kept the law from *aleph* to *tau*. The rabbis said that when God blessed his people, he blessed them from *aleph* to *tau*. His blessing was total and complete. Clement of Alexandria worked this out in his own way. 'The Son is neither simply one thing as one thing, nor many things as parts, but one thing as all things, whence also he is all things. For he is the circle of all powers rolled and united into one unity. Wherefore the Word is called *alpha* and *omega*.'[2]

Here then is a pictorial way of saying that there is nothing lacking in Jesus Christ. He is total and complete. He has all power, all wisdom, all knowledge, all holiness, all goodness.

[1] *Laws* 715e.   [2] *Miscellanies* 4.25.

Nothing that man can possess is anything but fragmentary; Jesus Christ is complete with the completeness of God.

(iii) But *aleph* and *tau*, and *alpha* and *omega*, have another symbolism. 'From *aleph* to *tau*', and 'from *alpha* to *omega*' both describe perfect continuity. They describe that which has no break, that which is unchanging, unvarying and uninterrupted. Here we have symbolised two great truth about Jesus Christ.

First, his life, his action, his power are continuous. He has been acting before history began, all through history, he is acting now, and will go on acting for ever until history is ended. He is the same yesterday, today, and for ever. Here is symbolised the eternity of the Son.

The second truth is more personal. The action and the help of Jesus Christ are continuous all through life. Childhood, youth, manhood, age, birth, death—there is nothing in any time of life which can separate us from him.

iv)   On two of the occasions on which he uses this phrase John expands it (Rev. 21.6; 22.14). It is the last one, as we saw, which particularly refers to Jesus Christ: 'I am the Alpha and the Omega, the first and the last, the beginning and the end.' The word *beginning* is *archē* and the word for *end* is *telos;* and each of these words is capable of a double meaning.

Archē can mean *beginning* in point of time and *telos* can mean *end* in point of time; and these meanings are certainly involved, for John calls Jesus the first and the last. This symbolises the truth that the Son was before the world began and will be when the world is ended. He has neither beginning nor end in any human sense of the term.

But *archē* can also mean *beginning* in the sense of *source* or *origin*, and *telos* can mean *end* in the sense of *goal* and *consummation*. This then means to say that Jesus Christ is the source and origin from whom life began and the goal and end to which all life moves. He is the creator of life and he is the one in whom life is consummated and perfected. This is exactly what Paul said when he spoke of Jesus as the one from whom, and through whom, and to whom are all things (Rom. 11.36).

We may put this much more simply and personally. It is from Jesus Christ that we have received life, and it is to Jesus Christ that we must give life back. From him we come, to him we must go.

There can be no higher title of Jesus than Alpha and Omega, the Beginning and the End, for the title is the title of God himself. But we may well believe that John was not thinking in terms of technical theology and of the connection between the Father and the Son as the theologians try to define it. This is not the language of theology, it is the language of adoration. John, like Thomas, confronted with Jesus, can only say: 'My Lord, and my God!' (John 20.28).

37

THE HEAD

ONE of the great Pauline conceptions is the conception of the Church as the Body of Christ; and the companion picture is the picture of Jesus Christ as the Head of the Church.

He is the head of the body, the Church (Col. 1.18). The reason why the heretics have gone astray, and why they are threatening to lead others astray, is that they do not hold fast 'to the Head, from whom the whole body, nourished and knit together through its joints and ligaments, grows with a growth that is from God' (Col. 2.19). God has put all things under the feet of Jesus Christ, and has made him the head over all things for the Church (Eph. 1.22,23). We are to grow up in every way into him who is the head, into Christ, from whom the whole body, joined and knit together by every joint with which it is supplied, when each part is working properly, makes bodily growth and upbuilds itself in love (Eph. 4.14,15). The husband is head of the wife as Christ is head of the Church, his body (Eph. 5.23). The head of every man is Christ (I Cor. 11.3).

In every language the head stands for supremacy, leadership, authority, even for the essence of life itself. It is so in the Old Testament.

(i) In the Old Testament we read of the national leaders who were the heads of the households and the heads of the people (Ex. 6.14; 18.25; Num. 1.4; 13.3; Josh. 14.1). The heads are associated with the princes (Num. 1.16; 10.4); with the elders (Josh. 23.2) with the judges (Josh. 24.1). The head is the symbol of leadership.

(ii) The Old Testament has the picture which we still use of the national leader as the head of the state. The people offer to make Jephthah their head (Judg. 11.8-11). Damascus is the head of Syria and Rezin is the head of Damascus. Samaria is the head of Ephraim, and the son of Remaliah is the head of Syria (Isa. 7.8,9). In the Psalm it is said to be David's thanksgiving that God kept him as the head of the nation (II Sam. 22.44; Ps. 18.43). The head is the symbol of royalty.

(iii) Supremely the title belongs to God, for God is the head above all (II Chron 29.11). The head is the symbol of divine authority.

(iv) So important is the head that often it can stand for the whole person. We often come upon the phrase that, if a man continues in his folly, his blood will be on his own head (e.g. I Kings 2.44). Blessings are said to be on the head of the righteous (Prov. 10.6). When David was among the Philistines, Achish the Philistine king said to him: 'I will make you keeper of my head for ever' (I Sam. 28.2). The RSV correctly modernises it into: 'I will make you my bodyguard for life.' The head is so much the centre of personality that it repeatedly stands for the whole person.

The Greeks used many of the same phrases. Where in English we might find a person addressed as 'Dear heart', Greek says. 'Dear head'.[1] Greek can speak of five hundred heads as we would more naturally speak of five hundred souls.[2] Greek speaks of staking one's head where we would say to risk one's life, and of throwing away one's head, where we would speak of throwing away one's life.[3]

The Greeks too could call the leader of the state the head. When Vindex the Roman general led the rebellion against Nero, he invited Galba to become Emperor, 'that he might

---

[1] Homer, *Iliad* 8.281; Euripides, *Rhesus* 226; Plato, *Phaedrus* 264a.
[2] Herodotus 9.99.   [3] Homer, *Odyssey*, 2.237; Herodotus 8.65.

serve what was a vigorous body in need of a head.'[1] In an Orphic hymn Zeus is called the head, the middle, and the one in whom all things find their end.

Clearly, the use of the picture of the head to denote one in power and authority is a universal picture. What does the phrase mean when it is applied to Jesus?

(i) In the head is concentrated the life of the body. It is with the eyes we see, with the ears we hear, with the nose we smell; and above all it is with the mind and brain we think. So Jesus Christ is the life of the Church; without him the Church is as dead as a body without a head.

(ii) It is the head which directs and controls the body. The head directs the action of the body. Without the mind the body can have neither aim nor purpose nor effective action. The mind controls the instincts and the passions of the body. Even so Jesus Christ must control and direct his Church. He alone can give purpose and direction to the Church and he alone can restrain the Church from human folly. As Armitage Robinson puts it: 'It is the function of the head to plan the safety of the body, to secure it from anger, and to provide for its welfare.' The head has the right to rule and must be obeyed. As J. B. Lightfoot says of the head in relation to the body, it has the 'inspiring, ruling, guiding, combining, sustaining power'. It is 'the mainspring of the body's activity, the centre of its unity, and the seat of its life'. And all that Jesus Christ is to his Church.

(iii) But there is another side to this. It is true that the head guides, directs, controls the body; but it is equally true that without the body the head is helpless. The head can think and plan, but its thoughts and plans cannot turn into action without the body. If the body needs a head to direct it, the head needs a body to use for its purposes. Even so, there is a real sense in which Jesus Christ is

[1] Plutarch, *Galba* 4.3.

helpless without his Church. If, for instance, Jesus Christ
wants a child taught, nothing can teach that child, unless a
man or a woman is prepared to accept the task. If Jesus
Christ wants a message taken to a nation, a church, or an
individual, he has to find some one to be his mouth, to speak
to the people, and to be the bearer of his message. It is at
once the glory and the responsibility of the Church that it
has to be the body through which Jesus Christ acts upon
the world of men.

Herein lies a great warning and challenging truth. When
we say that Jesus Christ is the Head and that the Church is
his Body, we mean that the Church cannot live and act
without Jesus Christ, and Jesus Christ cannot work out his
purposes in the world without the Church.

38

THE IMAGE OF GOD

TWICE in the New Testament Jesus is described by the word
eikōn. In the AV and in the NEB the word is rendered 'image'
on both occasions. In II Cor. 4.4 Paul speaks of Jesus as *the
image of God;* and in Col. 1.15 he speaks of him as *the
image of the invisible God*. Strangely enough, the RSV
renders 'likeness' in the first passage and 'image' in the second.

This is one of the great descriptions of Jesus, but in one
sense it is a highly dangerous description and exceedingly
liable to misinterpretation. It is intended to indicate the essential unity of God and Jesus, of the Father and the Son,
but it could be used and has been used to argue that the relationship between God and Jesus is not that of unity and identity
but only that of resemblance and likeness in the ordinary sense
of the word. It is therefore of the first importance to study
and to define the meaning of the word *eikōn*.

In the New Testament itself the word is quite common. It
is very commonly used for an image in the sense of an idol,
a graven image, a man-made representation of God (Rom.
1.23; Rev. 13.14,15; 14.9,11; 15.2; 16.2; 19.20; 20.4).

It is used in the normal sense of likeness, more or less
close, without any real identity. Those whom God foreknew
he predestined to be conformed to the *image* of his Son
(Rom. 8.29). Man is the *image* and glory of God (I Cor.
11.7; cp. Gen. 1.26,27). Man bears the *image* of the man
of dust and will bear the *image* of the man of heaven (I Cor.
15.49). The Christian is changed into the *likeness* of Christ,
from one degree of glory to another (II Cor. 3.18). In Christ
nature is renewed after the *image* of the Creator (Col. 3.10).

In all these cases the idea is certainly more that of likeness than of actual identity. But there is one significant use of the word. In Heb. 10.1 the old law is said to be but a shadow (*skia*) of things to come instead of the true form, the *eikōn*, of their realities. There *eikōn* means a real, true, accurate, essential reproduction and representation, as contrasted with that which is shadowy, vague, nebulous, unreal and essentially imperfect. It is the complete perfection of the reproduction which is there the point of the word.

We must now turn to the use of the word in secular

(i) It can mean what might be called an apparition in the mind. Euripides tells how Hercules was suddenly arrested in his murderous madness and his savage blood lust by the *appearance* in his mind of the goddess Athene.[1]

The mental vision of Athene is called an *eikōn*.

(ii) It can be used for an image in the mind. Plato describes how a man hears a word or sees some sight, and thereupon he forms in his mind a true or untrue *eikōn*. This is very much what we would call in idiomatic English a mental impression.

(iii) It can mean a comparison or a similitude. Aristotle cites examples of such similitudes.[2] The Samians are like children who cry when they accept the scraps. Demosthenes said that the people of Athens were like passengers who were sea-sick. These, says Aristotle, are *eikones,* similes.

It may well be said that so far these usages rather imply the difference of an *eikōn* from the real thing, and they well represent the danger into which the interpretation of this word can so easily run.

Now we come to certain uses of the word *eikōn* which bring us to the other side of the picture.

(iv) *Eikōn* can mean the reflection in a mirror. Euripides

[1] Euripides, *The Madness of Hercules* 1002.
[2] *Rhetoric* 1407a 11.

describes Medea 'ranging her tresses by a shining mirror, smiling at her own *image* (*eikōn*) there.'[1] Plato uses the word for the *reflection* of the sun in water.[2] Here we come upon the very important fact that there are a series of uses of *eikōn* which are connected with things which are the exact and perfect reproduction of an original.

(v) *Eikōn* can regularly mean an image or a statue. Herodotus (1.130) tells how Mycerinus king of Egypt made the hollow *image* of a cow of gilded wood as a resting place for the body of his dead daughter. He tells (1.143) how every high priest set up during his own lifetime a statue (*eikōn*) of himself in the Temple, and how the series of *eikones* goes back to the earliest times. Aeschylus uses the word for the *representation* of a monstrous beast on warrior's shield.[3] Lucian uses the word, as it is commonly used, for the busts of the gods.[4] Here again we are finding the idea of exact representation.

(vi) There is one further use of this word which is very significant. The diminutive form *eikonion* is what corresponds in Greek to the modern *photograph*. Apion the soldier writes home to his father Epimachus: 'I send you a little portrait (*eikonion*) of myself at the hands of Euctemon.'

There is a further development of this. The word *eikōn* becomes the regular word for the identifying description of a person which was subjoined to official documents, in particular with regard to the buying and selling of slaves. The *eikōn* was the official and accurate description of the person involved, and the means whereby he or she could be identified.

If we take it in this way, we may say that Jesus is the exact portrait and description of God.

---

[1] *Medea* 1162. [2] *Phaedo* 99d.
[3] *Seven against Thebes* 558. [4] *Alexander* 18.
[5] G. Milligan, *Selections from the Greek Papyri* 36.

There are two further strands still to add. First, in Philo, in whom Jewish and Greek thought unite, one of the principal conceptions is that of the Logos, the Word, who is God's instrument in creation, God's steersman of the universe, God's messenger to the world, and God's link and intermediary between men and himself. Again and again he calls the Logos the *eikōn* of God. The Word is the image, *eikōn,* of the unseen God.[1] The most sacred Word is the image of God.[2] The Word through which everything was made is the image of God.[3] The Word to Philo is the intermediary between God and man, and is the image of God.

Second, one of the dominant conceptions in later Judaism is the idea of Wisdom whose portrait is drawn in Proverbs 8; and Wisdom is 'the unspotted mirror of the working of God, and an image (*eikōn*) of his goodness' (Wisd. 7.26).

It can be seen that the Word *eikōn* has a great history. When Paul chose to use it, he was choosing to use a word not without its dangers, because it might be taken to mean that there was nothing more than a resemblance between Jesus and God; but the word can and does mean far more than that; it means an exact reproduction and representation, and in religious language it had come to describe One in whom God makes himself known to men.

We must now go on to try to see what Paul meant when he called Jesus the *eikōn* of God, and, before we do so, a debt must be acknowledged. Every one who has subsequently discussed this word has been heavily in the debt of J. B. Lightfoot for his full discussion of it in his commentary on Colossians, and on that discussion we too have very largely drawn.

As Vincent Taylor points out in his discussion of this word in *The Names of Jesus,* our task is made more difficult,

---

[1] *Concerning the Creator of the World* 8.
[2] *Concerning the Confusion of Tongues* 20.
[3] *Concerning Dreams* 1.41.

because of the fact that in English the word *likeness* tends to mean a rather faint copy of the original. The Oxford Dictionary defines *likeness* as 'an artificial imitation or representation of the external form of any object'. To begin on these lines would obviously be to set off on the wrong path altogether. Lightfoot identifies two main ideas in the word *eikōn*.

(i) There is the idea of *representation*. As R. C. Trench puts it, *eikōn* always implies an archetype from which the thing is drawn. The likeness implied in *eikōn* is not the kind of chance resemblance which might exist between two unrelated objects or persons; it is always a likeness to some archetype, some prototype, of which the *eikōn* is a likeness. Gregory Nazianzen describes *eikōn* as the *mimēma,* the imitation, the copy, the reproduction of the archetype.

That reproduction of the archetype may be deliberate, and, as it were, manufactured. For instance, in the New Testament itself, the king's head on a coin is called the *eikōn,* the image, of the king (Matt. 22.20; Mark 12.16; Luke 20.24). This is a likeness deliberately produced. The reproduction may be the result of a natural process. So, for instance, children are said to be *empsuchoi eikones,* breathing images, of their parents. In something the same way, on the Rosetta Stone (196 BC), Ptolemy Epiphanes is said to be 'the living image (*eikōn*) of Zeus'.

It is to be noted that this way of speaking does not necessarily imply a perfect and complete likeness; it simply implies that something or some one bears a more or less close resemblance to an archetype. For instance, man is said to be made in the *image* of God (I Cor. 11.7; Gen. 1.26,27). In the *Clementine Homilies* Christians are bidden to reverence the bishop, as the likeness, *eikōn,* of God. The closeness of the likeness can vary, and is to be found from the context and from the way in which the word is used.

If then we say that Jesus is the *eikōn* of God, it means that Jesus is the representation of God; God is the divine archetype and Jesus is the human likeness of him.

(ii) But, as Lightfoot points out, there is another idea in *eikōn*. There is the idea of *manifestation*. The *eikōn* is the visible manifestation of the invisible and the unseen, of that which in itself cannot be seen. Philo, for instance, says that we cannot look at the sun direct, but we can look at the rays of the sun; the rays of the sun are therefore the *eikōn*, the manifestation of the sun.[1]

Basil makes much of this idea.[2] It is because Jesus said that he who has seen him has seen the Father that we can go on to say that Jesus is the express image of God. We behold the Father in the Son. The Son is the image, the manifestation of the Father. We gaze at the unbegotten Beauty in the Begotten. Through knowledge of the incarnate Son we receive in our hearts the express image of the Father; the Father is known in the form of the Son. That is what it means to call Jesus the *eikōn* of God. Plummer, commenting on II Cor. 4.4, says that to call Jesus the *eikōn* of God means that Jesus is 'the visible representative of the invisible God'. Paul has the idea that the visible world is designed to show us the things which are invisible (Rom 1.20), and that man is made in the image of God (I Cor. 11.7). With this in mind, C. F. D. Moule, commenting on Col. 1.15, says: 'Christ is claimed to gather up in his own person that manifestation of the invisible God which was to be found both generally in nature (Rom. 1.20), and more particularly in man' (Gen. 1.26). To say that Jesus is the image of God is to say that he is the manifestation of the invisible God *par excellence*. As Vincent Taylor puts it, in Jesus Christ God comes to life and is expressed.

That is exactly what John meant when he said: 'No one

[1] Philo, *Concerning Dreams* 1.   [2] *Letter* 28.

has ever seen God; the only Son who is in the bosom of the Father, he has made him known' (John 1.18); and it is what Jesus meant when he said: 'He who has seen me has seen the Father' (John 14.9).

We may now go back and gather up the various strands in this word *eikōn*. It is true that there are cases in which the idea is that of a more or less distant likeness without any identity. But the word is used in direct opposition to *skia,* a shadowy outline (Heb. 10.1); it is used of the perfect reflection in a mirror; it is the nearest approach in the ancient world to the modern photograph; it is the word for the official, accurate and legal description of any person in cases of contract where that correct description is of the first importance. It has in it the idea of representation of an archetype, and manifestation of that which is in itself invisible.

The one remaining problem is how to render this word into English. There is no doubt that the word *likeness* is liable to serious misinterpretation. We may well say that Jesus is *the living image of God.* In him the unknowable God becomes knowable; the unapproachable God becomes approachable; the invisible God becomes flesh and dwells among us, and we see full displayed his grace, his glory and his truth.

39

THE CHRIST OF CREATION
THE FIRSTBORN OF ALL CREATION
THE BEGINNING OF GOD'S CREATION

THERE is in the New Testament a distinct line of thought which connects Jesus Christ with the creation of all things. For many of us this is a difficult conception. We must begin by setting down the passages in which the idea occurs.

It occurs in the Prologue of the Fourth Gospel, where we read: 'All things were made through him, and without him was not anything made that was made' (John 1.3). It occurs in the Letter to the Colossians in the passage which is sometimes known as 'the great Christology': 'He is the image of the invisible God, the firstborn of all creation; for in him all things were created, in heaven, and in earth, visible and invisible, whether thrones or dominions or principalities or authorities—all things were created through him and for him. He is before all things, and in him all things hold together' (Col. 1.15-17). It occurs in Hebrews where the writer speaks of him who was a Son, 'whom God appointed the heir of all things, through whom also he created the world' (Heb. 1.2). It occurs in the Revelation where the Risen Christ is called 'the beginning of God's creation' (Rev. 3.14).

Before we try to understand the meaning of these passages, it will be well to try to see what gave rise to them. It is to be noted that the idea does not occur in the early Gospels; it first emerges in the Fourth Gospel which was not written until the end of the first century. Again, it does not appear in the early letters of Paul; it emerges first in the

Letter to the Colossians, which was written towards the end of his life in his last imprisonment. This then is not a conception which was among the earliest beliefs of the Church; it is rather a conception to which the Church was made to move, in order to answer certain mistaken beliefs.

The problem of evil in the world, the problem of sin and of suffering, is a problem which has exercised men's minds ever since they began to think at all. In the ancient world there was a type of thought, to which the general name of Gnosticism is given, which explained the evil of the world by means of a thorough-going dualism. Gnosticism, put at its very simplest, held the following beliefs. Creation was not creation out of nothing; creation was creation out of already existing matter. There was an already existing 'stuff' from which the world was made. This matter had a flaw in it; it was evil from the beginning. Out of this flawed stuff, this evil matter, the world was made. God is altogether good, or, to put the antithesis more directly, Spirit, which is the opposite of matter, is altogether good. Because the God who is pure spirit is altogether good, it was impossible for him directly to touch this evil matter. So he put out a series of emanations or aeons. Each of these emanations was further and further from God, until at last there was arrived at an emanation who was so distant from God that he could touch and handle and shape this flawed matter. But there was more than mere distance from God in this. As the emanations became further and further from God, they became more and more ignorant of God, until in the end they actually became hostile to God. So the emanation at the end of the series, by whom the world was created, is distant from God, ignorant of God, and hostile to God. The explanation of the evil of the world is that the world is created out of flawed matter by a god who is ignorant of, and hostile to, the true God. Sometimes the Gnostics completed the picture by identifying the ignorant and hostile god with the God of the Old Testament, while the real and true God is the God of Jesus and of the New Testament. Here then is the picture of an essentially evil world, made out of bad stuff, by an inferior god.

It was in face of this that the Christian thinkers worked out their belief that Jesus Christ is God's instrument and agent in creation. They thus insisted that there are not two gods in opposition to each other in the universe, and they affirmed their faith that the God of creation and the God of redemption are one and the same. They would never have denied the evil of the world; but they would have said that the evil of the world is due neither to the material from which it is made nor to the inferior god who made it, but to the sin of man, which has defaced the creation of God and has kept it from being what God meant it to be.

In face of Gnostic dualism the Christians worked out the picture of the Son as God's agent in the creation and in the recreation of the world; creation and redemption are the acts of the one God, and both are through the one Son. It is well to remember that the conception of the Christ of creation was worked out to counter the dualism of Gnosticism. It would hardly be going too far to say that the idea of the Christ of creation was rather the product of circumstances than part of the original message of the Church. Let us now turn to the ways in which the Church expressed this new belief.

(i) We shall begin with the passage from the Revelation because it is the simplest. In it Jesus is called 'the beginning of God's creation' (Rev. 3.14). One of the strange features of this conception of the Christ of creation is that it is repeatedly expressed in language which is liable to the most serious misinterpretation. The word for beginning is *archē*, and the phrase the *archē*, the beginning of God's creation, can have two meanings. It can have a *passive* meaning and it can have an *active* meaning. As far as the Greek goes, and as far as the English goes also, to say that Jesus Christ is the beginning of creation can mean either that Jesus Christ was the first being to be created, or that he was the source and origin whereby all beings and things are created. Exactly the same word is used in Col. 1.18, and in 1.16 it has just been said that all things have been created through him and for him. It is therefore quite clear that *archē* is being used in its active sense, and that it means that Jesus is the source and the origin of all creation. 'In him was life.' From him both created and recreated life flow.

(ii) If the title 'the beginning of creation' produces difficulties, still greater difficulties emerge from the title 'the first-born of all creation'. The word for *firstborn* is *prōtokos*. Let us examine it.

(*a*) *Prōtotokos* can be, and frequently is, used simply in a time sense, meaning quite literally the first to be born in any family. 'I am Esau your firstborn,' says Esau to Jacob (Gen. 27.19), which is simply to say: 'I am your eldest son.' It was the firstborn, that is the eldest, sons who were destroyed by the avenging angel in Egypt at the first Passover (Ex. 11.5). The firstborn of men and animals were according to the Jewish law consecrated to God (Ex. 13.2; Num. 3.13). The word is even applied to Jesus in its literal sense in connection with his human birth, for he is called the firstborn son of Mary, her first child (Luke 2.7).

The word is commonly and regularly used in this sense in secular Greek. In an inscription a man refers to himself as 'a priest by the rites of the firstborn', meaning that he belongs to a family in which the eldest son inherits the office of the priesthood. A Greek epitaph tells of the death of a firstborn child who was two years old. It is perfectly natural to take *prōtotokos* as meaning firstborn in the sense of time. C. F. D. Moule in his commentary on Colossians points out that, if we were to interpret this phrase all by itself, without any reference to its context, and without any consideration of the rest of Paul's thinking, all it would mean is that Jesus Christ is the first of created beings, as it were, the eldest of the family; and it would include Jesus Christ in creation rather than identify him as the Creator. On this view Jesus would be a part of the created world, and not the eternal and uncreated Son.

(b) It is just barely possible, although it cannot be said to be likely, to take *prōtotokos* in an active and not in a passive sense, that is, to take it to mean, not *firstborn,* but *first begetter, primus auctor,* as the Latins put it, the first author, or the first begetter of all created things. This gives good sense, but the objection is that meaning of the word is very rare anywhere and non-existent in the New Testament and in the Greek Old Testament. Though theoretically possible, it is not a meaning which would strike any reader of the passage.

(c) Many of the early fathers radically altered the meaning of the Colossians passage. They held that the word *prōtotokos* is not descriptive of the pre-existent Christ in his life before he came to this earth, but that it refers to the incarnate Christ, to Jesus, and that it means that Jesus is *the firstborn of the new creation.* They cited Rom. 8.29 where Jesus is called 'the firstborn among many brethren', and where the reference is to the Resurrection, and where the meaning is that he was the first to be raised from the dead by God, thereby opening the path for others to follow to the new and recreated life. Again the meaning is good, but in the Colossians passage the clear reference is to the creation of the world, and, when the phrase is taken in its context, this meaning cannot well be read into it.

(d) The schoolmen of the Middle Ages took this phrase in a curious and an interesting way. They were strongly influenced by the thinking of Plato, and one of the fundamental Platonic conceptions is that there is a series of perfect patterns, archetypes, forms, ideas laid up in the heavenly places of which everything on earth is a pale and imperfect copy. So they said that when Jesus is described as the firstborn of creation, it means that he is the perfect idea, pattern, archetype of creation which existed from the beginning in the mind of God, and which was demonstrated and made actual on earth in him. That is to say, Jesus is the true demonstration of what creation ought to be, of what creation is in the mind of God. This in its own way is a great thought, but it is much too philosophic and abstract for the thinking of the New Testament.

(e) There is only one real solution to the problem. The word *prōtotokos* has quite commonly another meaning which has nothing to do with time at all. It means *first in place, first in honour*. It obviously developed this meaning because the eldest son has the first place and the first honour; but in course of time the idea of eldest faded from the word and the idea of chief honour became the dominating idea. This use of *prōtotokos* occurs in the Greek of the Old Testament. In Job in the speech of Bildad about the wicked man we read: 'By disease his skin is consumed, *the firstborn of death* consumes his limbs' (Job 18.13). The firstborn of death means the most terrible of fatal and deadly diseases. In Isaiah there is a passage in a prophecy of the good days of God which are to come: '*The firstborn of the poor will* feed, and the needy lie down in safety' (Isa. 14.30). The firstborn of the poor is the poorest man, the man, as it were, pre-eminent in poverty.

Polycarp describes the man who does not believe in the incarnation, who does not confess the testimony of the Cross, who perverts the oracles of the Lord to further his own lusts as 'the firstborn of Satan';[1] and it is said that he applied

[1] *Philippians* 7.1.

the phrase in particular to Marcion the heretic. The story
is that once Polycarp and Marcion met. 'Do you know me?'
said Marcion. 'I do know you,' replied Polycarp, 'the firstborn
of Satan.'[1] The firstborn of Satan means the man pre-eminent
in Satanic evil.

Just how far the word had taken on this meaning can be
seen by the fact that the Jewish Rabbi Bechai called God
himself 'the firstborn of the world'. The sense of pre-eminence
in honour has banished the sense of first in time completely.

Here is our clue. To say that Jesus is the firstborn of
creation is to say that the highest place in the universe is
his. It lifts him above and beyond all created things and
sets him in the topmost place.

But we have no sooner brought the matter to this length
than another problem faces us. Jesus is the firstborn of creation; by him all things were made; for him all things exist;
in him all things cohere. *How can this possibly be said
about a man who hung in shame and agony on a cross a
litle more than thirty years before?* How could anyone begin
to believe in the primacy of this Jesus in creation and in the
universe? There are three lines towards the explanation of
this.

(i) Firstborn was undoubtedly a title of the Messiah. The
use of the title as a Messianic title comes from the fact
that the nation of Israel is called God's firstborn. Moses
was to say to Pharoh: 'Thus says the Lord, Israel is my
firstborn son' (Ex. 4.22). 'I am a father to Israel,' God said
to Jeremiah, 'and Ephraim is my firstborn' (Jer. 31.9). God
says of his faithful man: 'I will make him the firstborn, the
highest of the kings of the earth' (Ps. 89.27). Inevitably
the title became a Messianic title; and, if it was a Messianic
title, it would inevitably sooner or later be applied to Jesus.
Here it is clear that the meaning is pre-eminence and honour.

[2] Irenaeus, *Against Heresies* 3.3.4.

(ii) As soon as Jesus was thought of as the Word, the idea of creation was bound to come in. In Genesis 1 we see the creative word of God in action. 'By the word of the Lord the heavens were made,' says the Psalmist (Ps. 33.6). To call Jesus the Word was necessarily to link him with creation.

(iii) As soon as Jesus was thought of in terms of Wisdom the idea of creation would come in. Wisdom was with God in the beginning of his work, before the beginning of the earth, like a master workman (Prov. 8.22-31). Wisdom is the worker of all things, more moving than any motion, passing and going through all things, the breath of the power of God (Wisd. 7.22-30). Wisdom is the firstborn before all creatures, created before the world, destined to last after the world has ended, eternal (Ecclus 24). Once Jesus came to be thought of in terms of Wisdom, he would again be necessarily linked with creation.

But we have simply pushed our problem one step further back. How could this crucified Jesus be thought of in terms of the Messiah, the Word, Wisdom, the Firstborn? *The answer lies in the Resurrection.* Jesus was the firstborn from the dead (Col. 1.18; Rev. 1.5). The fact of the Resurrection explains the complete pre-eminence in time, before time, and in eternity given to Jesus Christ. There could clearly be nothing beyond the power of him whom death was powerless to hold. The first place in the universe goes by right to him who vanquished death.

The one question remains. What is the meaning of this conception of the Christ of creation for us? Apart from any literalism, what is its permanent meaning? We shall deal with this more fully when we come to think of Jesus as the Word. At the moment it is sufficient to say this—the conception of the work of Christ in creation lays down the great fact that the power which redeemed the world is the same power as created the world. The God of redemption and the God of creation are one, and therefore at the basis of the world there is love. This is not so much an exercise in philosophic cosmology as an affirmation that creation is ultimately good.

THE BRIGHT MORNING STAR

PERHAPS the most beautiful title ever given to Jesus, and certainly the title most instinct with poetry, is given to him in Rev. 22.16, where he is called the Bright Morning Star. The title is a title with a history, and in later days it was to be associated with the events which saw the total and final destruction of the Jews as an independent power.

For the Jews the Star was a Messianic title, although in the earlier days it was not one of the common titles. Its basis as a title of the Messiah was in Num. 24.17 in the prophecy of Balaam: 'A star shall come forth out of Jacob.' Twice in *The Testaments of the Twelve Patriarchs,* one of the inter-testamental books, the Messiah is described as a star. He is so described in *The Testament of Judah* (24.1-6):

> And after these things shall a star rise to you from Jacob
> in peace,
> And a man shall arise from my seed, like the sun of
> righteousness,
> Walking with the sons of men in meekness and
> righteousness,
> And no sin shall be found in him.

In this book there occurs the unusual idea of the priestly Messiah who was to spring from the tribe of Levi. We have part of the description of him in *The Testament of Levi* (18.3-55):

> And his star shall rise in heaven as of a king,
> Lighting up the sun of knowledge as the sun the day.
> And he shall be magnified in the world.
> He shall shine forth as the sun on the earth,
> And shall remove all darkness from under heaven.

This title emerged again in the final disaster of Jewish history. In AD 70 the Roman armies under Titus had devastated Jerusalem, leaving hardly one stone standing on another. But time brings healing. We come to AD 132. At that time the greatest figure in Judaism was Rabbi Akiba. So expert was he in the Law that he was called a second Ezra, and it was said that the power of Moses was weak until Akiba came to interpret him. He was such a lover of his fellowmen and he so cared for the weak and the humble that he was called 'The Hand of the Poor'. In spite of Israel's misfortunes Akiba was sure that the coming of the Messiah was near. Just at this time there arose a popular leader, certainly a man of desperate courage and of great military skill. His real name is unknown, but Akiba saw in him the promised Messiah and called him Bar-Cochba, which means 'The Son of the Star'.

At first the revolt of Bar-Cochba was highly succesful, for the Romans had few soldiers stationed in Palestine, and from his headquarters at Bethar south-west of Jerusalem Bar-Cochba won a series of victories. Even the legate of Syria, Publicius Marcellus, had not sufficient forces to quell this rising. The Emperor Hadrian recognised the danger, and summoned from Britain the greatest Roman general of his day, Sextus Julius Severus. Bar-Cochba and his desperate men were no match for the full might of Rome now deployed against them. It was a war of annihilation; it is said that more than half a million Jews perished, and that the survivors 'glutted the slave markets of the East'. So grim was the resistance that the survivors had to be starved out of underground caverns and passages, where, it was said, they even took to cannibalism to stave off death or surrender.

Finally the revolt was broken. Bar-Cochba, the Son of the Star, the last Messianic claimant, was executed. Jerusalem was deliberately destroyed; the very name Judaea was wiped

off the map and the province became known as Syria
Palaestina. The Jews were forbidden on pain of death to
enter Jerusalem, or even to look on it from afar. The only
sad privilege that they were allowed was that each year on
the anniversary of the destruction of the Temple by Titus
they were permitted for that one day to enter the ruined city
and to weep on the ruins of the place where the Holy of
Holies had stood. This time Hadrian made certain that there
would be no more trouble. On the ruins of Jerusalem he
erected a new city called Aelia Capitolina, and on the site
of the ancient Temple he built a new temple dedicated to
Zeus Capitolinus. For the Jewish nation this was the end.
So the Messianic title of 'the Star' was to be connected with
the last terrible agony of the Jewish people.

It was almost inevitable that the Christians should take over
the title and apply it to Jesus. Justin Martyr, Irenaeus and
Cyprian all apply it to Jesus.[1] The application of the title
to him was made easier by the story of the star which rose
in the east and which led the Magi to the place where he
was born (Matt. 2.2-9).

This title says certain things about Jesus.

(i) The morning star is the brightest of all stars, and
this therefore sets Jesus in the forefront of splendour. Other
luminaries pale into insignificance compared with the morning
star, and other teachers and leaders pale into significance in
comparison with Jesus Christ. This gives him his place as
the supreme light of the world.

(ii) To us the title nowadays seems mainly a poetic title.
But in Old Testament times, especially in Arabic, the star
was the title for a prince, for one pre-eminent in royalty and
power. So this title enthrones Jesus as King of kings and
Lord of lords.

---

[1] Justin, *Dialogue with Trypho* 106; Irenaeus, *Against Heresies* 3.9.2;
Cyprian, *Testimonia* 2.10.

(iii) It is the function and the glory of the morning star to be the herald of the dawn. When the morning star rises, the full blaze of day is not far behind. So with Jesus there came the light which puts the darkness to flight.

There remains one other thing to add. We have already seen that this title occurs in *The Testaments of the Twelve Patriarchs,* and, if we continue the quotation from *The Testament of Levi* (18.8,9), we find something very suggestive, for this is one of the quite few passages which thinks of the Messiah not only in terms of the exaltation of the Jewish nation, but of the enlightenment of the whole world:

> And there shall none succeed him for all generations
> for ever,
> And in his priesthood shall the Gentiles be multiplied
> in knowledge upon the earth,
> And enlightened through the grace of the Lord.

A star is not something which any nation can keep to itself. A star is something which any man who can look up can see, and whose light and guidance any man can enjoy; and so the title of the Star sets Jesus forth as the Saviour of all mankind.

41

LORD

OF all the titles of Jesus the title Lord became by far the most commonly used, widespread, and theologically important. It would hardly be going too far to say that the word Lord became a synonym for the name of Jesus.

This did not happen all at once; it was rather the result of a gradual growth. In Mark there are only one or two occasions on which Jesus is called Lord in the full theological sense of the term (Mark 11.3; 12.57). In Matthew it is much the same. In Luke there are about seventeen occasions when the title in its full significance is applied to Jesus. But Dr Vincent Taylor reckons there are at least 130 occasions in the letters of Paul when Jesus is called simply Lord, apart from the occasions on which the title Lord is used in conjunction with some other title. The combinations in which Lord is used with some other word or title, with the number of occurrences of each given in brackets, are as follows: Our Lord (1); Our Lord Jesus Christ (28); The Lord Jesus Christ (18); Jesus Christ our Lord (3); Christ Jesus our Lord, or my Lord, or the Lord (6); Jesus our Lord (2); Our Lord Christ (1); Our Lord Jesus (9); The Lord Jesus (12); the Lord Christ (1); The Lord, Jesus Christ (1). This is to say that in one form or another Jesus is called Lord well over 200 times in the letters of Paul. Clearly here is a title which is at the very heart and centre of the Christian faith.

The word in Greek is *kurios;* the Christian Church did not invent the word; it found it already a great and noble word; and we must first study the secular use of the word in order to see the suggestions it would have for a Greek.

The first thing that strikes us when we study this word in detail is *the atmosphere of authority* which it carries with it. That authority operates in a variety of spheres.

(i) It is the word of *domestic* authority. It describes the authority of the father of the family.[1] It describes the man who is, as he ought to be, master, *kurios,* in his own household.[2]

(ii) It is the regular word for a *master as opposed to a slave.*[3]

(iii) It is the regular word to describe the *undisputed owner* of any property.[4]

(iv) Kurios very commonly describes the person who has *authority to make decisions.* It describes the commander who has the right to make *military* decisions, who can decide between peace and war, who can despatch troops on some vital engagement.[5] It describes the magistrate who has the *legal* authority to pass sentence of death,[6] or to exercise his own judgment when the law is not clear, or when the existing law does not cover the case.[7] It describes a law which is unalterable and unbreakable;[8] a legal decision which is valid and binding;[9] a treaty which has been ratified and whose terms must be observed;[10] a decree which cannot be transgressed.[11] *Kurios* describes authority in every sphere of public life.

(v) It can express *moral* authority. It describes the man who is able to win some moral victory. Aristotle, for instance, uses it to describe the man who has the strength of

[1] Aristotle, *Rhetoric* 1402a 1.　　[2] Epictetus 3.22.3.
[3] Aristotle, *Politics* 1269b 10.　　[4] Plato, *Laws* 929d.
[5] Thucydides 4.20; 5.63; 8.5; Xenophon, *Hellenica* 2.2.18; *Anabasis* 5.7.27.
[6] Plato, *Critias* 120d.　　[7] Aristotle, *Politics* 1287b 16.
[8] Aristotle, *Politics* 1286a 24.　　[9] Plato, *Critias* 50b.
[10] Lysias 18.15.　　[11] Demosthenes 14.1.

character and will never to allow himself to become in-
toxicated.[1] He uses it of the supreme good which, he says,
must be decisive (*kurios*) in all our actions.[2] He uses it of
Prudence when he says that Prudence has even more authority
over life than Wisdom.[3]

(vi)   It can be describe what English calls *sovereign authority*. *To kurion* (the neuter of it used as a noun) is the word
for the sovereign authority of the state.[4] Aristotle uses it,
for instance, of the sovereign power of the *ekklēsia*, the
governing body of the city of Athens.[5] It is used for what
in English we call a sovereign remedy. So, for instance, Plato
says that cross-examination is a sovereign remedy in the
purification of error.[6] Galen, the Greek doctor, uses it to
describe what we would call the *principal* parts of the body.[7]
Epicurus, to help people who had no training in reading or
study, reduced his whole system of philosophy to forty
sentences which he called the *kuriai doxai*, the sovereign
maxims.

It is true to say that there is no word in Greek so clothed
with authority as *kurios* is.

We must now go on to look at certain uses of *kurios*
which were part and parcel of the everyday speech of men
in New Testament times, and which certainly did much to
define its meaning when it was applied to Jesus.

(i)   *Kurios* was the normal word of courtesy and respect,
used in addressing an elder or a superior or some one held
in affection. It was used in the same way as the English
'Sir', the French 'Monsieur', and the German 'Herr'. In the
New Testament itself the courteous but disobedient son says to
his father: 'I go, sir (*kurios*)' (Matt. 21.30). Everyone in the Greek-

[1] *Nicomachean Ethics* 1113b 32.   [2] *Politics* 1282b 15.
[3] *Nicomachean Ethics* 1143a 34.
[4] Aristotle, *Politics* 1365b 27; Demosthenes 19.259.
[5] *Constitution of Athens* 43.3.   [6] *Sophist* 230d.
[7] Galen, 1.385.

speaking world would use *kurios* in this way every day in life.

(ii) *Kurios* in letters was used very much in the way in which we use the phrase 'Dear so and so'. It is perhaps a little more consciously respectful and a little less conventional than the English phrase. The soldier Apion begins his letter to Epimachus his father with greetings to 'his father and lord (*kurios*)'; as we would say, he begins 'My dear Father'. Apollinarius sends greetings to 'his mother and lady (*kuria*)'; as we would say, he begins 'My dear Mother'. It is the epistolary word of loving and affectionate respect.

(iii) There is a use of *kurios* which is very common in contracts in which a woman is involved. Under Greek law a woman had no rights; if therefore she was to enter into any contract or agreement, she could not do so herself; she had to be represented by her guardian who was called her *kurios*. In a marriage contract a certain Apollonia has her brother Apollonius as her *kurios*. In a census return Thermoutharion names another Apollonius as her *kurios*. The *kurios* is the legal guardian of the rights and interests of one who needs a protector.

(iv) *Kurios* became the standard and official title of the Roman Emperors. This did not happen all at once. In theory the Roman Empire was a democracy. It was, as it has been rightly put, a principate and not a *dominate*. That is to say, the Emperor was the first citizen (*princeps*), but he was not the master of a collection of slaves (*dominus*). *Dominus* is the Latin for the Greek *kurios*, and we have seen that *kurios* is the word for *master* as opposed to slave. For that reason the Roman Emperors were in the West very chary of the word *kurios*. Augustus and Tiberius refused to use it or to accept it in the West. In the oriental courts of the East it was very different; there the relationship of people to ruler had always been much more servile, and there *kurios* always had been a royal title. As far back as the third century BC the Rosetta Stone calls Ptolemy V Epiphanes by the title Lord. In an inscription in the temple of Isis in the island of Philae, dating from 62 BC, Ptolemy XIII is addressed as 'the lord king god'. In the East as far back as Tiberius the Roman Emperor was known as *kurios,* lord.

Slowly the title spread. By the time of Nero, at least in the East, *kurios* was the standard title for the Roman Emperor. That use occurs even in the New Testament. After examining Paul, Festus the Roman procurator was at a loss, and had no certain report to make to his lord, his *kurios,* the emperor, that is to say, to Nero (Acts 25.26). By AD 67 in Greece itself Nero was being called 'lord, *kurios,* of the whole world'.

When the Roman Emperor was deified and began to be regarded as a god, the use of *kurios* was naturally intensified; and by the time of Domitian, towards the end of the first century, all over the empire, in the West and the East alike, the inevitable title of every emperor was *kurios kai theos, dominus ac deus,* 'lord and god'. The commonest of all dating formulae in papyrus business documents is in the form, 'In such and such a year of Hadrian Caesar, the lord (*kurios*)'. *Kurios* had become the word of imperial power.

(v)   *Kurios* takes still another step. Especially in the East it became the standard title of every god. Deissmann says of it that it was 'a divine predicate intelligible to the whole eastern world'. The word *kurios* comes to be prefaced to every divine name. Apion, whose letter to his father Epimachus we have already quoted, writes: 'I thank the lord (*kurios*) Serapis, that, when I was in peril on he sea, he saved me immediately.' A runaway prodigal son writes to his mother: 'I make supplication for you daily to the lord Serapis.' As far back as Pindar it could be said of Zeus: 'Zeus giveth this; Zeus giveth that—Zeus who is lord (*kurios*) of all.'[1] *Kurios* had become the word of divine power.

[1] Pindar, *Isthmians* 5.53.

(vi)   There remains one last use of the word *kurios*. In the Septuagint, the Greek version of the Hebrew Old Testament, *kurios* is the regular word used to translate Jehovah or Yahweh, the sacred name. For any Greek-speaking Jew *kurios* had become the equivalent of the name of God.

It is not difficult to see the atmosphere which *kurios* brought into Christianity along with it. It is characteristically the word of authority in every sphere. It is the title of respect and affection; it denotes a legal guardian; it describes the Roman Emperor; it is the divine title of every heathen god; it stands for the very name of God himself. It is clearly no light thing to use of the Lord Jesus Christ.

We now turn to the use of *kurios* in the New Testament itself, and we are confronted with problems which are not altogether easy to solve. We begin with two uses of *kurios* which are quite straightforward.

(i)   There is what may be called the purely *human* use of the word. As in all Greek, so in the New Testament *kurios* is continuously used of men in a human sense. It is used of the *owner* of a vineyard or the owner of a colt (Matt. 20.8; 21.40; Mark 12.9; Luke 20.13,15; 19.33). It is used of the *master* as opposed to the slave. No man can serve two *kurioi* (Matt. 6.24; 16.13). The disciple is not above his teacher, nor the servant above his *kurios* (Matt. 10.24,25; John 13.16; 15.20). The servant is the subordinate and thus does not know what his master *(kurios)* is doing (John 15. 15). It is used of the owner of an estate (Gal. 4.1); of a husband in relation to his wife, as when Sarah calls Abraham her *kurios* (I Peter 3.6); of earthly masters who in their treatment of others must remember that they have a heavenly master (Eph. 6.5,9; Col. 3.22; 4.1). It is the word by which the Jews address Pilate (Matt. 27.63); by which the Greeks address Philip when they come with their request to see Jesus (John 12.21); by which Mary addresses the figure in the garden whom she takes to be the gardener (John 20.15). All these are the normal Greek uses of *kurios* as a title of human authority or respect.

We must note that this is a use which is specially characteristic of the parables. Again and again the parables are about the owner of some estate or the master of some servants or slaves; and the word for owner or master is *kurios*. In passages like this the AV is particularly misleading, for it nearly always translates *kurios* by the word lord in places where master or owner would be the correct rendering. It is so used by the servant to the master in the parable of the wheat and the tares (Matt. 13.27); of the unforgiving debtor (Matt. 18.25,27,31,32,34); of the faithful servant (Matt. 24. 45,46,48); of the talents (Matt. 25.18,19,20,21); of the fruitless fig-tree (Luke 13.8); of the wedding feast (Luke 14.21,22,23).

In all these cases *kurios* is used in its ordinary human sense.

(ii) There is the purely *divine* use of the word. At least 150 times *kurios* is used of God. It is the glory of the Lord *(kurios)* which shines around the shepherds (Luke 2.9); it is the Spirit of the Lord who is upon Jesus (Luke 4.18). The New Testament and the Old Testament alike constantly use *kurios* of God.

(iii) Now we come to one of the most difficult uses of the word, the use of it as applied to Jesus in direct address during his days in the body in Palestine. Again and again he is addressed as *kurie,* which is the vocative of the word, the form of address.

We have already seen that any such address can have a very wide range of meaning. It can be a conventional courtesy; it can be the address of a child to a parent, of a scholar to a teacher, of a servant to a master, of a slave to an owner, of a subject to his emperor, of a worshipper to his god. *Kurios* is a word whose meaning can be entered into at a wide variety of levels.

In regard to its use to Jesus certain very obvious facts stand out. Quite clearly *kurie* cannot be used in the same sense by the woman of Samaria and by John the Beloved Disciple. Clearly *kurie* cannot be used in the same sense by the Syro-Phoenician woman, meeting Jesus for the first time, and Peter affirming his faith that Jesus has the words of eternal life, or suddenly desperately conscious of his sin (John 4.11; Mark 7.28; Matt. 15.27; John 6.68; Luke 5.8). Still more clearly, *kurios* cannot possibly have the same content when it is applied to Jesus in his bodily days in Palestine as it has after his resurrection from the dead and his conquest of death. Quite clearly a new feeling would be in the mind and heart of the man who was addressing the risen and the glorified Christ.

In the days of his flesh no one fully knew who Jesus was; it took the Resurrection and the descent of the Spirit to reveal his full majesty and wonder. It would indeed be a reasonable working rule to say that *kurie,* when applied to Jesus in the days of his flesh, practically always means 'Sir' or 'Master', while *kurie* and *kurios* applied to Jesus after the Resurrection practically always mean Lord.

(iv)   We have already said that the use of *kurios* in regard to Jesus is a development. The first step is when Jesus is called *ho kurios,* The Lord, in narrative passages. If Jesus is called *kurios* in such passages, it means that the writer has come to call him Lord, and to use Lord as a synonym for his name. This growth can very easily be traced. This use does not appear in Mark at all except in 16.19,20, and these last verses are not part of the original Gospel. Nor does it appear in Matthew except in 28.6: 'See the place where the Lord lay', and even there the reading is doubtful. In Luke the situation is different; in that Gospel Jesus is called Lord in the narrative parts of the Gospel about twelve times. Frequently Luke introduces words of Jesus with the phrases:

'The Lord said' (Luke 11.39; 13.15; 17.6; 18.6). 'The Lord,'
he says, 'turned and looked at Peter' (22.61,62). This is even
more marked in John. John often quite simply calls Jesus
the Lord when he is telling of him (John 6.23; 11.2; 20.2,20,
25). In Acts Jesus is often called the Lord Jesus (4.23;
7.59; 11.20; 16.31; 28.31). And, when we come to the letters
of Paul, as we have already seen, Paul in one form or
another calls Jesus Lord more than 200 times. Clearly, by
that time *kurios* has become the standard word by which
Jesus was known.

The safest rule is that *kurios* applied to Jesus only has its
full meaning Lord after his Resurrection. It was indeed the
discovery of the Church that Jesus *is* Lord. It was the
Resurrection and the experience of him as the Risen Lord
which revealed to them that *kurios* was the only adequate
name by which to call him. And we must now go on to see
something of how the early Church did use that name.

(i) As we have already seen, *kurios* is pre-eminently the
word of the risen Christ. It is the Resurrection word, the
title of the Christ who lived and died and conquered death
and who is alive for evermore. It is certain that apart from
the Resurrection the word *kurios* would never have united
itself so inseparably with Jesus.

(ii) It describes Jesus in his office as the Messiah of
God. This becomes even clearer when we remember that
the word Christ and the word Messiah are the same word;
Christ is the Greek for *anointed* and Messiah is the Hebrew
for the same word. The Anointed One is the divine King,
because kings were made kings by anointing. It will often
give us much better sense if we translate the Greek word
Christos by the word *Messiah,* and if we remember that the
word Christ was not originally a name but a title, meaning
the Messiah, the Anointed One of God. The song of the
angels was: 'To you is born this day in the city of David a

Saviour who is Christ the Lord' (RSV). The NEB has, 'a
Saviour who is the Messiah, the Lord'. Moffatt has, 'a Saviour
who is the Lord Messiah'. God, as Peter said, has made Jesus
Lord and Christ (Acts 2.26), or, as the NEB renders it,
'Lord and Messiah'.

The words *Messiah* and *kurios* are intimately connected.
Kurios was the regular title of the Emperor; the Messiah is
God's Anointed King; and therefore *kurios* well expresses the
majestic, imperial, kingly power of the Messiah, and is therefore a fit title for Jesus in his Messianic office.

(iii) It is connected with Jesus in his office of Saviour.
He is our Lord and Saviour Jesus Christ (II Peter 1.11; 2.20;
3.2; 3.18). The person who is Lord, *kurios,* is also Saviour,
sōtēr. The kingliness, the majesty and the glory exist, not to
obliterate and to crush, but to save and redeem men.

(iv) The title *kurios* is very closely associated with Jesus
in his ultimate triumph. It is the word which is continually
used of him in connection with his coming again. The end
is the revelation of the Lord Jesus Christ from heaven (I
Cor. 1.7; II Thess. 1.7). It is for the day of our Lord Jesus
Christ that the Christian waits (I Cor. 1.8; II Cor. 1.14;
Phil. 3.3). It is the coming of the Lord Jesus which is the
Christian hope (I Thess. 2.19; 3.13; 5.23). It is for the appearing of the Lord Jesus Christ that the Christian looks
(I Tim. 6.14). He hopes for mercy from the Lord on that
Day (II Tim. 1.18). It is the certainty of the Christian that
the Lord will rescue him from all evil and give him a share
in his eternal kingdom (II Tim. 4.8,18). It is the Lord who is
at hand (Phil. 4.5; James 5.8).

To put it in technical terms, Lord, *kurios,* has become an
eschatological title of Jesus. When the Christians think of
Jesus as appearing in glory and triumph at the end of the age,
it is as *kurios,* Lord, that they see him.

(v) It is the word which is expressive of the authority of

Jesus. The Son of Man is Lord, *kurios,* even of the Sabbath (Mark 2.28). When Paul is settling some ethical problem, he is careful to say that it is not he but the Lord who is speaking (I Cor. 7.10); and when he is giving his own decision, if he has no commandment of Jesus to quote, and even if he is sure of the guidance of the Spirit, he says that the instruction comes from him and not from the Lord (I Cor. 7.12). A binding commandment is a commandment of the Lord (I Cor. 9.14; 14.37).

Kurios is the title which thinks of Jesus as speaking the last word with which there is no argument.

(vi) *Kurios* is very specially the word of worship and of prayer. It was natural that in their prayers men should call Jesus *kurios.* The heathen might have many gods and many lords, for *kurios* was the word by which the heathen addressed their gods, but in reality there is only one Lord—Jesus Christ (I Cor. 8.5). The table of the central act of worship of the Christian Church is the table of the Lord (I Cor. 10.21; 11.26,27). It is to the Lord that Paul takes his appeal for help in his struggle with the thorn in his flesh (I Cor. 12.8). When the assembled Church sings, it is to the Lord (Eph. 5.19).

So much is *kurios* the word of liturgy and worship, that the anglicised form of the vocative *kyrie* has woven itself into the prayers and the music of devotion, especially of the Roman Catholic Church.

(vii) We have left to the end what is certainly the most important historical use of the word *kurios.* The creed of the early Church was *Jesus Christ is Lord.* It was Paul's vision of the universe, and Paul believed that it was God's vision of the universe, that a day would come when every tongue would confess that Jesus Christ is Lord (Phil. 2.11). The test of salvation is to confess that Jesus Christ is Lord (Rom. 10.9). It is the Holy Spirit which leads a man to say that Jesus Christ is Lord (I Cor. 12.3). What Paul preaches is not

himself but Jesus Christ as Lord (II Cor. 8.6). There is one
Lord, Jesus Christ (I Cor. 8.6). There is one Lord, one faith,
one baptism (Eph. 4.5). 'Jesus Christ is Lord' was the basic
creed of the early Church.

It was precisely that creed that brought the Christian
Church into head-on collision with the Roman Empire. It
was that creed for which the Christians were martyred and
for which they were prepared to die. The Roman Empire was
a vast heterogeneous mass of men of all races and nations
and tongues. Above all it needed a unifying bond and power.
Very early men began to think of Rome as divine, for Rome
gave them a security and a justice they had never known
before. They made for themselves a goddess Roma. But the
spirit of Rome was embodied and incarnated in one man,
in the Emperor. At first it was the dead Emperors who were
regarded as having been elevated to be gods in the heavenly
places. But bit by bit even the living Roman Emperors began
to be regarded as gods; temples were erected to them; and
they were worshipped as divine. This began in the East where
men were much more susceptible to ideas such as this. At
first the Emperors were embarrassed by the very suggestion
of their divinity. They allowed the worship in the East but
they forbade it in the West. But the plain fact was that they
could not stop it. The worship of the Emperor spread all over
the Empire. And then the Roman government began to see
that here was the very unifying principle they needed; here
was the thing which could weld the empire into one. 'Caesar-
worship,' as Mommsen said, 'became the keystone of Roman
imperial policy.'

So the last step came. The Roman government made Caesar
worship compulsory from one end of the Empire to the other;
they made it the bond which held the empire together. Once
a year a man had to come and burn a pinch of incense to
the godhead of the Emperor and to say: 'Caesar is Lord.'

That was a test of his loyalty as a citizen of the Empire; and, having done that, he could go away and worship any kind of god he liked; but that affirmation of faith in Caesar he must make. This is precisely what the Christians would not do. They would not take the name of *kurios* and give it to anyone else in earth or in heaven. For them Jesus was Lord, and nothing would make them say, 'Caesar is Lord'. And so they chose to die for their faith, and they died in the agonies of the cross, the flames, the arena, the rack. *Kurios* was the one-word creed for which the Christians were ready to lay down their lives.

'Jesus Christ is Lord,' was and is the supreme affirmation of faith of the Christian Church, and Lord is not a word to be taken glibly and lightly on thoughtless lips.

42

THE WORD

THE New Testament was not written by theologians; it was written by missionaries. It was not written by men who were in the position of a man writing a thesis in a study or in a library; it was written by men who had a message and who were desperately eager to communicate that message to the world at large. This means that in one sense at least the New Testament interpretations of Jesus were almost all the product of circumstances. They were wrought out by men faced with an actual situation in which they had to find a way to communicate the gospel; and that gospel was not something for the scholars and the theological experts, it was something for the whole world.

At first the task was not so very difficult, for the earliest missionaries were Jews preaching to Jews. They spoke the same language and spoke in the same ideas as the people to whom they were speaking and preaching. But before long the situation changed and the problem became acute. The commission of the disciples was that they were to make disciples of all nations, and once they went out to the wider world they had to find a new set of interpretations. There was little good in talking to a Greek about a Messiah or a Son of David; these were terms which meant nothing to Greeks. Even the term 'Son of God' hardly met the case, for the Greeks knew all about sons of the gods, who were the product of the amours of the gods who had come to earth and seduced mortal maidens. If Jesus Christ was to be presented to the Greeks, some new way of communication had to be found.

A new way was found by the John who wrote the Fourth Gospel. He lived and worked in Ephesus some time about AD 100; he was faced with the problem of finding a way to communicate Jesus to the Greeks, and he found it in the interpretation of Jesus as the *Logos,* the Word. The greatest value of this interpretation was that it spoke with equal effectiveness to both Jews and Greeks. Starting from a Jewish background, and working from a Jewish conception, John had thought out an idea which was able to speak intelligibly and even compellingly to the wider world. Let us then, as John himself must have done, begin with the Jewish background of the idea of the Word.

(i) The basis of the whole idea is that for the Jew a word was not simply a sound in the air; a word was a unit of energy and of effective power. A word did not only *say* things, a word *did* things. We can to some extent understand this idea if we remember how effective towards action the words of some great orator can be. He can move men to laughter or to tears; he can set them out on some political course of action or on some military campaign. His words are dynamic units of power, not only producing an effect in men's minds, but moving them to action.

In the Old Testament the great example of this is the creative word of God. Every act in the drama of creation begins with the words: 'And God said' (Gen. 1.2,6,9,11,14, 20,24,26). The word of the Lord, said Jeremiah, is like a hammer that breaks the rock in pieces (Jer. 23.29.) The heavens were made by the word of God (Ps. 33.6,9). God's word does not return to him empty and ineffective; it *does* that which it was designed to do (Isa. 55.11).

To say that Jesus is the Word is to say for a Jew more than that he is the *voice* of God; it is to say that he is the dynamic and creative power of God in action.

(ii) Another development in Judaism greatly helped the

idea of the Word; it did not add anything to the meaning of the idea, but it did very greatly affect the use of the term.

In later Judaism the idea of God became ever more transcendent. God, as it were, became every more high and lifted up and therefore ever more distant from the world. Now the Old Testament is very anthropomorphic. It does not hesitate to speak of God in very human terms. It can speak of the hands and the arms and the feet of God; it can speak of God as someone who can be met as simply and directly as we can meet another human being. To the later Jewish thinkers this seemed all too human; and so in the Targums, the Aramaic translations and paraphrases of the Old Testament, very often where some specially anthropomorphic idea is used in the Old Testament, there is substituted the Word, the *Memra,* of God. For instance, in Ex. 19.7 we read that Moses brought forth the people out of the camp to meet with God. This for the Targumists was too human a way to speak of God; so it becomes the statement that Moses brought forth the people before the *Memra,* the Word, of God. Isaiah, in a passage of magnificent poetry, has: 'My hand has laid the foundation of the earth; and my right hand has spanned the heavens' (Isa. 48.13). This becomes: 'By my *Memra* I have founded the earth, and by my strength I have hung up the heavens.' Deut. 33.27 speaks of the 'everlasting arms' of God. In the Targums this becomes: 'The eternal God is thy refuge, and by his *Memra* the earth was created.'

The result is that the word *Memra,* the Word of God, is scattered hundreds of times all over the Targums. It became an entirely natural way to speak of God. The expression the *Memra*, the Word, had become a substitute for the name and action of God.

(iii) Still another development of Jewish thought contributed to the idea of the Word. In later Jewish thought

Wisdom began to occupy a very high place. 'Wisdom,' says the Sage, as it may be translated, 'is the principal thing' (Prov. 4.7). In the Old Testament this reached its peak in Proverbs 8. Wisdom speaks noble things (v. 6); her treasures are greater than gold or silver or jewels (vv. 10,11); by her kings reign and rulers decree what is just (v. 15); hers are the only enduring wealth and prosperity (v. 18). But the picture goes much further than that. Wisdom is the companion of God before the world began, and his agent and helper in creation (vv. 22-30). Here is the idea of Wisdom existing, almost as a person, before time with God and as the coadjutor of God in the world of creation.

This conception was developed between the Testaments. Ecclesiasticus tells how Wisdom was created by God before all things, and poured out upon his works (1.1-10), and to the end she shall never fail (24.9). We find the same idea in the Book of Wisdom. Wisdom holds all things together (7.27). She was present at creation and is God's creating agent (9.1,2,9). She is the breath of God and the effulgence of the glory of the Almighty (7.22).

It has to be remembered that the Greek word *logos* does not only mean 'word'; it also means 'mind' or 'reason'—a fact to which we shall have to return. This close connection of meaning helped in the association of the idea of Wisdom with the idea of the Word; and the connection of the Word with God and the creating power of the Word are still further underlined.

So Judaism provided the background of the idea of the Word, and especially the background of the idea of the closeness of the Word to God and the action of the Word in the creation of the world. But we began by saying that it was rather to the Greeks than the Jews that John was presenting the gospel. How then does the idea of the Word connect with Greek thought?

(i) We begin with the fact that we have already mentioned, and which is basic to the whole Greek side of the question. *Logos* has two meanings; it means 'word' and it means 'reason' or 'mind'. Both these meanings are in John's use of it. In English there is no one word which will bear both meanings. This is acknowledged by Moffatt, who abandons the attempt to translate *Logos* and who simply writes: 'The Logos became flesh and tarried amongst us.' It may well be that Moffatt chose the right way of dealing with this, for the two meanings of *logos* have to be kept constantly in view.

(ii) The idea of the *Logos* came into Greek philosophy with Heraclitus, who, like John, lived in Ephesus. Heraclitus wrote and thought in the sixth century BC. Heraclitus saw two principles in the universe. (a) Everything in this world is in a state of flux. Everything is changing and altering; nothing remains the same. No one can step into the same river twice. Between the time that a man steps out and steps in again the river has flowed on. Life is change. (b) In spite of this, the universe remains a dependable universe. The same action causes the same reaction; the same cause produces the same effect. The same seed will always produce the same kind of flower or the same kind of grain. The seasons come not erratically and unpredictably but in their own appointed order. (c) What is it that produces this order in the flux? What is the dependable law operative in the changing universe. That, said Heraclitus, is the *Logos*. 'All things happen according to the *Logos*.' The *Logos* is the mind, the reason, on which the whole order of the universe depends.

(iii) Heraclitus is a philosopher whose work exists only in fragments and as others tell of it. The idea of the *Logos* came to its peak in the Stoic philosophy, which was the most influential philosophy in the ancient world. The Stoics had two basic ideas. (a) They were pantheists; they believed that everything in this world is quite literally God. God himself is infinitely pure 'fiery spirit'. Some of that spirit became 'depotentiated'; it lost its 'tension'; it became dull and inert, and so became matter, but it is still the stuff of God. The life in everything is a spark, a *scintilla*, of the fiery spirit which is God. The Stoic was a man with God inside him living in world which is all God. (b) No thinkers have ever been so impressed with the order of the world as the Stoics were. They were fascinated by the unchanging, ever recurring pageant of the seasons. They were thrilled with the order of the heavenly bodies. They gloried in the mind of man. They insisted that a world like this could not be the product of any chance set of circumstances. You could as easily conceive of some one flinging down thousands of the letters of the alphabet and the plays of a master dramatist emerging as you could conceive of this world being the blind product of chance. There is clearly *mind* in this universe. Whose mind? The mind of God, the *logos*. The *logos* is the mind of God interpenetrating the universe like a soul, putting sense into it, and putting reason into man. It is by the *logos* that the universe is controlled and directed and that the chaos has become a cosmos. To the Stoic it is not too much to say that the *logos* is the most important thing in the world, because the *logos* is the mind of God.

(iv) There is still one strand in this Greek background. Philo, born in 20 BC, was an Alexandrian Jew. In him Greek and Jewish thought met, for he was steeped in both. He was a prolific writer, and in his books the *logos* is spoken of more than 1200 times. To him the *logos* is the image of God and in a unique sense the bridge between God and man. The *Logos* is God's instrument of creation, God's mind stamped on the universe, the tiller by which God steers the world, the bond which holds the world together, the High Priest through whom God communicates with men.

Philo took the Jewish and the Greek idea of the Word
and put them together, and for him it is by the Word that
the universe was made, it is by the Word that the universe
holds together, it is the Word which is the means of communication between God and man.

Let us then see what John is saying about Jesus when he
called him the Word.

(i) A word is the means of *communication;* it is by words
that we establish connection between ourselves and other
people, and that we communicate to them. In Jesus then
God is speaking to men, as God never spoke before and never
need speak again. 'Thus says the Lord' is the characteristic
saying of the prophets; and in Jesus all that God had ever
been saying to men became incarnate in a person. Jesus is
the *message* of God incarnate.

(ii)   A word is the means of *revelation.* The simplest of
all definitions of a word is that a word is the expression of
a thought. *Jesus then is the expression of the thought of God.*
This leads us directly to the other meaning of *logos—mind*
or *reason.* Jesus is the expression of the mind of God. It is
as if John said to the Greeks: 'For the last six centuries
you have been speaking about the mind of God in the universe. If you want to see what the mind of God is, look at
Jesus Christ. Here, full-displayed, is that mind of God about
which you have always been thinking and talking. The *logos*
has become flesh. The mind of God has become a person.'

This is another way of saying that in Jesus we see perfectly
expressed the attitude of God towards men. To put it in very
simple language, in Jesus we see how God feels about, and
feels towards, men. And when we look at Jesus, what do we
see? We see one who healed the sick and fed the hungry
and comforted the sorrowing and was the friend of outcasts
and sinners; and we can say: *'This is God.'*

Here indeed is a revelation. We have already seen how in

the Old Testament it is dangerous to approach God, that to see God is to die. But here is the God whom all men may come near. The typical story of Greek thought is the story of Prometheus. Prometheus was one of the gods; and in his heart there was pity for men. At that time men did not possess fire, so Prometheus took fire from heaven and gave it to men; and for this Zeus the king of the gods took him and chained him to a lonely rock in the middle of the sea to face the agonies of hunger and thirst, and prepared a vulture to tear out his liver, which ever grew again only to be torn out again. Here is the picture of one lonely god who pitied men while all the other gods grudged man everything he had. What a contrast with the God who so loved the world that he gave his only Son! The one basic characteristic of the Stoic idea of God was that God is *apathēs,* which means not apathetic but utterly incapable of all feeling. It is joy and sorrow, gladness and grief which make a tempest of life. If only a man could never love, he would never sorrow. If only a man had a heart insulated against all feeling and emotion, how much easier life would be! So the Stoics said that God alone had that peace which came of a heart which could not feel. What a contrast between the passionless God and the God who loves men so passionately that there is a cross in his heart!

Jesus is the revelation of the heart of God, and that heart is love.

(iii) As we have seen, there is one other idea in this conception of the Word which has no direct parallel in English at all. John connects the Word with creation. 'All things were made through him, and without him was not anything made that was made' (John 1.3). What is the meaning of this? We have already seen that in Jesus we have seen the mind of God, and that mind is love. If then we say that the Word was active in creation it means that creation is the product of the mind of God which we see in Jesus Christ. This means that the same love which redeemed us created the world, that love is the principle of creation as love is the principle of redemption. There is a time in life when this may seem simply a theological or philosophical truth; but there is also a time in life when it is the only thing in life left to hold on to. There is a time when life and the world seem quite clearly to be an enemy, when life seems out to break our hearts, to ruin our dreams, and to smash our lives. There comes a time when we seem to be living in a hostile universe. At such a time it is the greatest thing in life, sometimes it is the only thing left, to be able to cling on to the conviction that 'life means intensely and it means good.' For if we believe that it was this mind of God in Jesus Christ which conceived and created the universe then it does mean that, whatever it feels like, God is working all things together for good, and the world is out not to break us but to make us. If the Christ of creation and the Christ of redemption are one and the same, then there is light even in the darkest hour.

Jesus is the Word. He is God's ultimate and final communication to men; he is the demonstration to men of the mind of God towards them; he is the guarantee that at the heart of creation there is love.

Printed by Murray Printing Co.
Bound by Haddon Craftsman Inc.
HARPER & ROW, PUBLISHERS, INCORPORATED